MOTIVATING READING COMPREHENSION

CONCEPT-ORIENTED READING INSTRUCTION

WITHDRAWN

MOTIVATING READING COMPREHENSION

CONCEPT-ORIENTED READING INSTRUCTION

TOURO COLLEGE LIBRARY
Kings Hwy

Edited by

John T. Guthrie
Allan Wigfield
Kathleen C. Perencevich
University of Maryland, College Park

2004

LAWRENCE ERLBAUM ASSOCIATES, PUBLISHERS
Mahwah, New Jersey   London

KH

Lawrence Erlbaum Associates, Inc., Publishers
10 Industrial Avenue
Mahwah, New Jersey 07430

Cover design by Kathryn Houghtaling Lacey

Library of Congress Cataloging-in-Publication Data

Motivating reading comprehension : concept-oriented reading instruction / edited by John T. Guthrie, Allan Wigfield, Kathleen C. Perencevich.
    p. cm.
Includes bibliographical references and index.
ISBN 0-8058-4682-4 (cloth)
ISBN 0-8058-4683-2 (pbk.)
    1. Contents area reading—United States—Case studies. 2. Reading (Elementary)—United States—Case studies. 3. Reading comprehension—United States—Case studies. 4. Motivation in education—United States—Case studies.   I. Guthrie, John T.   II. Wigfield, Allan.   III. Perencevich, Kathleen C.

LB1573.75.M68 2003
372.47—dc22

                                                        2003056145
                                                        CIP

Books published by Lawrence Erlbaum Associates are printed on acid-free paper, and their bindings are chosen for strength and durability.

Printed in the United States of America
10 9 8 7 6 5 4 3 2 1

11/22/04

We dedicate this book to our spouses,
Stacey, Marguerite, and Stephen,
without whom this endeavor may never have occurred.

Contents

Preface

This book is one milestone in our quest to understand reading engagement and how to promote it in classrooms through Concept-Oriented Reading Instruction (CORI), an instructional program that merges reading strategy instruction, conceptual knowledge in science, and support for student motivation. We define reading engagement as the interplay of motivation, conceptual knowledge, strategies, and social interaction during literacy activities. We believe engagement in reading is crucial for the development of life-long literacy learners. The CORI program is designed to foster reading engagement and comprehension, through the teaching of reading strategies, teaching of scientific concepts and inquiry skills, and its explicit support of the development of student intrinsic motivation to read.

Collaborating with Lois Bennett, a fifth-grade teacher at Calverton Elementary School, John Guthrie began developing CORI in 1993. He and Allan Wigfield began to study the links between reading and motivation in 1994 and were joined by Kathleen Perencevich in these endeavors in 1996. We have collaborated with teachers, reading specialists, and educational psychologists in further developing CORI, including them in our publishing from the outset. These connections enable us to merge some recent theoretical developments in reading comprehension, motivation theory, and cognitive psychology with the resources and realities of classrooms in public schools. In 2000, Dr. Pedro Barbosa and his graduate students, biologists at the University of Maryland, joined our endeavor as co-investigators. They bring science expertise to the table, keeping us honest in the science applications of CORI and assuring exciting talk about ecology and children's learning of it.

In 2000, Guthrie, Wigfield, and Barbosa received a grant from the Interagency Education Research Initiative (IERI) that enabled us to embark on a project to assess how CORI and a multiple-strategy instruction influence elementary school-aged children's reading comprehension and motivation. The appendix to the book contains a brief description of the 5-year project. Initially, we worked with all teachers in grades 3 and 4 in four schools. Much of what we present in this book draws heavily on the first year of working with the 20 teachers who implemented CORI in two schools from September to December in 2001 and 2002. A substantial amount of data on student learning and development was collected, and we are writing articles for submission to journals based on these data. Rather than presenting the data in detail here, this volume is intended to communicate the major constructs that undergird our investigation, and to portray some concrete illustrations of the principles of learning, development, and instructional practices that are embodied in the current CORI implementation. We do this by presenting vignettes of teachers implementing CORI lessons on different topics, and by portrayals of students in these classrooms. We are grateful for the work of researchers and teachers whose commitments coalesce in this exciting inquiry.

All of the authors in this book have been deeply involved in the IERI-funded project of CORI's effects on reading comprehension and motivation. Each chapter describes a central aspect of CORI and its current implementation in third-and-fourth grade classrooms. In chapter 1, John Guthrie presents an overview of the CORI framework, describing how it is based in theories of reading comprehension, motivation, and theories of conceptual knowledge growth in science. He presents a detailed vignette from one exemplary CORI classroom. This chapter also serves as an overview of the remainder of the book. In chapter 2, Kathleen Perencevich discusses how teachers in third-grade classrooms implement the CORI framework during the 12 weeks of CORI instruction. She describes reading strategy instruction, science inquiry activities, and motivation support that occur during each week of CORI. John Guthrie, Allan Wigfield, and Kathleen Perencevich present, in chapter 3, the fundamental ways in which motivation is fostered in CORI classrooms. They focus, in particular, on how teachers *scaffold* students' motivation by providing the necessary level of support needed for students to develop intrinsic motivation to read and reading self-efficacy.

The next three chapters discuss some of the essential components and tools used in CORI. Reading strategies are the tools students use to comprehend text and are an essential part of the CORI program. In chapter 4, John Guthrie and Ana Taboada describe the reading strategies taught in CORI and how teachers first focus on one strategy per week, and then combine strategies in the second 6 weeks so children learn how to use them together. Science educational concepts also are a critical aspect of CORI. In chapter 5, Pedro Barbosa and Laurie Alexander discuss the role of scientific inquiry in CORI. They define ecological concepts related to plant and animal survival that students encounter through observation, experimentation, and reading. Another essential part of CORI is the reading and other materials teachers use to connect science activities to literacy. In chapter 6, Marcia Davis and Stephen Tonks describe how trade books are chosen for use in CORI classrooms, as well as how teachers select relevant materials from the World Wide Web. These materials provide the foundation for the CORI program.

A new CORI focus is special concern for struggling readers. John Guthrie, in chapter 7, describes how CORI teachers and reading specialists implement CORI with struggling readers, focusing first on reading fluency and then on reading strategies and reading–science integration. To illustrate how the CORI program was implemented in one third-grade classroom, chapter 8 presents Melissa Sikorski's detailed case study of Janice O'Hara's CORI classroom during the 12 weeks of CORI instruction.

The last three chapters of the book focus on the development of children's comprehension, motivation, and strategy use in CORI classrooms. In chapter 9, John Guthrie and Nicole Scafiddi describe the growth of children's comprehension skills. They present a rubric for gauging children's knowledge growth from basic facts to elaborate conceptual knowledge that is gained from the reading and science activities in CORI. In chapter 10, Allan Wigfield and Stephen Tonks discuss the development of children's motivation. They define key aspects of motivation, describe how children's motivation develops, and discuss how CORI influences children's motivation. In the final chapter, Ana Taboada and John Guthrie describe growth in children's use of reading strategies. They focus on growth in the cognitive sophistication and depth of children's questioning, presenting a rubric that describes different levels of students' questions.

We attempt to capture CORI in this book in a way that is meaningful to teachers, reading specialists, educational administrators, teacher educators, and educational researchers interested in the development of children's literacy. Thus, we hope the audience for this book is comprised of individuals in all of these groups. By using vignettes and anecdotes, we present CORI's implementation in vivid ways that practitioners can understand and perhaps use in their own classrooms. We also tie CORI to current theory in the fields of reading comprehension, motivation, and science education. It is our hope that this book not only presents the current implementation of CORI, but also provides innovative concepts, evidence from classrooms, and extensions to existing theories of reading comprehension, motivation, and science education.

Acknowledgments

We are privileged to acknowledge the contributions of many individuals to this book and the endeavor it represents. We thank the teachers in Grades 3 and 4 of the participating schools. We want to recognize these teachers of Monocacy Elementary School: Myra Buskirk, Rick Holtz, Kimberly Martin, Brenda Martz, Penni Stockman, Sally Trent, and Andres Wright; the following teachers of North Frederick Elementary School: Kimberly Aguilar, Wendy Bruchey, Jennifer Clausen, Joe Daly, Ann Duncan, Meghan McCoy, Sherry Mowery, Jennifer Nunn, Jean Samuel, Mary Straub, and Iva Wright; the following teachers of Whittier Elementary School: Amy Forsyth, Sandy King, Garnet Lynch, Angela McAllister, Heather McCarthy, Colleen Miller, Alex Owen, Stacey Shewbridge, Eileen Thuman, April Fridley Vierra, and Mary Zygmunt; the following teachers of Hillcrest Elementary School: Lydia Barse, Amy Broomall, Chad Connors, Suzanne Garrett, Laura Hill, Sheree Kastner, Brian Kilduff, Steve Ruefle, Greg Weir, and Todd Working; and the following teachers at Spring Ridge Elementary School: Karen Nori, Dawn Briscoe, Amber Johnson and Steven Moore. In addition, Michele Pickens, Christine Beherendt, Patti Kern, Judy Stup, and Janice O'Hara were reading specialists who helped enormously. The principals of each school were remarkably supportive, including: Jeri Cepura and Sherry Collete, Monocacy Elementary School; Grason Jackson, North Frederick Elementary School; Caroline Strum and Lynda Johnson, Whittier Elementary School; Carol Young, Hillcrest Elementary School; and Laura Guthrie, Spring Ridge Elementary School. The Frederick County Public School district was a model of administrative support and collaboration, especially Michele Krantz, Associate Superintendent, Jerry Strum, Curriculum Specialist, Steve Hess, Director of Curriculum and Evaluation, and Phil Browhan, Science Curriculum Specialist.

At the University of Maryland, substantial contributions were provided by the Dean of the College of Education, Edna Szymanski, and Charles Flatter and Jo Peng of the Department of Human Development. In addition to those who co-authored chapters, students providing invaluable expertise included Shelly

Alicia, Sharon Russell, Laurel Wagner, Jennifer Cromley, Sevgi Ozgungor, Sarah McAdams, Stephanie Wagner, Amy Wilson, Nicole Humenick, Angela McCrea, and Ben Rinicker. Professor Linda Baker of the University of Maryland Baltimore County gave a professional critique and editorial advice to an early draft of each chapter.

Ellen Kaplan devoted talent and energy to the editing process. She is credited with lending consistency and coherence to this volume, but should not be faulted for any errors. Thanks to Eileen Kramer, administrative assistant to the research project who contributed not only to the text, but also to the infrastructure that made the project possible.

The work reported herein was supported by the Interagency Educational Research Initiative (IERI) (Award #0089225) as administered by the National Science Foundation. The findings and opinions expressed here do not necessarily reflect the position or policies of the Interagency Educational Research Initiative, the National Science Foundation, or the University of Maryland.

—*John T. Guthrie*
—*Allan Wigfield*
—*Kathleen C. Perencevich*

About the Editors

John T. Guthrie is a professor of human development at the University of Maryland, College Park. He is also the director of the Maryland Literacy Research Center and the Principal Investigator on a 5-year IERI grant to study the increase of reading comprehension, motivation, and science knowledge using Concept-Oriented Reading Instruction in grades 3–5. His studies of motivational and strategic development in reading and the instructional contexts that increase long-term reading engagement have been published in the *Reading Research Quarterly*, the *Journal of Educational Psychology*, and the *Elementary School Journal*. Before coming to Maryland, John was Research Director for the International Reading Association. He began his career at Johns Hopkins University, where he founded a school for children with reading disabilities. John is a recipient of the Oscar Causey Award for Outstanding Reading Research and is a member of the International Reading Association Hall of Fame. John is married to Stacey and enjoys spending time with children and family.

Allan Wigfield is Professor of Human Development and Distinguished Scholar-Teacher at the University of Maryland, College Park. His research focuses on the development of children's motivation. He has authored more than 80 peer-reviewed journal articles and book chapters on children's motivation, and also has edited three books and four special issues of journals. Included in his publications are chapters on motivation in the *Handbook of Educational Psychology, Handbook of Child Psychology (5th ed.)*, and *Annual Review of Psychology*. Dr. Wigfield was Associate Editor of the *Journal of Educational Psychology* from 2000 to 2002 and currently is Associate Editor of *Child Development*, leading journals in the fields of educational and developmental psychology. He is a Fellow of Division 15 (Educational Psychology) of the American Psychological Association, and has won several awards for his research and teaching. Dr. Wigfield's research focuses on how children's motivation develops across the school years. In the literacy area, Dr. Wigfield has done research on the development of children's motivation for reading, and how different instructional practices influence children's reading motivation. He currently is collaborating with John Guthrie on an NSF-funded study of how two reading programs, Concept-Oriented Reading Instruction and Strategy Instruction, influence elementary school-aged children's reading motivation and comprehension. He is married to Marguerite Tom-Wigfield, and has a 14-year-old son, Dennis, and 12-year-old daughter, Noelle, who teach him much about motivation for reading and other activities.

Kathleen C. Perencevich is a doctoral candidate at the University of Maryland at College Park. Her current research explores how various classroom contexts support students' reading engagement. Specifically, her work examines the influence of autonomy-support and conceptual instruction on student motivation and learning. Her work has been published in several journals and edited books. She is a former classroom teacher. She is happily married to her wonderful husband, Steve, and they are enjoying their newest collaborative effort, Stephen Nicholas.

1

Classroom Contexts for Engaged Reading: An Overview

John T. Guthrie
University of Maryland

RATIONALE AND PURPOSES OF THIS BOOK

One of the aims of this book is to provide an extended description of the instructional context of Concept-Oriented Reading Instruction (CORI). Previous publications on this instructional framework have appeared in journals devoted to reporting empirical findings and book chapters in which the principles of CORI are outlined. However, neither of those publishing outlets allows the depth of depiction that is necessary to fully understand the principles and practices of CORI.

This detailed portrait is designed to be useful to both educators and researchers. Teachers who read this book should have a fuller picture of how CORI looks in the classroom and a feel for the dynamics of teacher–student interactions. The specific ways that teachers introduce books, link science activities to reading, provide strategy instruction, and sustain a motivating context are conveyed with many teacher vignettes.

For researchers, we believe there is an important role for a fine-grained reporting of contextual variables related to the educational and psychological principles of CORI. In educational psychology, principles such as "providing student choices" and "using stimulating tasks" are often presented as research-based instructional practices. Indeed, there are experimental and correlational studies supporting the connection between these practices and student achievement in reading. However, these principles, and others like them, depend crucially on other factors within the classroom. For example, "giving student choices" must be contextualized within tasks. What kinds of choices for what kinds of students are being offered? Our investigations reveal that choice can range from an empowering and cognitively challenging opportunity to an unwelcome burden and counterproductive event. The difference between these extremes depends on important factors that can be defined and identified. In other words, there are crucial conditions that determine whether choice is beneficial, how choice facilitates motivation, and whether or not student autonomy is valuable for student achievement in reading. By explicating the conditions under which student choice is beneficial, we provide a firmer knowledge base for the role of giving students choices as part of effective instruction.

An important aim of this opening chapter is to expressly state the principles underlying Concept-Oriented Reading Instruction and the linkages among them. Individual chapters in this book introduce the teaching practices related to strategy instruction, motivation for students, science education in CORI, and adapting CORI to struggling readers. Separate chapters focus on how the instructional practices appear in classroom contexts. Our first chapter addresses the following topics:

- Engaged reading.
- Classroom characteristics that foster engaged reading.
- Explicit strategy instruction in a context.
- Helping struggling readers in the Concept-Oriented Reading Instruction (CORI) classroom.
- Student benefits from CORI.
- Professional development for teaching CORI.

ENGAGED READING

Imagine a classroom in the later elementary grades. At one table, children are working on an extended project. The students have selected a topic, perhaps life in colonial times or threats to the Chesapeake Bay watershed. Students find books within the classroom and the school media center relevant to their topics. They treat books with care and learn new content with delight. Notebooks are brimming with organized clusters of information gleaned from multiple sources, including Web sites and reference materials. Embracing the challenge of figuring out the complexities of their topic, such as how the water cycle in the region influences changes in the Chesapeake Bay, students share resources and help each other piece together an understanding.

Students at the table are remarkable. They are good readers and good citizens who are working hard in school. We have seen them in almost every school and in many classrooms. Yet, educators face an urgent dilemma because such students are too rare. Too few learners gain this level of independent reading and learning competence. Without extensive assistance from teachers, students in the bottom half of the achievement distribution in many schools may never gain these competencies and self-confidence. How, then, do we build sustaining classroom contexts to help a large majority gain these attributes?

To understand and to create pathways for fostering reading comprehension within classrooms, we need a language for discussing what successful comprehenders do. We use the phrase *engaged readers* to describe students like the ones previously described. These students possess the four main qualities of engaged reading. The most obvious characteristic is cognitive competence, referring to comprehension skills and cognitive strategies for learning from texts. They are able to use background knowledge, form questions, search for information, summarize accurately, organize their new-found knowledge, and monitor their comprehension as they read books.

A second attribute of the engaged reader is motivation. Engaged readers want to learn; they take satisfaction in successful reading, and believe in their reading skills. Importantly, they persist in the face of difficulty and exert continuing effort until they have attained their goals for understanding a passage or have completed a portion of a project.

Third, engaged readers are knowledge-driven. For their project, they have consolidated what they already know. Having reviewed their prior knowledge, they take notes of what they can recall. They may have created diagrams to help themselves build an understanding of their topic. During reading, they consciously add to this initial knowledge base, expanding their conceptual structures deliberately.

Fourth, engaged readers are socially interactive in learning. At their table, there is a buzz of productivity. Discussions about distracting topics and interpersonal conflicts are relatively rare. In sum, engaged readers are strategic, motivated, knowledge-driven, and socially interactive (Baker, Dreher, & Guthrie, 2000).

The opposite of this portrait is all too familiar. Disengaged readers do not possess the cognitive strategies that enable them to be productive in independent work. Although some of them may have adequate skills for learning from texts, they lack curiosity about new ideas. They lack the desire to master new concepts in books. Often, they are not confident as readers. Many believe that if new information does not come immediately from texts, it is not possible to understand the material. Finally, these students are not socially collaborative in literacy activities. They see learning as a solitary activity; they do not want to "give away" their new knowledge, and they gain little gratification from sharing literacy activities.

Ample evidence suggests that when teachers create conditions that enable reading engagement to be extensive and satisfying, students' reading comprehension and their measurable achievement increase (Guthrie & Cox, 2001; Guthrie et al., 1998). In other words, students' growth in reading comprehension is substantially influenced by the amount of their engaged reading. Engaged reading is not merely a recreational activity. It is not simply a form of enjoyment, to be contrasted with the hard work of reading for meaning or new knowledge. Rather, engaged reading is valuable, and perhaps necessary, for reading achievement in the later elementary grades (Guthrie, Schafer, & Huang, 2001). Our model of the relationship between engagement and achievement is simple. Engaged reading is the primary pathway toward the competencies and expertise needed for achievement.

WHAT CLASSROOM CHARACTERISTICS FOSTER ENGAGED READING?

CORI classrooms are designed to meet students' needs. Becoming a comprehender in the later elementary grades is based on two needs; the first is mental, or cognitive. Students must be able to use cognitive strategies easily. They need to be able to tap into background knowledge, ask questions, and summarize frequently and appropriately. A second need is motivational, or affective. Students must want to learn, to have the desire to be good readers. We have seen that engaged readers possess these qualities—cognitive and motivational—woven together. Students who are good strategy users are usually motivated, and students who are motivated are often competent in using strategies.

Yet, teaching that supports the mental (or cognitive) and the motivational (or affective) are often segregated. For example, many teachers promote self-selected reading as an opportunity to read for enjoyment, but cognitive strategies are rarely taught during this time. Likewise, many teachers believe that strategy instruction is hard and cognitive, and they do not expect it to be enjoyable. We suggest that the challenge for educators is to support the cognitive and motivational sides of reading simultaneously. Possessing strategies for reading should help students increase their enjoyment in reading books for pleasure. Likewise, gaining motivation for reading should fuel strategy development. Therefore, we propose that the twin aspects of reading—the cognitive and the motivational—must be supported simultaneously in the classroom context.

A Theoretical Model

A graphic depiction of the theoretical framework that underlies the reading program is shown in Fig. 1.1. At the center of this figure is a box with desired student outcomes of achievement, knowledge, and reading practices. Outside the box, the four sides of the outer square represent processes of reading engagement. These consist of using background knowledge during reading, being strategic with texts, having intrinsic and extrinsic motivation to read successfully, and interacting with students in literacy activities. As we have suggested, the more students are engaged in reading and display these processes, the better their comprehension of texts is likely to be. On the outside of this figure are ovals, representing the classroom characteristics that give rise to high amounts of reading engagement among students. There is abundant evidence that a composite of these classroom attributes facilitates reading comprehension de-

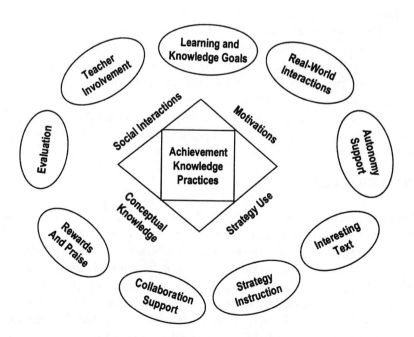

FIG. 1.1. Engagement model of reading development.

velopment. We do not suggest that one factor can produce improvement in reading comprehension. To the contrary, the pragmatic, applied aspect of our investigations leads us to conclude that all of the processes represented in the outer ring of this figure are necessary for engagement in reading. They interact dynamically to support the learner in long-term instructional endeavors (Guthrie & Wigfield, 2000; Skinner, Wellborn, & Connell, 1990). This theoretical model suggests that instructional context increases student engagement in reading, and reading engagement increases reading achievement.

Rationale for Concept-Oriented Reading Instruction

To provide long-term support for students' development of reading comprehension in the classroom, a team of researchers, teachers, and graduate students created a framework for teachers. With success, it expanded to other classrooms and schools, as chronicled in Guthrie and Cox (2001). We named the framework "Concept-Oriented Reading Instruction," to reflect the central position of conceptual knowledge in teaching reading comprehension. Following the experienced judgment of teachers and findings from empirical research on reading, the framework has two main aspects; (a) support for the cognitive strategies for knowledge construction during reading, and (b) support for the motivational development of learners. These two aspects are both served by teaching to contents or concepts in a discipline. When students are trying to gain conceptual knowledge, the difficult strategies of reading, such as summarizing, have an authentic purpose and are more readily acquired. Simultaneously, interest and motivation for reading are immediately aroused by concepts, such as how dinosaurs lived. Our notion is that important, interesting conceptual themes are a valuable context for teaching comprehension strategies and for sustaining the motivation required for long-term reading development.

CORI Framework

The CORI framework depicts the overall structure. Four strands include reading strategy instruction, inquiry science, motivational support, and reading–science integrations. Table 1.1 shows the framework for 12 weeks of CORI. The overall conceptual theme for this instruction is "Survival of Life on Land and Water." The first 6 weeks concentrates on life on land and focuses on the topic of "Birds Around the World." This topic emphasizes biodiversity and the adaptation of life. The second unit is "Survival in Freshwater Habitats," emphasizing pond ecology. These units fulfill school and district mandates.

TABLE 1.1

CORI Framework: Conceptual Themes: Survival of Life on Land and Water

CORI Phases	Weeks	A. Reading Strategy Instruction	B. Inquiry Science Activities	C. Motivational Processes	D. Reading-Science Integrations
Observe & Personalize	1	**Activating Background Knowledge** Relate experience to stories/folktales on bird theme. (Folktale/story- *Owl Moon*)	**Observing** Local habitat (e.g., field trip to local woods) observe land, plants, animals, and populations.	**Initiating Environmental Interest** Notice animals, behaviors, or plants that were new or interesting.	**Relating** Relate birds in story to field observations of birds and their surroundings.
	2	**Questioning** Ask multiple questions about bird survival in diverse land forms of the Earth.	**Designing Experiment** Pose hypothesis about bird feeding and design investigation.	**Student Choices** Write multiple, varied questions; post 3 favorite for class discussion.	**Compare and Contrast** Identify questions that can be answered by reading, science observation, or both.
Search & Retrieve	3	**Searching** Gather information from multiple expository texts and media to answer personal questions on birds, and their survival. (Story structuring- *White Bird*)	**Collecting Data** Dissect owl pellet and observe bird feathers.	**Extending Environmental Interest** Attention to new or interesting information from science investigation.	**Connecting Interests** Notice differences between birds in field and birds in legends or stories.
Comprehend & Integrate	4	**Summarizing** Express gist of information texts; write summary of several books. (Story structuring- *White Bird*)	**Representing Data** Make histogram to show owl pellet results.	**Interesting Texts** Students take ownership of ideas learned; show mastery of knowledge related to personal questions.	**Contrasting Domain Learning** Distinguish text and science avenues to learn about ecology and populations.

(continued on next page)

7

TABLE 1.1 (continued)

CORI Phases	Weeks	A. Reading Strategy Instruction	B. Inquiry Science Activities	C. Motivational Processes	D. Reading-Science Integrations
	5	**Organizing Graphically** Make a concept map of bird survival. Use up to 9 ecological concepts, containing links and relationships. Place on a team science poster. (Story structuring- *White Bird*)	**Organizing Investigation** Team makes poster of owl feeding study, showing scientific method and conclusions.	**Collaborating** In small groups, students exhange ideas and expertise on habitats, birds, and how they survive, as they make individual concept maps.	**Combining Conceptual Learning** Merge results from bird investigations with knowledge gained from books into concept map.
Communicate to Others	6	**Communicating To Others** Team teaching to audience. Re: Concept map on bird survival around the Earth. (poetry readings)	**Communicating to Others** Team teaching to audience. Re: Science poster on birds feeding investigation.	**Coordinating Motivational Support** Chart trail of curiosities and learning about bird survival.	**Coordinating Reading & Science** Chart trail of curiosities and learning about bird survival.
Observe & Personalize	7	**Activating Background Knowledge** Relate experience to folktales or stories on aquatic life theme.	**Observing** Teams build aquarium for snails, fish, insects, and plants. Field trip to nature center/collect specimens.	**Initiating Environmental Interest** Notice animals' features and behaviors that were new or interesting.	**Relating** Relate snail and frogs in story to observations of aquarium animals and their interactions.
	8	**Questioning and Activating** Ask multiple questions about aquatic regions and biomes on Earth and the animals inhabiting them using background knowledge.	**Designing Investigation** Pose 1-2 questions about food web study.	**Student Choices** Write multiple questions about selected aquatic animal and biome; post 3 favorite questions for class discussion.	**Compare/Contrast** Compare and contrast questions about bird life on land biomes with aquatic life in water biomes.

Search & Retrieve	9	**Searching, Questioning, and Activating** Gather information from multiple texts and media to answer personal questions on aquatic life in varied water systems. (Story structuring *Adventures of Frog and Toad*)	**Collecting Data** Gather data from aquarium to answer questions.	**Extending Environmental Interest** Attention to new interesting information in science investigation.	**Connecting Interests** Notice similarities between species in the aquarium and animals you read about.
Comprehend & Integrate	10	**Summarizing, Activating, & Questioning** Represent texts; summarize several texts to answer student questions extending background knowledge.	**Representing Data** Make table or histogram for data; draw conclusions; explain how locomotion contributes to survival.	**Interesting Texts** Students take ownership of ideas learned; show mastery of knowledge related to personal questions.	**Contrasting Domain Learning** Distinguish text and science avenues to learn about ecology and populations.
	11	**Organizing Graphically Activating & Questioning** Concept mapping information texts; write chapter book on ecological explanation of animal life in an aquatic biome.	**Organizing Investigation** Write steps, findings, and conclusions of food web investigation as a section of individual chapter book.	**Collaborating** In small groups, students exchange ideas and expertise in writing books; peer editing; illustrating; producing;	**Combining Conceptual Learning** Merge results from aquarium investigation on locomotion with knowledge gained from books into chapter book.
Communicate to Others	12	**Synthesis of Strategies/Communicating** Team teaching to audience about individual chapter book (poetry readings)	**Communicating to Others** Team teaching to audience about individual chapter on investigation.	**Intrinsic Motivation** Students display choices, collaboration, and competence.	**Coordinating Reading & Science** Chart trail of curiosities and learning about aquatic life survival.

In the first CORI unit (in Grade 3—"Birds Around the World"), the reading strategies are taught one at a time, in the sequence as listed in the table. Single strategy instruction enables lower achieving third-graders to understand, to gain command, and to transfer the strategies to a variety of texts. In the second half of this 12-week unit (Aquatic Life), the reading strategies are combined. Teachers first instruct students in combining background knowledge with questioning. As students use what they already know about a topic to formulate new questions about this topic, the questions become more elaborate, more interesting to learners, and more productive for reading comprehension. Teachers progressively combine the first five strategies for learning from information texts and for learning from literary and narrative texts. Obviously, structuring stories is a strategy that is specialized for literature and is taught in that genre. All of these strategies are described in chapter 11, and strategy instruction in the CORI content is conveyed in chapter 4.

The last phase of a CORI unit is "communicating to others," involving writing, creating posters, speaking, and communicating to an audience. Although it is not a reading strategy, it is an aspect of CORI that enables students to have a culminating activity for their reading and writing. A culminating activity requires students to synthesize knowledge gained from reading, to critically analyze their own text, and to monitor their comprehension of materials that they read and created.

Roles of text and text qualities weigh heavily in strategy instruction. For the 6 weeks of the "Birds Around the World" unit, students read at least 10 information books in full, 10 more information books partially, three or four stories, and two chapter books. A large amount of extended, engaged reading activity is a central purpose of CORI for teachers and depends on an abundance of well-selected, well-configured books. Chapter 6 is dedicated to the identification, organization, and the use of diverse texts in the classroom.

Science Inquiry. In the second column of the CORI framework (see Table 1.1), science inquiry activities are listed. Basic science processes are sequenced as they are in the benchmarks of the American Association for the Advancement of Science, the state of Maryland science goals, and the curriculum goals of Frederick County, in which the classrooms described here are located.

In this inquiry frame, the first phase is **observing**. For example, students may take a walk in a local habitat and chart the land, plants, animals, and signs of life. Next, students **design an investigation**. As the first theme is "Birds Around the World," teachers direct students' attention to birds during their initial observation. In class, students read books about habitats, animals, and birds, with a focus on owls. For science inquiry, students design an investigation about owls' feeding and the possible contents of an owl pellet. In the third phase, they **collect data** by dissecting owl pellets. This is an exceptionally exciting activity. Students take delight in making predictions about contents of the owl pellet. They carefully, but eagerly, dissect with tools and magnifying glasses. They are fascinated to classify the bones from the pellet. The following week, they **represent their data** by drawing histograms and charts. Finally, they **organize** their investigation by making a poster of their feeding study, which displays the scientific method and their conclusions.

In the CORI phase of **communicating to others**, students present their science report to a valued audience. During the second unit of CORI, weeks 6–12, students progress to design an experiment about aquatic life. They attempt to manipulate one variable, while holding other variables constant, in an aquarium study. In both sections of the CORI unit, "Birds Around the World" and "Survival in Freshwater Habitats," students learn about the conceptual theme by using the scientific method (see chapter 5).

Motivation Support. Motivation support for reading development is sketched in the third column of the CORI framework (see Table 1.1). Several principles for increasing interest in reading are employed. We focus first on situational interest. During the opening week, a habitat walk enables teachers to **initiate environmental interest** in the local area. Students notice the features of the habitat, and the plants and animals within it. These situational interests are quickly connected to books on the same topics as their observations. Having aroused initial interest in the local habitat immediately surrounding the school, as well as in books describing plants, animals, birds, and other features of the habitat, teachers then **encourage student choices**.

One aspect of choice is questioning. Teachers provide information about a wide range of habitats around the world. Diversity of landforms is taught, including wetlands, forests, grasslands, polar regions, deserts, and others. Across these diverse habitats, survival of birds is introduced. Students are encouraged to ask their own personal questions about birds and how they survive, as a basis for their reading and for **extending environmental interest**. These questions are central to the curriculum and motivating for the students.

Within the CORI unit, **interesting texts are used** on all possible occasions (see chapter 6). Teachers **enable students to collaborate** to learn from a variety of materials, exchange ideas, and develop expertise together. Such collaboration provides sustaining motivation for learning and using strategies from books. Chapter 10 is devoted to children's development of motivation, including intrinsic motivation, self-efficacy, extrinsic motivation, and social motivation. Our theoretical position on how the classroom context influences reading is also unveiled in that chapter.

Reading–Science Integration.   In the fourth column of the CORI framework, reading–science integrations are presented. These integrations enable students to link their real-world experiences to their book reading. Such links are especially useful to low achieving students because they provide a concrete referent for abstract words and concepts in a text. First, students **relate** their observations of birds in the local habitat to the characteristics of birds in a story, such as *Owl Moon* by Yolen. Next, students **compare and contrast** characteristics of birds or animals in stories (often birds of legends are magical) with those in the real world. Finally, students form concept maps, displaying their bird knowledge gained from books in combination with knowledge gained from their investigation of owls. This enables them to **combine conceptual learning** across reading and science. Students integrate text learning with observational experiences, which is valuable for the knowledge-building enterprise.

PROVIDING EXPLICIT STRATEGY INSTRUCTION IN A CONTEXT

Most basically, reading comprehension is learning from text. The reader interacts with the printed material to build new meanings. A relatively good reader can construct more, higher level meanings from a wider diversity of texts, than a relatively poor reader. Using a strategy helps students build interlinked knowledge that is taught. For each specific strategy, such as questioning or summarizing, attention is given to teaching the attributes of strategic reading that have been frequently discussed by others (Paris, Wasik, & Turner, 1991).

Attributes of Strategic Reading

In teaching cognitive strategies for reading, teachers need to foster the qualities of competence, awareness, and self-initiation. Competence in the strategy is the first quality students need. If students are attempting to summarize a paragraph, they need to gain skill in doing that strategy. Beyond competence, students need to feel a sense of awareness and to initiate strategies appropriately.

Students may perform the steps of summarizing without awareness of what the strategy is or how it will help them. CORI teachers explain that summarizing refers to recognizing the main idea and supporting details without including less important information. Awareness enables students to use the strategy liberally when it is useful. Through discussion, reflection on strategy use, and explanation of how strategies are different from each other, awareness is enhanced. Aware students know that background knowledge refers to previous experience or past learning, whereas questioning points toward what might be learned through reading in the immediate or more distant future. This awareness enables them to be deliberate and conscious about the use of strategies. Most simply, students show awareness if they know *when* to employ a strategy. Such understanding enables intentional, rather than merely habitual or prompted, use.

A crucial aspect of strategic reading is self-initiation. Self-initiating strategy users do not wait for the teacher's prompt or the requirements of a worksheet. They invoke a strategy, such as activating background knowledge or questioning, when they encounter a new text, when they are confused, or when they sense the need to deepen their knowledge in a particular reading event. Self-initiating strategy users are motivated. They want to learn from text. Because strategies are cognitively demanding, students who are not highly motivated are unlikely to be self-initiating. Unmotivated students depend on extensive prompting, encouragement, or requirements from the teacher. Teachers who are effective in fostering full strategy development place expectations on their students for initiating strategies, and they encourage students to implement strategies widely.

We expect that students should become competent, aware, and self-initiating in the use of reading comprehension strategies. Because very few students begin Grade 3 with any of these qualities, it is sensible to start with the development of competence. CORI, in Grade 3, emphasizes competence in activating background knowledge, questioning, searching for information, summarizing text, organizing text graphically, and structuring stories. To teach these strategies, it is valuable to have developmental benchmarks. For instance, benchmarks for questioning show what kinds of questions students ask when they are beginning to learn, and what kinds of questions students should be expected to ask as they become more effective questioners. These benchmarks can be goals for teaching. For example, our research led to the development of a four-level rubric in questioning, to be described more extensively in chapter 11.

Strategies Taught in the CORI Model

Drawn from a body of knowledge on strategy learning and our studies of searching for information (Guthrie, Weber, & Kimmerly, 1993), we selected strategies consistent with the National Reading Panel Report (2000). They are presented briefly here, and are detailed in chapter 11.

Activating Background Knowledge.   The strategy of activating background knowledge refers to recalling experiences and knowledge of texts before reading, for the purpose of linking new content to prior understanding. In activating background knowledge, students at the beginning of Grade 3 may be expected to recall knowledge that is not relevant to the topic or is trivial. A first benchmark of instruction is that students should activate knowledge that is relevant to the text topic and use important text cues, such as the title and headings, so that their knowledge statements link to the new text. The second, more advanced benchmark for instruction is that background knowledge should represent interconnected concepts and information related to the text topic. CORI teachers encourage students to improve their statements of background knowledge by increasing their relevance and using the text features to expand the conceptual richness of their statements.

Questioning.   Questioning refers to asking, or writing, a self-initiated question about the content of the text before reading. This content may include conceptual knowledge from expository text or literary information about narrative text. In the beginning of Grade 3, children's questions may possess minimal depth. A child's question may be a word or phrase rather than an interrogatory statement. Questions may be answered by a simple fact, or a yes or no response. A first benchmark is that students should pose questions that are stated as complete sentences, related to central concepts of the topic or the text. The second, higher level benchmark for instruction is that the students' questions should address multiple concepts, with supporting evidence, and a statement of interrelationships and patterns among concepts in the text. For example, advanced questioning about literature shows an elaborate understanding of character goals and actions, as well as events, plot, or facts about the characters.

Searching for Information.   Searching for information refers to seeking and finding a subset of information in the total text by forming specific goals, selecting particular sections of text, extracting accurate information, combining new and old information, and continuing until goals are fulfilled. Initially, third-grade students usually make vague and imprecise search goals. A first benchmark of instruction is that students are able to generate multiple goals, and use keywords to guide their search. Accompanying this, students should learn the most obvious access systems to text such as the index, table of contents, and topic sentences. A second, higher level benchmark of searching for information is that students identify multiple texts to use as sources for information, integrate information from multiple texts, and relate knowledge of cultural or historical information with text-based information about characters or events in literary texts.

Summarizing. Summarizing refers to forming an accurate, abstract representation of text after reading all or a substantial portion of material. Initially, in Grade 3, students may be unable to understand what it means to summarize a text. They struggle to identify central ideas or concepts within a text as short as one paragraph. A first benchmark for teaching summarizing can consist of enabling students to identify central ideas in a passage by locating keywords and identifying supporting factual information. A higher level benchmark consists of students writing summaries with all the important concepts identified, accompanied by full statements of accurate supporting evidence from the text.

Organizing Graphically. Organizing text graphically refers to constructing a spatial representation of text-based knowledge, which may include drawings, concepts maps, and diagrams. Initially, in Grade 3, students may be incapable of creating a spatial structure, such as a "t" chart, or drawing a concept map. An initial benchmark for teaching is that students identify key concepts and supporting terms. At first, students generate a graphic, with teacher support. As learners advance, the second benchmark for teaching is for students to build more complex concept maps and diagrams more independently. Their work should show a hierarchy of knowledge, clusters of supporting information, and dynamic relations with causal links among concepts.

Creating a Motivating Context for Strategy Development in Reading

Learning cognitive strategies is a challenging enterprise. To children, the strategies are abstract and difficult. Because the persistence and sustained attention required to learn them are demanding for young learners, building the right context is crucial. In CORI, reading strategies are taught in a context of inquiry, which affords teachers the opportunity to support motivation by (a) having knowledge goals for reading instruction, (b) providing hands-on activities related to reading, (c) giving students realistic choices, (d) using interesting texts for instruction, and (e) weaving collaboration into children's classroom lives.

Knowledge Goals. The first aspect of the CORI framework consists of knowledge goals. Teachers establish major concepts of ecology as the purpose for reading and learning. Many studies have documented that conceptual knowledge or learning goals are more motivating for students than performance or skill goals. For example, the comprehension skill of questioning is not as motivating in isolation from content as it is when it is immersed in a rich domain. In CORI, the knowledge goals relate to animals and plants and how they live in different environments. In Grade 3, the first 9 of the following science concepts are taught and in Grade 4, all 11 concepts are explored. The 11 science concepts that represent the knowledge goals for the theme of "Survival of Life on Land and Water" consist of the following:

1. All plants and animals have behaviors, traits, and adaptations designed to ensure the **reproduction** of the species.
2. **Communication** is critical to all aspects of plant and animal life.
3. All plants and animals must have adaptations for **defense** in order to survive.
4. Because most critical resources are shared in a limited supply, **competition** in plants and animals is often observed.
5. While feeding on plants is very common, **predation** is a frequently observed interaction among animals.
6. The search for food and the interactions involved in **feeding** are critical if animals and plants are to acquire the nutrition needed for growth and development.
7. **Locomotion** allows organisms to undertake all needed requirements of life and usually reflects a close adaptation to their habitat.
8. **Respiration** is an essential process for the acquisition of oxygen, without which most life cannot proceed.
9. Plants and animals exhibit physical structures and behavioral patterns that reflect **adaptations to the habitat** in which they survive.
10. The **niche**, or roles animals and plants play in their environment (e.g., scavenger).
11. **Habitat conservation**, which are the positive effects of plants and animals that serve to preserve the life-giving qualities of the environment.

These are the core concepts to which reading materials and comprehension activities are directed. More detail on science concepts and processes is provided in chapter 5.

These goals can be used as a common orientation for teaching many of the comprehension strategies and the reading of diverse texts. Teaching to such concept goals is what gave rise to the name *Concept-Oriented Reading Instruction*. Orienting students toward understanding as the main aim of reading instruction is more likely to foster long-term motivation than a focus on rewards and prizes (Stipek, 1996).

Hands-On Activities.   Having identified a few conceptual goals for instruction, the framework for CORI provides for hands-on activities related to the concepts. In science, this consists of observing and experimenting. As students pursue the unit "Birds Around the World," they observe their local habitat, the birds that live within it, and proceed to dissect owl pellets. For a substantial number of students, especially low-achieving learners, these concrete experiences are vital for reading comprehension. Observing provides immediate, tangible, sensory experiences that are motivating and memorable. Seeing the "real-world" in the classroom usually arouses situational interest, which can motivate reading (Hidi & Harackiewicz, 2000).

Hands-on experiences, in moderation, amply support a wide range of literacy activities. Our experience is that a good ratio of hands-on activities to literacy activities is 1 to 10. That is, one hour of hands-on activity will support at least 10 hours of extended, engaged reading, writing, and text-based discussion.

Student Choices.   At the beginning of a unit, the teacher elicits student questions that are related to the conceptual goal and to the hands-on experience. Because these questions are based on the students' background knowledge and are linked to learners' personal interests, the questions motivate a range of reading comprehension activities. When students realize that comprehending effectively helps them answer their personally formed and publicly stated questions, interest in reading is spurred forward. Although student questions are encouraged and posted in the classroom, questions are not "left hanging" without being addressed. Students read a variety of texts to answer their questions and enter answers in notebooks or on charts and posters, soon after questioning. During this quest for information, teachers encourage learners to choose texts and subtopics within texts. These choices enable them to link questioning and knowledge. Students learn that the question is a tool to fashion their understanding from text. Supporting meaningful choices increases reading motivation and moves students toward becoming "self-determining" readers (Deci & Ryan, 1992).

Interesting Texts.   To help students answer their questions about the conceptual theme of the unit, teachers provide interesting texts, consisting of trade books at different levels of difficulty, with an optimal mix of illustration, texts, headings, and formatting that foster concept development from text. In the terms of motivation theory, such texts provide situational interest (Hidi &

Harackiewicz, 2000). Interesting texts immediately command attention, which can be used to facilitate strategy learning in reading. Characteristics and roles of interesting texts are described in chapter 6.

Collaboration Support. A prominent feature of a CORI classroom is collaboration. For example, during instruction in the cognitive strategy of summarizing, pairs of students are likely to be asked to formulate a summary of a text paragraph. They work together to identify keywords and supporting details, and delete less important information. In this process, students enjoy the interpersonal interaction as they implement a strategy and check each other's application of the strategy to new material. Such collaboration relies on teachers' explaining the importance of give-and-take, speaking and listening, and respect for others. When it is successful, collaborating is intrinsically motivating. It is rewarding to be socially immersed during portions of reading instruction.

Roles of Inquiry Science in CORI

As indicated previously, inquiry science contributes to CORI by providing several important aspects of context. However, science learning is itself a goal of this teaching. Our science goals have been approved by the Frederick County, Maryland school district where we implement CORI. These goals are consistent with national, state, and district standards.

Beyond these external accountabilities, we believe that there are powerful commonalities between learning science and reading. At the heart of science are inquiry processes, including **observing, hypothesizing, designing experiments, collecting data, representing findings graphically and quantitatively, and writing to communicate with others.** Distinct parallels between these inquiry processes and the reading comprehension strategies include activating background knowledge (observing), questioning (hypothesizing), searching for information (designing experiments, collecting data), and organizing graphically (representing findings graphically and quantitatively). In our view, processes such as questioning in reading and hypothesizing in science can be taught in concert with each other. Teaching one should support learning of the other. Furthermore, both reading and science are ultimately aimed at gaining conceptual understanding. Students conduct science experiments to address a conceptual problem, not merely to perform the procedure. Likewise, students use a reading strategy to gain understanding and learn concepts. We believe that the integration of reading and science may be synergistic for both disciplines. More detail is provided in chapter 5.

HOW DO WE HELP STRUGGLING READERS IN THE CORI CLASSROOM?

Students entering the third grade are diverse, and many of them are not fluent in word recognition. They may be able to recognize a few sight words, but often they cannot decode unknown words easily. They cannot read quickly and smoothly enough to be expressive in their oral reading. Without word recognition fluency, students are often handicapped in comprehension. While reading a story, these students may succeed in understanding some facts, but will not "get the point." Rarely do these students have the skills to summarize even a paragraph. These "struggling readers" are identified and placed into groups of four to six individuals. Although these students participate in all whole-classroom CORI activities, they also participate daily in focused, small group instruction.

Oral Reading Fluency

Struggling reader instruction begins with activities to support oral reading fluency. This may include "whisper reading," in which students read aloud softly while the teacher listens to each of them read, providing support for word recognition. Support may include choral reading and attempts to read expressively. Within this dimension of teaching, repeated reading of selected text may occur. For example, half of the group may read a certain passage aloud, followed by the other half reading the same passage aloud. Groups attempt to become increasingly expressive and convey the meaning and tone of an information text or the characters in a story. These activities foster fluency, the bedrock of comprehension.

Simpler Strategy Instruction

For readers struggling with reading comprehension strategies, instruction is simplified. Teaching a particular strategy, such as questioning, may be limited to a single page, a single picture, or an individual character in a story. The scope of the question is constrained to give students a more focused target. Initially, students may be requested to ask one question rather than multiple questions. The teacher is likely to provide more extended, explicit modeling for struggling readers than is needed by the rest of the class.

Bridging From Text to Response

Extremely valuable for struggling readers is a bridge between the text and the normally expected outcome of using a strategy. Consider a lesson in summarizing. For stronger readers, it is sufficient for the teacher to walk students through the steps of summarizing: identify key words, locate supporting facts, delete unimportant information, and compose the summary. With such a guide, these on-grade students can write a brief summary.

Struggling readers need a bridge from the text to the written summary. A bridge may consist of a simple chart, guide, or map. For example, the teacher may identify four pages of a text, each to be summarized one at a time. On each page, she may identify one key concept and ask students to identify key words that support this concept. After entering key words or phrases on a chart, students may then say or write a brief summary about each page (see chapter 7).

Opportunity to Learn

Struggling readers in Grade 3 need multiple opportunities to learn a particular strategy. In one or two trial runs, they are unlikely to gain command of a strategy. One CORI teacher provided simplified instruction in summarizing for 9 days during the reading of a chapter book. By the end of that time, the students had gained competence in writing short summaries of a single page of the book and a beginning sense of self-efficacy for this strategy. Frequent opportunities for learning, under the conditions of support for fluency and simplified strategy use, are needed.

Texts used during instruction with struggling readers should address the topic of the conceptual theme as frequently as possible. However, it is often difficult to find easy-to-read texts on a science topic. Consequently, content-related texts are used during some of the focused instruction time for this group, and other less connected texts may be introduced.

HOW MUCH DO STUDENTS BENEFIT FROM CORI?

Ultimately, the most important evidence about the merits of this program is its benefits for children. If children gain in reading comprehension, increase in motivation, and acquire science knowledge, we judge that the instruction is successful. There are many forms of evidence regarding the effectiveness of an educational intervention. Here we provide case studies, vignettes of classroom discourse, and descriptive statistics about students' growth and development. As this chapter is being written, we are conducting an experimental comparison of CORI, strategy instruction, and traditional instruction, over 3 years, with 1300 students.

Experimental Evidence

In previous research, we statistically compared students in CORI classrooms with students in traditional classrooms (Guthrie & Cox, 2001). One of the studies was longitudinal, chronicling the growth of students' strategies and motivations within a CORI classroom. Whereas CORI students increased in intrinsic reading motivation and reading strategies for comprehension, students in traditional, basal-oriented classrooms gained in extrinsic motivation and did not improve as markedly in reading strategies. In two other investigations, we examined the year-long implementations of CORI in Grades 3 and 5, in comparison to traditional reading instruction within the same three schools. Students in CORI classrooms had higher reading comprehension scores than students in traditional classrooms in a performance assessment in Grade 3 (Effect size = .61) and Grade 5 (Effect size = 1.31), as well as traditional measures of text comprehension in Grade 5 (Effect size = .50; Guthrie et al., 1998). CORI students have been shown to transfer their strategies to new topics in Grade 3 (Effect size = .80) and Grade 5 (Effect size = .96), and comprehend traditional narratives in Grade 3 (Effect size = .69) better than traditional students (Guthrie et al., 1999). For motivation, CORI students were higher than traditional students on intrinsic motivation, especially curiosity (Effect size = 2.35) and involvement in reading (Effect size = 1.61; Guthrie, Wigfield, & Von Secker, 2000). In reading strategy use, CORI students scored higher than traditional students in a performance assessment (Effect size = .91) and a self-report measure (Effect size =1.7; Guthrie et al., 1998; Guthrie, Wigfield, & Von Secker, 2000).

These experimental findings permit us to conclude that CORI, as a total system, increases reading comprehension, motivation, and conceptual knowledge of learners beyond that afforded by traditional reading instruction. Our current research is directed to the issue of which dimensions of the CORI framework are most centrally important to enabling these benefits to occur for students in Grades 3–5.

HOW DO WE PROVIDE PROFESSIONAL DEVELOPMENT FOR TEACHING CORI?

Successful implementation of the CORI framework rests in the hands of teachers. This is not a program represented in a set of materials that can be purchased and used. It has no script that can be delivered in the classroom. Rather, CORI requires that teachers understand the principles of students' engaged reading and the instructional practices of the framework. Teachers learn to utilize this framework in concert with their own expertise and preferences. The CORI framework is customized, to a certain degree, by each teacher.

Performances of CORI

In the main professional development workshop, learning is performance-based. To begin the workshop, teachers participate in a mini-CORI learning activity for approximately 2 hours. During this activity, teachers go through the four CORI processes: (a) observe and personalize, (b) search and retrieve, (c) comprehend and integrate, and (d) communicate to others, with respect to a specific topic, such as bird feathers and how feathers help birds survive. This experiential learning enables teachers to perceive how students can link a hands-on experience (observing bird feathers with a magnifying glass) to literacy learning (reading books about the variety of feathers and their functions). Teachers participate in searching through books, locating resources, synthesizing information, and communicating to the rest of the group. All of these processes parallel the learning activities their students will undertake in a CORI classroom.

Performance-based learning is also provided for the cognitive strategies of reading comprehension. In the workshop, teachers execute each of the six strategies taught in CORI with materials relevant to their reading level and interests. For example, in discussing the role of activating background knowledge, teachers read a text about which they have very little, if any, conceptual knowledge, and compare this to their reading of a text for which they have a rich, abundant reservoir of information. This enables teachers to experience what their students encounter as strategy learners in the classroom.

Observing and Modeling Instruction

In this professional development workshop, teachers observe CORI in several forms. They view videotapes of CORI teachers providing the context for inquiry, reading strategy teaching, motivational support, and the integrations of reading and science. Expert CORI teachers attending the workshop provide examples of their lessons, their planning, and their implementation of CORI units. These prototypes of instructional design and teaching activities provide an abundance of concrete ideas for teachers to incorporate into their own personal planning and design for implementing CORI.

A CORI Teaching Guideline

During the middle of the workshop, teachers review a guide for implementing CORI, beginning with suggested activities for a week of CORI instruction. Adaptations necessary to make this framework efficient and effective for both low and high achievers and for smaller and larger classes are discussed. Although the initial portion of this 12-week guide is highly detailed, the specifications decrease over time to encourage teachers to become active designers following the CORI principles.

During each workshop day, teachers tailor this provisional framework to their own purposes. They adjust the length of teaching activities, make book selections from menus offered within the framework, and revise the students' writing expectations based on the needs of their students. Teachers also incorporate language arts requirements that may be particular to their school, reading strategies that will be especially important for their students, and other techniques that enable them to adapt this instruction to their classrooms.

Learning the Background

To gain a sense of the engagement perspective, teachers read professional journal articles and discuss students' reading engagement. They debate what it means to be an engaged reader and how strategies, knowledge, motivation, and the social milieu of the classroom are interrelated. Everyone joins into seminar-type discussions. The aim of this phase is to enable teachers to gain conceptual knowledge of the theoretical framework that is depicted in Table 1.1.

Continuing Development and Support

Professional development and support does not end once the school year begins. In a continuing forum for professional development, teachers attend one-day, monthly workshops to meet with mentors and project leaders. At these events, teachers describe what has worked and what areas need improvement. They present teaching activities that have been effective for improving reading and exchange the challenges they face. Brainstorming helps teachers find solutions collaboratively. Teachers' interchange ends with plans for their next stages of CORI implementation.

REFERENCES

Baker, L., Dreher, M. J., & Guthrie, J. T. (2000). *Engaging young readers: Promoting achievement and motivation*. New York: Guilford.

Deci, E. L., & Ryan, R .M. (1992). The initiation and regulation of intrinsically motivated learning and achievement. In A. K. Boggiano & T. S. Pittman (Eds.), *Achievement and motivation: A social developmental perspective* (pp. 3–36). Toronto, Canada: Cambridge University Press.

Guthrie, J. T., Anderson, E., Alao, S., & Rinehart, J. (1999). Influences of Concept-Oriented Reading Instruction on strategy use and conceptual learning from text. *Elementary School Journal, 99*, 343-366.

Guthrie, J. T., & Cox, K. E. (2001). Classroom conditions for motivation and engagement in reading. *Educational Psychology Review, 13*(3), 283-302.

Guthrie, J. T., Schafer, W. D., & Huang, C. (2001). Benefits of opportunity to read and balanced instruction on the NAEP. *Journal of Educational Research, 96*(3), 145-162.

Guthrie, J. T., Van Meter, P., Hancock, G. R., Alao, S., Anderson, E., & McCann, A. (1998). Does Concept-Oriented Reading Instruction increase strategy use and conceptual learning from text? *Journal of Educational Psychology, 90*, 261-278.

Guthrie, J. T., Weber, S., & Kimmerly, N. (1993). Searching documents: Cognitive processes and deficits in understanding graphs, tables, and illustrations. *Contemporary Educational Psychology, 18*, 186-221.

Guthrie, J. T., & Wigfield, A. (2000). Engagement and motivation in reading. In M. L. Kamil, P. B. Mosenthal, P. D. Pearson, & R. Barr (Eds.), *Reading research handbook, 3*, (pp. 403-424). Mahwah, NJ: Lawrence Erlbaum Associates.

Guthrie, J. T., Wigfield, A., & Von Secker, C. (2000). Effects of integrated instruction on motivation and strategy use in reading. *Journal of Educational Psychology, 92*(2), 331-341.

Hidi, S., & Harackiewicz, J. M. (2000). Motivating the academically unmotivated: A critical issue for the 21st century. *Review of Educational Research, 70*(2), 151-179.

National Reading Panel. (2000). *Report of the National Reading Panel: Teaching children to read—an evidence-based assessment of the scientific research literature on reading and its implications for reading instruction.* (NIH Publication No. 00-4769). Jessup, MD: National Institute for Literacy.

Paris, S. G., Wasik, B. A., & Turner, J. C. (1991). The development of strategic readers. In R. Barr, M. L. Kamil, P. Mosenthal, & P. D. Pearson (Eds.), *Handbook of reading research* (pp. 609-640). New York: Longman.

Skinner, E. A., Wellborn, J. G., & Connell, J. P. (1990). What it takes to do well in school and whether I've got it: A process model of perceived control and children's engagement and achievement in school. *Journal of Educational Psychology, 82*(1), 22-32.

Stipek, D. (1996). Motivation and instruction. In D. C. Berliner & R. C. Calfee (Eds.), *Handbook of educational psychology* (pp. 85-113). New York: Simon & Schuster Macmillan.

CHILDREN'S BOOK REFERENCES

Yolen, J. (1987). *Owl moon*. New York: Putnam & Grosset.

2

How the CORI Framework Looks in the Classroom

Kathleen C. Perencevich
University of Maryland

This chapter illustrates how Concept-Oriented Reading Instruction (CORI) looks in the classroom. Specifically, it shows how teachers implement CORI; how their instruction is aligned with the CORI principles of using a conceptual theme; connecting science inquiry with literacy instruction; emphasizing important motivational guidelines such as autonomy-support, collaboration, and support for reading efficacy; and directly teaching important reading comprehension strategies. The essence of CORI instruction is presented through multiple lenses, including rich descriptions of activities used in weeks 1–6 (see chapter 8 for a detailed description of weeks 7–12), vignettes from videotaped instruction, excerpts from teacher interviews, and displays and descriptions of student work. Throughout the chapter, CORI teachers use the principles in multiple and varied ways, and yet, reaching the overarching goals of promoting engaged reading, increasing reading comprehension skills, and gaining high conceptual knowledge in science.

Overall Instructional Plan

For 12 weeks, CORI teachers integrate reading and science and teach for two consecutive hours each morning. Two additional weeks before and after the 12 weeks of CORI instruction are used for week-long pretest and posttest reading–science performance assessments (see chapter 9). During the first 6 weeks of CORI, teachers teach reading comprehension strategies, science content, and science process skills using the "Birds Around the World" conceptual theme. In the next 6 weeks of CORI instruction, teachers use the "Survival in Freshwater Habitats" conceptual theme. Both themes focus on the survival of life in the ecosystem and use nine core ecological concepts to guide knowledge acquisition including: feeding, communication, locomotion, respiration, defense, predation, competition, reproduction, and adaptation to the physical environment. We choose to focus on these concepts because they are central to animal survival and understanding of ecological systems (see chapter 5). Throughout CORI, there is a special emphasis placed on support for student motivation and explicit support for reading and science integrations.

Birds Around the World.   This theme was chosen because birds survive in multiple biomes, and yet, in any biome, their survival depends on the nine core concepts introduced in CORI. CORI teachers follow a general framework, incorporating reading strategy instruction, inquiry science, motivational processes, and reading–science integrations. Additionally, teachers engage students in four major phases of learning: (a) observe and personalize, (b) search and retrieve, (c) comprehend and integrate, and (d) communicate to others.

Initiating Reading Engagement Through Personalization.   During weeks 1–3 of CORI instruction, teachers focus on instructing through observation, personalization, and search. In order to initiate student engagement in reading, CORI teachers begin by helping students interact with the real world (see Chapter 1). During the first few weeks of CORI, students observe birds in their natural habitats, personalize their learning goals by asking questions about birds that pique their interests, and search for answers to their questions. Inquiry science activities, which serve as a launch to questioning and searching, include: a walk in the local woodlands, multiple observations and mini-experiments with bird feathers, and an owl pellet dissection. These activities initiate questioning which give rise to students' creation of personal goals for learning about birds around the world. These inquiry science activities, when linked to the reading material in the class, help students gain conceptual knowledge both from reading and from experimentation. For example, students have access to at least five class or team sets of books and five individual books about owls to connect their curiosities and hypotheses about owl pellet dissection to learning conceptual knowledge from reading. It is crucial that students begin to realize that reading is the fundamental connection between their curiosities and their conceptual knowledge growth (see chapter 6).

Next, students search through interesting texts in order to gather information about their curiosities. During the first weeks of CORI, teachers directly teach reading comprehension strategies in the context of children's knowledge pursuit. CORI instruction focuses on six reading strategies selected from the National Reading Panel Report (2000; see chapter 4). For example, CORI teachers promote skills for **activating background knowledge** before reading about birds and observing birds in their natural habitats. They teach **questioning** skills and **search** strategies in the context of children's desires to learn about their personal queries about bird survival. Discussed later in this chapter are successful instructional activities that enable children to observe and personalize goals through questioning, searching, and retrieving important and relevant information about bird survival.

Sustaining reading engagement through knowledge growth. During weeks 4–6, students focus on comprehending and integrating their knowledge of bird survival. Comprehension strategies, such as **summarizing, organizing graphically,** and **story structuring** are taught explicitly, and students practice these strategies in multiple settings, with texts in multiple genres and levels (see chapter 4). Student goals for these reading strategies include: (a) becoming facile with the use of the strategy (e.g., competence building); (b) understanding the appropriate use of the strategy and its connection to knowledge growth (e.g., metacognitive awareness); and (c) learning to be independent and proficient users of reading strategies (e.g., self-initiation). In addition, students learn how to express their knowledge and use of strategies by communicating their scientific knowledge to others. The second half of this chapter illustrates how teachers successfully teach these reading strategies and how students communicate their scientific expertise to their peers. The first teaching phase of CORI, observe and personalize, is depicted in Table 2.1.

OBSERVING AND PERSONALIZING
IN JEAN SAMUEL'S CLASSROOM

On this first day of CORI, third-grade students walk into their classrooms to find them filled with theme-relevant learning materials. In one corner of the room, they notice a perky pet parakeet. Another corner houses brilliant peacock, ostrich, and pheasant feathers. Posters describing the conceptual theme, "Birds Around the World," fill the room, as do charts depicting important concepts of study, including feeding, respiration, and competition, among others. On the walls and bulletin boards are descriptions of the essential reading strategies students will be learning: activating background knowledge, questioning, searching for information, summarizing, organizing graphically, and story structuring. Another bulletin board depicts a growing vocabulary word wall and the beginning of a concept map that will expand as learning occurs.

TABLE 2.1
Observing and Personalizing in the CORI Classroom

CORI Phases	Reading Strategy Instruction	Science Inquiry Activities	Motivational Support	Reading-Science Integrations
Observe & Personalize	**Activating Background Knowledge** Relate personal experiences to stories and information texts on birds around the world.	**Observing** Observe and record information about birds in local habitats. Take a field trip to local woods and observe plants, animals, and populations.	**Interacting with the Real World** Support students in noticing birds and bird features that are new or interesting in order to pique curiosity for reading.	**Relating** Relate birds in stories to field observations of birds and their surroundings.
	Questioning Ask multiple questions about bird survival in diverse land forms in order to initiate text reading.	**Designing Investigation** Pose hypotheses about owl feeding and design owl pellet investigation.	**Students Choosing** Choose three favorite questions for class discussion and posting. Choose and take ownership of favorite sub-theme to study.	**Comparing and Contrasting** Identify questions that can be answered through reading, and science observation.

However, most apparent in this lively third-grade classroom is the sheer abundance of books. There are books about different biomes around the world. There are books about the survival of birds. There are books about specific species of birds, such as owls and penguins. Importantly, there are both expository and narrative books at multiple reading levels, ranging from Grades 1–6.

Holding a book about polar regions in one hand and pointing out the window at a woodland habitat with the other hand, teacher Jean Samuel, of North Frederick Elementary School in Frederick, Maryland, lures her students into a discussion about how animals survive in multiple biomes. "Would an owl be able to live in the Arctic?" The children shake their heads. "Would a penguin be able to live in our schoolyard woods?" she queries. In unison, the children exclaim, "No, of course not." They giggle at the mere thought of it.

Maintaining their piqued curiosity, Mrs. Samuel describes the conceptual theme for the next 6 weeks. "We will be studying different places or habitats where birds live. Some birds live in deserts, some birds live in polar areas, and some birds live right in our backyard. So, we will study how these different birds survive around the world." She exclaims, "Now, let's think about how plants and animals survive in our own backyard. In a few minutes, we will take a walk in our backyard woodlands and collect everything we see. But first, take out your journals, and with a partner, write down all of the plants and animals you expect to see on our woodland walk." Kate and her partner, Tyrone, write that they expect to see rabbit tracks, a squirrel, a bee, a chipmunk, a hole, a butterfly, a dog, a bird, a bird nest, trees, bushes, and leaves. Soon, students gather their materials for a woodland walk.

They bring along their CORI journals to take notes, draw, and label everything they see. The students are divided into teams, each bringing along a disposable camera to take pictures and a large net to collect specimens for team terrariums. During the walk, pairs of students complete a chart depicting plants and animals they observe, signs of life that they encounter, and locations of these plants and animals. For example, Kate and Tyrone report seeing yellow dandelions, grass, flowers, bugs, nuts, pinecones, worms, a spider, a cricket, two caterpillars, a big bird in the tree, and two bird feathers on the ground. They fill their net with the caterpillars, leaves, grass, some nuts, and a cricket. They also write personal questions that arise during their walk. For example, Kate poses three questions; "How do birds tell his baby how to fly?" "How does a bird talk?" and "How old does a tree get?"

When they return to the classroom, the teams excitedly place their specimens in their team terrariums. At this point, Mrs. Samuel asks students to share their prior knowledge and personal questions with each other. One student proudly announces, "I know what a blue jay looks like, but my question is, what does it eat?" After browsing bird books for a few minutes, students make a list of their questions about birds on the board.

After this short activity, Mrs. Samuel asks her students to take out their personal copies of the book *Owl Moon*, by Jane Yolen. In pairs, students will read this delightful story of a young girl who goes owling with her father. First, students look through the book and write some predictions about what the girl and her dad might see on the walk. As they have just experienced their own woodland walk, students excitedly begin writing about what the girl and her Pa might see on their walk. Kate writes what she knows about owls: "I know that owls are nocturnal. They hunt at night and they don't make a sound when they fly. They live in trees." Next, Kate makes her story predictions: "I predict that they take a walk at night and look for an owl. Maybe they will see an owl. It will be under the moon. That might be the way *Owl Moon* got the title."

As this first morning of CORI comes to an end, Mrs. Samuel tells her students some of the activities they will be doing in the upcoming weeks. They will describe how the walk in *Owl Moon* is similar to and different from the woodland walk they experienced. They will begin to answer their personal questions by exploring books, and they will be observing, reading, and learning about birds around the world. They will dramatize *Owl Moon* in an expressive reading activity. Furthermore, they will be dissecting an owl pellet and making hypotheses about how owls feed and compete for food.

WHY ARE REAL-WORLD INTERACTIONS IMPORTANT?

Students in Jean Samuel's class begin their literary experiences by interacting with their natural world. The overarching goal of real-world interaction is to set the stage and create purposes for engaged reading. In CORI, students interact with concrete objects, specimens, and events using their senses of sight, hearing, touch, or smell, and by recording their experiences through writing, drawing, or photography. Real-world interactions can range from broad (e.g., woodland walk) to specific (e.g., carefully drawing and labeling the parts of a cricket, leaf, or bird feather). Observations must be purposeful, not simply "fun." The main goal is two-fold, serving both motivational and cognitive functions. Cognitively, real-world interactions help students activate experiential knowledge in order to pursue a reading event. Motivationally, real-world interactions help to pique student curiosities and foster questioning, which create personal goals for knowledge seeking. Establishing a purpose for reading that is personally significant is an essential goal of observation in CORI.

Cognitively, real-world interactions help students activate their background knowledge. It is well known that facile readers relate their background knowledge to ideas in text and relate ideas in one text to another (Dochy, Segers, & Buehl, 1999). In addition, background knowledge is often revised during reading to account for new information in text. Real-world interactions help students bring their background knowledge to the forefront before and during reading. Often, students come to school with sparse experiences about the world around them. Certainly, they have seen birds fly outside, but most third- grade students have never actually touched a bird feather. Likewise, they may not have noticed the oft-undetected hidden world of insects, rabbit holes, or bird nests that Mrs. Samuel's students saw during their woodland walk. Thus, the real-world interaction affords experiences to children who may have impoverished experiences about the conceptual theme and activates other students' awareness about the theme. Real-world interaction is needed to prime students for engagement in reading.

Motivationally, it is well-documented that students are typically interested in things that they know a little something about (Alexander, Jetton, &

Kulikowich, 1995; Bergin, 1999). Real-world experiences are exciting, as they arouse curiosity and evoke a sense of wonder about the world. This arousal represents situational interests that we believe can develop into long-term motivations for reading (see chapter 10). For example, the energy aroused by the woodland walk did not simply end with the walk; rather, it was directed into reading interesting text. In the vignette, Jean Samuel used a woodland walk as a concrete, tangible activity to launch the theme of bird survival and the reading of *Owl Moon*. The captivation and attention students feel during real-world interactions often induce intrinsically motivated behaviors. They often report losing track of time, desiring to continue working despite hurdles and difficulties, and perhaps most importantly, aspiring to learn more about what they observed, through reading.

The curiosity piqued during real-world experiences prompts students to ask questions. Student questioning serves a different purpose from teacher questioning. When teachers ask questions, they are the directors of the curriculum. Questions teachers ask may or may not kindle student interest. In contrast, when students ask questions, the theme becomes personally relevant and meaningful, which is a central principle for increasing motivation in reading (see chapter 3).

> Jean Samuel relays her feelings about questioning and personalization: Before I became a CORI teacher, I posed a lot of the questions myself and had students look for the answers in order to get the information from the text. Now, I try not to do that anymore. I want to allow my students to come up with their own questions and I see that they are much more authentic. Some of the questions are much deeper than I would have expected. I have seen such a shift when they are posing their own questions. For example, one very interesting question that came up when we were observing the peacock feathers was, "How do the peacocks move their tail feathers up and down when they have so many feathers?" I responded that we would have to read and discover the answer to the question. I didn't answer the question like I used to. Rather, I wrote the question on the board. We had so many great questions and I started writing them as a PowerPoint presentation. The students kept coming back to their questions during their research. It was exciting to them because they were their questions, not mine.

Figure 2.1 depicts some of the questions Jean's students asked about birds.

When students experience the world in their own personal ways, their experiences are unique to them and thus set the stage for self-direction and ownership of the learning topic. What lies before them is not simply *any* bird feather or owl pellet, but their *personal* bird feather or owl pellet. Recall that during the walk, Kate asked how birds learn to fly. During the week, she would have her question answered both by observing bird feathers to learn about flight and reading about wing feathers. When texts and Internet sources are fused with real-world interac-

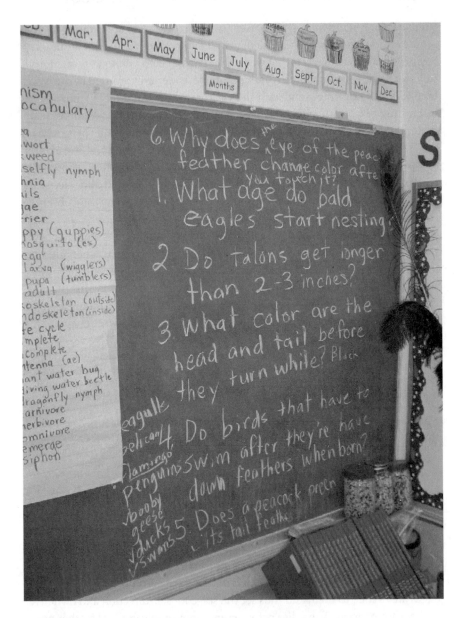

FIG. 2.1. Jean Samuel's board of students' questions about birds.

tions, students realize how both experiences and books can fill the gaps in their knowledge. Students become bona fide scientists as they ask important questions, make hypotheses, read to gather information, and experiment.

Thus, student questions become the learning goal—the very purpose for reading. Imagine the excitement Kate felt when she found the answer to her question, both through observing flight feathers and reading about those very feathers in books. She wrote in her journal, "I wanted to know how birds fly. My observation showed me that my wing feather was very light. It was 5 inches and 1¼ wide. It had some black in it and a wide, long stem in the middle, which attaches to the bird." From reading, Kate learned even more about her question. She wrote, "Did you know that the wing feathers are the most important feathers? They can help the bird fly. They are many different sizes and shapes and the air flows over the feathers when it flies. The tail feathers are cool too, because they help keep a bird's balance and help them steer."

In sum, questions serve as the springboard for learning, but also as a reminder of the merging of students' interests and their prior knowledge. Teachers help to legitimate these learning goals by publicly posting them for all to see. Students often write questions on sentence strips and on PowerPoint presentations for their peers. Students typically share their questions with each other and the whole class.

OBSERVATION AND PERSONALIZATION: THE CORI TEACHER'S ROLE

Students do not interact automatically and effectively with observational phenomena. Teachers must scaffold the observations of birds, bird feathers, owl pellets, or the growing leaf. Support for what to observe, how to record data, and how to interpret trends in data is necessary for the enrichment and fulfillment in a real-world interaction. Teachers support observation and real-world interactions by supplying students with an abundance of resources and tools to help guide students to discovery. For example, in the vignette, Mrs. Samuel provides scaffolds, asks enticing questions, and encourages her students to be thorough with their observations by drawing and labeling, photographing, magnifying objects with hand-held microscopes, and measuring specimens. Importantly, Mrs. Samuel provides her students with charts to organize their detailed observations. The class often shifts from an animated community that shouts with joy as a cricket tries to jump out of its terrarium, to a very serious and quiet group that measures each bird feather with skillful precision in order to fill in their observation chart.

Real-world interactions must be coupled with multiple sources of text (Newman, 1999; see chapter 6). Students' excitement and questions may be short-lived if they cannot follow them up immediately with related reading ac-

tivities. Reading should occur on the same day as the extended real-world interaction, when possible. With access to shelves of multilevel trade books, Internet
sources, and reference books, Mrs. Samuel has the resources necessary to fulfill
students' inquiries. Many of these books are provided to CORI teachers, and
they find others in the school's media center.

Mrs. Samuel constantly relates student observations to text by asking questions
like, "How was your woodland walk similar to or different from the walk that took
place in *Owl Moon*?" or "How does this book's description of owl feeding relate to
what you dissected in your owl pellet?" CORI teachers anticipate students' interest
and questions, and provide the necessary resources for them to pursue their learning goals. The real-world interactions and related reading occur alternatively in a
spiral of observing scientific phenomena in order to launch engaged reading and
reading to understand and critically evaluate the scientific observation.

It is important to note the extensiveness of the third-grade teacher's scaffolding with regard to questioning. Questioning, although crucial for personalization, is not an easy task for a third grader to accomplish. In the beginning
weeks of CORI, student questions are not necessarily correct in form and lack
conceptual content. Teachers provide extensive teaching, modeling, and scaffolding to help students write high-level conceptual questions (see chapter 11).
Quite often, students initially ask questions that may not be answerable from a
text. Therefore, CORI teachers use multiple ways to encourage students to ask
additional questions, write questions that are text-relevant, and use teammates
to foster more questioning.

A TEACHER'S VIEWS OF OBSERVATION
AND PERSONALIZATION

Teacher Penni Stockman, at Monocacy Elementary School in Frederick, Maryland describes observation in her classroom:

> Yesterday, students sat in convenient teams of their choosing and dissected owl
> pellets. They shared their excitement with their teammates as they measured,
> weighed, and dissected the owl pellets. Next, it was time to collect data and make a
> team graph. We put the team graphs together to form a class chart to figure out the
> number and types of bones we found as a class and, of course, to figure out what an-
> imals owls eat, because that is one of our core concepts. The children were excited
> and amused to realize that our class had found so many bones from so many ani-
> mals that owls eat. Many of our books connected because they had owls in them
> and described the process of owls making pellets. When they see it in a book, they
> make the connection, "Oh wow, we've seen this." I asked them, "Why didn't I just
> show you the book? Why did we actually tear the owl pellet apart? Why didn't I just
> show you a picture of an owl pellet and then read you a story about an owl?" "You

know what they said? 'Because we wouldn't have learned as much or been as interested in the book. It wouldn't have been as exciting.'"

Table 2.2 indicates the next instructional phase of CORI, search and retrieve.

SEARCH AND RETRIEVE

It is Week 3 of CORI in Penni Stockman's classroom. Students are busily studying about bird survival. Hanging on the classroom walls are biome posters containing students' background knowledge and questions about particular birds living in multiple biomes. For example, under the desert biome poster, one question reads, "How do birds protect themselves from the sun in the desert?" In addition, students' favorite questions are posted on the bulletin board entitled "Information Seekers." The teacher understands the importance of using student questions as a launch to students' search and retrieval processes.

On this day, students are gathered into teams each with a personal copy of *All Kinds of Habitats* by Sally Hewitt on their desks. In addition, a crate filled with approximately five to seven books on various biomes, including: *Looking at: Animals in Hot Places* by Moira Butterfield, *A True Book: Deserts* by Darlene Stille, and *Life in the Rainforests* by Lucy Baker. Teachers selected these texts for direct strategy instruction lessons on searching through expository texts. Shared characteristics of these books include high-quality use of text features, such as table of contents, indices, captions, bolded words, glossaries, subtitles, clear main ideas, and illustrations that match and extend the accompanying text (see chapter 6).

TABLE 2.2
Searching and Retrieving in the CORI Classroom

CORI Phases	A. Reading Strategy Instruction	B. Science Inquiry Activities	C. Motivational Support	D. Reading–Science Integrations
Search & Retrieve	**Searching** Gather information from multiple texts and media to answer personal questions about birds and their survival.	**Collecting Data** Dissect owl pellet and observe bird feathers. Categorize bones in pellets and collect data on feather experiments.	**Expanding Knowledge Goals** Expand goals from conceptual theme to guide reading. Show mastery of knowledge related to personal questions.	**Connecting Interests** Notice similarities between birds in field or experiment and birds in stories or information texts.

Mrs. Stockman begins her searching-for-information lesson. For students to answer their personal questions about birds, they must be facile searchers. Therefore, CORI teachers spend a significant amount of time teaching students to search for answers to their questions. First, she asks students to browse their *All Kinds of Habitats* text with their teammates to uncover particular text features that the author uses to help get the point across. She circulates in the classroom to take the pulse of the working groups. She praises students for their successes and if there is confusion, she pulls the class together for a quick discussion of the students' working knowledge and their difficulties. Teams eagerly write down all of the text features they are finding.

Mrs. Stockman asks students to hold up their texts, pointing to an important text feature that will help them find the answers to their questions about birds in various biomes. Tanya is pointing to a caption and illustration in her text. As Penni writes the text feature on the board, she asks, "Why do you think that feature is important?" Tanya responds that it helps to explain the picture. Robert points to his index, while Jacob is pointing to his table of contents. Mrs. Stockman continues writing all of the text features and helping students explain their potential functions. For example, she explains the difference between a table of contents and an index and asks students to think of an example of when it might be better to use one over the other.

Next, it is time for students to practice searching. Mrs. Stockman has prepared some questions in advance that will challenge her students to search through the texts effectively. She starts with an easy task of having the students use the table of contents, but then moves to more difficult questions that require the use of a synonym in the index or a search in two sections of the text.

Mrs. Stockman queries, "How do polar bears protect themselves from the cold?" Students excitedly search through their *All Kinds of Habitats* text. Some students use the index and find that polar bear information is located on page 18. Others use the table of contents and find that information about polar lands is located on pages 18–19. Students are gratified that there are many avenues to use to answer the question. Mrs. Stockman reminds students that they must support their answers with text evidence. Jemez explains to his classmates that he found his information on page 18 by using the index. He explains that polar bears survive in the cold because they have thick fur and an extra layer of fat to provide warmth. Lucinda notes that she finds the boxed text helpful in case she wants to research other animals that have thick fur and live in the snow.

After a few questions whereby students practice single feature use of texts, Mrs. Stockman moves to a more challenging task. She asks, "How are rainforests and woodlands different?" Notice that this question requires a search through at least two chapters of the book in order to answer the question. Students must not only use important search features such as the table of contents and index, but they must use subtitles and main ideas, and integrate information across multiple parts of a single text. Students work with partners to search and gather their information. Mrs. Stockman reminds students to be prepared to justify their answers with text evidence.

The teacher pulls the class together, "Okay, tell me one difference between rainforests and woodlands. Come on. Think about it." Cecile excitedly explains that different animals live in the rainforests than live in the woodlands. "Excellent," Mrs. Stockman exclaims, "How did you find that information?" Cecile says that she needed to look in two parts of the book to read about all of the different animals in each biome. "Like on page 9, I read that woodpeckers live in the woodland trees and on page 17, there is a picture of a toucan in a rainforest tree." Darren says that the plants are different, too, and he quotes from page 16, "Plants grow here [in the rainforest] that cannot be found anywhere else in the world."

Students are still very excited about the prospect of finding the answers to questions from their books. Now it is time for them to practice on their own. Mrs. Stockman tells the class that they will be searching for answers to the biome questions that they asked and hung around the room. During the week, students use their books to find the answers to the questions they asked about bird survival in various biomes. In the weeks to come, teams of students will also be researching a bird of their choice and these search skills come into play throughout the remainder of the CORI unit.

Mrs. Stockman fosters their growth in searching by expanding their practices to multiple text integration, use of multimedia for search, and use of concepts in their search process. For example, in one lesson, students find differences in their bird's survival, using as many core concepts as possible. In another lesson, students build a classroom chart of all the different birds being researched in order to show the diversity of animal adaptations and survival of bird life in multiple regions of the world.

During Week 3 of CORI, students are also searching and retrieving scientific information. The students dissect owl pellets and spend time searching books and field guides to classify the different bones found in the pellets. Another essential aspect of this phase of CORI is the integration of science observation and experimentation with reading and the extension of environmental interest through reading. Teachers help students notice similarities between birds in the field and in experiments, and between birds in stories and information texts.

WHY IS SEARCHING AND RETRIEVING IMPORTANT?

Students in CORI classrooms learn to search for information in the context of asking questions that are important to them. The search process occurs both with reading expository texts and collecting scientific data. In both cases, students are seeking answers to questions they ask. This is the fundamental key that unlocks the strategy instruction stalemate that all too often occurs in elementary classrooms (Pressley, Yokoi, Rankin, Wharton-McDonald, & Mistretta, 1997). In typical reading classes across the country, reading strategy instruction occurs in isolation of content (Allington & Johnston, 2002). When reading strategies are compartmentalized from important content, it is likely that they will not be remembered when the use of the reading strategy is crucial. However, CORI students learn to search for information in the context of answering their own personal questions (Guthrie & Cox, 1998). It takes great effort for a third grader to learn the difference between the table of contents and an index, for example. In addition, much persistence is needed in order for students to self-initiate and practice using appropriate text features in appropriate reading situations. It has been well documented that before reading, good readers develop a reading plan and identify texts and sections of text which are goal-relevant (Dreher, Davis, Waynant, & Clewell, 1998; Guthrie, Weber, & Kimmerley, 1993). During CORI, students' questions set the stage for goal-relevant reading to occur. Importantly, in as much as knowledge generation is a crucial aspect of CORI, searching instruction aids students in gaining important knowledge about the scientific concepts.

Searching through texts to learn information and collect scientific data is beneficial both cognitively and motivationally. Cognitively, the ability to search is crucial for reading and learning scientific information. A number of studies have shown that students' abilities to search through expository texts increase their reading comprehension (Symons, MacLatchy-Gaudet, Stone, & Reynolds, 2001). For example, in our CORI classrooms, search significantly predicts text comprehension (Guthrie & Cox, 2001). That is, students who have advanced searching skills are better text comprehenders than those with limited searching abilities.

Motivationally, facility in searching and other reading strategies increases students' self-efficacy for reading (Schunk & Zimmerman, 1997). When students feel competent in themselves as strategy users, their general efficacy toward reading will be likely to increase. Note that Mrs. Stockman began her instruction on searching using a relatively easy text. The topic was one on which the students had already written background knowledge and asked personal questions. In order for students' competence to grow, Mrs. Stockman slowly raised the instructional bar to keep students at the edge of their competencies. Thus, not only are they receiving accurate feedback about their abilities during the search process, they, too, are experiencing successes in small increments as the instructional challenge increases. Indeed, the fundamental aspect of searching in CORI that differs from other instructional programs and curricula is that the search is dependent fully on students' questions. It is the student who initiates the search goal, and thus searching becomes an intrinsically motivated event. Students in CORI classrooms constantly share their knowledge about posted questions that they answered through searching. Of course, this sharing generates the deepening of knowledge and the hunger for more questions.

SEARCH AND RETRIEVE: THE CORI TEACHER'S ROLE

The teacher plays a critical role in teaching students to search and retrieve information from text. Teachers provide a variety of supports for strategy learning, including modeling, explaining, coaching and scaffolding, peer discussions, practice, and student reflection. Strategies such as searching involve many steps and processes that must be taught directly at the beginning of each day. Students also need extensive practice using the strategy with teams, partners, and independently.

Importantly, most third graders need scaffolds in order to help with reading comprehension strategies. CORI teachers provide extensive scaffolds for the strategy of searching to come to fruition for students. In order to help students use an index to locate important concepts, one CORI teacher provided a chart for students to write synonyms under each concept. For example, Sarah chose owls for her bird research project and asked many questions about the concepts of survival. For each of the concepts, she wrote words that would help her search for information on the body parts needed for each concept (e.g., jaw and talons for feeding), the behaviors exhibited for each concept (e.g., swooping and flying for locomotion), and the environmental biome features present for each concept (e.g., nests, trees, or barns for reproduction).

Another chart used by a CORI teacher contained words that students brainstormed before searching about the different biomes. For example, when thinking about grasslands, Sandy filled in a chart of words about a description of the biome (e.g., grassy, meadow), plants that might live there (e.g., trees), animals that might live there (e.g., fox, snake, tiger), and birds that might live there (e.g., vulture).

Another simple, yet effective, idea is to have students write the main question on the top of a page and leave room for questions that arise during the search process. Students then write comprehensive notes and answers to all of the questions. Many CORI teachers give students Post-it notes to attach onto text pages that refer to a particular concept. This is especially helpful with the integration of searching for information across multiple texts.

Last, a very effective teaching tool in CORI classrooms is an oversized chart of synonyms. Whenever a student comes across a good synonym for a concept, he writes it on the chart for all to see. Thus, if a struggling reader becomes "stuck" in the search process, the growing chart can help to overcome the reading hurdle.

Search instruction is also dependent on appropriate text selection. Texts should be chosen based on qualities that aid with the search process. All too often, teachers teach search skills out of a traditional basal text. There are a number of problems with this instructional strategy. For one, most basal readers do not have an index. Also, the table of contents is merely a list of the text's titles in the basal and the page number on which the selection begins. In contrast, many good expository trade books contain a conceptually ordered table of contents, authentic indices and glossaries, and likely, subtitles and bolded words to aid in the search process. Another authentic and fundamental use of search skills is the Internet and websites, as a plethora of future reading will be done directly from computers (see chapter 6). CORI students practice their search skills in these various contexts, thus ensuring that transfer of skills is more probable.

A TEACHER'S VIEW OF SEARCH AND RETRIEVE

Melissa Burton describes her personal goals with regard to strategy instruction and specifically the strategy of search in her classroom:

> One of my goals when teaching reading strategies is to help the children understand how the strategies can be integrated. We talk about how strategies are really dependent on each other and are not used in isolation. Being able to use one helps you to use another. For example, having a question leads students to gather information in order to find the answer to that question. For the ultimate goal, I want my students to be able to search through expository texts to find information and express their knowledge about what they found.

When asked how she chooses which books to use for direct instruction of the search strategy, Melissa responds:

> I chose this particular book to teach from because the topic was very appealing since students had some background knowledge about it and previously they had asked questions about the topic. The book had many appropriate text features and the size of the book was manageable for instruction. Also, the organization of the book really roused them to search for the information that they needed.

I'm very decisive about the books I choose to teach from. It is never random. Now [as a CORI/Strategy Instruction (SI) teacher], I am choosing books that fit the particular reading strategies, as opposed to just choosing books based on content or curriculum goals. The criterion has changed for me. Strategy instruction comes first, content next, and then there is some deliberation about the variety of text sources (e.g., trade books, literary selections, websites, articles, and pamphlets). In fact, one piece that was useful was from a kid-friendly website that had very good search properties. One thing we've noticed is that these search skills transfer; that searching in language arts is the same as searching in science and social studies. When children are able to write in their journals about their search processes, they see how it connects when they are writing a lab report.

Another thing I consider is where the students are in their development of the strategy. So, in the beginning, I use very easy, accessible texts because the strategy learning is difficult and new. But as they became more familiar with the strategy, I shift the level of books to ones that are still on their reading level, but a bit more challenging in order to use the strategies.

Really, the most gratifying thing about teaching this search strategy is that the kids choose for themselves, the question they want answered and the important ideas they want to select from the texts that answer their questions. I think that using kids' questions to start the search process really empowers them. It's very personal to them. They are reading for a purpose—their own purpose, not one set up by me. Although I knew what my goal was today, they feel a sense of ownership in it too.

Table 2.3 indicates the instructional activities used in the next phase of CORI teaching, comprehend and integrate.

COMPREHEND AND INTEGRATE

During Weeks 4 and 5 of CORI, teachers focus on helping students comprehend and integrate various incoming information into a coherent form. Recall that our definition of reading comprehension is not merely enjoyment of text, although that is one crucial aspect; it is also that children gain new knowledge from reading text (Dreher, 2000; see chapter 1). Knowledge generated about the ecological concepts is fundamental to our view of reading comprehension (Erikson, 2002). In CORI, children are encouraged to express their new knowledge in a cohesive and coherent form. Therefore, during these weeks of instruction, it is crucial that students be able to integrate all of their search information and effectively summarize it. Students need the ability to summarize not only chapters of a single text, but information from multiple texts and other sources, such as the Internet. Students are also learning to organize information they are gathering from science observations. Students must organize the data from their observations into a useful and informative form, such as a team or class histogram.

TABLE 2.3
Comprehending and Integrating in the CORI Classroom

CORI Phases	A. Reading Strategy Instruction	B. Science Inquiry Activities	C. Motivational Support	D. Reading–Science Integrations
Comprehend & Integrate	**Summarizing** Express the gist of information and literary texts; write summaries of several books.	**Representing Data** Make histogram to show owl feeding preferences.	**Using Interesting Texts** Use multiple texts and internet sources to find information about a bird of choice.	**Contrasting Domain Learning** Distinguish text and science avenues to learn about ecology and populations.
	Organizing Graphically Construct a concept map about one bird's survival. Use up to nine ecological concepts, containing links and relationships.	**Organizing Investigation** Make a poster of owl pellet study, showing scientific method and conclusions.	**Collaborating** In small groups, exchange ideas and expertise on habitats, birds, and how they survive. Exchange literacy knowledge regarding strategy use.	**Combining Conceptual Learning** Merge results from bird investigation with knowledge gained from books.

Two fundamental reading comprehension strategies are summarizing and concept mapping (Alexander, Graham, & Harris, 1998; National Reading Panel, 2000). Connecting these two strategies to students' knowledge of ecological concepts facilitates both conceptual knowledge growth and an awareness of the usefulness of the strategy (Brown, 1997; Guthrie et al., 1998). When reading, there is an interaction between the reader and the text. The goal for the reader is to actively construct meaning from the text. Summarizing and concept mapping are two important tools students use to represent text in a coherent and conceptual form. Multiple vignettes of summarizing and concept mapping instruction are provided in chapters 4 and 11, respectively, that illustrate different methods CORI teachers employ to help students learn and use essential reading comprehension strategies. Initially, CORI teachers were surprised and struggled with the extensive amount of comprehension instruction necessary for students to actually use the strategies in meaningful ways. Thus, rather than give one instructional vignette for summarizing or organizing graphically, I described multiple tasks that teachers used to help students become proficient with these reading strategies.

In as much as the heart of CORI instruction is conceptual, all teachers use the concepts as springboards to summarizing and organizing. In fact, this simple change, from instruction that is topical to instruction that is conceptual, makes organizing and summarizing a much less laborious task. For example, no matter what organism students are studying in CORI, they come to realize that the core ecological concept of communication is essential for all organisms and thus must be featured in a conceptual organizational scheme of survival. Therefore, in addition to creating summaries and concept maps of individual texts, many CORI teachers also help students to organize and summarize, based on the nine core ecological concepts. They do this with class concept maps, team maps, and individual maps, as well as detailed, labeled illustrations. Often, students wrote summaries about their concept maps and vice versa. For example, teachers ask students to share their concept maps with a partner and have the partner summarize the information on the map. This instructional strategy helps both the map designer and the person learning from the map. It assists the students in realizing where there might be gaps in their own knowledge or in their expression of their knowledge.

With regard to literary text, summarizing still reflects the main idea and supporting details of the text, but the summary is typically expressed in a cause–effect mode. Thus, rather than circling a main idea for a selection, students often must express in one sentence what happened during a few paragraphs or a page of text. During chapter book reading, CORI teachers create reading guides wherein students express, in two or three sentences, what happened in a chapter of the text. Furthermore, students draw an illustration of their written summary. One CORI teacher uses a "Map-It-Out" strategy where students express a main idea and the key supporting points to back up the main idea and then write a summary expressing these key points.

To express their science knowledge gleaned from experimentation and observation, students draw histograms and write summaries about what their histograms depict. For example, Rose writes:

> I learned many things by looking at the histogram I made. I learned what some owls eat and where some owls live. I learned what different bones look like. Our pellets showed that our class owls had six rat bones, 20 bird bones, nine rodent bones, and seven vole bones and we all found a lot of fur in our pellets. I learned how hungry owls could get!

When students organized their information, they became more curious about owls and wanted to learn more through reading. When asked what was most interesting about the owl pellets, Rose referred to the knowledge she learned about owls from reading, not simply from the fun part, dissecting. "The most interesting thing was organizing the bones and reading about which bones they were. I like that the bones were all different and that owls eat so many animals. I liked doing the research on the owl." Additionally, many CORI teachers ask students to draw food webs of owls. This activity helps merge observation, comprehension, and knowledge growth in science. Students combine their information gained through dissecting the owl pellet with knowledge gained through reading about owl eating habits. Students begin to realize depth of knowledge about owl survival through feeding and competition.

During their own personal research on a bird of their choice, students self-initiate and practice the skills of summarizing and organizing. CORI teachers have students create individual bird maps and then team maps on all the birds in a particular biome. Students compare maps and write summaries about the survival of birds in various biomes.

WHY ARE COMPREHENDING AND INTEGRATING SKILLS IMPORTANT?

For children to become engaged readers, competence in comprehending and integrating information is essential. Cognitively, this competence is fundamental to gaining new knowledge from text. Knowledge is dynamic and ever-growing, and reading strategies, such as summarizing and organizing text, help students become aware of where their knowledge began and where their growth in knowledge grew. For example, in the chapter 11 vignette, Amy Broomall's students not only express knowledge from the text, but as their knowledge and understanding of the text grows, they constantly revisit and reorganize their concepts and topics to better describe their connections to each other. Similarly, in the vignette in chapter 4, Ann Duncan's students express their new knowledge by putting text ideas into their own words, and yet still express the main ideas and supporting details in the text. Thus, the competent reader is the strategic reader.

Motivationally, competence in comprehension and integration is essential for intrinsic motivation. There is a reciprocal relationship between understanding and enjoying text. It is obvious that students who struggle with understanding the meaning of what they read cannot enjoy the nuances of the text meanings. When students' goals are to pursue new knowledge, a change takes place in their stance toward reading. No longer is the goal to satisfy the teacher or compete with classmates; rather, the goal is to become curious about the text information, to extend their personal knowledge, and to express their knowledge in socially satisfying ways.

A TEACHER'S VIEW OF COMPREHEND
AND INTEGRATE

In this interview, Amy Broomall describes her teaching of graphic organizing:

Today I taught the graphic organizing strategy for the first time. The first and most important thing I did to prepare for this lesson was to find a good text to teach organizing. After that, everything falls into place. I knew I eventually wanted the children to independently make their own concept maps.

I try to relate organizing to their lives, so I talked about how we organize our papers in folders, to prime their knowledge of organizing before the lesson. In general, we do some journaling and I always try to relate the strategy to their lives. My goal is to continue teaching graphic organizing. Next week, we will use two texts about the same topic and I will have students organize that information.

We are doing the populations theme and thinking about dispersal and that is why I chose the topic of birds. For this theme, students are learning about habitats, organisms living in various habitats, and their survival skills. We also learn about animal adaptations in order for them to survive in these habitats. Today, I wanted them to learn about communication, habitats, and bird flight using this text. With regard to reading, everything has to do with these important scientific concepts. During language arts or science, students are always asking me which folder to put their work into. To me that shows that they don't feel a separation between reading and science, which is great.

When choosing this book, I thought about the level of the text. It related well to our science theme. It had some challenging vocabulary and some vocabulary they could find success with. It had words and concepts that were easily recognizable to pull out for organizing. In the beginning, when I'm teaching a new reading strategy, I try to find a text that is accessible for most of the students. It took me a while to find this text for today's lesson. First, we read the text independently, then with partners, to make sure they understood the content. Then, I began direct teaching of the organizing strategy.

I always try to start the strategy first. So, I modeled a concept map with them for the first few pages of the text. I start the concept map, then I call on them to ask them for help with the organizing. They always have a part in deciding how to do the reading strategy. For example, I ask them to use their own words on the map, not just the words in the text. Since doing this type of teaching (i.e., SI), I typically use students' questions as a launch to teaching most of the reading strategies, so it is more personal to them. For example, Katie wrote her prior knowledge and questions about birds before reading this text and learning this organizing strategy. The students seem to be making the connection between using the strategy and becoming better readers.

I had students work with partners to share their thoughts and find more success. In terms of motivation, these students love the topics of animals and plants. I definitely think that they enjoyed organizing those words. They were so involved in today's lesson. You could see that they were on task. They love using these reading strategies. For example, they love telling everything they know.

I was worried about this reading strategy of organizing, but after today, I can see they are really getting it. I felt really good about the students being able to come up with verbs to connect the concepts. Even my struggling readers really shined today. One little girl wrote about her motivation; she wrote that writing her background knowledge and writing about what she learned after organizing the book was like reading the text again!

Table 2.4 depicts the instructional activities in the fourth and final phase of CORI teaching, communicate to others.

Communicate to Others

It is now the moment students have been anticipating. It is time to express their new knowledge to their peers and other audiences. Students have chosen the method and form for their personal expression. Some students have created posters and written reports, others have made dioramas or concept maps with accompanying index card reports, others have written books about their bird, and still others have designed murals describing their biome and all of the birds in it. One student created a video of his bird-watching experiences, along with his written report.

One aspect important to CORI is to help students integrate the knowledge learned from expository and literary texts, as well as from scientific observations. Remember that presenting to this group of "experts" is a challenging task, for all of the students have a grasp of the concepts. When it is time for questions, students need to be ready to answer very high-level conceptual questions.

It is finally Elizabeth's turn to present her expertise about the three birds she researched: the pileated woodpecker, the broad-winged hawk, and the ovenbird. Elizabeth wrote a chapter book and designed a poster to illustrate the nine ecological concepts: feeding, locomotion, respiration, communication, defense, predation, competition, reproduction, and adaptation to habi-

TABLE 2.4
Communicating in the CORI Classroom

CORI Phases	A. Reading Strategy Instruction	B. Science Inquiry Activities	C. Motivational Support	D. Reading–Science Integrations
Communicate to Others	**Communicating Literacy** Teach an authentic audience about bird survival and your literacy strategies.	**Communicating Science** Teach an authentic audience about scientific content and process learned in experiment.	**Coordinating Motivational Activities** Chart trail of curiosities and learning about bird survival.	**Integrating Reading & Science** Write a combined report about experiment and content learned from texts.

tat. Figure 2.2 indicates what one third grader, Elizabeth, wrote to describe the concept of locomotion.

Figure 2.3 indicates what Elizabeth wrote to summarize all the ecological concepts.

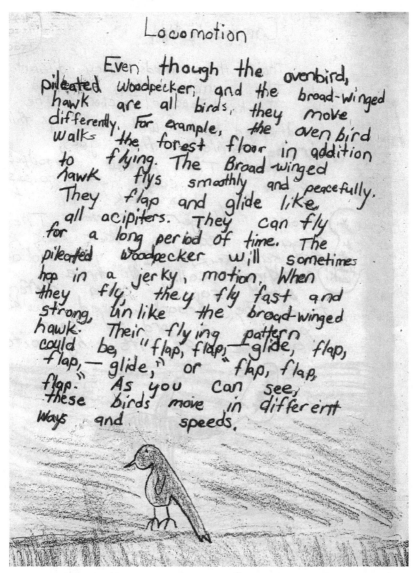

FIG. 2.2.   Elizabeth's description of the concept of locomotion.

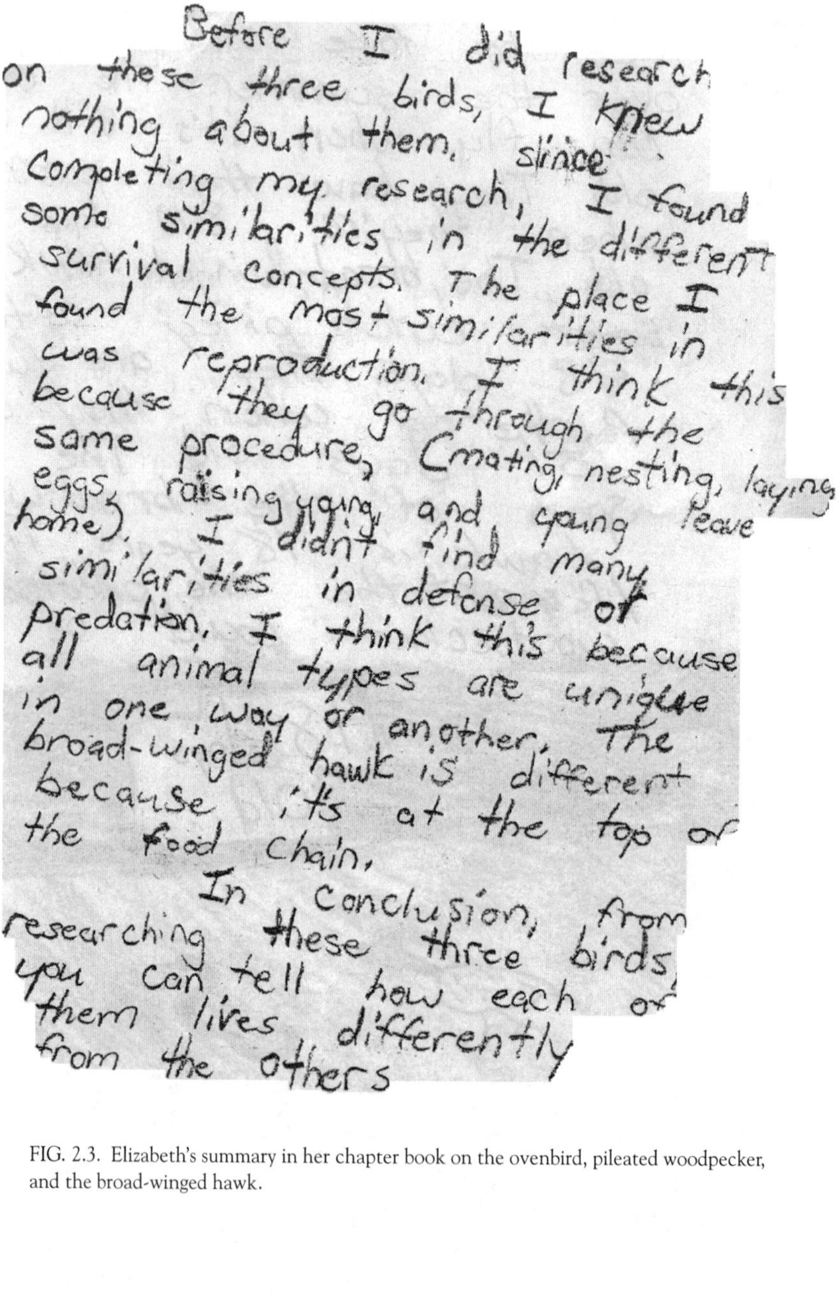

Before I did research on these three birds, I knew nothing about them. Since completing my research, I found some similarities in the different survival concepts. The place I found the most similarities in was reproduction. I think this because they go through the same procedure, (mating, nesting, laying eggs, raising young and young leave home). I didn't find many similarities in defense of predation. I think this because all animal types are unique in one way or another. The broad-winged hawk is different because its at the top of the food chain.

In conclusion, from researching these three birds, you can tell how each of them lives differently from the others

FIG. 2.3. Elizabeth's summary in her chapter book on the ovenbird, pileated woodpecker, and the broad-winged hawk.

WHY IS COMMUNICATING TO OTHERS IMPORTANT?

In CORI, self-expression is a key element of engaged reading. Self-expression refers to the many approaches students use to display their new knowledge and expertise. CORI teachers afford control to students in the form of honoring their voices and allowing them to direct movement of curricular decisions (see chapter 3). In her work on communities of learners, Brown (1997) explained, "Students and teachers each have ownership of certain forms of expertise, but no one has it all" (p. 12). In CORI classrooms, self-expression is crucial because students are the experts; the teacher is not the sole distributor of relevant knowledge.

Students have perceptions of their purposes for being or not being involved in literacy activities. Oldfather and Dahl (1994) found that intrinsic motivation was significantly related to student self-expression. Students' self-expression that is valued is referred to as the *honored voice*. When student voices are honored, students know that their opinions and personal views on topics of study and interpretations of text are valued. Oldfather and Dahl (1994) found that students who felt their voices were honored also experienced much more ownership in their literacy activities. In CORI, students lead discussions, share ideas, initiate topics, and take turns deciding when to shift the discussion. When their voices are honored through this sharing of expertise, they feel ownership over their learning.

Self-expression is an essential aspect of CORI because it helps students to develop an ownership of their interpretations of text (Tharp & Gallimore, 1993) and become efficacious in their abilities to dethrone the authority of text (Bandura, 1982). If children become reliant on teachers to interpret texts for them, and if the learning environment restricts children to respond only to teacher-initiated, literal questions about text, then students' opportunities to craft their own personal interpretations about text become severely limited.

When students shape tasks and goals to represent what they value and those interests that hold personal significance, then they will be more engaged with the content (Lambert & McCombs, 1998). Ryan and Deci (2000) stated, "For a high level of intrinsic motivation, people must experience satisfaction of the needs both for competence and autonomy" (p. 58). When students receive challenging instruction and work on conceptual tasks, they need choice and input into the management of the task. This is when self-expression is particularly beneficial. In her chapter book, Elizabeth wrote passionately about her knowledge of her chosen bird. The excitement she felt is the reward for 6 weeks of in-depth study on her woodpecker, and her pride in her work was obvious.

A TEACHER'S VIEW OF COMMUNICATING TO OTHERS

In Jean Samuel's CORI classroom, several forms of communication occurred through the CORI units. Jean describes how her class communicates their new knowledge to others:

> We read that beautiful book, *The Silver Swan*, and were almost in tears at the end. The children loved it. As we reread it, and discussed what we could learn about swans from the book, we discovered that although it was a narrative selection, it taught us about many of the core concepts in CORI. The children worked by themselves, and then in pairs, to analyze the text for factual information. We shared what we found together and then organized our findings into the core survival concepts. We discovered that certain concepts were covered and others were not. Feeding was not an important concept in the book and we got very little information about it. We combined predation and defense because they were closely related, when the fox was trying to catch the female and the male struggled to protect her. These concepts were very important. Another concept that the children found a lot of information about was reproduction. This included the care in finding and building a nesting sight, taking care of their eggs, and also teaching the young. When the students wrote their reports, it was to share that although the author wrote the book for pleasure, you could also learn important facts about swans in their natural environment. The children put all of their gathered information into paragraphs and wrote excellent reports.

> Another CORI class project was the owl pellet dissection. The whole process of dissecting the owl pellets was a highlight of the unit. They wrote their findings in report form and then made excellent posters to communicate their findings. We worked on a format that was pleasing to the eye; children need to learn how to organize their information into a form that is artistic, yet not fanciful. Once their reports were done, the bones from the pellet identified and glued to paper, the poster was constructed, and the children were able to compare their findings with other children's findings. The posters were displayed outside the class for the school to view.

> The children chose a bird and examined websites, books available in the classroom and library, and their own resources at home to gather information on the nine core survival concepts. They were to create a visual representation of their bird, a written report, and present an oral report about their bird. This was important because they were putting into practice all that they had learned in the project. They chose the bird, wrote questions that required research to find the answers, organized the information they gathered, and wrote an organized report about their bird. Finally, they presented their research to their peers, orally, as well as with their visual. When they finished, they answered classmates' questions. This was an important phase because the children began to compare their findings with other's findings and saw similarities and differences. For example, most children didn't include respiration in their reports because they had not chosen water birds. The two or three who chose birds that survive near oceans (puffins, penguins) found it necessary to include respiration, because their birds could stay underwater for different lengths of time.

> For our freshwater unit, we brainstormed a different communication piece for their chosen organism. We found a book that had a wonderful format and we tried to duplicate it in our poster displays. One comment the children made was, "This is the greatest project!" They still needed to do the research, but the poster contained their

information in a different way. Many were superb! Some students creatively used humor to convey their information.

The children have gained a great deal of knowledge, and the depth they go into a topic is phenomenal! Our last venture has been studying sharks. We started with activating background knowledge, posing questions, and then researched to find answers. Next, we graphically organized our information and found areas that needed more. We went to other sources (I have about 20 books about sharks, plus what was in the library, plus information from the Internet). My husband also dissected a shark for the children. They then wrote a report about sharks. As they were writing a paragraph, they discovered they didn't have enough information in certain areas. Individually, they returned to the books to read more so they could fully explain each specific topic. One report is 11 pages long! The students are now making dioramas of sharks in their habitat. They even made their own boxes. They definitely know how to fully research a topic!

Jean concluded her interview on the CORI concept of communicating to others with these thoughts:

Learning has been great fun for the children, but in order to confirm what they've learned, they need to let others know what they know by writing about it, drawing, or doing some artistic representation of it, and then, somehow, sharing their knowledge with others. As they have shared their information, others have challenged what they've said with, "I don't think that's right. I didn't read that anyplace. Show me where you found that!" When the one challenged shows them, it's quite a proud moment.

CONCLUSION

CORI teachers use the four instructional phases of observe and personalize, search and retrieve, comprehend and integrate, and communicate to others around a conceptual theme to help their students build new knowledge. Teachers model and scaffold reading strategies to teach them to their students. Strategies alone, however, do not make students engaged readers. Rather, engaged reading is fostered in a classroom environment that piques students' curiosities through observation and questioning, gives students the ability to search and comprehend multiple texts about topics they find interesting, and that legitimates students' knowledge growth through communicating with others.

REFERENCES

Alexander, P. A., Jetton T. L., & Kulikowich, J. M. (1995). Interrelationship of knowledge, interest and recall: Assessing a model of domain learning. *Journal of Educational Psychology*, 87, 559–575.

Alexander, P. A., Graham, S., & Harris, K. R. (1998). A perspective on strategy research: Progress and prospects. *Educational Psychology Review, 10(2)*, 129–153.

Allington, R. L., & Johnston, P. H. (2002). *Reading to learn: Lessons from exemplary fourth-grade classrooms*. New York: Guilford Press.

Bandura, A. (1982). Self-efficacy mechanism in human agency. *American Psychologist, 37(2),* 122–147.

Bergin, D. (1999). Influences on classroom interest. *Educational Psychologist, 34,* 87–98.

Brown, A. (1997). Transforming schools into communities of thinking and learning about serious matters. *American Psychologist, 53(3),* 399–413.

Dochy, F., Segers, M., & Buehl, M. (1999). The relation between assessment practices and outcomes of studies: The case of research on prior knowledge. *Review of Educational Research, 69,* 146–186.

Dreher, M. (2000). Fostering reading for learning. In L. Baker, M. Dreher, & J. Guthrie (Eds.), *Engaging young readers: Promoting achievement and motivation* (pp.68–93). New York, NY: Guilford Press.

Dreher, M., Davis, K. A., Waynant, P., & Clewell, S. F. (1998). Fourth-grade researchers: Helping children develop strategies for finding and using information. In T. Shanahan & F. Rodriguez-Brown (Eds.), *National Reading Conference Yearbook, 47,* 311–322. Chicago: National Reading Conference.

Erickson, L. H. (2002). *Concept-based curriculum and instruction: Teaching beyond the facts.* California: Corwin Press.

Guthrie, J. T., & Cox, K. (1998). Portrait of an engaging classroom: Principles of Concept-Oriented Reading Instruction for diverse students. In K. Harris (Ed.), *Teaching every child every day: Learning in diverse schools and classrooms* (pp. 70–130). Cambridge, MA: Brookline Books.

Guthrie, J. T., & Cox, K. E. (2001). Classroom conditions for motivation and engagement in reading. *Educational Psychology Review, 13(3),* 283–302.

Guthrie, J. T., Van Meter, P., Hancock, G. R., Alao, S., Anderson, E., & McCann, A. (1998). Does Concept-Oriented Reading Instruction increase strategy use and conceptual learning from text? *Journal of Educational Psychology, 90,(2),* 261–278.

Guthrie, J. T., Weber, S., & Kimmerly, N. (1993). Searching documents: Cognitive processes and deficits in understanding graphs, tables, and illustrations. *Contemporary Educational Psychology, 18,* 186–221.

Lambert, N. M., & McCombs, B. L. (1998). *How students learn: Reforming schools through learner-centered education.* Washington, DC: American Psychological Association.

National Reading Panel. (2000). *Teaching children to read: An evidence-based assessment of the scientific research literature of reading and its implication for reading instruction.* (NIH Publication No. 00–4769). Jessup, MD: National Institute for Literacy.

Newman, S. B. (1999). Books make a difference: A study of access to literacy. *Reading Research Quarterly, 34,* 286–311.

Oldfather, P., & Dahl, K. (1994). Toward a social constructivist reconceptualization of intrinsic motivation for literacy learning. *Journal of Reading Behavior, 26,* 139–158.

Pressley, M., Yokoi, L., Rankin, J., Wharton-McDonald, R., & Mistretta, J. (1997). A survey of the instructional practices of grade 5 teachers nominated as effective in promoting literacy. *Scientific Studies of Reading, 1,* 145–160.

Ryan, R. M. & Deci, E. L. (2000). Intrinsic and extrinsic motivations: Classic definitions and new directions. *Contemporary Educational Psychology, 25,* 54–67.

Schunk, D. H., & Zimmerman, B. J. (1997). Developing self-efficacious readers and writers: The role of social and self-regulatory processes. In J. T. Guthrie, & A. Wigfield (Eds.), *Reading engagement: Motivating readers through integrated instruction* (pp. 34–50). Newark, DE: International Reading Association.

Symons, S., MacLatchy-Gaudet, H., Stone, T. D., & Reynolds, P. L. (2001). Strategy instruction for elementary students searching informational text. *Scientific Studies of Reading, 5,* 1–33.

Tharp, R. G., & Gallimore, R. (1993). Teaching mind in society: Teaching, schooling, and literate discourse. In L. Moll (Ed.), *Vygotsky and education* (pp. 175–205). Cambridge: Press Syndicate of the University of Cambridge.

CHILDREN'S BOOK REFERENCES

Baker, L. (2001). *Life in the rainforests*. London: Two-Can Publishing.
Butterfield, M. (1999). *Looking at: Animals in hot places*. Austin, TX: Raintree Steck-Vaughn.
Hewitt, S. (1999). *All kinds of habitats*. Danbury, CT: Children's Press.
Morpurgo, M. (2000). *The silver swan*. New York: Penguin Putnam.
Stille, D. R. (1999). *A true book: Deserts*. Danbury, CT: Children's Press.
Yolen, J. (1987). *Owl moon*. New York: Putnam & Grosset.

3

Scaffolding for Motivation and Engagement in Reading

John T. Guthrie
Allan Wigfield
Kathleen C. Perencevich
University of Maryland

One of the fundamental purposes of CORI is to foster children's reading motivation. To develop a classroom context that supports the long-term growth of the disposition to read and gain new knowledge from text, teachers use a well-formed instructional framework. The aim of this instructional context is not merely to promote fun, games, and entertainment, but rather to facilitate children's development of long-term goals, beliefs, and dispositions toward reading. In explaining this framework, we discuss *motivation, engagement, and scaffolding.*

Of course, motivation for reading is not created in a day. A student does not suddenly possess the desire to read widely and deeply. Such an attribute grows and expands over time, with experiences and a supportive environment. Imagine all the attitudes, behaviors, and dispositions of a highly motivated student in Grades 3–5. Here we briefly describe this student with our notions of motivation and engagement, and we supply more research-based detail in chapter 10. Then, we explain how scaffolding works for motivational development.

READING MOTIVATION

In our view, reading motivation encompasses several aspects of the learner emphasizing intrinsic motivation and self-efficacy (Eccles & Wigfield, 2002). These all improve when scaffolding for motivation and engagement are successful.

Intrinsic Reading Motivation

Intrinsic motivation is the disposition to read for its own sake and for the enjoyment of reading. Intrinsically motivated readers readily find books and pursue them in free time (Ryan & Deci, 2000). Such enjoyment in reading is not limited to light, entertaining, or trivial texts, but includes material with deep conceptual content or complex literary themes. As a consequence, avid, intrinsically motivated readers are typically high achievers who score well on a variety of tests and receive top grades in school (Sweet, Guthrie, & Ng, 1998).

Intrinsically motivated students are curious, desiring to gain understanding about a topic or author of particular interest (Deci, 1992). Curiosity is integral to intrinsic motivation for reading because it represents a personal quest for learning about a person, topic, or event, for its own sake (Harter, 1981). These children do not attempt to satisfy a curiosity in order to receive an external reward. Satisfying a curiosity is its own reward, and the reading act that helps satisfy a curiosity is performed for its own sake. Curious readers are likely to have relatively high levels of perceived autonomy because they seek out books and information tailored to their interests. They make choices and control their reading activities for the purposes of gratifying and expanding their curiosity. This disposition is highly related to students' desire for mastery of content through reading. In the motivation literature, this is termed a mastery orientation (see chapter 10).

Involvement in reading is a characteristic of intrinsically motivated students. Involved readers may be so absorbed that they lose track of time during a text interaction. Their intrigue with the content, whether literary or informational, is so strong that they concentrate without much effort and attend to details that bring to light the full meanings of the author. Deep involvement in text entails a high measure of cognitive engagement. While reading, the learner is thinking and pondering, sometimes slowly and sometimes rapidly. This cognitive engagement leads to full experience of the text and deep understanding of content after reading. An involved reader is frequently satisfying a curiosity and will choose books that provide this experience of immersion in favorite topics and pursuits (Wigfield & Guthrie, 1997).

Intrinsically motivated readers show a preference for challenge in their reading. They seek opportunities to read complex material that deepens their knowledge. They pursue literary authors and books to understand and internalize their themes, irrespective of obstacles they encounter. In contrast, students with low intrinsic motivation shun difficult texts and recoil from thought-provoking tasks. They read to complete the tasks and minimize their effort.

Possessing the attribute of *perceived autonomy*, intrinsically motivated students see themselves as independent learners who are in control of their reading. They are aware that they can find books that interest them and are empowered to give themselves satisfying experiences through reading. These children are self-directed readers and learners who can start and stop their reading activities in appropriate situations. They begin reading a self-selected book freely when the opportunity arises and put it away when the time has shifted to a different academic activity. Most distinctive for these learners is their capacity to make good choices. They know how to choose books, activities, and partners for learning that will facilitate their growth and enjoyment, and they participate actively as decision makers in their own reading pursuits.

Reading Efficacy

Self-efficacy in reading is necessary for continuing advancement in achievement. Students who have high self-efficacy believe they can tackle difficult texts and are confident that their efforts will be beneficial to them. Students with low self-efficacy will state, "I can't do this," when confronted with a text that appears lengthy, complex, or cognitively challenging. Lack of belief in their capacity to comprehend undermines their initiation and use of whatever comprehension skills they possess. A student's level of self-efficacy is deeply dependent on his perceived success on important reading tasks (Schunk & Zimmerman, 1997). Children's development of self-efficacy in reading is related to their development of intrinsic motivation for reading (Baker & Wigfield, 1999). If students do not believe they have the capacity to read well, they will not believe they are in control of their book-related activities. Low self-efficacy makes it unlikely that a student will frequently choose to read or pursue curiosities through texts. As a consequence, self-efficacy and intrinsic reading motivation are moderately associated with each other (Wigfield, 1997).

READING ENGAGEMENT

When children are intrinsically motivated to read, believe they are capable of reading, and integrate literacy into their view of themselves, they are more likely to become engaged readers. *Reading engagement* is defined as linkages between motivations, interactions with text, social interactions, conceptual knowledge growth, and use of strategies (Baker, Dreher, & Guthrie, 2000). These things are linked because it is hard to imagine seeing students' motivation increase without seeing their interactions with text and social interchanges expand. Although the affect of motivation for reading is internal to the individual, motivation also connects students to texts and to other students. Engaged readers are not only motivated and socially interactive but are also using their background knowledge to gain new understanding. As this understanding is often hard-won, engaged students are strategic in reading a variety of texts. They employ such strategies as questioning and summarizing to learn from books.

Social Interaction

Engaged readers are socially interactive, sharing topics and titles with each other or participating in book clubs. If engaged readers need help understanding a word or event in a text, they can readily turn to their peers. They use their social network to undergird their understanding and to enhance their enjoyment in learning from books. Socially interactive readers may readily collaborate with other students on a project, taking separate aspects of a large topic and synthesizing their information from reading. They may share vocabulary meanings, comprehension strategies, note-taking techniques, and other tools for comprehending books. Their collaborative activities enable them to make good choices, succeed in accomplishing their aims, expand their zones of curiosity, and deepen their involvement in reading. These constituents of intrinsic motivation and social interaction are documented to be mutually enhancing (Stipek, 1996).

Knowledge Growth

Central to engaged reading is expanding knowledge and experience through text interaction. When students are motivated for reading over extended periods of time, they are usually following the plot of a favorite mystery or expanding their knowledge of a familiar topic. They direct their energy to authors, types of genre, or topics they want to explore.

Strategy Use

Reading strategically is a constituent of engaged reading. Students who are motivated over a long period of time have usually learned effective cognitive strategies. They often keep track of plots, organize new understanding, and know how to give accurate summaries to their friends or classmates. They possess strategies that enable them to expand their experience with books. Such strategies are central to reading comprehension. Links between motivations and strategies enable readers to fulfill their purposes and grow into proficiency (Guthrie, Schafer, & Huang, 2001).

Motivation to read and engagement in reading do not develop automatically. These processes are strongly influenced by children's individual experiences with reading, and also by the kinds of classroom environments they encounter as they learn to read. When teachers create supportive classroom environments, children's motivation and engagement to read are enhanced. In CORI, we talk about supporting the classroom environment for motivation by using scaffolding.

SCAFFOLDING PROCESS

Teachers and researchers are familiar with the term *scaffolding,* which refers to teacher support for learning in which both teacher and learner are co-participants in a learning activity. In the beginning of this joint endeavor, teachers typically perform high proportions of the joint activity, while students contribute a smaller amount. As student expertise increases, teachers transfer responsibility for performance in an activity more completely to the student. For instance, a teacher may begin scaffolding for student questioning by providing ample support, such as a topic and the first half of a written question, enabling students to complete the question using their own words. The provided topic and starter half-question are scaffolds for the beginning portion of the process of posing questions. Later in the instruction, the student may identify a topic and compose a question independently.

Most research on scaffolding focuses on how scaffolding fosters children's cognitive development. We believe children's motivation can be scaffolded as well. Indeed, scaffolding for motivational development is highly similar to scaffolding for a comprehension strategy, such as asking questions over text. The scaffolding process consists of teachers and students jointly engaging in an activity, with teacher contributions prevailing at the outset and students assuming increasing responsibility for complete performances during the course of instruction. This scaffolding process enables students to acquire motivation and engagement in the classroom.

Within the classroom, teachers have command of extremely valuable resources for fostering motivational development. These resources, which are highly related to the contextual variables described in the previous section, can be used to build a scaffold for students' motivational development (Hidi & Harackiewicz, 2000). Resources consist of types of instructional support that teachers can, and frequently do, provide for students in reading. The scaffolding framework provided here illustrates how these resources can be organized to support students' reading motivations and can be shifted over time to enable students to develop motivations for reading that will be internalized and enduring.

In CORI classrooms, scaffolding for motivational development in reading includes the coordination of the following supports for reading and writing activities: (a) conceptual knowledge base, (b) real-world interactions, (c), use of comprehension strategies, (d) provision of texts and technology, (e) choices and reflection, (f) social interactions, (g) expression of text understanding, and (h) environmental features in the classroom (time, place, tools for literacy). Teachers organize these aspects of their instruction, and shift them over time, to support motivational development.

In any reading activity in the classroom, there are books to be read, purposes for reading them, strategies to be used in learning, and a place for working. These are some, but not all, of the attributes mentioned previously. For any given reading activity, the students and teacher are working together to direct the reading activity. Some balance of decision making exists between teachers and students. To the degree that teachers are deciding all of these aspects of a reading event and students are complying with her requests, the activity is teacher-directed. On the other hand, to the extent that these aspects of the reading event are decided by individual students or influenced by student input, the activity is more student-directed.

The term *scaffold* refers to a support system for student performance. A high level of scaffolding for reading is represented by a high level of teacher direction in the reading–writing activities. In other words, when the teacher is determining the content of reading, the texts that will be used, the strategies for use, and the degree of student choice and social interaction, a high level of scaffolding is present for the reading activity. Each of these aspects of the scaffold may be considered a "plank," each of them giving a form to the platform for the entire activity. On the other hand, if these aspects of a reading activity are under student control, a relatively low level of scaffolding for performing the reading activity is present in the classroom learning scene.

Teachers foster students' motivational development in reading when they adjust the level of scaffolding to meet the students' capacities for motivated, engaged reading—for example, their curiosity, autonomy, involvement, efficacy, and social exchanges. Students naturally vary in the level of motivated reading they are disposed to pursue. If scaffolding is too high and teacher direction too strong, students' motivation will be decreased. Likewise, if the scaffolding is too low and student self-direction is too high, student work will often be unproductive, leaving both students and teachers frustrated. Therefore, it is the match of the level of scaffolding for motivation to children's motivational development that determines the extent to which motivation is facilitated in classroom environments. Teachers must be aware of students' level of motivation, and match the level of scaffolding they provide to deepen that motivation. The way in which these matches can be formed and sustained is discussed next.

SCAFFOLDING FOR MOTIVATIONAL DEVELOPMENT

This section discusses the various reading and writing activities in CORI mentioned earlier and how teachers can scaffold these activities for motivational development, beginning with conceptual learning goals, which provide both cognitive and motivational benefits to learners (Pintrich, 2000).

Conceptual Learning Goals

When children are at the initial stages of learning comprehension strategies and gaining confidence in constructing meaning from larger sections of information books or literature typical of third and fourth grade materials, teachers usually provide conceptual background that enables the students to understand the new information in text. A high scaffold at this stage of learning consists of presenting a multilevel, highly detailed knowledge framework as background for the text. For instance, in teaching wetlands as a biome, teachers may present contrasts of wetlands with other biomes, general purposes of wetlands (filtering water), and wetlands as abundant habitats for wildlife. A highly developed scaffold provides such information over several days, enabling children to acquire full conceptual understanding to be used in reading new texts. Teachers with a complex scaffold at this phase of learning frequently mention these major concepts and important facts within the knowledge domain to keep students alert to new information they are acquiring from text. With respect to motivation, these scaffolding activities can pique students' curiosity and enhance their desire to gain new knowledge through reading. Students use newfound information to learn more from texts. The initial stage of curiosity (using knowledge to create a desire for learning new knowledge) occurs.

At a lower level of scaffolding for motivation, teachers present a more limited conceptual background for reading a new text. This may consist of a one-time mention, in limited terms, of the relevant knowledge domain. For instance, the teacher may say, "Wetlands support many kinds of life and different species, so let's read to learn more about them." Although this is vague and short term, it is an orientation to the topic and purpose for reading. Such a low scaffold is more guidance than none at all, which would consist of simply saying, "Now read this text that I am giving you to understand it as well as you can." This latter request contains no topical information or orientation to any specific reading goal. With the low scaffold, students partially direct their own knowledge acquisition. They have a wider set of options about what and how to read to satisfy their curiosity.

Real-World Interaction

As part of the scaffold for children's reading about science concepts, teachers often provide science observations and hands-on activities. These are sensory experiences in which students see, hear, feel, smell, touch, and manipulate the physical environment for purposes of inquiry. It is necessary to have simple, clear links between the real-world interactions, the main conceptual framework, and the knowledge goals being pursued. The teacher who provides a high scaffold supports students' situational interest by suggesting that they notice and discuss the aspects of the science observation that are new and interesting to them. Perhaps students are observing insects or mammals and discussing how and why they fly, walk, or hide as they do. With the scaffold of real-world interaction, teachers create the opportunity for children's situational interest to emerge. Children are fascinated by the world around them including birds, salamanders, boggy marshes, or dinosaurs that roamed the planet in past times.

When connected to texts, these situational interests arising from simple science observations enhance students' motivational process of involvement in text. With books available related to their observations, students seek pictures, information, and explanations for what they have seen. Their immersion in the text is a powerful motivational attribute that we refer to as *involvement in text interaction*. In a high scaffold for real-world interaction, teachers may organize one or more observations per week. However, it is important not to spend too much time pursuing real-world interactions, but to use the situational interest generated by them to increase book exposure and amount of time engaged in reading for conceptual learning.

At a low level of scaffolding, real-world interaction is rarer, making it more remote from text. For instance, a teacher may simply ask students to recall their science observations consisting of a habitat walk, an owl pellet dissection, or an experiment with wetland plants. Texts related to these experiences take on the excitement and involvement of the real-world interaction. Students do not need to continually participate in real-world interaction. Refreshing students' memories and briefly describing the past interaction may rekindle some of the original interest that the experience afforded them. Their original involvement in real-world interaction transfers to texts on related topics through a shift from high to low scaffolding.

Text Support

A highly developed scaffold for reading motivation includes appropriate text provided by the teacher. To promote cognitive engagement in reading, teachers select texts that are at students' independent reading level, meaning that they can correctly recognize at least 95% of the words. Although vocabulary and content within the text may be new, the word recognition difficulty is moderate. Teachers provide a high scaffold for text involvement, selecting content that is at least moderately familiar to the students. In studying the wetlands, teachers choose a book or chapter from a book that overlaps partially with students' existing information recently gained from the unit or brought from prior experience to the text. Such moderate familiarity affords students the opportunity to activate and use their background knowledge to gain new content understanding and allows students to readily learn strategies such as questioning or summarizing.

Most important for purposes of scaffolding for motivation is readable text on a moderately familiar domain that is interesting and that enables students to learn content they find appealing. To enable students to become immersed in text, teachers pose intriguing questions and enable students to form a few of their own questions over text. Teachers provide ample time, encouraging students to dwell on new information and combine it with their previous understandings so they can explain what they have read to others. Time and opportunity for text involvement encourages absorption in content that is evident when students say, "Hey, this is interesting, look what I found!"

A lower level of scaffolding for motivational development through text consists of less teacher support for the processes of immersion in text. With a low scaffold, a teacher may enable students to select a text, rather than choose it for them, and may encourage students to learn something of interest and value to them on a slightly new topic. With this lower scaffold, students are responsible for finding a suitable topic or author and directing their own involvement with the content and materials. The teacher can encourage students to read what is interesting to them and to select books from which they will learn, which serves as a minimal guide for students' self-direction in learning to become involved with text.

Choice and Control

A vital aspect of scaffolding for motivational development is supporting students in the process of making choices and taking control of their reading activities. As discussed earlier, perceived autonomy can be highly motivating to children. However, if children are given too many choices before they can manage them, motivation can suffer. They will choose poorly and may become very frustrated. Conversely, students ready for autonomy, but given little, will also lose motivation. Again, the scaffolding match between students' characteristics and teachers' instruction is key.

Under the conditions of a high scaffold, teachers provide limited options and request choices within a relatively narrow range. For instance, the teacher may have provided conceptual background for a topic, assured a minimum amount of real-world interaction, and asked students to form questions about this topic. Then, she may give students a choice of two chapters to read in an information book to learn more about this content domain. This choice is extremely limited but, nevertheless, may be a valuable initial stage in students' learning to direct their own reading. In addition to providing limited, yet functional, options, teachers may ask students to give reasons for their choices. As students state why they preferred one chapter or topic over another, they articulate their interests and backgrounds. Giving a reason for one's choice not only legitimates the choice itself, but legitimates the interest that led to the particular selection. Accompanying these aspects of providing choices, a teacher may assure that explicit links are made between the choice and other activities in the learning unit. For instance, the teacher may remark that the students' choices between two chapters in an information book may be connected to two different topics previously described in the content domain (e.g., defense and predation in animal life) and to two different observational activities in their science learning (e.g., hiding for defense and hunting at night for predation). These links help students realize that choices are not empty and inconsequential, but are functional parts of their forward progress as readers in the content domain.

At a lower level of scaffolding, the teacher may provide more opportunity for children's self-direction. She may broadly prompt students to choose a subtopic and a text for their learning. For example, in CORI a teacher may say, "Choose three or four concepts of ecology and locate several animals that can be used to illustrate these concepts." This reading activity is within the domain of life science, is related to familiar texts within the classroom, and calls on multiple comprehension strategies. A comparison request calls for intertextual reading and integration, although the specific texts to be compared are not designated by the teacher. Therefore, this is a lower level of scaffolding, which students with substantial previous instruction experience and expertise would be able to utilize to foster their choices and their acquisition of higher levels of self-directed reading. Teachers may appropriately take several months to shift from a high scaffold to a low scaffold for choice.

Social Interaction

When teachers provide a high scaffold for motivational development using social interaction, they afford students opportunities to participate in multiple social structures, such as whole class and pairs reading. For instance, the teacher may discuss background knowledge with the entire class, ask the class to read a passage, and discuss important ideas within it. She may then ask students to form pairs and read and discuss the next section of text. By explaining new knowledge to a peer, a student participates in the process of socially interacting to form new knowledge structures from text. The process of battling out the meaning of a text, and assuring full coverage of its content in deciding about the interpretation of material, enables children to learn the art of social interchange and dialogue in a literacy situation. With a high level of scaffolding, the teacher may further assign students to work in teams and may provide roles for each individual within the team. At the initial stage of learning with the highest scaffold, a teacher defines the group. Roles may vary, consisting of one person as the oral reader, another as the individual listing new vocabulary, a third as the summarizer, and a fourth as the reporter to the class or another team. As students develop independence in working in teams, the teacher may not need to assign roles as explicitly or frequently.

At a low level of scaffolding for motivational development, teachers may initiate social interactions less explicitly and less frequently. For instance, the teacher may allow a team to choose a book, divide it into sections, read each section with team members taking responsibility for them, and summarize the content of the book for the class. This prompt requires students to determine their social structure, make choices, and utilize appropriate comprehension strategies for the purpose of integrating these sections of the book. This weak scaffold places a high level of responsibility on students, and young learners cannot be expected to succeed with this without extensive experience in reading and learning under these conditions.

Using Comprehension Strategies

Our purpose in scaffolding for motivational development is to enable students to gain self-efficacy through success in understanding what they read. At the beginning of a unit, a teacher may ask students to perform some of the comprehension strategies she has been teaching. For instance, she may ask students to activate their background knowledge and pose questions about a new topic. Using the example of wetlands, students will recall their prior learning and create goals for the next steps in their reading. The successful completion of these strategies of activating background knowledge and questioning enables students to make choices that will be productive for their learning. This use of comprehension strategies enables them to choose subtopics for further learning, texts that will be valuable for them, or other reading strategies (such as writing down key words) that will help them learn. Furthermore, the successful use of known strategies for comprehending text enables students to gain confidence in their ability to read a new and formidable chapter or book. This sense of empowerment fosters students' self-efficacy as readers.

When using a high level of scaffolding for comprehension strategies, teachers heavily prompt students in the use of a strategy by providing many suggestions, questions, and cues during the students' performance of the strategy, assuring that their questions are fully formed and well-phrased. With a high scaffold for comprehension strategies, teachers often request that students write down the outcomes of using the strategy. Students activate knowledge not only by brainstorming and discussing, but also by writing their previous conceptual knowledge about a topic. In addition, students may share their questions orally. In a high scaffold, teachers frequently ask students to use their comprehension strategies during an extended lesson. They may often request that students remember prior knowledge, and specifically elicit information to comprehend a new book or section. When students see their successful performance and gain confidence in using a strategy, their reading efficacy increases. Their efficacy often relies on heavy prompting, written outcomes, and frequent use, which are all part of a strong scaffold for comprehension strategies. Also, it is important for teachers to tell students directly how the strategies they are learning increase their reading skills, thereby helping to build students' self-efficacy.

In a lower level of scaffolding for strategy use, the teacher may give one initial prompt for using a strategy prior to a new reading activity. Students may share their outcomes of the strategy (previous knowledge or their questions) by saying them aloud or mentioning them to their partner, rather than writing them down. This lighter, briefer request for strategy discussion supports children's strategy awareness, and thus enhances their self-efficacy.

Expression of Text Understanding

When the teacher provides a high scaffold for reading motivation, she is explicit and detailed about how students should show their text-based comprehension.

She states the mode of expression consisting of reading, writing, drawing, or other possibilities. She defines the content to be shown, including the specific types of information expected and the organization of that information. A high scaffold includes descriptions of the format for length, use of conventions of English, and other aspects of production. For example, with a high scaffold, a teacher may say, "Write a five-line summary of the second chapter in the information book on wetlands and be sure to use a topic sentence that includes the main idea and provides supporting details." This request explicitly requires the mode, content, and format, but does not predetermine the central concepts or supporting details to be identified by the student.

A more relaxed scaffold would provide more student opportunity for choice of text, mode, or format of responding. For instance, at a low level of scaffolding, a teacher may merely request that the students make a poster of what they have understood from reading two books on the wetlands. She may suggest that this poster include drawings and summaries of important concepts. This provides students some latitude in selecting specific topics, identifying length of statements, and exploring a variety of ways to show what they know through illustrations, graphs, stories, or poems. This scaffold, moving from high during initial instruction to lower during later periods of instruction, where students have gained fuller command of reading strategies and self-directed learning, affords students the opportunity to engage in several motivational processes. This progression is likely to occur across several months.

At this same low level of scaffolding for expression of text understanding, students can exercise their curiosities by choosing topics that interest them. They can identify books they are confident in using, which extends their efficacy as readers. They can make a range of choices, illustrating their competence in directing their learning, and can share the endeavor with classmates. Whereas these processes may be likely to occur with suitable long-term scaffolding for motivational development, they will not be likely to appear immediately if students are merely given a low scaffold, without previous opportunities for acquiring these motivational processes for cognitive engagement in reading and writing. We have observed that students' belief in the importance of reading (integrated reading motivation) is enhanced when they exercise a lot of freedom of expression as they present or display what they have learned from extended reading activities.

Environmental Features and Resources

In a high scaffold for motivational development, a teacher may provide the physical infrastructure needed to completely perform a reading and writing activity. That is, she may provide the time, place, paper, pencil, and other materials and resources for a simple literacy event. This may enable students to exercise their autonomy in selecting a text. Ample resources may enable students to become involved in reading to learn and readily share information with classmates. However, as students gain expertise in self-direction, and as their motivational processes become more fully formed, the teacher reduces the scaffold by permitting students to choose some portions of these environmental supports. For instance, the teacher may allow students to work at any location in the room. With a slightly lower scaffold, the teacher may give students a choice about which resources to use for their composition, for instance, handwriting or the computer word processor. She may also enable students to choose and determine the time for performing a specific activity (*Write your poem* **now** *or write your poem* **later**, *but complete it by the end of* **tomorrow**).

At the low level of scaffolding, a teacher may provide one main resource, such as time (**Now** *work on your expressive reading*). The student would be expected to supply the other resources, including the books, materials, partners, and location for working. The low scaffold is not mere neglect. It assumes students' experience, competence, and responsibility for selecting those resources productively to assure learning during this literacy experience. A low scaffold is not an opportunity for chaos and loss of learning. Rather, it is an occasion for motivational processes of curiosity, involvement, self-direction (control), efficacy, and social interaction to occur within the mainstream of classroom activities.

HOW MOTIVATION DEVELOPS IN A SCAFFOLDED CONTEXT

Engaged Readers in the Later Elementary Grades

In Grades 3, 4, and 5, intrinsically motivated and engaged readers occupy many classrooms in many schools. These are the students who read avidly on their own, pursue their interests, and gain knowledge they enjoy sharing with others. They exhibit the motivational attributes of being curious readers, becoming deeply involved with texts, making good choices while directing their own reading, having a sense of confidence and efficacy that is realistic, and participating in social interchanges during reading. These are the qualities of a self-determining reader, and may be developed in an appropriately scaffolded classroom context.

Shifting From Higher to Lower Scaffolding for Motivational Development

As students learn to self-initiate their reading, make good choices, and increase the depth with which they become involved in reading and sharing what they have learned, teachers may lower the scaffold slowly. Effective instruction consists of subtly shifting the responsibility from the teacher to the learner. Over time, the shift may go from 90% teacher responsibility and 10% students' responsibility to 50% teacher and students' responsibility. In this phase, the direction and decision making for reading interactions are shared. Teachers and students jointly define the conceptual domain to be explored, discussing, for example, which books to use and what forms of expression of text understanding to expect. There is no one ideal prescription for a middle-level, moderately strong scaffold. Some teachers may choose to support motivational processes more fully on some planks of the scaffold, whereas other teachers may use other planks more consistently. However, the common aim is to reduce the level of teacher provision of each dimension of the scaffold and to assure that students are supplying each dimension for themselves.

One hazard of scaffolding is a shift from high to low that is too rapid for the students. If the teacher leaps prematurely to a low level of scaffolding, students will be lost, frustrated, and will find ways to avoid reading, rather than to embrace it. Too little guidance from the teacher, and too much option for the students too early in development, is a punishing experience for all. If students are unable to fulfill their own goals or the teacher's aims because they have too many choices or do not know how to make good choices, they may feel like failures. On the other hand, a high scaffold maintained indefinitely does not support motivational development. If the teacher continually defines the content, supplies the text, makes the choices, and determines forms of student expression, students' motivation can hardly develop. How can learners expand their curiosity, involvement, and interest without any latitude for their reading activities? Over-scaffolding students, irrespective of their level of achievement, occurs when teachers maintain the scaffold, even though students are capable of participating in the motivational processes of choosing and becoming involved without a high level of teacher direction. In the absence of opportunity, motivational processes do not occur, cannot develop, and will not coalesce into the self-determining reader (see also Ryan & Deci, 2000). Optimal shifts of scaffolding begin with a high scaffold for motivation and slowly reduce in strength, extent, and duration. Movement to a lower scaffold is determined by the students' uptake. When students show the capability and disposition to make choices, pursue curiosities, interact productively in social groups, and learn from text independently, teachers give them relatively lower levels of scaffolding.

Multiple Scaffolds in the Classroom

A large number of classrooms in Grades 3–5 are heterogeneous in ability, having two or three grade levels of achievement within them. In Grade 4, reading achievement levels can easily range from Grades 2–6. Consequently, the teacher must afford these diverse readers a variety of scaffolding levels. Whereas the fourth-grade level readers within a classroom may be able to learn productively from text and develop motivationally from a moderate to low scaffold, the lower achieving students within the same classroom may require a high scaffold. Although outstanding educators orchestrate these multiple scaffolds continuously, all teachers can learn to balance them. For example, a relatively high scaffold for reading a certain information book may be applied to the entire classroom. Then, a more advanced group of higher achieving students in the class can be provided a lower scaffold and be expected to continue their reading along the line that was previously begun. The teacher may then attend to a lower achieving and/or less motivated group of students, offering them a higher scaffold for their comprehension and motivational development. The teacher may juggle these two levels, enabling both groups to proceed. Although other, more complex patterns of scaffolding may appear in the classrooms of some remarkable teachers, it is valuable and necessary for multiple scaffolds to be provided simultaneously in a majority of regular classrooms. To illustrate these points, we now present two classroom vignettes, one demonstrating a high level of scaffolding, and the other a lower scaffold for motivation.

HIGH SCAFFOLDING VIGNETTE: PENNI STOCKMAN'S LESSON

It is the sixth week of school and the fourth week of a CORI unit for third-grade students who have been studying the conceptual theme, "Birds Around the World," in Penni Stockman's classroom. Her students are slightly below-average readers who are only occasionally motivated to read. They need her high scaffold for motivation. During the weeks before this lesson on graphic organizing, students learned a number of other reading strategies, including activating prior knowledge, questioning, searching for information, and summarizing. In addition, students participated in numerous real-world observations and experiences, including bird watching, owl pellet dissecting, examining bird feathers, walking in local habitats to find evidence of bird life, and feeding birds. They have a plethora of books in the classroom with multiple genres and levels of text. For example, students have been practicing their expressive reading with partners using the book *Owl Moon* by Jane Yolen. Additionally, they have begun team research on a bird of their choice and will create an information book about the bird's many aspects of survival. For example, one team is studying the egret and how it survives in a wetland habitat. In their chapter book, they will discuss the various aspects of survival, including communication, locomotion, competition, and defense, among others.

It is important that students understand how to organize all of the animal information they are gathering from multiple texts. Therefore, Penni will begin a week-long instruction on the reading strategy of graphic organizing, using direct instruction, scaffolding, and independent practice as the main elements of her cognitive strategy instruction lessons. In addition, Penni will also use scaffolding for motivation to help students become autonomous learners who are collaborating effectively, making appropriate choices, getting involved in the books and the project they are writing, and taking on challenges and risks in learning, while helping students maintain high levels of piqued curiosity. In this vignette, we focus on how Penni scaffolds for motivation during this very demanding cognitive task.

Penni works from a large blackboard using concept words and magnets to help students understand how to organize information. Keeping in mind the importance of collaboration, Penni asks the students to sit very close to her and the board, forming a semicircle on the floor. In this way, she configures the students' social environment, ensuring that everyone is close enough to attend, get involved, and be full participants in the lesson (environmental scaffold for social support and involvement).

On the blackboard, Penni has multiple index cards, circle cards, and one card that is the shape of a house displaying either a biome word (e.g., rainforest, wetlands, woodland, grassland, desert) or a bird name (e.g., heron, egret, blue bird, penguin, elf owl, etc.). She begins, "Today, we will work on organizing graphically. What are these words?" Penni points to the biome words on the board.

One student exclaims, "Biomes" (autonomy—student feels free to speak without having to raise hand and be called on). "Now, take a look at these words. Can you understand the way they are displayed now?" Penni inquires. The students respond that the words are very disorganized, to which Penni asks, "How then could I organize these words to figure out which bird lives in which biome?"

One student explains, "First, take the house card and put that on top, because all of these words are about bird homes." Penny complies with the student's request. Another student says that the words in the circles are important because they depict the biomes, so they should go across the board as headings. Again, Penni complies with the student's request (autonomy support—students are coming up with the organizational procedure themselves).

Penni asks, "So then what should we do with the bird names?" One student says that they should be placed under the biome headings to show where the bird lives. Penni reinforces the idea saying, "Oh, so here is a bird. What heading should I put it under?" One student says, "Wetlands." At this point, Penni randomly hands out bird name index cards to all of the students and they place the cards under the appropriate categories (conceptual knowledge—support for curiosity). When students have completed this activity, they vote on whether the names are categorized correctly (collaboration support).

Next, Penni explains, "Now we have the words in some order, but we have to come up with a way to show how these words are related. What could we do to show their relationships?" One student says, "You could draw lines connecting them." Penni asks, "How?" as she draws a line between a penguin and an owl. The student says, "You can't do that." Penni inquires, "Why not?" (knowledge challenge piquing student curiosity).

The student explains, "Because you are connecting across categories and you can't do that. All of the arctic birds have to be connected together under the arctic category."

"Ohhh!" Penni says, "So I had better erase this line?" "Yes," the boy explains. (autonomy support—allowing student to be the expert, while teacher simply follows his directive).

"OK, so, how then should we connect these words?" Penni asks again and waits (environmental support—gives thinking time).

Students contemplate the words for a moment. One student says that they could put all of the biomes in a circle and make a web to connect them. Penni explains that they just organized these in categories and don't want to move them, just connect the words. Another student says, "Spread out the words and connect them like a ladder." Penni asks the class if they agree (collaboration and support).

"Great, it looks like we all agree. Before we start connecting, though, we had better check to make sure the birds are in the right categories." (comprehension strategy—support for graphic organizing). Students discuss words and categories with each other and begin telling Penni where to move particular words that are misplaced.

Penni asks, "Where is my rainforest team?" (collaboration support—teams are becoming experts on birds in particular biomes). "Does a flamingo live in your biome?" (autonomy support personalizes the question "your biome"). Students seem to remember that although they may not be experts about each bird, they do know their own biomes. They excitedly talk with their teammates about their biome birds and figure out with their teammates which birds are not in the right biomes. They tell Penni to change the ostrich to the grassland. Penni then asks students to think about the Gila woodpecker. She reminds them that they know some other animal with "Gila" in it that may help them. "Remember the Gila monster?" "Oh yeah," says one student, "they live in the desert."

"Great!" Penni says. "That's not cheating you know, that's using your resources" (conceptual knowledge scaffold for curiosity).

Penni scaffolds some other changes by pointing out students' prior knowledge of the concepts they are studying, like feeding, asking, "Where do bald eagles like to build their nests?" and "What do egrets eat?" (conceptual knowledge scaffold). Penni also uses some of the real-world experiences to help scaffold students' knowledge. "We observed this bird's cousin's feathers the other day. Do you remember where this bird might live?" (real-world experience scaffold).

The students are very excited about their newly formed organizational structure that they constructed together. Now, Penni lowers the scaffold. She guides students to practice with partners using the organizing strategy. She provides some motivational scaffolds to help students maintain engagement. Penni explains, "When you go back to your seats, you will be working with a partner (collaboration). Use the book *Feathers and Flight.* (autonomy support—high text scaffold—teacher chooses text). You will read pages 4–12 (autonomy support—high text scaffold—teacher chooses pages to read) with your partner and find the main idea and supporting details. I made a sheet with some main words from this reading to help you get started (comprehension strategy scaffold—provides partial chart with main ideas). However, there are many more important words. There are also shapes on this sheet. What kinds of shapes do you see?"

Students call out, "Ovals, squares, rectangles, squiggly shapes."

"Hmmm," Penni ponders aloud, "When you look at these shapes, which do you think is going to be the main idea? Which is different from the rest?" (conceptual knowledge scaffold for curiosity—helping students recognize the main idea).

One student says that *plumage* is different. Penni says, "Yes, plumage is the main idea of this section of text. I want you to organize these words and add your own words to be organized (autonomy support), but you must read in order to organize these ideas. Then, cut the words apart and make a graphic organizer to show how all of these words are connected and related. You and your partner will make a concept map. You can choose whichever way you want to make your map. You could do it like we did on the board, or a web, or any way you want, as long as you are showing the main ideas and supporting details in an organized map (autonomy support—students choose how to display their own knowledge). Also, you may choose your partner. Make sure, however, that whoever you choose, you can work well with. If there is a problem, I will assign a partner to you (collaboration support). "OK, let's review the directions." Penni writes the directions on the blackboard as students tell her what to write (environmental scaffold for autonomy and self-direction).

Students choose their partners and go to their own space in the classroom. Each student is equipped with the book *Feathers and Flight*. Some students read aloud together with their partners, while others decide to read independently and then discuss what they read (autonomy support—students deciding how to complete the task. Students are very engaged and show great levels of independence).

Penni walks around to check on the progress of each pair. She gives students plenty of time to read and concentrate on the task at hand (environmental scaffold). After approximately 15 minutes, Penni calls the class to attention to check understanding and provide a partial model for struggling students. "OK, boys and girls, turn to page 8 of your book, to the section on tail feathers. On this page, you will find supporting words that explain the functions of tail feathers. For example, this section says, 'Most birds use tail feathers to steer.' *Steer* is a supporting detail of *tail feather* and should be in your organizer" (comprehension strategy scaffold).

Penni reads aloud some other sentences from the text to give additional examples. "So, you want to make sure that the text is supporting the words that you categorize. Also, some other words may be related to each other. Remember, when we do our summarizing strategy, we use the circle (main idea), underline (supporting details), and cross out (irrelevant details) strategy. When we organize, we are doing the same thing. We are choosing the most important ideas to organize (comprehension strategy scaffold for efficacy). If you go one section at a time for each type of feather, the organizing task will be easier."

Based on Penni's prompts, many students go back to the text to justify their words and reorganize them as necessary. Students excitedly glue the words on their maps. Multiple pairs use different strategies for organizing their text and words. Penni calls the class together. "I'd like a couple of partners to share their work on organizing. Show us your map and tell us how you organized the words" (personal expression scaffold). One pair of students explains their map and connections they made for an organizer in chart-like form. Another pair shares their map that is a concept web. Penni enthusiastically announces, "I'm impressed with your work. As you can see, there are many different ways to organize, as long as you can explain how and why you organized the way you did." (autonomy support scaffold—multiple pathways to the correct response).

LOW SCAFFOLD FOR MOTIVATIONAL DEVELOPMENT: JEAN SAMUEL'S LESSON

In mid-November, Jean Samuel's third-grade students had been in her CORI classroom for 2 full months, and they were in a unit on life in aquatic environments. These students were above average in reading competence, and most had developed relatively high intrinsic motivation and self-efficacy. Consequently, Jean's scaffolding was appropriately lower than Penni's level. Jean's class had taken a field trip to a local stream and collected crayfish and aquatic life. All had performed an experiment in an aquarium to examine how fish escape from predatory insects (by hiding in grasses and gathering together). Then they were ready to examine aquatic survival more widely. Jean set up their project with a broad goal, "How do different animals survive in a freshwater habitat?" In discussion, the class decided that many animals live in aquatic environments including mammals, reptiles, amphibians, birds, spineless animals, and fish. She gave them a list of animals, including beaver, otter, deer, piranha, angelfish, electric fish, swan, crane, geese, heron, salamander, frog/toad, snail, and crayfish. Trade books in the classroom contained information on each animal. She asked students to work in pairs and choose at least four of the main concepts of survival they were investigating, including defense, communication, predation, feeding, competition, reproduction, respiration, locomotion, and adaptation to the physical environment. They were expected to select one class of animals, choose three animals in that class, locate books on those animals and the aquatic environment, select at least four concepts, read extensively to learn, organize their newfound information, and write a statement to teach students in another class what they learned. During a 6-day activity, Jean gave 5 to 7 minutes of guidance at the beginning of each 45-minute period, emphasizing the students' resources and decisions to be made.

With this level of scaffolding, Jean provided some knowledge goals, relevant texts, choices of animals, collaboration structure, and organizational plans for the writing. Students were able to exercise their **curiosity** by selecting subtopics, make **choices** about topics and texts, get **involved** in reading and learning about a self-identified aspect of survival, and **collaborate** with a partner in learning and writing. This context afforded students the opportunity to engage in all processes of intrinsically motivated, self-determined reading. However, this low level of scaffolding, which occurred in November, was only successful due to prior high scaffolding earlier in the year. Her scaffolding for motivation in early mid-September looked like Penni Stockman's higher scaffolding described previously.

RESEARCH ON CONTEXTUAL VARIABLES
INFLUENCING READING MOTIVATION

Most aspects of the scaffolding described in the previous section are based on aspects of the classroom context (variables) that have been investigated previously. That is, the use of a conceptual theme, real-world interactions, support for choices, interesting texts, use of strategies, and social interaction have been related to reading in various studies. We briefly review selected studies and offer a short critique focusing on two important limitations of this research. Note that two aspects of instructional scaffolding have not been investigated in motivational research: expression of understanding and physical features of the environment. Consequently, they are not addressed here. Our justification for incorporating them into the scaffolding framework is that they are evident in our extensive videotapes of CORI classrooms.

Supporting Student Autonomy

Autonomy support refers to instruction designed to offer students some control over their own learning, including what and how to learn. Central components may include choice, ability to negotiate tasks with regard to level of difficulty, interest, organization and procedures, evaluation, and standards of success. Also, this includes student decision making about significant features of instruction, self-expression, honoring voices, and ownership of ideas in reading.

Our perspective on autonomy support encapsulates the idea that the student shares in the responsibility of decision making in the classroom milieu, but is not the *sole* decision maker (Garcia & Pintrich, 1996). Additionally, autonomy support is not defined as permissiveness or lawless confusion. It is certainly possible to set limits on children's behaviors in an autonomy-supportive manner (Deci & Ryan, 1994; Eccles, Buchanan, Flanagan, Fuligni, Midgley, & Yee, 1991; Koestner, Ryan, Bernieri, & Holt, 1984). It is the structure and guidance that helps to foster autonomy. McCaslin and Good (1996) coined the term *co-regulation* to express the interdependent relationship between the student and teacher in making decisions and choices in the classroom context. However, in order for students to become co-regulators of their literacy in the classroom, teachers must scaffold a number of motivated reading activities.

When students perceive ownership of their goals, they report high intrinsic motivation and reading engagement (Au, 1998; Morrow, 1996). For example, Au (1998) created a curriculum to foster student ownership. In this curriculum, teachers utilized multiple strategies for instruction such as reading comprehension, writing process, language and vocabulary, word reading strategies, and voluntary reading. However, students were important contributors because their language patterns outside the classroom were imported into discussions in reading lessons. In a year-long implementation of this program, student ownership increased significantly. In another study of literacy instruction, fifth-grade students who led discussions, shared ideas, initiated topics, and took turns deciding when to shift the discussion, reported an increased interest in taking responsibility for constructing personal literacy goals (Turner, Parkes, & Cox, 1995). Furthermore, ownership also contributes to reading comprehension and amount of reading (Morrow, 1996). In a controlled experimental study, Morrow (1996) gave students ownership over reading in independent reading and writing centers. Students increased in reading comprehension and amount and breadth of reading, as indicated by measures of print exposure.

Autonomy support contributes to achievement, as well as to motivation (Deci, Nezlek, & Sheinman, 1981; Miserandino, 1996; Weinert & Helmke, 1995). In a longitudinal study of first to fourth graders, a positive relationship was found between autonomy support and academic achievement (Weinert & Helmke, 1995). Also, autonomy support in the classroom was significantly related to positive attitudes toward learning and on-task behavior. In another investigation, a teacher's orientation toward autonomy support increased perceived competence and mastery motivation among students (Deci, Nezlek, & Sheinman, 1981). In this study, 889 children in Grades 4, 5, and 6, in 36 classrooms, completed self-report measures of intrinsic motivation (curiosity, preference for challenge, and independent mastery), perception of the classroom context along a continuum of controlling to autonomy supportive (deCharms, 1976), and a measure of self-esteem. Also, teachers completed a measure to assess their style with regard to autonomy or control. There was a strong correlation between autonomy support and intrinsic motivation among students. Specifically, an autonomy-supportive climate was significantly correlated with students' preference for challenge and curiosity. Interestingly, the influence of autonomy-support on student motivation was relatively immediate and remained stable over the school year. In addition, Miserandino (1996) found that a social context that supported perceived autonomy and curiosity predicted improvements in grades over the school year.

What Exactly Do Autonomy-Supportive Teachers Do?

Reeve, Bolt, and Cai (1999) reported that teachers high in autonomy support listened to students more often and allowed students to handle and manipulate the instructional materials and ideas more often than those teachers categorized as low autonomy-supportive. With regard to discourse, autonomy-supportive teachers were more likely to ask about student wants, respond to student-generated questions, and volunteer perspective-taking statements meant to relay to the student the teacher's understanding of the student's emotional state. Autonomy-supportive teachers were less likely to give solutions or use directives. Further, Reeve et al. (1999) found that, compared with their controlling counterparts, autonomy-supportive teachers created a student-centered atmosphere, encouraged student initiative, nurtured competence, and provided rationales for school tasks.

Knowledge Goals Support Motivational Development

A conceptual theme can be a motivational support for reading because it can support students' curiosity, desire for understanding, and goals to master material. A conceptual theme is represented by a few abstract principles in a content domain (Chi, DeLeeuw, Chiu, & Lavancher, 1994). At high levels of understanding about the conceptual theme, students have acquired explanatory concepts that can account for facts, observations, and a range of phenomena. Examples of conceptual themes include survival in ecology, weather patterns in earth science, and simple machines in physics.

Conceptual themes are a productive starting point for designing instruction because they invite teachers and students to form content-learning goals and sub-goals (Lipson, Valencia, Wixson, & Peters, 1993). From a motivational perspective, a conceptual theme supports mastery goals. With a thematic unit, teachers focus on students attaining conceptual goals, rather than emphasizing ability-based practices, which tend to undermine mastery orientation (Roeser, Midgley, & Urdan, 1996). Conceptual goals for reading have been shown to increase interest, enjoyment, and willingness to pursue learning difficult text. When conceptual themes are the organizational frame for lessons, students pose high-level questions, which enable them to generalize and think productively (Meece, Blumenfeld, & Hoyle, 1988).

Real-World Interactions for Motivational Development

At the outset of learning the conceptual unit, the theme can be initiated through real-world interactions. Drawing on classroom-based research, investigators have found that students "can become lifelong science learners. Science courses offer models to provide a firm foundation for their future experiences so they can continue to link to connect their scientific ideas to the activities they normally pursue" (Linn & Muilenburg, 1996, p. 23). The authors suggested that when real-world experiences can be linked to academic activities such as reading, student motivations and comprehension strategies are supported. It has also been shown that when students experience meaningful hands-on activities, the links are tightened between their mastery goals (desire for understanding) and their use of reading strategies for learning (Bruning & Schweiger, 1997).

Real-world interactions, such as collecting specimens in a stream or experimenting with predatory insects, are exciting for a large majority of students. This excitement represents situational interest that can develop into long-term motivation for reading (see chapter 10). If the energy aroused by fascinating phenomena is directed into texts, engagement in reading increases. Ross (1988) reviewed experiments showing that "hands-on" experiences in classrooms increased the quality and number of questions students asked, and increased their attention to learning. Anderson (1998) reported an experiment in which students who observed live animals in connection to reading about them recalled new knowledge more fully than students who read the same material but did not perform the same observations.

Interesting Texts

An interesting text matches the topical interest and the cognitive competency of the reader. If a book is relevant and easy to comprehend, it is more likely to be interesting than if it does not possess these qualities (Schraw, Bruning, & Svoboda, 1995). Interesting texts, furthermore, contain vivid details and attractive illustrations. These texts entice students to spend more time with them and read a larger number of words than books that are less interesting to them personally (McLoyd, 1979). One of the more robust predictors of reading achievement in elementary schools is the number of books in the classroom. With a national sample of students in the United States, Elley (1992) reported that the number of trade books per student within the classroom predicted reading achievement, after important potentially confounding variables of parental education, income, and general school resources were controlled. These findings were confirmed in 20 nations in the study.

The availability of books in classrooms varies substantially (Allington, 1984). In his survey, Allington showed that well-endowed, stocked classrooms had more than 20 books per student, whereas book-poor classrooms had fewer than four books per student. Not only does access to interesting texts appear to correlate with achievement, but this access varies substantially across classrooms.

Students in book-rich classrooms fare well. For example, Au and Asam (1996) confirmed that student ownership of literacy (which is similar to intrinsic motivation for reading and writing) was increased in a program in which a diversity of interesting reading material was provided. Moreover, Pressley, Rankin, and Yokoi (1996) observed that teachers who are nominated as outstanding by their supervisors frequently attempt to motivate learning by displaying books and reading books aloud in ways that emphasize their interest-value for students.

Social Collaboration for Literacy Motivation

Collaboration in the classroom has been studied in many investigations. Central to the notion of social collaboration is interdependence among the learners. Individuals who are interdependent members of groups coordinate their efforts, share information, and build on each other's thinking as they seek to understand texts. Furthermore, when different forms of expertise are distributed across members within a community of learners, collaboration becomes highly functional and fosters conceptual learning (Brown & Campione, 1998).

Beneficial effects of social collaboration on cognitive engagement in learning from text have been shown for narrative and informational text. Almasi (1995) documented the benefits of sharing diverse perspectives on literary works by showing that students who openly expressed different interpretations in discussion groups gained deeper literary understandings than students who were not provided the opportunity for diverse interpretations. Using expository texts, Meloth and Deering (1994) showed that when student teams were encouraged to use strategies of searching, integrating, and evaluating, their conceptual learning was increased. Across a range of texts, Guthrie, Schafer, Wang, and Afflerbach (1995) showed that when students interacted socially by sharing literacy with friends and family, their reading outcomes improved. Social interaction increases a range of cognitive competencies for comprehension and expands students' motivation to read widely and frequently.

Comprehension Instruction Supporting Student Reading Efficacy

As discussed earlier, reading efficacy beliefs refer to individuals' assessments of their ability to read well. When individuals believe they can successfully complete activities, like reading a story or book, they will persist at the activity, attempt to read difficult books or stories, and choose to return to the activity when they have the opportunity (Bandura, 1997; Schunk & Pajares, 2002). Therefore, when teachers foster students' reading efficacy, many good things happen.

What are the seeds of a strong sense of self-efficacy? Bandura (1997) stated that there are several main influences on students' self-efficacy; we focus on the three most relevant to children's reading achievement. First and foremost is students' performance. When students achieve success in school, their self-efficacy grows. As their successes build, so does their self-efficacy (Schunk & Zimmerman, 1997). A second influence on self-efficacy is watching others successfully complete an activity. When students see others accomplish a task, they often think they can do it themselves. This is especially true when the person doing the activity is a peer. Teacher modeling can also help students learn to accomplish an activity. A third influence, encouragement from others, is where teachers can have particularly strong power. When teachers provide encouragement and support, student self-efficacy can grow.

With respect to reading efficacy and achievement, the fundamental tools taught in CORI classrooms are the reading strategies. In the first 6 weeks of CORI, teachers introduce individual reading strategies to students and work with them until each strategy is mastered. During the second 6 weeks, strategies are combined so that students learn how to use them together. This strategy instruction provides all students with the fundamental tools they need to read a variety of different texts and materials, thereby allowing them to become strong readers. Such successful performance will likely enhance their competence and reading efficacy, leading them to read increasingly challenging books.

Limitations of Research Literature on Classroom Motivation Supports

Studies in the research literature are often dedicated to documenting the extent that a classroom context variable, such as a teacher's autonomy support, influences a student variable, such as perceived autonomy or intrinsic motivation. Although the variable of autonomy support is accurately identified, it is usually studied in isolation from other variables that may affect it dramatically. For example, in a correlational study, Reeve, Bolt, and Cai (1999) reported that students were more highly motivated in classrooms where teachers were classified as high autonomy-supportive than low autonomy-supportive. In an experiment, Reynolds and Symons (2001) reported an experimental study with a choice and no-choice condition to determine the effect of choice on students' motivations. Although we concur with the conclusions from these investigations, we suggest that they should be qualified by adding consideration of variables in the environmental context.

Our rationale is that a variable such as autonomy support does not exist in isolation. In any study, just as in any classroom situation, a student making a choice must choose something—a book, a task, a partner. A chooser must select some concrete object or event. The autonomous action cannot appear in a vacuum. The circumstance in which the choice occurs is likely to be vital to the choice itself. For instance, if a student is choosing among books, the difficulty, topics,

graphic appeal, length, and vivid details of the text will influence whether the
choice occurs and whether it evokes a positive affect. Choosing between two difficult, boring, inaccessible books will not lead to motivational benefits for the
learner. Yet, these qualifying conditions are not described systematically in previous research. In the Reeve et al. (1999) studies, high-autonomy teachers are embedded in the choices offered to students in the classroom context, but the
context is not described in detail. Likewise, in valid experiments such as the one
by Reynolds and Symons (2001), the texts for the choice condition are carefully
constructed, but the text characteristics are not fully described as part of the
study. Therefore, we have little information about the necessary enabling conditions for teachers' autonomy support. The same limitation applies to all of the
studies on the variables we use as part of the motivation support system in CORI.
However, CORI teachers provide scaffolding that fuses variables into a composite
to enable these supports to function dynamically.

A second limitation of previous research is the investigation of polar extremes
in motivation. For example, investigations often report the consequences of
teachers who are highly supportive or not at all supportive of students' autonomy.
Some studies focus on autonomy-supportive teachers or controlling teachers who
discourage or preclude students from making choices (Deci, Schwartz,
Sheinman, & Ryan, 1981). Likewise, experiments usually have a choice condition or a no-choice condition (Cordova & Lepper, 1996; Reynolds & Symons,
2001). Although these are valuable studies, they do not yield information about
the process of shifting from a high level of autonomy support to a low level, or vice
versa. Therefore, these investigations have not shown how changes in the environment are related to development of motivation.

The process of scaffolding for motivational development addresses these
limits of the existing research literature by placing the scaffolding process in a
context, and by describing the shift from high to low support for the motivational process (e.g., encouragement of students' independence). As the examples of high scaffolding in this chapter illustrate, a single "plank" in the scaffold,
such as autonomy support, must be connected to topics to be learned from a text
and other features of context. In the beginning of scaffolding, the teacher gives
third graders microchoices about a topic or a limited menu of texts to be read.
Across a wide age range, students need scaffolds for choice, which enable them
to exercise autonomy in a responsible manner (Guthrie & Davis, 2003).

Scaffolding not only embeds the variables, but matches these processes to
the learners' needs and optimally reduces the support for them over time. At the
start of instruction, the scaffold for curiosity, involvement, autonomy, and social interaction will be high. Students cannot exercise curiosity for a long time,
over many texts, and across situations independently, without plenty of oppor-

tunities and guidance. A high scaffold at the outset makes an initial level of text-based curiosity successful and gratifying for the learner. A teacher would not provide beginning third graders with a totally open opportunity to "Choose any book in this school to read for the next hour." Students need guidance in making choices and in how to use time to gain enjoyment and information from their selections. After offering high scaffolding for choice making, teachers reduce their guidance and students gain autonomy in directing their reading.

The optimal level of scaffolding is the support needed by students to increase their level of self-determined reading. If the scaffold remains high indefinitely, students' motivational development is precluded. If the scaffold is always low, many students will not experience the motivational processes that lead to intrinsically motivated, self-determined reading. Shifting the guidance from high scaffolding, which enables students to perform processes of intrinsically motivated behavior, to low scaffolding, which affords students the opportunity and classroom infrastructure for high amounts of self-direction in their reading, increases motivation and engagement.

CLOSING

Looking at all students in a given grade (say Grade 4) in a school, teachers can easily identify some students who are highly motivated, self-determined readers. Most, but not all, are able, high-achieving students. Some teachers view these students' motivation as self-made. These learners enter their classrooms as motivated readers (or not). Simultaneously, teachers rarely view themselves as agents of motivational growth. Although they know that extrinsic incentives such as points, rewards, or extra recess will energize and control students briefly for an activity, teachers often do not imagine that they influence students' motivation to read in the long term. Yet, teachers are more powerful than they realize. They are endowed with all the resources to move students up the ladder of self-determined literacy. By scaffolding for motivational development, teachers can profoundly foster students' reading engagement and self-directed reading.

REFERENCES

Allington, R. L. (1984). Oral reading. In P. D. Pearson (Ed.), Handbook of reading research (pp. 829–864). New York: Longman.

Almasi, J. F. (1995). The nature of fourth graders' sociocognitive conflicts in peer-led and teacher-led discussions of literature. Reading Research Quarterly, 30, 314–351.

Anderson, E. (1998). Motivational and cognitive influences of conceptual knowledge: The combination of science observation and interesting texts. Unpublished doctors dissertation, University of Maryland.

Au, K. H. (1998). Social constructivism and the school literacy learning of students of diverse backgrounds. *Journal of Literacy Research, 30*(2), 279–319.

Au, K. H., & Asam, C. L. (1996). Improving the literacy achievement of low-income students of diverse backgrounds. In M. F. Graves, P. van den Broek, & B. M. Taylor (Eds.), *The first R: Every child's right to read* (pp. 199–223). New York: Teachers College Press.

Baker, L., Dreher, M. J., & Guthrie, J. T. (2000). *Engaging young readers: Promoting achievement and motivation.* New York: Guilford.

Baker, L., & Wigfield, A. (1999). Dimensions of children's motivation for reading and their relations to reading activity and reading achievement. *Reading Research Quarterly, 34*, 452–476.

Bandura, A. (1997). *Self-efficacy: The exercise of control.* New York: Freeman.

Brown, A. L., & Campione, J. C. (1998). Designing a community of young learners: Theoretical and practical lessons. In N. M. Lambert & B. McCombs (Eds.), *How students learn: Reforming schools through learner-centered education* (pp. 153–186). Washington, DC: American Psychological Association.

Bruning, R., & Schweiger, B. M. (1997). Integrating science and literacy experiences to motivate student learning. In J. T. Guthrie & A. Wigfield (Eds.), *Reading engagement: Motivating readers through integrated instruction.* (pp. 149–167). Newark, DE: International Reading Association.

Chi, M. T. H., DeLeeuw, N., Chiu, M., & Lavancher, C. (1994). Eliciting self-explanations improves understanding. *Cognitive Science, 18*, 439–477.

Cordova, D. I., & Lepper, M. R. (1996). Intrinsic motivation and the process of learning: Beneficial effects of contextualization, personalization, and choice. *Journal of Educational Psychology, 88*(4), 715–730.

deCharms, R. (1976). *Enhancing motivation: Change in the classroom.* New York: Irvington.

Deci, E. (1992). The relation of interest to the motivation of behavior: A self-determination theory perspective. In K. A. Renninger, S. Hidi, & A. Krapp (Eds.), *The role of interest in learning and development.* Hillsdale, NJ; Lawrence Erlbaum Associates.

Deci, E. L., Nezlek, J., & Sheinman, L. (1981). Characteristics of the rewarder and intrinsic motivation of the rewardee. *Journal of Personality and Social Psychology, 40*(1), 1–10.

Deci, E. L., & Ryan, R. M. (1994). Promoting self-determined education. *Scandinavian Journal of Educational Research, 38*(1), 3–14.

Deci, E. L., Schwartz, A. J., Sheinman, L., & Ryan, R. M. (1981). An instrument to assess adults' orientations toward control versus autonomy with children: Reflections on intrinsic motivation and perceived competence. *Journal of Educational Psychology, 73*(5), 642–650.

Eccles, J. S., Buchanan, C. M., Flanagan, C., Fuligni, A., Midgley, C., & Yee, D. (1991). Control versus autonomy during early adolescence. *Journal of Social Issues, 47*(40), 53–68.

Eccles, J. S., & Wigfield, A. (2002). Motivational beliefs, values and goals. *Annual Review of Psychology, 53*, 109–132.

Elley, W. B. (1992). *How in the world do students read?* Hamburg: International Association of the Evaluation of Educational Achievement.

Garcia, T., & Pintrich, P. R. (1996). The effects of autonomy on motivation and performance in the college classroom. *Contemporary Educational Psychology, 21*, 477–486.

Guthrie, J. T., & Davis, M. H. (2003). Motivation struggling readers in middle school through an engagement model of classroom practice. *Reading & Writing Quarterly, 19*, 59–85.

Guthrie, J. T., Schafer, W. D., & Huang, C. (2001). Benefits of opportunity to read and balanced instruction on the NAEP. *Journal of Educational Research, 96*(3), 145–162.

Guthrie, J. T., Schafer, W. D., Wang, Y. Y., & Afflerbach, P. (1995). Relationships of instruction of reading: An exploration of social, cognitive, and instructional connections. *Reading Research Quarterly, 30*, 8–25.

Harter, S. (1981). A new self-report scale of intrinsic versus extrinsic orientation in the classroom: Motivational and informational components. *Developmental Psychology, 17,* 300–312.

Hidi, S., & Harackiewicz, J. M. (2000). Motivating the academically unmotivated: A critical issue for the 21st century. *Review of Educational Research, 70*(2), 151–179.

Koestner, R., Ryan, R., Bernieri, F., & Holt, K. (1984). Setting limits on children's behavior: The differential effects of controlling versus informational styles on intrinsic motivation and creativity. *Journal of Personality, 52,* 233–248.

Linn, M. C., & Muilenburg, L. (1996). Creating lifelong science learners: What models form a foundation? *Educational Research, 25,* 18–24.

Lipson, M. Y., Valencia, S. W., Wixson, K. K., & Peters, C. W. (1993). Integration and thematic teaching: Integration to improve teaching and learning. *Language Arts, 70,* 252–271.

McCaslin, M., & Good, T. (1996). The informal curriculum. In D. Berliner & R. Calfee (Eds.), *Handbook of educational psychology* (pp. 662–670). New York: Macmillan.

McLoyd, V. (1979). The effects on extrinsic rewards of differential value on high and low intrinsic interest. *Child Development, 50,* 1010–1019.

Meece, J. L., Blumenfeld, P. C., & Hoyle, R. H. (1988). Students' goal orientations and cognitive engagement in classroom activities. *Journal of Educational Psychology, 80,* 514–523.

Meloth, M. S., & Deering, P. D. (1994). Task talk and task awareness under different cooperative learning conditions. *American Education Research Journal, 31*(1), 138–165.

Miserandino, M. (1996). Children who do well in school: Individual differences in perceived competence and autonomy in above average children. *Journal of Educational Psychology, 88*(2), 203–214.

Morrow, L. (1996). *Motivating reading and writing in diverse classrooms: Social and physical contexts in a literature-based program.* Urbana, IL: National Council of Teachers of English.

Pintrich, P. (2000). An achievement goal theory perspective on issues in motivation theory, terminology and research. *Contemporary Educational Psychology, 25,* 92–104.

Pressley, M., Rankin, J., & Yokoi, L. (1996). A survey of instructional practices of primary teachers nominated as effective in promoting literacy. *Elementary School Journal, 96*(4); 363–383.

Reeve, J., Bolt, E., & Cai, Y. (1999). Autonomy-supportive teachers: How they teach and motivate students. *Journal of Educational Psychology, 91*(3), 537–548.

Reynolds, P. L., & Symons, S. (2001). Motivational variables and children's text search. *Journal of Educational Psychology, 93*(1), 14–23.

Roeser, R. W., Midgley, C., & Urdan, T. C. (1996). Perceptions of the school psychological environment and early adolescents' psychological and behavioral functioning in school: The mediating role of goals and belonging. *Journal of Educational Psychology, 88*(3), 408–422.

Ross, J. A. (1988). Controlling variables: A meta-analysis of training studies. *Review of Educational Research, 58,* 405–437.

Ryan, R. M., & Deci, E. L. (2000). Intrinsic and extrinsic motivations: Classic definitions and new directions. *Contemporary Educational Psychology, 25,* 54–67.

Schraw, G., Bruning, R., & Svoboda, C. (1995). Source of situational interest. *Journal of Reading Behavior, 27*(1), 1–17.

Schunk, D. H., & Pajares, F. (2002). The development of academic self-efficacy. In A. Wigfield, & J. Eccles (Eds.), *The development of academic motivation.* (pp. 16–29). San Diego: Academic Press.

Schunk, D. H., & Zimmerman, B. J. (1997). Developing self-efficacious readers and writers: The role of social and self-regulatory processes. In J. T. Guthrie & A. Wigfield (Eds.),

Reading engagement: Motivating readers through integrated instruction (pp. 34–50). Newark, DE: International Reading Association.

Stipek, D. (1996). Motivation and instruction. In D. C. Berliner & R. C. Calfee (Eds.), *Handbook of educational psychology* (pp. 85–113). New York: Simon Schuster Macmillan.

Sweet, A. P., Guthrie, J. T., & Ng, M. (1998). Teacher perceptions and student reading motivation. *Journal of Educational Psychology, 90*(2), 210–224.

Turner, J. C., Parkes, J., & Cox, K. E. (1995). Perspective on literacy research and practice. In K. A. Hinchman & D. J. Leu (Eds.), *Forty-fourth yearbook of the National Reading Conference*, (pp. 126–136). Oak Creek, WI: National Reading Conference.

Weinert, F. E., & Helmke, A. (1995). Learning from wise Mother Nature or big brother instructor: The wrong choice as seen from an educational perspective. *Educational Psychologist, 30*(3), 135–142.

Wigfield, A. (1997). Children's motivations for reading and reading engagement. In J. T. Guthrie & A. Wigfield (Eds.), *Reading engagement: Motivating readers through integrated instruction* (pp. 14–33). Newark, DE: International Reading Association.

Wigfield A., & Guthrie, J. T. (1997). Motivation for reading: Individual, home, textual, and classroom perspective. *Educational Psychologist, 32*(2), 57–135.

CHILDREN'S BOOK REFERENCES

Biddulph, F., & Biddulph, J. (1993). *Feathers and flight*. Bothell, WA: Wright Group.

Yolen, J. (1987). *Owl moon*. New York: Putnam & Grosset.

4

Fostering the Cognitive Strategies of Reading Comprehension

John T. Guthrie
Ana Taboada
University of Maryland

At the center of Concept-Oriented Reading Instruction is the process of fostering competence in reading comprehension. In this chapter, we define the main reading strategies children are taught. Through vignettes of teachers explicitly teaching reading comprehension strategies, we describe how to organize and provide good reading strategy instruction in CORI. Finally, we describe how teachers modify their instructional approach to give special attention to struggling readers within the CORI classroom.

Strategies for comprehension cannot easily be taught in isolation. Children must be immersed in rich content to learn comprehension strategies easily. To nurture students in strategy learning, CORI provides an inquiry context. The previous chapter described this context, which included a conceptual theme for an extended unit of learning, hands-on experiences related to the theme, an abundance of interesting texts for instruction, and collaborative activities. All of these provide an environment, a home, for learning the strategies of comprehension. In many ways, the context of CORI and the strategy instruction within CORI depend on each other. With a strong conceptual context for learning "big ideas," children can readily grasp comprehension strategies. As comprehension strategies are assimilated, practiced, and used, children find they can learn important content from books.

LINKS OF STRATEGY INSTRUCTION IN CORI
TO THE RESEARCH BASE

Synthesis of Research-Based Knowledge

At the turn of this new century, in 2001, the field of reading took the occasion to look back over several decades of reading comprehension research. At least three sources provide summaries and perspectives on this body of literature (Collins & Pressley, 2002; Gersten, Fuchs, Williams, & Baker, 2001; and National Reading Panel, 2000). Extremely prominent in these recent syntheses is the work of the National Reading Panel (NRP). This panel identified research on comprehension that met specific criteria for the validity of each study. The report outlined the criteria that emphasized replicability. Each study had to be adequately described, defined, and conducted in such a way that the public could follow the study and others could repeat the investigation as the original investigators did. This panel also required that studies be quantified so that the amount of benefit to learners from an instructional approach could be estimated. In total, the panel identified the following types of comprehension instruction in which more than three studies per area that met the criteria were conducted: (a) comprehension monitoring, (b) cooperative learning, (c) curriculum integration, (d) graphic organizing, (e) listening actively, (f) mental imagery, (g) prior knowledge, (h) question answering, (i) question generation, (j) story structuring, and (k) summarizing. In addition, the panel noted that at least 38 studies had examined multiple strategies in which several of these strategies were combined. Furthermore, about six investigations were focused on explicitly training teachers in comprehension instruction for multiple strategies. The importance of teaching these strategies to young learners has been emphasized by teachers such as Keene and Zimmerman in *Mosaic of Thought* (1997) and researchers in reports such as the National Reading Panel Report (2000). We have used these strategies in CORI since our first report in 1996 (Guthrie et al., 1996).

Relating CORI Strategies to the Research Literature

The strategies, as we name them in CORI, are highly similar to several strategies identified as effective in the NRP report. We use the term *searching* to refer to the complex activity of forming a goal or a question, identifying books related to the goal or question, and retrieving information that addresses the question. This is a broader strategy than question answering as examined in the NRP report. The panel reviewed studies in which students answered "why" questions after reading small portions of text, such as sentences or brief passages. Searching for information includes this activity, but also includes other processes of forming goals, locating information, and synthesizing answers from several texts. Otherwise, strategies in CORI and the ones located in the research base by the National Reading Panel are highly similar. Five out of the six strategies in CORI were rated as being among the seven best and most well established strategies in the experimental research literature. We included activating background knowledge in CORI, although it was not on the "short list" of the NRP, because this strategy is very important for learners, relatively familiar to teachers, and we believe the evidence supports its use within the CORI framework.

Attributes of Comprehension Strategies

There are two salient attributes for each of these strategies. First, each strategy distinguishes good readers from poor readers at a given grade level. These strategies reliably discriminate experts from novices in reading. For example, in Grade 4, good readers may be expected to be much more proficient in questioning than poor readers at that grade level. The second attribute is that each strategy can be taught to young learners in the later elementary grades. Given suitable texts for learning, appropriate explanations, and modeling, students will learn the strategies. Generally, they will be able to use them productively, with a new text, within the same topic domain that they were taught. For most of the strategies, it has been documented experimentally that learning a strategy increases not only proficiency in the strategy, but performance on other reading comprehension tasks. In other words, the strategy transfers to new areas and increases knowledge gained from text. These are remarkable strengths, and they suggest that the strategies are potentially powerful tools for learners in the classroom.

The research literature contains descriptions of how these strategies are taught within the investigations. A large majority of teachers were the investigators providing the **direct explanation** and **modeling**. That is, the teacher explained what the strategy was and how it would help students' comprehension. Furthermore, the teacher provided the demonstration by modeling the strategy and showing the students how she would perform it with a specific text. Most of the investigations also provided scaffolding, where teachers offered guidance and practice with a strategy and encouraged students to use it with new reading materials.

Limits of Research-Based Knowledge

Despite these remarkable attributes of strategies for comprehension, there are several issues that investigators have not researched. One issue is developmental sequence. It has not been established whether some strategies are important for younger learners, whereas others are more easily taught at a later stage of learning. Furthermore, the development of students' competence within a strategy is not mapped out. For example, developmental benchmarks for children's questioning have not been investigated frequently by other researchers. We suggest that understanding the benchmarks, or levels, of learning that students progress through is informative for teachers. These benchmarks serve as goals for instruction and topics for reflection by learners to facilitate their awareness and their competence.

A second issue focuses on how strategies should be connected to content knowledge. It is obvious that questioning must be questioning about a topic, and summarizing must be summarizing of content. However, the breadth and depth of learning about content, as it is related to children's understanding of how to use strategies, has not been firmly established.

The CORI framework provides one example of how a knowledge domain functions as a context for strategy teaching. Some strategies must be tailored to the content. For example, organizing graphically is different for information text and literary text. With information texts, a graphic organizer, such as a concept map, reflects abstract concepts and supporting information for the concept. On the other hand, a graphic organizer for a literary text may include the goals of characters and the changes in the plot. These different contents may produce quite different graphic structures. Knowing how to compose a graphic organizer for information text is not an assurance that students can transfer this skill to a literary text and vice versa. Therefore, each of the strategies must be tailored and practiced within the specific topic areas (science, history, literature, math) in which students are expected to use them.

With issue three, we suggest that strategy instruction is always provided in a rich context. However, the nature of that richness has not been profiled in the existing research base. Elements in a strong classroom context usually include providing student choices (autonomy), encouraging social discourse for learning from texts (collaboration), providing concrete experiences related to books (hands-on activities), writing extensively about what has been learned from reading, and communicating new understandings gained from literacy activities to audiences inside and outside the classroom (Guthrie & Cox, 2001; Guthrie & Wigfield, 2000). CORI provides a framework for building these elements into the classroom with a long-term plan. The CORI framework provides enabling conditions for strategy learning.

STRATEGY INSTRUCTION IN CORI

Single Strategy Instruction

As the CORI framework shows, in the first 6-week unit on "Birds Around the World," six strategies are taught. These are allocated to one strategy per week in succession. The sequence is: activating background knowledge, questioning, searching, summarizing, organizing graphically, and structuring stories.

Our rationale for the single strategy instruction is that beginning third graders benefit from this simplification. During normal reading, proficient readers use multiple strategies. They are likely to use prior knowledge, think of questions in their minds, and organize what they are learning spontaneously. Even in third grade, advanced readers use multiple strategies simultaneously. However, lower achieving third-grade readers may be at the end of first-grade or the beginning of second-grade reading levels. These children have little awareness of what strategies are, how to perform them, or how they influence reading comprehension. Even gifted and talented learners in third grade benefit from the awareness of strategies that single strategy introduction provides. More advanced students can develop the language of strategies (i.e., using terms such as *activating background knowledge*, etc.) and linking the questions to new understandings artfully, while lower achievers gain basic competence in doing a strategy fully.

Combined Strategy Instruction

In the second 6-week unit of the CORI framework, strategies are merged and are referred to as *multiple strategy instruction* (Trabasso & Bouchard, 2002). Combined strategy instruction is provided with attention to how these different mergers take place. A principle for linking two strategies is to use the result of one strategy in doing the next one. For example, suppose students are learning about grasslands and how animals live in them. When introducing a new book on rivers as a habitat for different kinds of plants and animals, the teacher might ask for questions. Students may come up with thoughts such as, "What lives in a river? What do river animals eat?" These are acceptable and appropriate responses, but they are low-level questions.

By combining the strategy of activating background knowledge with the strategy of questioning, these questions can be improved. For example, the teacher could ask students to brainstorm about rivers. Students might volunteer that rivers are: "water," "moving water," "muddy sometimes," "filled with rocks," "beginning small in a mountain," and "increasing in size as they move toward the sea." In brainstorming about animals that live in the river, they may identify creatures such as fish, salamanders, and bugs. Following brainstorming, the teacher could ask, "Use your prior knowledge to write new questions." Students might respond by forming such inquiries as, "How do fish find bugs in moving water?" or "Why doesn't water wash away the home of an otter?" These questions are at a moderately high level on our rubric for questioning (see chapter 11) because they require complex explanations. The previous questions were lower level on the questioning rubric, merely requesting a simple description. By using the results of their first strategy, activating background knowledge, in performing their second strategy of questioning, students' strategies have improved. This is likely to increase the depth of understanding the richness of new knowledge gained from reading the book introduced by the teacher.

Cognitive Strategies Taught Within CORI

Before discussing how CORI teachers provide instruction, we describe the comprehension strategies that children learn within our framework. We believe that it is best to provide a few strong strategies that children are able to command firmly.

Activating Background Knowledge. Activating background knowledge refers to students recalling what they know about the topic of a text before reading and during reading for the purpose of learning the content as fully as possible and linking the new content to prior understanding. As students approach a new book, or a new section of a book that they are reading, they are likely to ask, "What do I know about this topic?" Often, the title of the book or a picture in the book will prompt this reflection. When students gather their recollections and think about how their previous experiences may relate to the topic of a new text, they set the stage within their minds for learning from the book.

Students who are most proficient in using what they already know to gain new understanding show several qualities. These students do not merely think of a few disconnected words. Rather, they represent their previous knowledge as an interconnected, causally related set of concepts. More proficient users of this strategy employ the strategy flexibly, as needed. During the reading of every sentence or every section of a book, the process of activating previous knowledge is not necessary. However, when the student is confused, when an obstacle in the text is encountered, or when a new vocabulary word is read, the process of activating background knowledge is a powerful tool for learning.

The cognitive strategy of activating background knowledge is an instrument of the learner. It is the student who activates background knowledge. When a teacher brings a new book to the class, she may often provide background information about the topic and content of the book. If the students will be reading about an octopus, most teachers introduce the topic with a discussion about what an octopus looks like, where it lives, and its unique features. Although this is a valuable practice, this is not student activation of background knowledge. This is teacher provision of relevant content that can aid learning. In contrast, the student process of activating background knowledge is a support system that students provide for themselves, before and during reading. Teachers may ask students, "What do you know about this topic?" and thereby help the students get their process of activating started. Ultimately, only the student can perform the process of activating background knowledge in reading.

Questioning in Reading.   Questioning refers to students asking or writing self-initiated questions about the content of a text, before and during reading, to help them understand the text and the topic. Students' reading processes change dramatically when they pose questions about the topic of a book or text before reading. Their questioning serves several roles in the comprehension process. First, if they are students' personal questions, they come from the students' knowledge. They flow out of personal experiences and represent those experiences as the students encounter new ones.

Just as important, a question represents a child's investment. It is his request for information, and his desire to know. Children identify closely with their questions. They feel proprietary about their own questions and are affectively attached to them. In this light, questions create motivation for learning from a text. They link children's interests to the content of their reading.

Questions are best formed after perusal of a text or brief discussion of its content. Children cannot ask questions about an unfamiliar topic. Likewise, they cannot form questions about an unknown book. Therefore, providing the opportunity to preview a text and its title, pictures, captions, and sections, before beginning the questioning process, fosters student questioning.

As children begin questioning, they focus on simple facts and rudimentary information. In reading a book about a whale, children may begin by asking, "How big is a whale?" As they progress, children move toward questions about basic processes or structures. They may ask, "How do whales talk to each other?" As children gain knowledge about a topic, their questioning is more focused and more deeply probing. At this higher level, they may ask, "How far do whales have to swim to fill up their big stomach?" At the highest level we have observed among third graders, children may ask questions that relate large concepts to each other such as, "How do whales defend their babies from enemies?" Such a question interconnects defense and the processes of reproduction and rearing and, therefore, is a higher order question.

Searching for Information.   Searching for information refers to students seeking and finding a subset of information in the total text by forming specific goals, selecting particular sections of text, extracting information accurately, combining new and old information, and continuing until goals are fulfilled. Searching for information can be contrasted with comprehension of a total text. During total text comprehension, students begin reading with the first word of a text, such as a story, and continue in a linear fashion to the last word, comprehending all portions and all sentences of the text. In contrast, students who are searching for information are highly selective. They begin with a larger text, such as a long book, and find particular portions that are relevant to the project, problem, or question being asked. The purpose of searching is not to read the entire text, but to read and learn from only the most relevant portions of the text.

Four essential processes are utilized during the search strategy: (a) forming a learning goal, (b) effectively using text features to guide searching, (c) comprehending relevant text related to goals, and (d) monitoring the fulfillment of goals. Students who are proficient in searching for information are able to form clear goals. By clearly stating their purposes for reading and by forming good questions, students set up firm goals to pursue in their search. The next phase in their searching is to locate sections of a text related to their learning goals. For example, if students are learning about elephants, they may ask questions about elephant migration, habitat, and communication. In this case, students locate relevant sections by using the table of contents, index, pictures, topic sentences, and other text features that enable them to search effectively.

The search process continues until students have located text relevant to their goals. Then, students read for details, important factual information related to their goals. They focus on the relevant information closely and comprehend it as fully as possible. Simultaneously, students relate this information to their question or purposes for reading. They monitor their understanding to determine whether their question has been answered and whether the text is satisfactory for their purposes. Searching for information may often include multiple texts, resources such as Web sites, and other media. A challenge for learners is to organize and integrate these resources into a coherent understanding.

Summarizing During Reading.   Summarizing refers to students forming an accurate, abstract representation (the gist) of the text after reading all or substantial portions of the material. Students with excellent comprehension are likely to be summarizing as they read. Should a teacher interrupt a good comprehender during reading, the student could likely identify main ideas and supporting facts in what she has read. She is continually building a mental representation of the text. A weak comprehender who is interrupted is far less likely to be able to delineate central concepts and important facts in text he has read. This process of summarizing during reading is a valuable tool for full comprehension.

On the surface, a summary seems simple. However, it can be more complex than we first imagine. Consider how a reader summarizes a paragraph. There are several processes involved. First, the individual identifies important high-level concepts in the paragraph. Often, this can be accomplished by locating key words within the text. These important concepts, or key words, might be considered the "main idea" of the text. A second process consists of identifying key supporting information. This may consist of words or phrases, rather than full sentences. A third process is to identify and to omit less relevant details. Often, the most striking information within a paragraph is vivid details. Sometimes this information is valuable, but more often than not, it is distracting and irrelevant. Selecting the more important from the less important supporting information is a central process in summarizing. Finally, if the learner is expected to write a summary, she will compose a brief statement (one to four sentences) representing the summary.

Third-graders find the process of summarizing more challenging than we first expected. Grade 3 students have not learned all the phases of locating central concepts, identifying supporting information, and avoiding the inclusion of unimportant information in the summary. Therefore, instruction on this cognitive strategy must be carefully scaffolded with multiple opportunities for learning. The following is an illustration of this strategy.

A Vignette on Summarizing Instruction

Ann Duncan, a third-grade teacher at North Frederick Elementary School in Frederick, Maryland, is teaching students a CORI unit on aquatic life. Students have taken a trip to a pond and have brought back specimens to the classroom. They are observing an aquarium with guppies and snails while jotting notes in their science journals. Aligned with this, Ann is teaching the reading strategy of summarizing.

Ann opens the lesson by explaining what summarizing is and how it helps children with their reading. She begins:

> The strategy I am teaching today is summarizing, and actually being able to write a summary and understand what to write. They kind of go together ... you're reading, you understand, and you're thinking about what you're reading. You're making those connections to your real life. On top of that, I'm going to then take you through the summarizing process. How do you summarize? What is a summary? The first part of our strategy is going to involve our actually understanding what we read. Actually, this past week, we've been talking about organisms that live in our aquarium. We've observed one of the organisms, which is the snail. We came up with lots of ideas about what a snail does, what helps it to do a lot of these aspects of survival, such as what does it do to defend itself, and what body parts does it have that helps it to defend itself? I also hear people talking about the locomotion part of the snail. What helps it move from one place to another?

Ann walks to the side of the classroom. Ecology concepts are posted on display boards. They include the nine core concepts that have been studied since the beginning of the year: feeding, locomotion, predation, reproduction, respiration, communication, defense, competition, and adaptation to habitat. Icons are associated with each of these abstract terms to help the third graders remember them. For instance, a telephone represents communication and a baby in a cradle represents reproduction. Ann has explained the human analogies to these concepts in relation to their study of animals, birds, insects, and now, aquatic life. Having laid the conceptual foundation for this lesson on summarizing, Ann introduces the text:

> We observed snails in our aquaria early this morning. As I walked around the classroom, I heard students talking about how they move and how they eat. Now, we will read about the food for a snail. We will use this book, *Snails*, and read one page from it now. In front of you is a page that I photocopied for us to read. I will read it aloud and you follow along with me. Now I'm going to stop at certain points, and I'm going to say stop and talk. You talk about what we just read with your partner, at those times.

Ann organizes and pairs a few students who do not have partners at their tables. Then she reads aloud:

> Snails are herbivores. Herbivores are animals that eat plants. Land snails eat grass, leaves, and dried plants. Freshwater snails eat algae and other plants. Algae are small floating plants. Ocean snails eat seaweed. Stop and talk.

Now, students chat about the meaning of what they just read. The classroom is alive with interchange. After three "read and discuss" cycles, Ann proceeds to her summarizing lesson:

> Now please look here and I want your attention. Look at this page on the overhead projector. Now, I am going to give you some strategies for summarizing what you just read. A summary, first of all, should give you an understanding of what you just read, okay? It tells me, Mrs. Duncan, that you know what? That Sarah, she understands what she just read. There are two parts to a summary, okay? First of all, there is the main idea. You have a main idea in your summary. Secondly, you have what is known as supporting ideas, ideas that support that main idea of your summary. Your summary is only about three to four sentences.

A student responds to Ann's last statement by saying, "That's fun because you don't have to write very many sentences."

Ann Duncan places the first paragraph from the text on the overhead projector and proceeds:

> In this paragraph, I want us to circle the most important point, which is the main idea. This is about snails and food, so food is the most important word. This is my main idea, and I will circle it. You do this on your page.

All of the students find the word in the first paragraph on their photocopied page and circle it.

Ann continues her instruction:

> You never want to underline whole sentences. You want to underline key words that help you understand what you just read. What other word in the first sentence will help me understand about snails and feeding?

Ann's student, Andres, replies, "Herbivores."
Ann responds:

> Yes, that is an important word. Let's underline it. An herbivore is an animal that eats plants. Are there any important ideas that are going to help me understand how snails feed and eat? Okay, so you want to underline each plant. Any important supporting ideas about snails and how they feed or what they feed on? Plankton is another important word. Plankton are small flat worms. We are underlining supporting words or supporting ideas in each sentence that help us make sense of how a snail feeds. Now, you're going to take your main ideas and we are going to actually write a summary with our main ideas.

Ann walks to a different side of the classroom to a large sheet of white paper hanging on a chalkboard. She asks students for information and writes their summary on the paper. She asks class members for the main ideas and supporting details in each paragraph. She writes one sentence for each paragraph into her summary on the paper in large words.

Ann asks one student to read the paragraph, which she does, but the final sentence is unclear. Ann questions the student, "Does that last sentence make sense?"

"No," the class choruses in response.

"How can we fix it?" Ann asks. Students make various suggestions as Ann enters them on the chart.

Denise reads the summary:

> Our main idea is about snails and how they eat and how they use their body parts to eat. Some snails are carnivores, they eat meat, and others are herbivores, they eat plants. Snails have long black tongues called radulas. A radula is covered with tiny sharp teeth that help to bring the food into its small body.

Ann then asks the pairs of students to write a summary of the next page. Students followed her model. They identify the main idea by circling key words. Next, they underline supporting information in the form of key words and phrases. Last, they place a line through unimportant details. Then, also in pairs, students write a three-to four-sentence summary of this page from the book. Individuals read their summaries aloud to the class. As they work, Ann circulates among the pairs answering questions, coaching, and encouraging. Students were able to follow her framework; they easily read and took their initial steps in this exceptionally challenging job of summarizing a page of print. As they progressed and gained experience, their confidence slowly increased and their smiles were shared. Students placed their steps of writing the summary into their reading journals. Their pages with key words circled, supporting information underlined, and less important information deleted, were placed in their journals. Their written summary was retained as a reminder of their first step toward learning to summarize a text.

Organizing Graphically.   Organizing graphically refers to students' construction of a spatial representation of text-based knowledge that may include drawings, concept maps, charts, and diagrams. Students who comprehend a text deeply are usually able to represent it in a spatial format. That is, they can draw a t-chart, formulate a diagram, or draw a concept map invoking appropriate text information. Many third graders require extended support in learning this process.

One frequent form of organizing information graphically is concept mapping. In this process, students begin by identifying a central theme or principle that is addressed throughout the text. In this case, the text may consist of an entire book, a section of a book, or a single page in an information book. Having found the most abstract topic or main idea, students then generate related and more specific topics and connect them to the central one. Next, supporting details or specific attributes of each concept can be added to the concept map. An example is shown here with the hierarchical structure of the principle, concepts, and facts or features (see Figs. 4.1 and 4.2). Links among the aspects of content depict relationships. Students label the links by placing a word on the link that enables them to write a sentence connecting the two contents, such as "is," "is needed for," "have," or "use." Links may also be described more abstractly as "necessary for," "part of," or "example of."

Graphic organizing, as a cognitive strategy in reading comprehension, may occur during reading. Such a process does not have to be delayed to the end of a unit, although that is a common practice and can be valuable. Used during reading, graphic organizing disrupts the reading process. However, the interruption can afford the opportunity for metacognitive processing, such as, "What do I know and how shall I organize it?" Concept maps can be made for a single page or a single section of text as a tool for summarizing and building a knowledge base from reading. Students learn to generate concepts, use symbols to link their concepts, and organize their thinking. By reflectively arranging their understanding, students learn how to structure what they know. Such structuring lays a foundation for future reading.

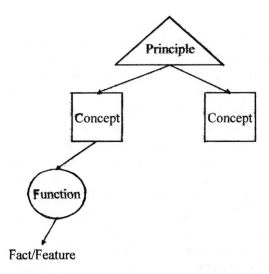

FIG. 4.1. Abstract example of a concept map.

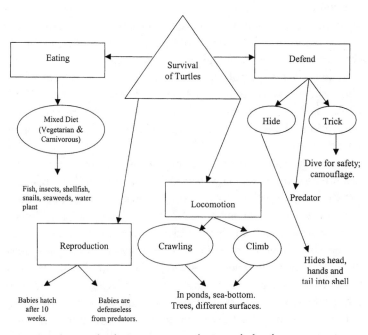

FIG. 4.2. Specific example of a concept map on the survival of turtles.

Structuring Story.   Students' understanding of the setting, plot, characters, motives, themes, and their relationships in literary texts is referred to as *structuring story.* We use this word order to emphasize the cognitive activity with a verb, as we do for all the strategies. At the beginning of third grade, students' comprehension of a story is often well developed. They may have enjoyed extensive narratives for many years at home and during early schooling. Beginning third-grade readers are often aware of how to follow the twists and turns of a plot. They may also be able to identify one or two important attributes of the main character. In addition, some third graders can identify the motives of characters fully and relate these motives to the events in the plot. With teacher support, these students can identify the central theme of a literary piece or the moral of a fable. To aid students in story structuring, teachers encourage them to draw diagrams and charts of their understanding of a piece of literature. Classroom enactments of literature allow students to link their experience to their more abstract conceptualization. An enactment acts as a graphic organizer of a literary piece.

Instruction for Combining Reading Strategies

Good comprehenders combine all of the strategies mentioned previously in this book. Even third graders who are relatively proficient may use additional strategies, such as monitoring their comprehension, and integrating them with the strategies presented here. Although we separate the strategies for initial instruction to help the majority of students learn them, we devote equal attention to enabling students to combine strategies productively. In the CORI framework, weeks 7–12 are dedicated to combining and integrating multiple strategies. The National Reading Panel Report (2000) referred to this as *multiple strategy instruction.*

Our combining process begins with linking the strategy of activating background knowledge with questioning. Although many students base their questions firmly on their knowledge of the topic, many do not. A small amount of explicit instruction and practice in the combining process is salutary for all students.

Combining strategies is an abstract idea. To make it concrete, we ask students to take the following steps: (a) do one strategy; and (b) use the results of the first strategy to do a second strategy. For example, students can be asked to use the strategy of activating background knowledge for a particular text. Suppose the topic of their text is trees and how they grow. Students begin by brainstorming what they know about trees, including the facts that trees have trunks, leaves, roots, green color, and birds living in them. Following such a simple activating process, students may ask a question such as, "Do the roots have to go deep to help the tree grow tall?" This question is interesting and more complex than a simple one that might have been asked before activating background knowledge. Without any activation, students might have asked, "How do trees grow tall?" Although this question is worthy, it is not as probing nor as likely to generate complex outcomes as the more informed question. By combining the results of their strategy of activating background knowledge into their strategy of questioning, students form deeper, more intriguing questions. Their questioning strategies improve as a result of first using the activating strategy.

This pattern of combining strategies works across many combinations. An example of this pattern is to ask students to combine the strategy of questioning (asking many diverse, relevant questions about a text and its topic) with the strategy of searching for information. Their search will be more elaborate if they did not first perform the strategy of questioning. Likewise, given a large text of several pages, making a graphic organizer of the text can be an excellent precursor to summarizing the same text. As students develop command of combining several strategies, they can fuse activating background knowledge, questioning, searching for information, summarizing, and organizing graphically as they perform larger, more integrated inquiries with multiple texts. The process of combining and integrating is natural for higher level learners in Grade 3 and above. However, it is valuable for learners and prudent for the teacher to provide the building blocks of single strategy instruction, and then to combine strategies comprehensively.

As students move to Grades 4 and 5, they are expected to understand large patterns of relationships in content texts. For instance, in life science, students may be expected to understand complex food webs in multiple biomes as they simultaneously interact. An example of this would be a food web of insects, plants, and fish in a river that intersects with a food web of grazing mammals and predators in the neighboring grassland. The concepts of eating, locomotion, communication, predation, and reproduction would be illustrated in these webs, as well as the fact that these concepts are interlinked. For students to understand patterns of relationships, they need multiple, high-level strategies operating simultaneously. To form complex networks of knowledge, students need to be able to activate background knowledge, search for information, question, and use multiple strategies effectively. Therefore, the integration of strategies in the later elementary grades accompanies the curriculum expectation that the students will form linkages among multiple concepts and content domains, such as science and social studies. Teaching students to combine reading comprehension strategies should be aligned with teaching students the patterns of relationships among concepts in the content areas.

Strategy instruction is aligned with the content objectives of teaching. As shown in the CORI framework, the reading strategy of activating background knowledge is taught at the same time that teachers provide a general introduction to a science activity. Therefore, activating background knowledge in the science activity, which is natural at the outset of content lessons, is taught simultaneously with activating background knowledge for reading related to that topic. Likewise, questioning during reading is taught along with hypothesizing and questioning during science exploration. We believe that these comprehension strategies and science processes can complement each other.

Comprehension strategy instruction can and should be provided for students with approximately a beginning second-grade reading level. Texts used during strategy instruction should be easily read. Students' word recognition accuracy should be 90% to 95%. Otherwise, students are struggling with the word recognition process and their attention to comprehension strategies is limited. Under these conditions, their learning will be minimal. Of course, cognitive strategies can be taught with listening activities and story read-alouds at any level of reading difficulty.

Explicitness of Instruction

As we have stated, the context of a conceptual theme is provided with hands-on activities connected to the conceptual theme and student questions as a guide for developing points of focus within the content area. Within this context, we provide explicit strategy instruction. The term "explicitness" refers to how thoroughly the teacher is directly explaining, modeling, and guiding student learning in the cognitive strategy. In contrast to explicit strategy instruction, some teachers are implicit in their teaching. That is, implicit instruction permits students to figure out the strategies as they learn meaningful content. We believe the research evidence in Grades 3–5 documents that implicit strategy instruction is too often ineffective, especially for lower achievers (Gaskins & Elliot, 1991). Beginning third-grade students are generally in need of explicitness. One exception to this may be beginning third graders who are gifted and talented, reading at a fifth grade or higher level.

Explaining the Strategy. At the outset of instruction, it is useful to provide a brief explanation about the strategy. In general, we want students to learn the **who, what, why, when**, and **where** of cognitive strategies for reading. The discussion of these points can occur throughout the instruction. At the outset of teaching, teachers can provide a discussion of what it means to "activate background knowledge." It means, "Using what we know." It means, "Thinking about our experiences before we read." It means asking ourselves, "How does this connect with information I already know?" To the degree that students are able to follow the message, teachers can explain **who**—all readers use background knowledge during reading, **when**—we use background knowledge before and during reading many different types of texts, and **why**—what we know helps us build our knowledge more securely. All of these points cannot be made in the initial discussions, but they can be built on over time. Awareness of these strategy aspects will assist students in becoming skillful and deliberate in their employment of comprehension strategies as readers.

Modeling and Scaffolding. The first step in teaching reading comprehension strategies is modeling. It is important to begin with a topic that is familiar to students. Learners should not be struggling to gain new content at the same time they are attempting to understand what a new cognitive strategy is and how to use it. Initially, strategies should be introduced with text that is highly familiar to learners.

Students should have good word recognition for a text that is relatively brief, such as one page. It is not usually feasible to begin teaching a strategy, such as summarizing, expecting students to summarize an entire story. Although students may be capable of beginning at this level, the majority of beginning third graders will find such a large unit of text frustrating.

Teacher modeling consists of a demonstration. The teacher shows the students how she would use a particular strategy for the lesson with a specific text. All students should have the text visible to them, perhaps on their desks and on an overhead projector.

Immediately following the modeling, teachers may provide a scaffolding activity. The essence of scaffolding is the teacher doing the strategy with the learners. The teacher may lead the way in this joint endeavor if students are unsure how to proceed. As students gain confidence or skill, teachers may reduce the scaffold and provide them with more freedom and more opportunities for leadership in the joint process of doing strategies together.

For example, a teacher may say, "Let's turn to page 2 in our books." The teacher may say, "On page 1, I showed you how I used my knowledge to learn about bird feathers. But page 2 is on bird nests. What do we know about bird nests?" As students answer, the teacher accepts and affirms their information. She proceeds by saying, "Read the first three sentences quietly to yourselves." After discussing the meaning of those sentences with the students, the teacher may say, "What is the next paragraph about?" As the students answer, noting it addresses the different locations of nests for different species of birds, the teacher can ask, "What do we know about where birds place their nests?" As students answer, information is affirmed. The students complete the reading of the page silently. In closing, the teacher may observe, "While you read, you activated your background knowledge. You used what you knew about birds and bird nests to help you better understand the text."

At a later time, explicit strategy instruction in activating background knowledge may include writing. Teachers request students to write sentences describing what they know about the topic of a text that they will be reading. After reading and discussing the text, students can express what they learned. They can compare their prior knowledge based on their written statements with their newfound understanding. The request for writing is a continuing scaffold to help students externalize their process of activating background knowledge. This request for writing can apply to any of the reading comprehension strategies.

Guided Practice.   As students gain basic competence in using a strategy, teachers provide for extended practice. Teachers may provide guidance to assure that practicing and using strategies occur. In providing guided practice, teachers introduce students to a range of different texts. Students may learn that activating background knowledge can occur for texts on mammals and reptiles, as well as the original book on birds with which the strategy was taught. Students learn that activating background knowledge (or all of the strategies) can happen across genres. Each strategy is used with literary works such as legends, fables, or fiction books. Almost all strategies are adaptable to multiple genres. However, there are important distinctions in how strategies are applied to different genres. Summarizing a story can be quite different from summarizing a page in an information book. Consequently, the use of a given strategy, such as activating background knowledge or summarizing, should be explicitly taught for different genres.

Independent Use of Strategies.   Independent use of strategies requires that students know how and when to use them on their own. Proficient readers do not use all of the strategies all of the time. By definition, a strategy is a tool we use to increase comprehension of text. When comprehension is going well during the reading of a particular text, students may not need to disrupt their reading and attempt to employ a strategy. However, if the comprehension process needs support, strategies should be used. For example, if a student is confronted with a new text, a confusing point of information, new vocabulary words, or a text that is not comprehensible, the student should stop and employ one or more comprehension strategies.

Students who can competently use a cognitive strategy for reading comprehension possess a skill for making meaning. It is self-evident that such a strategy will be valuable only if it is used. Students must not only know how, but they must decide when, to employ a strategy or a set of strategies. For good strategy users, self-initiation is the essence of their proficiency in comprehension. Good strategy users decide appropriately, on their own, when and how to use their cognitive strategies.

If a strategy is always teacher-initiated, it will not be valuable to the learner. If the teacher must prompt students to use their strategies, their learning is incomplete. To promote and assure independent strategy use, teachers can provide multiple opportunities for employment of strategies that have been taught. Requiring students to display the results of their strategies in their journals or portfolios, gives students visible evidence of their work. Students who are successful in self-initiated strategy use can be acknowledged, while learners who are not self-initiating frequently and effectively can be encouraged or provided a scaffold.

Scaffolding Novices and Experts

At the heart of strategy instruction is the process of teachers working together with students as they use a strategy. Extremely high levels of teacher support are necessary for the novice learner. At the highest level of teacher support, the teacher models the full process of using the strategy. At a slightly lower level of support, the teacher provides a scaffold, and the students begin to participate in the strategy-using process. Here, the teacher may provide examples of partial strategy use. She will frequently ask questions and guide student participation closely. The teacher is doing 90% of the strategy use and the students are contributing 10%.

At the lowest level of scaffolding, the teacher may simply request that the students perform a given strategy with a pre-selected text. For example, the teacher may say, "We will begin the new book on peoples of the rainforest. You should use your strategy of questioning for this book." In this case, the teacher would expect students to peruse the book briefly, think of questions that they have about the topic, share questions with their friends, and record several key questions in their strategy journals. Even this minimal request provides prompts and constraints. If students are successful at this low level of scaffolding, teachers have probably spent many previous weeks or months on questioning instruction.

At a moderate level of scaffolding, the teacher may ask the students to perform key aspects of the strategy, but not display the strategy or model it for them. At this level, the teacher may structure the task, for example, by selecting one page of text to be used. The teacher may direct the students' attention by suggesting that they read two bolded headings on this page of text. Further, the teacher may request that the students write their strategy outcomes in their journals. This moderate level of scaffolding does not contain a display or model, but rather directed attention, selected tasks, and guided performance.

It is possible to provide moderate scaffolding strategies for either novices or experts. The difference is how much competence in reading a particular text the student possesses. There are several occasions for a moderate level of scaffolding: if the students are low achievers; if the particular text is difficult. If the strategy has not been learned; or if the content of the text is unfamiliar. The highest teacher support is modeling, which is valuable at the outset of teaching a strategy. As students gain command of a given text topic, can read the words, and can perform the strategy, the teacher lowers the level of scaffolding. For students in Grades 3–5, scaffolding may occur across levels, ranging from high to low. Even relatively expert readers in Grades 3–5 can benefit from low levels of scaffolding in order to increase their use of strategies across different reading situations.

Adapting Scaffolding

One essential process in effective strategy instruction is adjusting the scaffolding. When students are frustrated because strategy learning seems difficult or unproductive, it is likely that the level of scaffolding has been too low. For third graders, a low level of scaffolding for summarizing consists of requesting, "Please write a summary." This frustrates many learners. Furthermore, a scaffold that is moderate when it should be high will also be frustrating. Likewise, students who are relatively expert with a given text on a given topic will not want a highly detailed and explicitly displayed model on how to use a strategy that is familiar to them. Too much scaffolding can be boring and counterproductive.

Adapting the scaffold is vital, not only for student learning, but also for motivation. If students are learning under the right level of scaffolding, they will be successful. Gaining competence in strategy use makes students aware, and thus proud, of their work. A scaffold that is attuned to the learner's needs is assuring the student's progress in a complex task. From their skills, students gain a sense of confidence and self-efficacy. Under the opposite conditions of a misaligned scaffold that is too high or too low for learners, students will be disaffected. They will become frustrated or bored. In the extreme case, they will likely withdraw from literacy learning activities.

A MORE DETAILED EXAMPLE: INSTRUCTION FOR STUDENT QUESTIONING

Many teachers empower students by enabling them to ask questions. When students ask questions, they gain a sense of direction for their learning. As they read to answer their questions, students are often delighted to find answers. Disappointment usually follows when the answers are absent from a book. Questions are powerful tools for teaching and learning. How do we help students use questions to read?

A Rubric for Students' Questioning

To build a guideline for instruction in questioning, we formed a rubric for children's questions. This rubric is a statement of levels (from 1 to 4) that represent the quality of students' questions. Lower numbers on the rubric represent lower quality questions and higher numbers denote those with higher quality. We judge the quality of students' questions by the power and effectiveness of the questions as enablers of reading comprehension. Students who ask lower level questions on a text are likely to show lower reading comprehension than students who pose higher level questions. This was our initial expectation, and it has been confirmed in research with hundreds of students. (Findings are reported in chapter 11.)

Factual Information.   These Level 1 questions ask for a simple fact. The answers may be yes or no, and they are often relatively trivial. For example, the question, "How big are sharks?" requests a factual statement.

Simple Description.   At Level 2, students ask about an important concept of a topic. The answer to this question will contain many facts and generalizations.

Complex Explanation.   At Level 3, questions ask for an explanation about an important concept and request evidence for the explanation. The question itself may be complex, containing significant amounts of student knowledge.

Pattern of Relationships.   Questions at Level 4 request a principled understanding, with evidence for complex interactions among multiple concepts. In science, this may reflect interdependencies of species and biomes. (see chapter 11).

Using Questioning Benchmarks as Instructional Goals

It is valuable to teach children to ask questions as they read. According to the research on strategy instruction, children who receive questioning instruction become better comprehenders than children who are given no questioning instruction. It is helpful to use the students' developmental benchmarks as goals when teaching this skill. Children who ask simple Level 1 questions have learned a valuable skill, yet they can be encouraged to ask questions at Level 2, which is simple description. As they grow from asking factual questions to simple description questions, these children advance in their questioning and progress in their reading comprehension. Likewise, as children progress from simple description to complex explanation (Level 3), their reading and thinking about text becomes more elaborate. When students move toward asking questions about patterns of relationships (Level 4), they are creating the occasion for high-level comprehension and synthesis across multiple texts.

Principles of Questioning Instruction

These principles apply to all of the strategies, but they are illustrated here for the strategy of questioning.

Questioning Instruction is Content-Focused and Hands-On Related. It is valuable to build an initial base of prior hands-on experiences related to a conceptual theme. In the CORI unit "Birds Around the World," teachers provide students with the following activities prior to questioning: (a) observation of local habitat of their backyard; (b) mapping the characteristics of the habitat; (c) discussion of landforms different from their backyard, such as deserts or polar regions; (d) drawing a variety of landforms; (e) charting animal life in various biomes; and (f) use of multimedia to broaden their exposure. With such a staged setting, students' questioning is grounded in information about landform diversity and bird survival. This enhances the possibility for higher level questions and creates the conditions that enable children to compare questions with each other.

Make Questioning Instruction Text-Based. Teachers provide students with books, pages of information, or pictures with captions, prior to questioning. Briefly browsing these materials benefits students in several ways. It often prompts their thinking and enables them to form a question. It provides them a set of topics addressed in a text that might be answered with their questions. Browsing a text helps the students and teachers avoid the frustration of asking questions that cannot be answered with available texts and materials. In their initial browsing, students can use headings, pictures, captions, and other text features to prompt or to provoke questioning and thinking.

Support Beginning Questioning With Scaffolds. Teachers can help beginning third graders form a question by giving them half of a question and letting them finish it. Support can be given by providing a cue card with a question word, or walking students through text features such as bolding, subtitles, and captions. Teachers should encourage students to discuss questions with partners or teams before posing them to the whole class.

Support Advances in Awareness and Self-Initiation. Teachers can enable students to progress in the rubric from lower to higher levels. Once beginning stages are established, higher benchmarks can be goals for questioning. When students are at Level 2, Levels 3 and 4 can become aims for questioning instruction. To support students' advancement teachers can:

- Have students evaluate their own questions.
- Have students choose their favorite question to answer.
- Allow students to "take ownership" of their questions.
- Have students rewrite questions to move them up in rubric levels.
- Encourage students to write several questions before reading.
- Encourage students to add questions to their lists during reading.
- Encourage students to write questions with their partners.
- Have students improve their questions collaboratively.

Assure Learning From Text Via Strategy Use. It is vital for students to read, write, and discuss in order to answer their questions. Questions posted in the classroom should not remain on the wall for an extended time without being addressed by reading and discussion. The questions and answers can be written on an illustrated poster. Questions can be presented in class and entered in journals. This makes questioning a strategy for reading, rather than an isolated activity. By coordinating students' questions with their answers gained from reading, teachers foster students' awareness. They enable students to see that questions are a tool for learning, a way of building their knowledge from text into higher levels.

Simultaneously, questions are a way to personalize learning. When students pose their questions, they are making a personal commitment or a statement of individual interest. Answering their questions through reading fulfills this commitment. Students feel ownership of the question and the answer. This builds confidence and efficacy for learners as questioners in a literacy environment.

A Vignette of Sally Trent's Questioning Instruction

The following vignette is an example of strategy instruction from the classroom of Sally Trent, a CORI teacher at Monocacy Elementary School in Frederick, Maryland. In Mrs. Trent "Survival and Environments" unit, students have completed their observations of the giant diving beetle in their aquariums. This is a predatory bug that can devour fish. In addition to observing, students conducted an experiment to determine whether prey would escape into plants when the giant diving beetle was introduced into the aquarium. They are in the process of performing that experiment. Students are also raising questions to learn more broadly about how this giant diving beetle survives.

As the scene opens, a team of five third graders is gathered around their small aquarium observing the plants, snail, guppies, and giant diving beetle. Their excitement is intense, as they feed the creatures and observe who eats who or what eats what. Sally places a poster on the bulletin board with two intersecting circles, one referring to giant diving beetles and one referring to people. She asks the students to record characteristics that are unique to people, other characteristics that are unique to the giant diving beetle, and characteristics that are common to both. On the circle referring to the beetle, the students write "claws," "pinchers," "beak," and "tube on its rear-end for breathing"—their favorite characteristic. On the people circle, students place many characteristics such as "nose," "toes," and "lips." In the intersecting section, students list "eyes," "stomach," "legs," "feet," and other shared characteristics.

When the chart is completed, Sally draws their attention to core ecological concepts. The concepts of predation, locomotion, feeding, competition, respiration, defense, communication, and reproduction are posted on the bulletin board, with icons, on colored paper. Her students have studied these same concepts in the unit "Birds Around the World." Their knowledge is deepening as they examine how the giant diving beetle has the same aspects of survival in an aquarium.

Sally asks, "What is predation?" After some wait-time, Julia offers, "How does our bug find food?" Sally affirms, "So if we are looking at predation, we are looking at what eats our bug or how our bug eats others. Okay, feeding, what is this?" Kathleen says, "It is what it eats." "Yes, eating," says Sally.

Next, Sally asks, "What is reproduction?" Sally proceeds through a brief review of all of the knowledge goals related to the environmental science unit.

Stepping to the other side of the classroom, Sally pauses, waits for quiet, and then says, "Now you will ask a question for each of these core concepts. You have a good bit of information about the giant diving beetle, but I'm sure there are more things you want to know. You are always asking me questions, now you can ask questions for yourselves. So, I'm going to give each group eight sentence strips because there are eight concepts, one question on each."

Sally then moves to a bulletin board with the questioning rubric that was discussed previously in this chapter. She asks, "What questions are we asking? We are asking about something we don't already know. We know that it eats fish. We've seen it. So do not ask what it eats. We have a good idea of how it eats, so do not ask how it eats. We know it breathes through its tail, so do not ask, 'How does it breathe?' You can question other parts of its breathing, such as does it have lungs?"

She instructs the students to work in teams at their tables to write one question for each concept. Students are excited and busily talk, write, and fill in their strips.

Next, Sally writes the students' questions on the projection screen as they read them aloud. Questions are grouped under concepts such as feeding and predation. Under feeding students have asked:

- How many animals can it eat in an hour in the wild?
- Why do they only eat the insides?

A student volunteers a question and Sally responds, "Say that again because I like your question." She writes the question on the overhead, "How does it use its pinchers to get its food?" She highlights it, following students' suggestions, to show that it is a high-level question (Level 3). Soon the questions are recorded from all teams for the class to see. The high-level questions are most visible because of their highlighting.

Continuing her instruction, Sally gives an advanced lesson on searching for information. In the previous unit, "Birds Around the World," students participated in an initial series of learning activities for using the text features such as index, table of contents, bolding, and topic sentences to locate and integrate answers to their questions. Now, they revisit this strategy of searching for information to answer questions. Using a class text on bugs, they review and identify the features used in searching. These features include captions, sidebars, headings, bolded words, and the index. This lesson ends as students have identified the books they will use to answer their questions and the features they will rely on in their next day's search. Their quest for information and their pursuit of knowledge about the core concepts through reading has begun.

CLOSING

Comprehension of a book is more than a collection of strategies. Acts of understanding are pursuits toward meaning. While interacting with a text, a reader "changes his mind," perhaps forever. A shift so significant is not made against the will of the reader. Just the opposite, the reader's will and intention drive comprehension. They fuel the quest to learn from text. In a word, comprehension is at the service of motivation, which is unfolded more fully in chapters 3 and 10.

REFERENCES

Collins, C. C., & Pressley, M. (2002). *Comprehension instruction: Research-based best practices.* New York: Guilford.

Gaskins, I., & Elliot, T. (1991). *Implementing cognitive strategy training across the school*. Cambridge, MA: Brookline Books.

Gersten, R., Fuchs, L. S., Williams, J. P., & Baker, S. (2001). Teaching reading comprehension strategies to students with learning disabilities: A review of research. *Review of Educational Research, 71*(2), 279-320.

Guthrie, J. T., & Cox, K. E. (2001). Classroom conditions for motivation and engagement in reading. *Educational Psychology Review, 13*(3), 283-302.

Guthrie, J. T., Van Meter, P., McCann, A. D., Wigfield, A., Bennett, L., Poundstone, C. C., Rice, M. E., Faibisch, F. M., Hunt, B., & Mitchell, A. M. (1996). Growth of literacy engagement: Changes in motivations and strategies during Concept-Oriented Reading Instruction. *Reading Research Quarterly, 31*, 306-332.

Guthrie, J. T., & Wigfield, A. (2000). Engagement and motivation in reading. In M. L. Kamil, P. B. Mosenthal, P. D. Pearson, & R. Barr (Eds.), *Handbook of reading research* (Vol. III, pp. 403-424). Mahwah, NJ: Lawrence Erlbaum Associates.

Keene, E. O., & Zimmerman, S. (1997). *Mosaic of thought*. Portsmouth, NH: Heinemann.

National Reading Panel (2000). *Teaching children to read: An evidence-based assessment of the scientific research literature on reading and its implications for reading instruction* (NIH Pub. No. 00-4769). Jessup, MD: National Institute for Literacy.

Trabasso, T., & Bouchard, E. (2002). Teaching readers how to comprehend text strategically. In C. C. Collins & M. Pressley (Eds.), *Comprehension instruction: Research-based best practices* (pp. 176-200). New York: Guilford.

CHILDREN'S BOOK REFERENCES

Holmes, K. J. (1998). *Snails*. Mankato, MN: Capstone Press.

5

Science Inquiry
in the CORI Framework

Pedro Barbosa
Laurie Alexander
University of Maryland

INTRODUCTION

At its simplest, CORI attempts to provide an atmosphere of inquiry and exploration that helps draw students into what, for many, is a new or poorly developed domain, the world of reading. CORI exercises the mind in order to
motivate students to accept, learn, and use reading skills. The science component of CORI parallels its overall philosophy in that hands-on exploration,
questioning, and content-based inquiry about the biological world motivate
students to incorporate into their lives the empowerment of reading. The philosophy that drives the science component parallels CORI in that it is, at its
core, *Concept-Oriented Science Instruction* (COSI).

The specific challenge of the *science* component of CORI is threefold: to
stimulate and encourage scientific curiosity; to use the process of science; and
to understand the interrelatedness of life. We aim to stimulate and foster scientific curiosity by encouraging hands-on experiences and developing observation skills with the aid of structured activities and a framework of conceptual
thinking. The second challenge is met by having students understand the process of science by conducting experiments to test hypotheses. The process of
science is reflected in the "Scientific Method," an approach that guides how scientists solve problems and test hypothetical explanations of what they observe
but do not understand. Yet, this method is nothing more than an outline for

problem solving. It is an approach used to systematically resolve the unknown by observing, gathering sufficient information to formulate a clear question, deciding on a way to unambiguously resolve the question, and drawing a conclusion based on the results of inquiry. Students learn that the process of science inquiry enables one to accurately describe, contrast, and explain the living world. The third challenge is met with a core element of the science component of CORI, that is, a mechanism that facilitates understanding the interrelatedness of the living world by exploring educational concepts. Science education in CORI entails the implementation of Concept-Oriented Science Instruction (COSI). COSI is based on the tenet that the life of all plants and animals revolves around certain common and crucial activities and interactions. Thus, the interrelatedness of life can be understood by exploring certain educational concepts that concentrate on those activities and interactions. As we discuss later, science activities in CORI are centered on a set of biological and ecological concepts or processes that we term *educational concepts*. The foci allow students to easily and readily expand and extend the knowledge acquired through reading and their own scientific research. These CORI educational concepts were selected not only because they represent important ecological and biological phenomena, but also because they are areas of science that are supported by grade-appropriate reading material.

At the heart of CORI is a focus on motivation that both drives and links science and reading (Fig. 5.1). COSI seeks to stir and develop the natural curiosity and enthusiasm of children. Their inquisitive nature and willingness to explore can, under the right conditions, be turned into a powerful tool for science inquiry that includes observation, experimentation, and reading. When we make a link and build a bridge between reading and science, the stage is set for a life-long learning from books based on confidence, critical thinking skills, and a rich relationship with nature itself.

THE PROCESS OF SCIENTIFIC INQUIRY

CORI Science Goals

The COSI goals of CORI fall into three broad categories, distinct in the scale of engagement and level of understanding. The three goal categories are: (a) science process goals, (b) science content goals, and (c) science concepts goals. When focusing on science process goals, we seek to develop and encourage the ability to observe, infer and ask questions based on observations, and construct logical but hypothetical predictions (hypotheses). Further, we seek to have students evolve the ability to develop ways of ad-

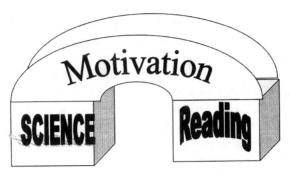

FIG. 5.1. Bridging disciplines for more effective reading.

dressing (or testing) their hypotheses, using concrete and verifiable and/or observed information about the natural world (which represent science content goals). Finally, it is our goal to develop in students the ability dis-cover and/or recognize seminal patterns in nature that describe and drive bi-ological interactions among plants, animals, and their environments (science concepts goals).

Making observations, generating hypotheses, and gathering facts serve as the currency with which science process skills are articulated. Focusing activities and discussions around 11 key educational concepts facilitates reaching science concept goals, and to some extent, science content goals. The overall objective of the CORI approach is that science content be acquired through hands-on experiences with careful observation. With this foundation and the guidance provided by a set of key educational concepts, good questions that lead to testable hypotheses can be generated. In the classroom, the science exercises and experiments are used to provide students with an opportunity to participate in clear, specific, and relatively simple observations and tests of a hypothesis. Using the educational concepts to discuss the relevance of results to other organisms, interactions, or habitats, can then broaden the relatively narrow results of the science observations and experiments. Ultimately, our expectation is that these experiences will serve as a motivating force, leading students to seek information by reading books at various points in the process. As this is happening, other components of CORI will facilitate the acquisition of needed reading skills.

However, in order for science inquiry to be a critical component in increasing motivation and reading skills, there must be a link between science exercises/experiments and classroom books. The questions that students formulate with the guidance of teachers must not only be linked to, or supported by, student observations, but also must be supported by classroom books, particularly if students are to formulate hypotheses and design experiments. Focusing discussions around the educational concepts generates contrasts and comparisons that, in turn, make other concepts/interactions, other organisms, or other habitats relevant to the experiments conducted by students. As Fig. 5.2 shows, children's questions and science knowledge are a combination of learning from experiments and learning from books.

Science processes and learning from books are intentionally fused. In fact, a strength of CORI is that it provides a framework in which motivating students to read and learn science is integrated seamlessly (Fig. 5.3). To help accomplish this fusion, one component of the teacher activities in the CORI framework is "reading–science integration." For example, after a local habitat walk, third-grade students read *Owl Moon* by Yolen, contrasting their experience with the

What I know about frogs and what adventures they might have.	What I learned about frogs and their adventures after reading *Animal Lives*.	What I know about ponds and what lives there.	What I learned about ponds and what lives there after reading *Pond Year*.

-don't open their mouths to breathe (respiration)
-tadpoles → frogs (reproduction)
-eat insects (feeding)
-tails (locomotion)
-hedgehogs are enemies (feeding, protection, predation)
-related to toads
-can only see things in motion (defense, locomotion)
-swim in water but live on land (locomotion)
-lily pads to catch flies (locomotion, feeding)
 	
    Adventures
• look for food
• sit and dive
• lost
• hop
• chase animals
	• run away from enemies
	• enemy is hedgehog
	• don't have to open their mouths to croak
	• croak is an instrument
	• swallow food whole
	• red bellies
	• water is their safety
	• frogs can breathe w/ closed mouths
	
	    Adventures
	Traveled from hibernating area to pond
	• run from enemy
	• swim away if they feel threatened
	• croak to attract mate
	• dive into water
		deer
		dragonfly (larva)
		cattails
		swans
		otters
		mud puppies
		crayfish
		snails
		algae
		water striders
		raccoons
		snakes
		herons
		eastern loons
		mosquitoes
		turtles
		beavers
		salamanders
		toads
		ducks
		lily pads
		tadpoles
			muskrats (Sept.)
			water boatman
			eggs
			tadpoles → frogs
			crayfish
			  (also called crawdaddies)
			salamanders
			newts
			  (are red/brown)
			lady slippers
			frog eggs
			  (are transparent)
			water striders
			frozen
			damselflies
			thick algae
			  (in summer)
			water lilies
			dragonflies
			foggy ponds
			bears
			flower lilies
			frogs
			berries
			ticks

FIG. 5.2. Effects of reading on science knowledge.

FIG. 5.3. The seamless integration of the components of CORI.

walk taken in the story by the child and her father. More generally, students use and integrate information from their books, hands-on experiences, and observations in order to pose good questions and develop testable hypotheses. For example, after discovering bones in an owl pellet dissection activity, students read avidly about the food webs of owls and many other animals. We encourage students to read books to gain additional information and to conceptually explain their observed phenomena. However, we set a key prerequisite for the text available to students, that is, the books should not "give away" the outcome of a science inquiry activity, whether a test of a hypothesis on the response of fish to predators or a hypothesis on beetle preferences for light and darkness. Simultaneously, we insure that the science information in available books sheds light on important educational concepts.

THE CONCEPTUAL BASIS OF SCIENCE INQUIRY

An objective of the science component of CORI is to enable students to visualize commonalities among living organisms, based on the nature of the interactions among plants, animals, and their environment. This goal represents an effort to have students apply *science process skills* using *science content* (i.e., science facts), providing insights into unifying principles of biology and ecology. Students gain in their knowledge of key concepts and biological phenomena that represent, or are part of, broad patterns applicable across many different types of plants, animals, or habitats. The educational concepts underlying COSI are reflected in the following propositions:

1. **Reproduction** involves the application of certain behaviors, traits, and adaptations designed to insure that plants and animals can produce individuals of their own kind.

2. **Communication** is the transfer of information among and between plants and animals.

3. **Defense** describes what plants and animals do, how they do it, and where they do what is necessary to prevent being eaten or injured by other organisms.

4. **Competition** describes the interactions among plants and animals that result when two or more organisms need to acquire a critical resource that exists in limited supply.

5. **Respiration** refers to the organisms' process of gaining oxygen from the environment.

6. **Predation** refers to the process of animals capturing and eating other animals.

7. **Feeding** describes the behaviors and interactions involved in an organism's attempts to acquire the nutrition that it needs to grow, develop, and reproduce.

8. **Locomotion** defines the ways and means by which organisms move from one location to another.

9. **Niche** refers to the organism's role in a habitat (e.g., whether it is a scavenger, predator).

10. **Adaptation to habitat** refers to traits and behaviors of plants and animals that insure normal and self-sustaining interactions with the environment.

11. **Habitat conservation** refers to behaviors of plants and animals that preserve the conditions of the habitat that enable it to sustain life.

We have observed that third-grade students can be taught all of these educational concepts individually. For example, when one third-grade student was asked what she knew about how animals live in grasslands, she wrote, "What I know is golden wheel spider cartwheel. Gorillas can crawl when they are two months old. Roadrunners go 23 mph." She had learned several examples of locomotion of animals. However, she did not spontaneously link locomotion to another concept, such as feeding or defense.

Fourth-grade students can readily learn the interactions of educational concepts from their reading. Asked to compare life in rivers and grasslands, one student wrote:

> Rivers and grasslands are alike and different. Rivers have lots of aquatic animals. Grasslands have mammals and birds. Rivers don't have many plants but grassland have trees and lots of grass. Rivers have lots of animal like fish trout and stickle backs.

They also have insects and mammals, like the giant water bug and river otters. Grass-lands usually have lions, zebras, giraffes, antelope, gazelles, and birds. In rivers the food chain starts with a snail. Insects and small animals eat the snail. Then fish eat the small animals and insects. Then bigger animals like the heron and bears eat the fish. Snails also eat algae which grows from the sun. In the grasslands the sun grows the grass. Ani-mals like gazelle, antelope, and zebra eat the grass. Then animals like lions eat them. This is called a food chain of what eats what. In a way the animals are helping each other live. Animals have special things for uses. Otters have closable noses and ears. Gills let fish breath under water. Some fish lay thousands of egg because lot of animals like eating fish eggs. Some animals have camouflage. Swallowtail butter fly larva look like bird droppings. That is what I know and about grasslands and rivers.

This student presented two food chains, one for each biome. The educa-tional concepts of predation, feeding, and defense were related to each other through the use of food chains. In the classroom, discussions revolving around the educational concepts further develop the interconnections among them. More details on these knowledge structures are provided in chapter 9.

In general, central to the CORI approach is that the use of the key educational concepts is expanded, from Grades 3–5. Third grade is the first exposure that stu-dents have to the educational concepts in these forms. Thus, a primary aim is to move away from teaching science as a series of fascinating and seductive isolated facts and to begin to give students the experience of thinking conceptually. This achieved, in fourth grade the primary aim is to begin to encourage students to see and understand the inherent connections between pairs of educational concepts. As students gain a familiarity with conceptual thinking, the relative amount of time spent on straightforward versus more sophisticated educational concepts may shift, or advanced versions of a concept may be substituted. For example, al-though the concept of niche, which refers to an organism's *profession*, may not be considered in great depth in third grade, it receives greater attention in the fourth and fifth grades. That is, in fourth grade, the educational concepts requiring a bit more sophisticated thinking can be emphasized to a greater extent than in Grade 3, whereas other educational concepts can be emphasized in fifth grade to a greater extent than in Grade 4. For example, we in Grade 4 place more emphasis on **Habitat Conservation** (the conditions in a habitat that assure normal and self-sustaining interactions among organisms and between organisms and the en-vironment) than in Grade 3. Finally, in fifth grade, students are encouraged to see all the educational concepts as one unified set of phenomena central to all living organisms reflecting each species' adaptation to other organisms and to its own role in its habitat as illustrated in Fig. 5.4.

It should be noted that there is nothing unique about the "educational con-cepts" listed. Although important, they merely represent a manageable set of educational concepts. Indeed, the choice of some concepts may be influenced by classroom practicalities. Certain educational concepts are not included in

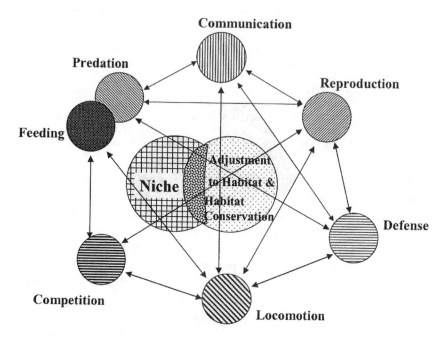

FIG. 5.4. Conceptual science foci: The interrelatedness of life.

CORI, either because they cannot be easily conveyed in a hands-on approach, are considered too advanced for students in Grade 3, or frequently, are not well supported in age-appropriate classroom books. Nevertheless, under appropriate circumstances, other educational concepts could be useful alternatives. These include, but are not limited to, essential aspects of science such as mutualism, evolution, parasitism, control of bodily systems, sensing the environment, growth, circulation of bodily fluids, digestion, ecosystems, communities, populations as entities, biodiversity, and mechanisms of inheritance.

THE SCIENTIFIC METHOD: AN APPROACH TO PROBLEM SOLVING AND SCIENCE INQUIRY

Science as a Hands-On Experience

Children are natural investigators, and therefore natural scientists. Scientists learn about nature primarily from direct experience, not by reading about it. Although it may seem contradictory to the goals of CORI, the first step in the successful integration of CORI and COSI is to put down the books. At the heart of learning science is the motivational power of direct observations and hands-on investigation of natural phenomena. Giving students the opportunity to make their own discoveries of nature sparks an enthusiasm for science that leads to an irrepressible desire to learn more by reading. Additionally, adding simple discipline to the process, by turning observations and questions into hypotheses and experiments, without stifling the spontaneity and the spirit of open-ended exploration, gives students confidence in their ability to conduct investigations of natural phenomena. They also acquire a motivation to read which, invariably, has a positive impact on all facets of their education.

So where do the books come in? CORI proposes that secondary sources of science content (i.e., books on science) are much more effective tools for learning when they build on the foundation of a child's own relationship with nature and enthusiasm for discovery. This relationship with nature, developed by exploring local habitats at home, school, camp, or in local parks is powerful. It connects children to the world around them. Once established, it remains intact for a lifetime and will continue to motivate them to ask questions and, if we build the connection to books, to read.

Experiential learning is essential in science, but scientists and educators also depend on secondary sources of information to obtain vital science content. Reading is required in order to research a question prior to beginning an experiment, adding to the direct observations one has made. Reading is also an important way to extend learning that begins by making direct observations. A student who has observed a fox entering a burrow near his school is likely to become engaged by books about the life history of foxes, wolves, or even dogs. Similarly, interest may be stirred in reading about other organisms that live in burrows, or in asking why organisms live in burrows. Interest generates questions; some specific questions, or components thereof, can be explored in the classroom and in books. The level of personal involvement and commitment that students feel after observing their world, asking questions, and designing and conducting an experiment to explore an interest can produce a very powerful desire to read.

GENERATING QUESTIONS: TRANSITION INTO HANDS-ON SCIENCE INQUIRY

When we say "hands-on science inquiry," we mean the use of the scientific method in an experiment. Experiments are learning tools for problem solving in elementary science education because they actively involve students in the process of inquiry. Predicting the answer to a question, developing a controlled approach for investigating it, recording and quantifying the responses, and interpreting the results engages students' minds in ways that passive viewing and recording of descriptive observations alone do not.

In short, doing experimental science turns students from watchers into doers. It turns them into scientists. As Kneidel (1993) said about her graduate school experiences in *Creepy Crawlies and the Scientific Method*, her excellent book on kids' science experiments:

> What was the big deal about doing experiments? I learned that instead of memorizing stuff that other people had discovered, I was creating knowledge. I was contributing to the accumulated body of knowledge. I understood then that science is not an already existing set of facts, but an ongoing process of discovery, and that I had become part of this process. By teaching children to do experiments, we give them that feeling too, that science is an ongoing process and that they are part of that process. It's an exciting feeling. It ceases to be intimidating and becomes a source of pride.

The success of the scientific method arises from the fact that it provides a flexible framework for investigating a wide range of questions. In fact, the usefulness of the scientific method as an investigative tool is not limited to science researchers, or to people of any particular background or age. It is, in fact, a disciplined process for general problem solving applicable to science questions at all levels, and to many nonscience questions as well.

The steps in the scientific method and how they interface with CORI are:

1. **Observe:** Spend time observing and taking notes on the organisms or habitats under study. In CORI, this stage is guided and structured in three ways:
   a. Using the **key educational concepts** to relate organisms to their habitats and to each other;
   b. Defining an overall **theme** or **framework** for each science study unit, such as "Hidden Worlds," "Woodlands," or "Wetlands";
   c. Providing well-planned **student worksheets** to focus students through observations in the field or in the classroom.

As students look for evidence of the educational concepts (locomotion, communication, feeding, etc.), many questions naturally arise. Careful observation leads to better questions, so students become better questioners by becoming better observers of nature. Teacher guidance is essential in helping students learn how to focus their observations (through student orientation and the use of worksheets). Relating what they observe to one or more of the key concepts (in class discussion) is also important. The development of hypotheses and experimental investigations are based on the observations that are made and questions that arise from the observations.

2. **Formulate a question**: In order to set up an experiment, it is necessary to narrow the students' large range of questions to one specific question, or to a small set of related questions. With help, the students can formulate a particular question that they would like to answer with their own experiment, or as part of a group. Books are used to provide background information for developing a question and hypothesis, but not to "answer" the question.

The success of an experiment depends, in large part, on choosing a good question. Many scientists are great scientists not merely because of their skill in solving problems, but because of their wisdom in the choice of question posed. Children are motivated by being able to pursue their own interests, just as we are. Young students, however, often ask questions that are not really suitable for a science experiment, or are beyond the scope of the realities of third-, fourth-, or fifth-grade classrooms. Left with unanswerable questions, students may be disappointed and will certainly not develop any science or reading skills. The teacher's role is to guide student questioning toward good hypotheses that lead to meaningful science experiments. Spontaneity and exploration (both mental and physical) are absolutely critical to this process. However, the passion generated in students must be guided by a great deal of discipline to insure that the process succeeds as a learning experience.

3. **Develop a hypothesis**: Students will address their question(s) by developing a testable prediction that will be subjected to experimental testing. For preplanned exercises and experiments, the objective in this step is to guide students to the desired hypothesis in a way that flows naturally from their questioning process. In this case, careful structuring of observations and discussions facilitates the task of leading students to a preplanned hypothesis. When students design their own experiments, the objective is to help them formulate their hypotheses in a way that can be experimentally tested with the materials and information available. In this case, developing a hypothesis—that is, turning a question into a testable prediction—is sometimes a more difficult step than it may first appear to be. We discuss this important transitional step for both preplanned and stu-

dent-designed experiments in more detail in the section "The Role of the Teacher."

4. **Plan and perform the experiment**: A plan and procedure must be developed to test the hypothesis (prediction). This plan also includes listing the materials needed, the number of observations and repetitions needed, and a quantitative way to measure and record the results. For both preplanned and student-designed experiments, this step is ultimately influenced and limited by the organisms and materials available in the classroom, and some creativity may be required to make an experiment practical enough to work in a real classroom. Some of the best science experiments ever done used only common, every day materials and very simple procedures!

5. **Record results**: The outcome of experiments should be recorded in a fashion that facilitates discerning patterns and drawing conclusions. Approaches to recording results may include using worksheets, graphs, tables, or histograms. Whatever method is used for recording data, it must be quantitative.

6. **Conclusions**: These are based on the interpretation of results obtained and attempts to explain the outcome of the experiment. This step includes looking at the implications of the findings and usually leads to the development of new questions, thus beginning the process anew at a deeper level of investigation.

GUIDANCE THROUGH WORKSHEETS

Good student worksheets are key to adding discipline and organization to the learning process. Therefore, worksheets used during observations and experiments must be thoroughly and carefully planned. Student charts and data sheets provide the structure for all stages of a science investigation, including observation, hypothesis testing, analysis, interpretation, and presentation of results. They focus students by guiding them to key aspects of the habitats, organisms, or interactions being observed, or to the most important variables in experiments. Our experience has shown that for inquiry-based science education, consistent use of well-designed student charts can be one of the most effective ways to integrate all of the steps required to complete a full investigation and to achieve a higher level of student investment in the learning process itself. The primary purpose of worksheets is to capture all of the principles, concepts, and methods that are being taught. Thus, they are designed to:

1. Reinforce the steps of the scientific method by urging students to record observations, make predictions, discuss methods, record variables, take measurements, and interpret and report results.
2. Encourage students to quantify observations and provide evidence to support conclusions.
3. Relate factual information to concepts.
4. Develop inferential thinking, as students reason from their results and look beyond the conclusion of one experiment to develop new questions and hypotheses.
5. Support a collaborative learning experience by encouraging the development of class hypotheses, compiling team and class results, interpreting data, and presenting group findings.
6. Sharpen observation by focusing student attention on the diversity of life's adaptations, and the interactions among organisms and the environment that shape plant and animal communities.

TESTS OF HYPOTHESES THROUGH OBSERVED CORRELATIONS OR MANIPULATION

There are two general ways in which students can test their hypotheses. Both approaches can be used in the classroom. Although they represent different approaches, both offer the opportunity to gain insights into the hypothesis being tested. In an observational or correlational study, students design an experiment where, by watching an animal, an interaction, or habitat without disturbing or manipulating it, they attempt to establish whether two so-called variables are associated. That is, students attempt to determine if two, or more, experimental variables (e.g., things, events, or conditions) are associated by quantifying some change when the variable is present and absent. The correlation between the presence or absence of the experimental variable and the measured change provides evidence of association, although not evidence of cause and effect. In the alternative approach (i.e., manipulative experimentation), the student establishes or creates two sets of conditions or situations, one in which, by appropriate manipulation, an experimental variable (a thing, event, or condition) is present and one in which it, and only it, is absent. That is, all factors except the experimental variable are the same. If the expected phenomenon (based on the hypothesis) is observed only in the presence of the manipulated variable, then the hypothesis is supported. This approach does provide evidence of cause and effect. Correlational experiments are most useful when it is impossible to control all variables except the one of interest. Examples of correlational experiments include those in studies evaluating the effects of some factor, such as coffee, on people. Although one certainly can have a group of people that drink coffee and one that does not, individuals in each group can vary in many ways that can influence results of the experiment. Thus, some may smoke cigarettes, exercise, eat fatty foods, for example, whereas others may not. Manipulative experiments are used to test predictions made as a result of observations (or suggested by current information), or used to investigate phenomena that were not directly seen, but were suggested by what was observed or read. All of the preplanned experiments in CORI are manipulative, and several examples are given at the end of this chapter.

The success of a manipulative experiment depends on (a) controlling all other variables so that measured differences between the normal (control) and manipulated conditions can be attributed to the manipulated change and (b) taking accurate measurements of the effects of that single change. Without control of other variables that could affect the outcome, and without clear quantification of the results, a manipulative experiment will likely be more confusing than educational. For example, in the *mealworm beetle, light/dark preference* experiment, if the dark sides of some of the tubes were larger, wetter, or warmer, than the light sides of the tubes, it would have been impossible to know which of these variables explained the mealworm beetles' choices. Similarly, if some students waited longer than others to make an observation (10 minutes for one student versus 5 minutes for another, for instance), the results might have been misleading because the second beetle was not given enough time to find the preferred condition.

Whether experiments are observational, manipulative, preplanned, or student-designed, doing them is key to developing cognitive skills for quantitative and critical thinking. They are also highly motivating when done properly because they actively engage students with a question, and (usually) produce the most satisfying kind of information—real results through personal discovery.

THE ROLE OF THE TEACHER IN SCIENCE INQUIRY

How do teachers help students become good experimental scientists, capable of articulating questions and hypotheses and designing experiments to test them? Here are some suggestions:

1. Teachers play a critical role because they encourage children to ask questions that can be answered directly from what they see, in addition to recognizing that other questions require more work (i.e., more reading or observation) in order to develop more focused questions. Being encouraged to ask and answer questions directly from what they

can see builds students' confidence in their ability to come up with the "right answer," and makes the entire process of asking and answering science questions much less intimidating.

2. Teachers encourage the use of the scientific method to move students beyond what they can observe directly. Direct observation is usually sufficient to answer simplistic questions that require a "yes or no" answer, or that can be answered by simply itemizing what they see (e.g., How many eyes does this spider have? Will a salamander eat a piece of fruit? Will a mealworm pupa survive in the freezer?). Tests show that students are often stumped by very simple questions that require the use of standard problem-solving methods. Yet, these are the very kinds of questions that the scientific method was designed to address. For example, if third graders want to raise tadpoles, they need to know what habitat conditions are best for their kind of tadpoles. They could look it up, of course, but what if this was not an option? Rather than giving up, students who have been taught to use what they know about tadpoles from observation and reading to come up with likely habitat conditions (the predictions) can develop simple experimental comparisons to test their ideas and find the best solution. Likewise, instead of asking if a mealworm pupa would survive after being frozen, students could design a simple, controlled experiment to determine the effects of temperature on survival and development of mealworm larvae or pupae by testing a range of temperatures (including 32°F) on a number of different beetle larvae or pupae. The results of such an experimental test are not only scientifically valid, but they also let the students discover for themselves how a key environmental factor (temperature) affects the life cycle of a living organism (the mealworm beetle) and other similar organisms. The student is also able to transfer his new knowledge to other organisms and habitats by considering how temperature might affect other phenomena such as reproduction, locomotion, or feeding.

Freeing children to use their own minds to explore solutions to questions that, on the surface, have no answer encourages the asking of such questions. In addition, it requires them to read to gather information that will enable them to test their hypotheses.

3. In discussions with students, teachers provide a general conceptual framework within which students can ask more specific questions, make predictions, and design experiments. Broad ecological questions can be broken down into smaller, testable ones that are suitable for experimental investigation. An example of this is given in the *guppy predator* experiment described at the end of this chapter.

4. An essential task for the teacher is to give students many opportunities to practice using the scientific method in the classroom. Getting comfortable with asking and answering science questions, and using the scientific method, is largely a matter of practice. Doing three or four small, simple experiments is better for young students than doing one larger, more complex one; that is, if students are required to apply the scientific method in a disciplined way, do a quantitative analysis of the data, and discuss the ecological interpretations of the results.

5. Teachers show students how to use the CORI framework and methods to experiment with new ideas or questions of their own. Students should be allowed to explore their own curiosity about the amazing world of nature, trying out things for which there are no preplanned experiments or guidelines, and to have fun discovering answers on their own. If a teacher's background does not include a lot of science, this idea may seem a bit daunting, but it need not be. Teachers already possess the critical skills needed to accomplish all of this. With some practice using the scientific method, and a willingness to follow new inquiries wherever they lead, teachers can guide students through the design of new science experiments with success and confidence. When things go wrong (and they do sometimes), it is important to remember that even unexpected results of experiments provide opportunities to learn about science and the process of science inquiry. Over the long run, a teacher's personal experience and enthusiasm for the study of science will inspire and encourage her students more than anything else.

Both teachers and students must start with preplanned experiments in order to learn and become comfortable with an experimental approach to asking science questions. To be true to the COSI component of CORI, one must feel free to break free of the guidebooks and focus on helping students design new experiments to answer genuine questions. Here are some tips.

Step 1: Teachers Can Practice Doing Experiments on Their Own

Teachers should try out as many preplanned experiments as possible. Even though the steps of the scientific method are straightforward, the only way to get good enough at using it and helping students design new experiments is for the teacher to work through many experiments himself. This experience makes hypothesis testing a natural part of a teacher's thinking, and provides useful experience on what works and what does not.

There are many sources of good experiments, including fellow teachers and the Internet. A place to start is Kneidel's (1999) book titled *Classroom Critters and the Scientific Method,* or her book of experiments with invertebrates titled *Creepy Crawlies and the Scientific Method* (1993). Both have a large number of excellent experiments that use readily available organisms and materials. For each experiment, background information, needed materials, a stepwise procedure, ready-to-use worksheets, clear explanations of variables and controls, and follow-up questions for student discussion or additional experimentation are provided.

Step 2: Learn to Recognize "Testable Questions"

As the teacher leads students through the CORI process, it is important for him to listen to the questions the students ask. The teacher must be able to decide which ones will likely lead to good hypotheses and to good science experiments and which ones will not. The students should be guided to a good set of questions, in the same way that they need to be guided to a particular question and hypothesis in preplanned experiments. Students should be helped to understand why some questions are "testable" (i.e., where responses can be observed and quantified, the methods can be accomplished with the available materials and in the available time, the relevant variables can be controlled and manipulated, the questions are not easily answered by casual observation, and the inquiry relates to one or more of the educational concepts), and why some are not. All questions are valid, but they are not all testable, given the methods and information available. Students may sometimes have difficulty recognizing the difference, but it is important to try.

Step 3: Develop a Standardized Set of Student Worksheets

It takes a lot of time to develop good worksheets, so establishing a standardized format that can be modified for content as needed will greatly improve your ability to create new experiments for student questions. Use of standardized worksheets will not only save valuable time, it will also help students think through some of the design issues as they develop an experiment. The science content and science lessons will be different for each experiment, but the basic steps, structure, and format will have already been thought through and written down.

Step 4: Talk to Other Science Teachers

Another way to gain expertise in science experimentation is to benefit from the successes and mistakes of other teachers. There is no better way to do this than to talk directly with a more experienced science teacher about his classroom experiences, or better yet, to visit the classroom when students are designing or conducting experiments. Many science teachers also put their experiments and helpful advice on the Internet. The World Wide Web is a very rich source of ideas and advice.

Step 5: Learn What Materials and Tools Are Available for K–12 Science

K–12 teachers are probably the most resourceful people on earth. They already know how to accomplish their educational objectives with limited materials and too little time, and can think fast on their feet when things go wrong in the classroom. In addition to creatively inventing the endless ways to use a cardboard box in science experiments, browsing science supply house catalogs such as those from Delta, Wards, and Carolina Biological Supply may be useful. Teachers may find new materials that can expand the scope of students' inquiry and simplify the job of finding materials to achieve science goals. Many items are expensive, but many are not, and some are bound to fall within a school's budget. It certainly never hurts to ask.

Step: 6 Participate in Science Programs Provided by the Local Government or Environmental Groups

There are many excellent science programs currently available to schools for little or no cost, and the number of such programs is rapidly increasing. At the time of this writing, a large initiative has been implemented by the Environmental Protection Agency (EPA) to increase the funding available for science outreach to schools. With this funding, there are many new workshops, field trips, classroom visits from members of science research organizations, opportunities for students to participate in ecological studies or restoration of local habitats, and other hands-on activities being added to the large number of resources already available. Other government groups may follow suit. The best place to start looking for such programs or resources would be through state Departments of Natural Resources, county Department of Parks and Recreation, or equivalent agencies. The EPA website and that of other government agencies also have a great deal of information for educators and students (including science experiments), and should be checked periodically. The objective of many of these new science programs is to remove obstacles to science education (including basic problems, such as transportation limitations) and to develop teachers' skills in scientific processes and methods.

A VIGNETTE OF THE GUPPY–PREDATOR EXPERIMENT

The following vignette is an experiment done by third-grade students who have just completed a CORI study unit in which they explored pond ecosystems through science observation and reading. The question to be answered experimentally was: "Do fish in ponds use the underwater plants as shelter from predators?" The students used guppies and a predator model in classroom aquaria to conduct their investigation.

This experiment was an optional activity for a CORI unit on pond ecosystems. The CORI teacher in this classroom decided that an extra experiment was a good way to conclude her students' study of ponds because it gave them a good opportunity to apply what they had learned to a new question. Even better, by closing the unit with an active inquiry, the questioning process and the steps of the scientific method would be fresh in the students' minds as they moved to the next study topic.

On the day of the experiment, the schedule allowed only 2 hours to set up, conduct, and discuss the experiment. Given the choice of letting students set up their own tanks or spend more time in discussion before starting the experiment, the teacher decided to set up the student tanks herself, with the help of her aide, allowing more time for students to discuss questions and plan the experiment. Therefore, at the start of the period, the tanks were all ready at the back of the classroom (but out of the students' line of sight) and the students were looking at the teacher with expectant faces.

She began by simply asking the students to name as many pond organisms as they could. The student response was immediate, and their knowledge of pond communities was impressive. They knew what kinds of fish, insects, mammals, birds, crustacea, mollusks, and even microbes were associated with pond habitats. Every student contributed at least one answer, and most included information about how the organism lived, in a discussion based on the science concepts of locomotion, feeding, reproduction, etc. The animals that students had observed and worked with in the unit's prior science activities were named, but most of the answers were pond animals learned about primarily by reading books. The connection between what students had experienced directly and what they had only read about was evident in the quality of the answers. All were equally vivid and accurate, regardless of their source (reading or direct observation). One boy, who provided a wealth of information about daphnia, added that he had already decided to become a daphnia scientist when he grew up. "I wish my parents didn't make me spend so much time on homework (in other subjects) so I could spend more time studying daphnia," he said with genuine frustration.

At first, no one mentioned a very common and important type of pond organism. "Can you guess what it was?" The teacher said that one group was still missing and baited the students with a few questions, but there was only silence and puzzled looks from the students until a small girl in the corner of the room said quietly, "Plants." "Oh, of course, plants!" said everyone else right away. "Are plants important to pond ecosystems?" the teacher asked. "Oh yes, very important!" was the reply, and the students identified several roles that plants play in pond ecosystems, including food (Feeding), habitat, shelter (Adaptation to Habitat), and structure for invertebrates to lay their eggs (Reproduction). Some of the comments were expressed as questions, which the teacher encouraged by opening class discussions to answer them.

Gradually, the teacher focused the discussion on the idea that plants provide shelter for small animals to hide from larger predators. The students reasoned that small fish normally swim in open water, as well as in and around plants, but hide in the plants to protect themselves when a predator shows up. She asked the class how they would design an experiment to investigate this role of plants. With her guidance, they figured out how they could use their student tanks and classroom guppies to do a test of the prediction that small fish (prey) would seek shelter in plants when a big fish (predator) was present, but not when it was absent. By planting half the tank, leaving the other half unplanted, and observing where the fish swam when a predator was present or absent from the tank, they could find out whether their prediction was correct or not. The students clearly identified the single experimental variable (the presence or absence of a predator), the importance for keeping all other conditions the same (same amount of water, same number of guppies, same choice of plants or no-plants), and the importance of doing repeated observations before reaching a conclusion.

The teacher solved the problem of finding a predator big enough to actually scare the guppies. She gave the students plans for making a *model predator* that they would control. The students liked this idea instantly, because it meant that they could "become" the predator themselves. They came up with a plan for deciding who among the team members would build the predator and who would control it during each of the experimental observations.

Before proceeding with the experiment, the students reviewed the steps of the scientific method, using placards on the wall that explained each step, and showed where they were in the process. They then formed groups of 4 or 5 students and collected their materials for the experiment, including the tanks that were ready and waiting at the back of the room. The first team's task was to write down the materials needed, predictions, and their reasoning on preprinted student data sheets. Personally recording what has already been discussed and planned is an important first step in getting the teams organized to begin, and to cement the experimental approach firmly into each student's mind. Each student completed her own data sheet, but many worked together to develop answers, and those who finished their answers quickly were asked to help the other teammates.

The model predator was constructed from tin foil pressed into the shape of a fish and attached to a pencil. Engaging the students in the predator model-making process had scientific significance, as well as creative expression. When the experiment actually began, one student had control of the predator model while the other members of the team closely watched the responses of the fish, timed each observation, counted the number of fish on each side of the tank at the end of each observation, and recorded the data on the their team data sheets for later analysis. All students of the team were fully engaged in the observation activities.

After the full set of observations had been made, the students calculated and recorded their team results. To pull the teams back together as a class, the teacher reminded the students that each team had only part of the answer, and that all counts had to be included before the final results could be evaluated. To reunite the class, the teacher had team representatives come forward one at a time to report their team's findings and add their data to a histogram of class results that had been drawn on the blackboard. Putting the class results on the blackboard (in addition to the student data sheets) focused the students on their common question, and reminded them that no one team or individual had enough data to make a complete assessment.

To everyone's delight, the class results confirmed the students' predictions, even though there were a few observations that showed the fish behaving differently than expected. The students were very comfortable with using a histogram to chart their results, and readily interpreted the bars on the chart to mean that the fish showed a strong tendency to move to the planted side of the tank when the "predator" was present, but not otherwise.

The last task before cleaning up was for each student to record the class data and conclusions on his data sheet, and write down ideas for future experiments. Discussions included predator–prey interactions in real-life situations and doing the experiment differently with other animals and methods. There was much excitement in the air, making it difficult for anyone to settle down to finish his or her final writing task. To compound the problem, it was now time for recess. The dangling sentences on the final page of some data sheets were compensated for by the well-written material on the preceding pages and by the looks of accomplishment on the smiling faces of the students as they filed out the open door to the playground.

PRINCIPLES OF LEADERSHIP AND STUDENT ENCOURAGEMENT: A KEY TO IMPLEMENTING THE SCIENTIFIC METHOD

The experiences of CORI teachers who have successfully taught students to become better readers by integrating science books into hands-on science have provided general perspectives that may be useful to others. They are encapsulated here in five principles of leadership and encouragement.

Principle 1: Let Discovery Happen

Students need to discover things for themselves in order to learn, as well as develop their own relationships to the natural world. This means letting students pursue open-ended questions about what they are seeing (within the limits of time, safety, and teacher experience). You will not always know the answers to the questions yourself, but this is OK! In fact, this is exactly what makes science so interesting and exciting. The diversity of life is so great, and still so greatly unknown, that we are all making new discoveries about "familiar" habitats and organisms practically every day.

Even when you do know the answer to a student's question, if you follow rather than lead the students' investigation of a question, you often end up learning something new about it yourself. This does not mean that students "run wild" in science class. Unstructured exploration can be fun, but it is rarely, if ever, good science. Focus, structure, and clear goals are essential to making students' science investigations meet educational objectives, but having fun is equally important because it keeps the spirit of inquiry alive and well in the process. How are both of these objectives met? Read Principle #2.

Principle 2: Use Biological Concepts, Rather Than Facts, to Focus Students' Observations and Investigations

The eleven key educational concepts of CORI (reproduction, communication, defense, respiration, competition, predation, feeding, locomotion, niche, adaptation to habitat, and habitat conservation) give students a transferable framework for learning about new organisms, interactions, habitats, and ecosystems. Use of educational concepts, rather than facts alone, is recommended for science inquiry because concepts transfer from one habitat or organism to the next, whereas facts do not always transfer. This approach encourages students to become independent investigators and to feel confident about launching inquiries in new ecological and biological domains because they are armed with knowledge that can be transferred to similar phenomena and used to uncover new facts about unfamiliar organisms and habitats. Using educational concepts rather than isolated facts to focus and engage students in a life science investigation frees both the student and the teacher to be guided by genuine curiosity.

A set of key educational concepts also provides structure for organizing new knowledge gained from observation, experimentation, and reading. Most students readily acquire information on their own, but need help from teachers to integrate this new information into a framework of understanding. To use the educational concepts as tools, however, a secure grasp of their meaning must be developed very early in the curriculum. The first goal of the CORI teacher is to help students (a) develop conscious knowledge of their intuitive understanding of these basic life processes, (b) learn to recognize and differentiate the words that represent them, and (c) recognize the full scope of their application to all living things.

The educational concepts themselves are intuitively familiar to most elementary-age students from prior experience, but some students initially have difficulty using the terms. The difficulty is often related to reading ability; poorer readers may fail to recognize the "long words" (locomotion, competition, predation, etc.) or to correctly relate them to the underlying concepts. Others may have difficulty separating similar-looking words such as "communication" and "competition."

In one such classroom, a CORI teacher developed a set of simple, graphic icons to represent each of the key science concepts. For reference, she gave the students handouts with the icons and terms side by side. To help students develop an association of the words with the icons, she also created a wall-size chart with the icons and educational concepts. Thus, a picture (icon) of a telephone was placed next to the term "communication" on a classroom chart, or a picture of a racer crossing the finish line next to the term "competition." Group decisions about the best icon to use for each term can be used as a tool to teach the meaning of each concept. Similarly, students can use their own experiences to identify how the key educational concepts relate to humans, and then to other animals. After this exercise, the students had little or no difficulty recognizing and using the terms and were able to apply the educational concepts in the science investigations that followed. This approach is very effective, not only in helping to elucidate the meaning of the educational concepts, but in helping to relate different types of animals to each other. It also reinforces how the concepts are common to all types of animals.

Principle 3: Use Simple Experiments to Teach Students How to Articulate and Test Their Own Theories About the World

Open-ended observation and discovery are the essential first steps of the scientific method. However, without the subsequent step of *experimentation* (i.e., coming up with a scientific way to test a new idea), the process of science inquiry is incomplete. Using the scientific method to design and conduct experiments builds general problem-solving skills that will endure for a lifetime. It gives students a powerful method for trying out their own ideas about how the world works. It teaches them how to follow a rigorous line of questioning and to use data as the objective basis for reasoning. It also helps develop numerical and oral language skills as students quantify and communicate new knowledge to others.

It is often tempting to try to design and conduct an experiment to address a large number of questions arising from observations, or to address as many educational concepts as possible. It may seem that reducing the complex world of a pond or wetland to a simple experiment involving one tiny aspect of that world will cause the students to lose the sense of excitement and wonder they experienced in their first encounters with that habitat. In fact, what often happens instead is that scientific experimentation results in a deeper sense of excitement and discovery as students commit themselves to the hands-on, experimental test of a single idea. Students will actually learn more from doing an experiment that has clear, simple results than from a complex experiment that has confusing, difficult-to-interpret results.

A simple experiment to see whether mealworm beetles are more attracted to light or darkness can lead students to the realization that "light" and "darkness" are each associated with many different environmental factors, such as high vs. low temperatures and dry vs. moist conditions. A discussion of the ecological implications of changes in single factors, like light, is far more beneficial for students at this stage than the complicated experiments that would require them to untangle multiple, correlated, and/or interacting factors. The guidelines for student discussion of this example are provided in the *mealworm beetle light/dark preference* experiment.

Principle 4: Study Nature Close to Home

Children need to learn about ecosystems and organisms in other parts of the world, but do not neglect the fascinating ecosystems that exist in your own community, county, and state. Valuable science lessons are waiting nearby, and there are at least three good reasons to study them:

1.   Children who have grown up in an area have already acquired a large amount of background information about local habitats, plants, and animals from direct experience. Activating this background knowledge sets the stage very effectively for a science inquiry. Scientific investigation (structured observation and experimentation) of familiar organisms and ecosystems enhances the ordinary day-to-day experience of them.

2.   Familiar as they may seem, closer inspection of local natural habitats in your own area will reveal strange new worlds. No matter where students live, they need walk only as far as the edge of the sidewalk or yard to find bizarre creatures that look as if they just crawled out of a science fiction movie. Careful observation of familiar animals such as insects, squirrels, and birds will reveal interesting, often complex, behaviors that surprise the observer. All such "strange familiar" (Teale, 1972) animals and plants make superb fountains of science discoveries for students, young and old. The new discoveries will enhance students' curiosity about the world they see around them every day.

3.   Children will be the caretakers of our country's natural resources when they grow up. They will benefit greatly from developing a close relationship to nature early in life, especially one that is built on the deep sense of belonging that comes from familiarity with the place that they call home.

Principle 5: Get Beyond the "Wow!"

The last principle is perhaps the most important of all, because it gets at the heart of true science education. This principle separates teachers who may influence students' lives for a year or two from those who will influence the direction of students' lives forever.

Introducing young people to the wonders of nature is one of the most rewarding and enjoyable parts of teaching the *sciences*. We enjoy it in part because we share in the excitement of each new student discovery and see the world afresh through each child's eyes. In CORI science instruction, each unit or module is launched with a discovery activity designed to excite or stir the student's interest, such as a visit to an outdoor nature area or observing a new animal in the classroom. This approach boosts curiosity by emotionally engaging and motivating students as they begin a new science study unit.

Anyone who has taught science to elementary-age children knows that it is easy for students to get excited about science lessons without actually learning anything from them. This often happens with so-called "science" programming on television, too, presentations that dazzle viewers with images of wild danger or natural beauty and stimulate high levels of interest, but do not teach any real science. The same effect can be achieved by simply bringing a snake, bird, or insect into the classroom for students to observe. It does not require any special talents, skills, knowledge, or materials.

The objective of teachers is to educate. If science instruction leaves students in an overstimulated, undereducated state, then the process, although perhaps entertaining, does not result in science education. Successful science instruction leaves students excited not only about observing strange new animals or habitats, but also about their own accomplishments using observation, complex questioning, and experimentation to develop a better understanding of the wonders they observe.

RELATIONSHIPS OF SCIENCE IN CORI TO CURRENT VIEWS ON SCIENCE EDUCATION

Our view of inquiry science is consistent with existing constructivist perspectives in science education. Conceptual understanding is widely acknowledged as a central goal of science education. The premium placed on conceptual understanding is illustrated by its prominence as an objective in the National Assessment of Educational Progress (NAEP) science assessment (O'Sullivan, Reese, & Mazzeo, 1997). The NAEP defines characteristic elements of knowing and doing science to include conceptual understanding, scientific investigation, and practical reasoning. Furthermore, O'Sullivan et al. (1997) suggested that conceptual understanding involves a diversity of scientific information including facts and events, as well as concepts, principles, laws, and theories that scientists use to explain and predict observations of the natural world.

A focus on conceptual understanding is consistent with Reif's (1990) emphasis on the explanatory nature of understanding and Linn's (Linn & Muilenburg, 1996) emphasis on the usefulness of science concepts for practical reasoning. This view of conceptual understanding is also consistent with the National Science Education Standards (National Research Council, 1996), which underscore students' ability to "construct and analyze alternative explanations, and communicate scientific arguments." These perspectives are consistent with our view that conceptual understanding is a multitiered structure of knowledge and process that can predict and explain particular facts, events, or interactions, and can be used for problem solving in a variety of situations.

Inquiry-centered approach to science education enables children to ask questions, experiment, develop theories, and communicate their ideas. The National Research Council issued the National Science Education Standards (NRC,

1996), which are founded on the proposition that science inquiry includes "opportunities for students to ask questions, plan and conduct investigations, use appropriate tools and techniques to gather data, think critically and logically to develop explanations, and communicate scientific arguments" (p. 23). It is argued that the benefits of inquiry science for student learning include the acquisition of deep understanding about science concepts (Smith, 1991; Strike & Posner, 1992; White, 1993). In an extended case study of inquiry science using a cognitive apprenticeship metaphor, Roth and Bowen (1995) examined student outcomes and educational processes. They reported that after studying abiotic and biotic features in small plots of land, students performed highly on measures of problem solving and conceptual understanding. In addition to promoting deep conceptual understanding, science inquiry is often thought to increase elements of the science process, such as data gathering, organizing information, interpreting, and communicating conclusions (Metz, 2000; NRC, 1996).

Substantial instructional scaffolding and technology is often argued to be valuable for helping students gain proficiency in inquiry (Krajcik, Blumenfeld, Marx, & Soloway, 2000). Some authors (Kuhn, Amser, & O'Loughlin, 1988) even propose that experience in the science processes is necessary for understanding principles in a science domain. Roth and Roychoudhury (1993) reported that students in Grades 8–12 who were involved in inquiry laboratory sessions in physics increased their science process skills, including their ability to identify and define pertinent variables, interpret and analyze data, plan and design an experiment, formulate hypotheses, and draw warranted conclusions.

The relationships of text to science inquiry are seldom highlighted in science education. On occasion, texts are viewed as impediments, but more frequently as supplements, providing a source for "secondary inquiry" in science topics (Palinscar, Magnusson, Marano, Ford, & Brown, 1998). There is evidence that students can gain conceptual understanding from reading science texts. For example, Romance and Vitale (1992) investigated an integrative curriculum at the elementary school level that emphasized science process skills and reading. Students in the experimental group surpassed students in a control group in science knowledge and reading comprehension in the Metropolitan Achievement Test. Confirming this result, Morrow, Pressley, Smith, and Smith (1997) reported that students who were provided science text reading opportunities gained more knowledge of science facts and vocabulary, as well as reading achievement, than a control group.

In sum, a number of educators propose that inquiry science is strongly facilitative of both conceptual knowledge and the acquisition of science processes (Glynn & Duit, 1995; Minstrell & van Zee, 2000). One approach to enabling students to meet the challenge of reading science text is to integrate reading and language arts instruction with inquiry science in the curriculum, which has been recommended by Parker (1994) for elementary teachers, and Brister and Drake (1994) for K–12 teachers. Unfortunately, few data are available to evaluate the effectiveness of science inquiry integrated with reading, although preliminary studies are positive (Guthrie et al., 1998). The current CORI approach is one framework for the integration of science inquiry with reading, and its benefits for students are under investigation.

REFERENCES

Bristor, V. J., & Drake, S. V. (1994). Linking the language arts and content areas through visual technology. *T.H.E. Journal, 22*(2), 74–77.

Glynn, S. M., & Duit, R. (Eds.) (1995). *Learning science in the schools: Research reforming practice.* Mahwah, NJ: Lawrence Erlbaum Associates.

Guthrie, J. T., Van Meter, P., Hancock, G. R., McCann, A., Anderson, E., & Alao, S. (1998). Does Concept-Oriented Reading Instruction increase strategy use and conceptual learning from text? *Journal of Educational Psychology, 90,* 261–278.

Krajcik, J. S., Blumenfeld, P. C., Marx, R. W., & Soloway, E. J. (2000). Instructional, curricular, and technological supports for inquiry in science classrooms. In J. Minstrell & E. H. van Zee (Eds.), *Inquiring into inquiry learning and teaching in science* (pp. 283–315). Washington, DC: American Association for the Advancement of Science.

Kuhn, D., Amser, E., & O'Loughlin, M. (1988). *The development of scientific thinking skills.* Orlando, FL: Academic Press.

Linn, M. C., & Muilenburg, L. (1996). Creating lifelong science learners: What models form a firm foundation? *Educational Researcher, 25,* 18–24.

Metz, K. E. (2000). Young children's inquiry in biology: Building the knowledge bases to empower independent inquiry. In J. Minstrell & E. H. van Zee (Eds.), *Inquiring into inquiry learning and teaching in science* (pp. 371–404). Washington, DC: American Association for the Advancement of Science.

Minstrell, J., & van Zee, E. H. ((2000). *Inquiring into Inquiry Learning and Teaching in Science* Washington, DC: American Association for the Advancement of Science.

Morrow, L. M., Pressley, M., Smith, J. K., & Smith, M. (1997). The effect of a literature-based program integrated into literacy and science instruction with children from diverse backgrounds. *Reading Research Quarterly, 32,* 54–76.

National Research Council. (1996). *National science education standards.* Washington, DC: National Academy Press.

O'Sullivan, C. Y., Reese, C. M., & Mazzeo, J. (1997). *NAEP 1996 science report card for the nation and the states.* Washington, DC: National Center for Education Statistics.

Palincsar, A. S., Magnusson, S., Marano, N., Ford, D., & Brown, N. (1998). Designing a community of practice: Principles and practices of the GIsML community. *Teaching and Teacher Education, 14*(1), 5–19.

Parker, D. (1994). Earth, stars, and beyond: A learning ahana at work. *Kamehameha Journal of Education, 5,* 93–100.

Reif, F. (1990). Transcending prevailing approaches to science education. In M. Gardner, J. Greeno, F. Reif, A. Schoenfeld, A. Disessa, & E. Stage (Eds.), *Toward a scientific practice of science education* (pp.91–139). Hillsdale, NJ: Lawrence Erlbaum Associates.

Romance, N. R., & Vitale, M. R. (1992). A curriculum strategy that expands time for in-depth elementary science instruction by using science-based reading strategies: Effects of a year-long study in grade 4. *Journal of Research in Science Teaching, 29*(6), 545–554.

Roth, W., & Bowen, G. M. (1995). Knowing and interacting: A study of culture, practices, and resources in a grade 8 open-inquiry science classroom guided by a cognitive apprenticeship metaphor. *Cognition & Instruction, 13*(1), 73–128.

Roth, W., & Roychoudhury, A. (1993). The development of science process skills in authentic contexts. *Journal of Research in Science Teaching, 30*(2), 127–152.

Smith, E. L. (1991). A conceptual change model of learning science. In S. M. Glynn, R. H. Yeaney, & B. K. Britton (Eds.), *The psychology of learning science* (pp.43–63). Hillsdale, NJ: Lawrence Erlbaum Associates.

Strike, K. A., & Posner, G. J. (1992). A revisionist theory of conceptual change. In R. Duschl & R. Hamilton (Eds.), *Philosophy of science, cognitive psychology, and educational theory and practice* (pp. 147–176). Albany, NY: SUNY Press.

White, B. (1993). Thinkertools: Causal models, conceptual change, and science education. *Cognition and Instruction, 10,* 1–100.

CHILDREN'S BOOK REFERENCES

Kneidel, S. S. (1993). *Creepy crawlies and the scientific method: More than 100 hands-on science experiments for children.* Golden, CO: Fulcrum.

Kneidel, S. S. (1999). *Classroom critters and the scientific method.* Golden, CO: Fulcrum.

Teale, E. W. (1972). *Strange lives of familiar insects:* Apollo Editions.

Yolen, J. (1987). *Owl moon.* New York: Putnam & Grosset.

6

Diverse Texts
and Technology
for Reading

Marcia H. Davis
Stephen Tonks
University of Maryland

In CORI classrooms, teachers typically use a range of texts and trade books for instruction. To an observer who has walked by a CORI classroom or stepped in for a brief visit, it may appear that CORI consists mainly of using diverse texts and trade books for teaching. Some individuals have perceived CORI to be a literature-based instructional program. However, this is a misconception on several grounds. The fundamental aim of CORI is to enable students to improve their reading comprehension through teaching that is centered on "big ideas," or major concepts, of a discipline relevant to content learning in a grade level. A variety of trade books and texts serve this purpose and motivate students through their intriguing content and adaptability to the motivational supports in CORI. These interesting texts afford students optimal amounts of choice and collaboration, which are major motivational principles. Trade books described in this chapter enable students to learn deeply about a conceptual topic, pursue subtopics of their own choosing, acquire comprehension strategies for learning from multiple genres, including information and literary texts, and synthesize information from multiple sources in order to communicate to an audience.

An emphasis on diverse texts for reading instruction in CORI can be expressed as a general teaching practice in the following terms: *Use an abundance of interesting texts for reading instruction.* Teachers who are able to implement this practice frequently and widely in their classrooms are usually accomplished in improving reading comprehension and motivation of their students. To ensure this teaching practice is met, teachers can take the following approaches to using texts in CORI:

1. Identify books and texts that represent informational and literary aspects of the conceptual theme of the unit.
2. Provide diverse difficulty among books on the conceptual theme to enable all students to participate in reading acquisition and conceptual development.
3. Link books to science activities by providing a conceptual base for investigations, links to science observations, and explanations of science findings.
4. Align books to the requirements of strategy instruction, with different texts serving unique roles across a range of comprehension strategies.
5. Select texts that are interesting to students by virtue of their appearance, readability, topic, and connection to classroom activities.
6. Enable struggling readers to read texts in and out of the classroom that are aligned with the content and adapted to their needs for fluency and simplified strategy instruction.
7. Incorporate multimedia into each of the previous practices.

In this chapter, we explain how CORI teachers employ these practices.

USE AN ABUNDANCE OF INTERESTING TEXTS FOR READING INSTRUCTION

This generalized statement represents a basic principle that subsumes all seven of these practices. The principle implies a wide range of teachers' plans, selected materials, and instructional practices throughout a CORI unit. Previous implementations of CORI utilized this principle (Guthrie & Cox, 2001). The explication provided here can be applied to those previous reports of CORI, although the details have been improved in recent CORI implementations. Using an abundance of diverse texts in content domains for reading instruction in later elementary grades has been widely documented as effective in enhancing reading comprehension. In one investigation of 575 teachers in three school districts, this practice was found to distinguish classrooms that were gaining in the statewide accountability test from classrooms that were declining in that test. Teachers whose instruction was typified by such statements as, "My students organize and use our classroom library" and "Our media specialist helps us develop literature-based units" showed statewide test scores that increased over 3 years, whereas teachers who did not employ these practices showed test scores that decreased over the same 3-year period. Furthermore, this finding was sustained for students at all achievement levels. Several literature reviews confirm that students' reading comprehension strategies are best learned, and most readily transferable, if they are acquired in a topic where the students possess substantial amounts of conceptual understanding. Being in a familiar content area fosters reading comprehension development (Guthrie, Schafer, Von Secker, & Alban, 2000). Each of the practices supporting the use of an abundance of interesting texts for reading instruction is described next.

1. Identify Books That Represent Informational and Literary Aspects of the Conceptual Theme of the Unit

In CORI, students learn conceptual themes in science beginning with "Survival of Life on Land and Water." Within this overarching theme in each Grade 3 classroom, students delve into the unit "Birds Around the World" for a period of 6 weeks. This unit emphasizes diversity of biomes across the globe and the myriad adaptations of animal life, including birds, to these biomes. In Grade 3, a variety of books, including trade books, are identified pertaining to this theme, including information texts, literary texts, and informational narrative. We define an *informational text* as *written material that communicates a substantive amount of content of a subject matter topic through exposition.* This exposition may present conceptual knowledge with hierarchical relations, cause–effect patterns, a factual information base, or other structures typical of information books (Chambliss, 1994). We define *literary text* as *written material that conveys an aesthetic experience through narrative or symbolic portraits of fictional or imaginary characters.* Literary texts include stories, fictional chapter books, fables, fairy tales, and poetry. A third type of text used in CORI is informational narrative. In these texts, a narrative sequence is presented (a story is often told) and the substantive content of a subject matter domain is simultaneously conveyed (Schmidt, Gillen, Zollo, & Stone, 2002). This is a partial mixture of the informational and literary types of text described previously (Rice, 2002).

An example of informational narrative that might be used in the unit "Birds Around the World" includes *One Day in the Woods* by Jean Craighead George, a narrative about a girl who finds an owl, duck, and squirrel on her trip to the woods. This book is appropriate for students at grade levels 3 and 4, whereas an informational narrative entitled *Owl Babies*, by Martin Waddell, is attractive to struggling readers in Grade 3. One example of informational literature is *Joyful Noise* by Paul Fleischman. The poem in the book entitled "A

Digger Wasp" begins "I will never see my children; they will never gaze on me."
As this poem for two voices proceeds, we go through the life cycle of a digger
wasp, which contains many shocks and surprises. These books can all be enjoyed in expressive activities or analyzed closely for the concepts of survival
embedded within them.

To illustrate the selection of texts and the relationships among the texts, we
describe a few of the selections for the unit "Birds Around the World." In the literary category, *Owl Moon*, by Jane Yolen, introduces students to the theme of
birds through an aesthetically pleasing story. Additional literary selections include *A to Z Mysteries: The Falcon's Feathers* by Ron Roy and *White Bird* by Clyde
Bulla, a chapter book about a boy and his adventures with an injured bird, that is
appropriate reading midway through the unit.

In this same unit, an information book entitled *All Kinds of Habitats* by Sally
Hewitt is used to initiate content instruction. The diversity of biomes around
the world, including deserts, freshwater, mountains, grasslands, woodlands,
oceans, and seashore are displayed with magnificent illustrations and depic-
tions of animal life within them. This book sets the stage for comparing biomes
and bird survival in diverse habitats. Information books include *Welcome to the
World of Owls* by Diane Swanson and a three-book set with titles *Eggs and Baby
Birds* by Anne Shirley and *Feathers and Flight* and *How Birds Live*, by Fred and
Jeanne Biddulph. Included within sets of books in the classroom are titles such
as *Bird Beaks* and *Birds' Nests*, both by Diana Noonan, *Birds of a Feather* by
Evelyn Davidson, and *Owls* by Lynn M. Stone. These books provide diversity of
information about habitats and the concepts of survival described in chapter 5,
which include eating, predation, locomotion, reproduction, and others.

In addition, literary books, such as *On the Wing* by Douglas Florian, provide
opportunities for expressive reading while simultaneously enabling students to
broaden their content learning about ecological processes (Donovan &
Smolkin, 2001). We suggest that half of the time be allocated to students' information book reading and half of the time be allocated to literary text and informational narrative book reading. Learning from multiple genres enables
students to use their reading strategies widely and to gain perspectives on the
conceptual theme with stories and literary departures. During a 120-minute
language arts period in CORI, teachers typically use both informational and literary texts, lending variety to the reading diet.

Using a range of information and literary texts in a conceptual theme for reading instruction is consistent with research literature in several areas. Emphasis on
a conceptual theme in instruction is consistent with the known contribution of
learning goals to students' motivation. A diversity of evidence from correlational

and experimental studies confirms that when students are dedicated to learning, rather than merely demonstrating their competence in a test or getting a good grade, their motivation for academic tasks increases. Students with learning goals, compared to students with performance goals, tend to use higher level reading and learning approaches to text and classroom assignments (Miller & Meece, 1997). Corroborating this finding, students who are oriented to mastery of content, rather than merely completing the task and finishing an assignment, are likely to be cognitively engaged with text and understand their texts deeply (Anderman, 1999). In other words, a conceptual theme can be motivating and lead to deeper understanding through higher engagement in reading.

Conceptual themes have also been shown to contribute to reading comprehension by enabling students to learn strategies within a familiar knowledge domain. For example, the strategy of questioning cannot be easily applied in a content in which students have no information. It is nearly impossible to frame any question, especially a deep and probing one, without some prior knowledge of the topic. Therefore, as students gain information in a conceptual theme, their questioning improves and expands to reach higher levels (Alexander, Kulikowich, & Jetton, 1994). Likewise, when a student is using such strategies as summarizing and searching for information, he needs content knowledge. How can a student monitor the quality of his summary or accuracy in searching for information without some content knowledge? A rich information base empowers a learner to monitor an evolving summary or an ongoing search. In the absence of self-monitoring, students are unable to learn from text and are extremely limited in their knowledge about whether their strategies are working for them (Baker & Brown, 1984). Therefore, the conceptual theme facilitates both motivational and conceptual needs of the student learning comprehension strategies.

For both informational and literary text, accuracy is a consideration. Not all information books are totally accurate (Rice, 2002). Textbooks, newspapers, trade books, and the Internet may contain inaccurate information. For younger elementary students, information is often oversimplified to the point of being misleading. For example, books may refer to a mushroom as a plant, when in fact it is not a plant, but a fungus. However, because authors do not expect younger children to comprehend the word *fungus*, they substitute the word with *plant*. Many books actually address frequent misconceptions. For example, a book may point out that although some people call a mushroom a plant, in actuality, it is a fungus.

In literary works such as stories, legends, or poems, scientific inaccuracy may be evident. For example, an eagle may feel sorry for a lost boy, or a turtle may live a thousand years. Teachers can easily discuss these notions found in a literary work (e.g., a legend) and relate them to scientifically accurate information found in an informational text. In this way, students can learn accurate information while enjoying the literary text (Smolkin & Donovan, 2001).

2. Provide Diverse Difficulty Among Books on the Conceptual Theme to Enable All Students to Participate in Reading Acquisition and Conceptual Development

Among classrooms in today's schools, there is a wide variety of abilities. In many classrooms, students are heterogeneous in reading achievement. Frequently, we see a third-grade classroom with students at second-, third-, and fourth-grade equivalence in achievement. Occasionally, Grade 3 classrooms may span from mid-first-grade reading achievement to strong fourth-grade achievement, depending on the neighborhoods served by the school and the policies of the principal. On other occasions, it is possible to see Grade 3 classrooms with all students achieving at a Grade 3 level, due to homogeneous grouping by the principal or instructional leaders in the school.

The CORI design responds to this variety among classrooms by providing texts that are aligned with the reading achievement levels of students in the class (see Table 6.1). To accomplish this, teachers use the following:

- Whole-class sets of trade books on the conceptual theme at the middle level of the classroom range. If there are students from Grades 2–4 in the third-grade classroom, these class sets would be approximately Grade 3 in difficulty.
- Both easier and more challenging books in team sets for groups within the classroom. In other words, each team or group of 3 to 6 students will share a limited set of texts, in addition to the whole class sets.
- Individual texts for a wide range of topics with aspects of the conceptual theme, including both easy-to-read and more challenging texts for each topic.

The rationale for these three methods of text selection is the value in providing whole-class lessons on reading comprehension strategies and certain concepts in the theme. For example, a teacher may wish to have all students examine a text while she discusses and teaches questioning as a reading comprehension strategy. A full-class discussion of the content of a few pages of a text, and the brainstorming of appropriate questions that might be asked about that text, are often valuable for all students. In addition, more explicit instruction on writing questions and then answering with the class-shared text is beneficial for higher and lower achievers alike.

TABLE 6.1
CORI Classroom Text Selection

	How many books?	What are they used for?
Class Sets	One per student	Whole-class strategy instruction
Team Sets	One per group	Generalized searching and strategy practice (guided reading)
Individual Sets	One per classroom	Specialized area searching

Diverse texts provided in the team sets (one for each group of 3 to 6 students) allow students of differing reading achievement levels to participate in guided reading and practice of reading comprehension strategies. For example, having texts at Grades 2–4 enables all students to participate. If the teacher's emphasis is on having students ask high-level questions about how birds use locomotion differently in different habitats, lower achieving students may read an easier book showing that penguins swim in the Antarctic, whereas higher achieving students may read a more challenging book conveying that some ducks fly in the air, as well as swim in the water. Students from different achievement levels can use different texts to gain factual support for the common concept that birds adapt their locomotion to their habitats. In one reading activity, teachers enable all students to improve their questioning through practice on texts that suit their reading levels. Students' sense of confidence as readers and sense of belonging in the classroom are improved as they read books on a common topic at various levels of difficulty that match their abilities. For example, a classroom discussion on birds and how they move could be sustained due to the diverse texts on a common conceptual theme, and the text diversity assures great opportunity for participation across the achievement spectrum (Holiday, Yore, & Alvermann, 1994).

When students have acquired familiarity with the topic domain and sufficient reading strategies to pursue content learning through multiple texts, teachers provide books on more diverse topics. For example, in the "Birds Around the World" theme, teachers provide books on birds in woodland, freshwater, grassland, and polar habitats, with easier books (below grade level) and more challenging texts (above grade level) available on topics in all of the domains that will be studied, enabling students to learn concepts of survival and to improve in reading strategies.

For the CORI unit "Birds Around the World," we compiled 19 books that lend themselves to whole-class and small group instruction. Of these 19, teachers were to select three titles as class sets and five titles as team books. One field guide was also included. In addition to the 19 class and team books, 24 individual books were selected for the classroom collection to fit the five different specialized areas of bird life. Included in these 24 books, we recommended literary books consisting of two chapter books, four stories, and one poetry book. This enables teachers to spend an equal amount of instructional time in literary and informational text. We recommend a similar configuration of texts for the Grade 3 unit on freshwater, aquatic life, suggesting the following:

1. Select one or two stories to introduce the general theme.
2. Choose at least two general information books to introduce the content theme. Ensure that books have good expository text qualities: for example, table of contents, index, and glossary.
3. Choose books that lend themselves to reading strategy development (e.g., teach questioning, search, summarizing, etc.).
4. Choose three to six team sets with multiple levels of difficulty to ensure accessibility to all students and diversity from general to specific information.
5. Choose two to four stories or legends that are vivid and exciting to supplement the theme.
6. Choose one to three chapter books as class sets that are accessible to most students.

The difficulty of trade books and texts in content domains is judged on the basis of multiple criteria (Shymansky, Yore, & Good, 1991). With teacher collaborators, we examined seven characteristics of information books that were related to teachers' ratings of difficulty. These were number of pages, number of sentences per page, average number of words per sentence, average number of illustrations per page, average number of words per page, average number of letters per word, and number of text access features, such as an index and table of contents. Nine teachers rated 12 books that had been used previously during their class instruction; eight were a type of information text and four were literary text. These teachers rated each book relative to their third graders, using a scale provided by the researchers. This scale ranged from easy (1) to difficult (5), as shown in Appendix A. The rank order of difficulty of information books, including the one informational guide, according to teacher judgment, was most closely related to the number of sentences per page. Easier books had about two sentences per page, whereas more challenging books had 9-11 sentences. For literary books, teachers' ratings aligned with sentence length more closely than other text characteristics. Although merely indicators of the layout and composition of these books, the indicators show an important difference between information and literary genre for reading instruction, and they provide a criterion for selection of books.

Investigations of difficulty in information texts have been reported by Donovan and Smolkin (2001) and Dreher and Singer (1989). These authors suggested that overall depth and breadth of a book should be considered. For example, in some trade books one specific animal is described, whereas other trade books cover 10 to 15 animals in one text. Books that present multiple animals may provide too much disconnected information for a young reader, unless a single theme is selected, such as predation, which may provide a common link across the animals. Dreher and Singer (1989) suggested that teachers discuss how the information in one section relates to the events or concepts in another to reduce the difficulty of the text. Related to these issues, new vocabulary determines the content challenge level. If many new words and concepts are represented per page, the book may be relatively more difficult for most students.

Not all students in the classroom have high enough oral reading fluency to read and comprehend texts on the average classroom reading level. To assure that all students are able to attain oral reading fluency for the texts on which comprehension strategy lessons are provided, teachers need to provide some classroom texts that are lower in difficulty. Research on the relationship between fluency of oral reading and comprehension contains two major findings. First, there is a substantial correlation between fluency and comprehension, provided that the range of ability levels in the classroom is varied for both fluency and comprehension (Paris, Carpenter, Paris, & Hamilton, 2002). Across a span of reading levels from Grades 1–4 (at least), higher oral reading fluency is associated with higher text comprehension. This relationship is sustained, irrespective of whether the measure of fluency is centered on discourse, such as a 100-word passage from a text, or centered on word lists, such as those found in some standardized tests (Torgesen, Wagner, & Rashotte, 1999). A second finding is that interventions that significantly increase oral reading fluency have not always shown transfer to comprehension tasks (Stahl & Kuhn, 2002). With training, students may markedly improve their reading fluency, although this fluency may not necessarily result in better understanding of their written materials. This experimental finding may be due to the possibility that both oral reading fluency and comprehension correlate with other variables (such as world knowledge) that influence both of them.

Another explanation is that fluency is a necessary, but not a sufficient, condition for comprehension of a text. If this is true, students who learn a given text fluently should be able to learn to comprehend that text readily. In other words, substantial improvements in fluency should facilitate the speed of learning, although they do not guarantee immediate comprehension improvement. This interpretation is consistent with our experience. When teachers enable students to read a given passage of 100 to 300 words fluently and expressively, they are able to learn how to pose questions, write summaries, and comprehend the designated text. By using classroom texts with diverse difficulty, teachers can assure that all students attain oral reading fluency for the texts, and as a prerequisite, comprehension is assured.

3. Link Books to Science Activities by Providing a Conceptual Base for Investigations, Links to Science Observations, and Explanations of Science Findings

Books are chosen with the conceptual theme as the main guideline, for example, "Birds Around the World." There is a range of possible observational and experimental science activities that may be connected to this theme, including a habitat walk, a bird watch, collecting bird nests, observing bird feathers, dissecting an owl pellet, and analyzing birds' communications. An optimal set of books complements these science activities in two ways. First, books provide a conceptual base for looking at objects and specimens. If a student has learned and discussed the idea that different types of feathers provide different types of survival benefits for birds, such as flying, warmth, nesting, and mating, the student is likely to observe feathers in more detail. Thus, a conceptual base, gained even from relatively light book reading, gives students a background for science observations.

Books further relate to science by providing key information on specific observations. For example, pictures, captions, and factual information in texts can enable students to match their observations of a bird nest, a pond surface, or a grassland terrain with further information. It is stunning how extensively the photographs, illustrations, and drawings in books provide a bridge between simple observing and deeper text-based learning. On several occasions, we observed a student noticing a picture matching an observation ("This is just like the nest I saw"), reading the caption to explain the type of bird or location of the nest, and then branching into text to explain the observation and the caption. The flow from environmental observations to full text reading is frequently bridged by an illustration and accompanying caption.

Critically important for students' development of knowledge about the world is the role of text as a source of concept learning. Although students may observe physical features of an animal, bird, or insect, it is rare that students can generate conceptual explanations of the features or phenomena. Although a student may observe the shape of a tree, location of an anthill, or speed of a beetle, rarely can she explain the reasons for the shape, location, or speed. Most of those reasons come either from text-based interactions or lectures from the teacher. Of course, if the student has chosen to read on a topic and is pursuing the text, the newfound knowledge will be more intriguing and valued than information received from a teacher's presentation. Therefore, texts are a source of conceptual knowledge acquisition that is unlikely to be found under observation-only educational conditions. Many CORI books are organized according to concepts in life science and ecology, such as defense, predation, eating, reproduction, and locomotion, and students' reading activities enable them to go beyond the physical attributes observable in a first-hand encounter or a science experiment. Consequently, information books foster students' development of explanations for their science observations and experimental findings.

Empirical support can be garnered to undergird the practice of linking books to science in an integrated curriculum. For example, Romance and Vitale (2001) reported that an integrated approach to science and reading instruction that provides hands-on science, with an emphasis on process skills and reading and language arts with information books, increases students' reading achievement. Reading comprehension scores on standardized tests (Iowa Test of Basic Skills and Scholastic Assessment Test) for Grades 4 and 5 students receiving an integrated reading–science approach were significantly higher than scores in classrooms where reading, language arts, and science were taught separately. This program differs from CORI because it places less emphasis on motivation. Furthermore, the results of a different study showed that reading instruction that encompasses science text and literary genres simultaneously produced higher reading achievement than instruction emphasizing only literary materials (Morrow, Pressley, Smith, & Smith, 1997). Although there is relatively little use of information books in the primary grades (Duke, 2000), the tide is turning, and the value of expository text for motivation and comprehension development is being discovered by innovative teachers (Rice, 2002).

4. Align Books to the Requirements of Strategy Instruction, With Different Texts Serving Unique Roles Across a Range of Comprehension Strategies

Trade books are not all equally valuable for teaching a given comprehension strategy. Books are selected based on the content for the conceptual theme and their utility in enabling students to begin their strategy learning or expand their strategy development. For example, a book that is ideal for teaching summarizing may not be the best choice for instruction in searching for information. Next, we discuss the attributes for books aligned to teach strategy instruction.

Activating Background Knowledge. For instruction in activating background knowledge, it is valuable to have a book that is at least moderately familiar to students. They must have some background knowledge to activate! For example, in the unit "Birds Around the World," a book on eagles is a promising choice because most students have heard about eagles, seen them, or viewed pictures of them. At the same time, students can immediately learn more about eagles that is valuable for their conceptual development in learning about survival. A book about black holes in space would not be a good choice for teaching third graders to activate background knowledge due to their low level of information on the topic. Moreover, an extremely simple text on a familiar topic may not be valuable, as the student may not learn anything new from the text. For instruction in activating background knowledge using literary or narrative texts, a familiar character in a familiar location, such as a sister of the narrator on a trip to a park, provides the moderate level of familiarity that enables students to recall experiences and characters like the ones in the text.

Questioning. For questioning instruction, it is valuable to have a book that is well organized to promote browsing or skimming. To guide reading and thinking before questioning, we recommend that students take a "book walk" where they can browse a book silently and familiarize themselves with the broad topics of the text, before generating questions. Organizational features such as chapter headings, illustrations with brief captions, and bolded headings, enable students to identify important topics in the book that might form the basis of their questions. The text should also contain sufficient depth of coverage to enable students to answer questions once they have posed them. A shorter and simpler text may not have the answers to many questions, causing frustration for the students.

Searching. For instruction in searching for information, it is most important to use a text with all the features that make it amenable to a search process, including a table of contents, index, pages numbers and headings on each page, glossary, bolded words, pronunciation guides, captions for all illustrations, and labels on diagrams. Books that contain these features need not be complex. Simple books like the *Rookie Read about Science* series by Alan Fowler contain the majority of them, and the *Eyewitness* series by Dorling Kindersley displays these features superbly.

Summarizing.   Using trade books to teach summarizing requires careful selection. First, a student should be able to read all of the sentences and paragraphs fluently and expressively. Reading a text aloud, expressively, in a whole class or group setting, enables students to form an initial representation of the content. The amount of text given to students for instruction in summarizing is the single most important factor in determining the success of lessons. If the text is too short (such as two sentences), there may be nothing of substance to summarize. However, if the text is too long (such as a five-page section of a complex information book), students may be unable to perform all of the summarizing processes needed to successfully capture this body of information, particularly when they are first learning summarizing. For example, teacher Ann Duncan provided an initial summarizing lesson with relatively low-level learners during the third-grade aquatic unit. This lesson was on summarizing one page of the book *Snails* by Kevin Holmes. The text follows:

Food

Most snails are herbivores. An herbivore is an animal that eats plants. Land snails eat grass, leaves and rotting plants. Fresh water snails eat algae and other water plants. Algae are small, floating plants. Ocean snails eat seaweed.

Some snails are carnivores. A carnivore is an animal that eats meat. These snails eat small fish and other snails. They also eat small, dead animals. Snails have radulas. A radula is a long, flat tongue. A radula is covered with tiny, sharp teeth. Snails use radulas to eat. Snails rub plants and animals with their radulas. This loosens pieces of food. Then snails pull the food into their mouths.

After extensive, explicit instruction, the class constructed the following summary:

The main idea is about snails and how they eat. Some snails are carnivores. They eat meat. Others are herbivores that eat plants. Snails have long black tongues called **radulas**. A **radula** is covered with tiny, sharp teeth that help bring food into its small body.

As students' proficiency and confidence in summarizing increase, the length of text should increase from a paragraph to a page to a section to an entire book.

Organizing Graphically.   Instruction for enabling students to graphically organize their knowledge during reading depends on a text that is suited to this comprehension strategy. If students are building a concept map that contains broad concepts with subordinate concepts and supporting facts, then text should contain these elements. An optimal text has features such as headings, illustrations, and bolded words that enable students to identify central information and supporting details. In addition, a text should be one that can be read fluently, like texts used for summarizing, to enable learners to quickly gain information at the word and sentence levels. Because the task of organizing graphically requires students to synthesize word-level, sentence-level, and paragraph-level information, these texts must be relatively easy to read and understand. Although graphically organizing information from text may appear to be a complex task, struggling readers can be taught this strategy. For example, in the CORI struggling readers' strand of instruction, teachers use the book *How Birds Live* by Biddulph, to teach graphic organizing. In this book, a section on beaks includes information on different shapes, colors, sizes, and functions of beaks for various types of birds that enable them to survive in different conditions. For struggling readers at the beginning second-grade level, this relatively concrete topic can be used to teach concept mapping with a superordinate concept such as survival, subordinate concepts such as eating and communicating, and supporting facts such as curved beaks for eating among predators and rounded bills for grass-eating ducks.

Structuring Story. For instruction in story structuring, literary texts of various lengths and complexities can be used. For example, in "Birds Around the World," the basic elements of stories (setting, character, plot, resolution) are initiated with the brief story of *Owl Moon* by Yolen and extended in the chapter book *White Bird* by Bulla. With either book, students should be able to read the text fluently and with expression, on their own, before undertaking the challenge of identifying story elements. Although it is possible to teach the elements of narrative structure by reading text aloud to children, students will not learn to apply these story elements to text. Without interacting with the print themselves, students often fail to learn how the qualities of setting and the twists of plot reveal themselves in books. Therefore, matching text difficulty to students' oral reading ability is a valuable aspect of teaching story structuring as a reading comprehension strategy.

Features of Text. In the research literature on strategy instruction, more attention is given to the type of strategies being taught than to the actual texts used in the studies. However, it is evident, on examining the individual studies, that texts were carefully chosen. For example, in a study of searching for information in expository text, investigators carefully selected texts that included features such as index, table of contents, pages numbers, headings, bolded words, and others (Reynolds & Symons, 2001). These features are indispensable to a successful investigation of the search process. However, many texts do not include all of these features, and therefore may not be appropriate for instruction on searching. This alignment of text characteristics and strategy instruction has not been extensively studied in experimental investigations but is clearly necessary for effective instruction. Likewise, this alignment of text and strategy instruction can be seen in studies involving summarizing. In these studies, an appropriate amount of text has been selected for the learners. The length of the text is a characteristic that is aligned to the strategy of summarizing. For instance, in investigations cited within the National Reading Panel Report, (2000) third to fifth graders were asked most frequently to summarize text consisting of 100 to 300 words. Rarely were entire books or complete stories used for this instruction. Although we want students to be capable of summarizing complete books and stories, it is sensible to begin with smaller chunks and more manageable portions. This amount should be increased as students' summarizing skill increases.

As stated earlier in the chapter, it is important to select texts that are on a familiar topic to students when teaching many of the reading strategies. Well known in the research on strategy instruction is the importance of a substantial, declarative, knowledge base. It has been illustrated, for example, that questioning is learned more readily in a familiar knowledge domain than in an unfamiliar one (Rosenshine, Meister, & Chapman, 1996). Other strategies, such as activating background knowledge and comprehension monitoring, are learned rapidly and applied more extensively if they are initially performed and taught in familiar content domains.

Finally, the information structure in the text influences its appropriateness for teaching different reading comprehension strategies. For example, organizing graphically using concept maps is more easily taught if the knowledge structure within the text is hierarchical with superordinate concepts, subordinate concepts, and supporting facts. These different forms of information are readily identified by students and can be organized and easily placed into spatial organizational structures. In sum, it is apparent that the strategy selected for instruction should be matched to texts in terms of their appropriate chunk size, availability of text features, content familiarity, and information structure within the materials.

5. Select Texts That Are Interesting to Students by Virtue of Their Appearance, Readability, Topic, and Connection to Classroom Activities

Characteristics that make texts interesting include appearance, readability, and topic (Schraw, Bruning, & Svoboda, 1995). Positive appearance can be determined by the number and color of pictures, interestingness of the title, font, color and layout of the text, number of headings and breakup of the text, and length of the book (Lapp, Flood, & Ranck-Buhr, 1995). Pictures are often the first characteristic a young reader uses to evaluate the interestingness of a book. Pictures capture the attention and help maintain interest in the task for texts, on computers as well as books (Cordova & Lepper, 1996).

Readability is a surprisingly important feature of interestingness. If students perceive the text to be "easy-to-read," they rate it as potentially more interesting than if they perceive it as "difficult." Perceived ease of reading is determined, as stated previously, primarily by the amount of print and the layout of illustrations. For information books, the number of sentences per page is a key indicator. Very simple books have two or three sentences and one or two illustrations per page in a 10 to 15-page book. More difficult books have 8 to 15 sentences per page, more illustrations, and more differentiation of headings. When a student sees a more difficult text his reaction is likely to be, "I am not interested in that" or "I don't want to read that." Often this affective response is not the same as the low efficacy statement "I can't do it," as the student may feel that although he is capable, he may not want to put in the effort to complete the task.

Usually, if the topic is appealing (Schiefele, 1996), the text is more likely to be read with interest than if the topic is neutral or unappealing. Most topics perceived as appealing are at least moderately familiar. Few people of any age have keen interest in a topic that is totally unknown to them. A base of knowledge brings the student a sense of expertise that adds to reading interest. Faced with a text on a familiar topic, a student may feel confident about enjoying it and learning from it.

In CORI, students become motivated to read through hands-on science experiences. Activities such as a habitat walk, dissecting an owl pellet, or experimenting with predators in an aquarium activate background knowledge and fuel the desire to learn more. In this context, texts aligned with the science goals and activities will be interesting. If the theme is the adaptation of birds (and other species) to biome diversity, and science observations bring this theme concretely to life, then books on this theme will be interesting. Interest that naturally springs from the tangible experiences of observing is quickly transferred to texts. Occasionally, illustrations are useful bridges between experience and text. Readers at all levels may say "I saw that before" (pointing to a picture of a fish's dorsal fin, or a vole) and then read about how fish use their different types of fins or how owls hunt voles at night.

6. Enable Struggling Readers to Read Texts In and Out of the Classroom That Are Aligned With the Content and Adapted to Their Needs for Fluency and Simplified Strategy Instruction

Often there are levels of struggling readers within a classroom in the later elementary grades (see chapter 7). For example, in a third-grade classroom, half of the students may be on grade level at the beginning of the school year, 30% to 40% of the students may be early second-grade level readers and about 10% of the students (two or three individuals) may be beginning first-grade level in reading achievement. They need assistance outside, as well as inside, the classroom. For beginning second-grade level students in the third-grade classroom, differentiated teaching is needed. Such students benefit from opportunities for gaining oral reading fluency and learning comprehension strategies on texts they have learned to read fluently. Without fluency for a given text, it is very difficult for these students to comprehend at the level of retelling or to use a strategy with the text. These needs can be met by a distinct stream of texts that are aligned with the content of the conceptual theme and that are designed to facilitate fluency development and simplified strategy learning.

For the unit "Birds Around the World," struggling readers are given the following sequence of strategy instruction and texts within CORI, as shown in Table 6.2.

An initiating activity for instruction in activating background knowledge can be provided with *Owl Babies*. The first page of the book contains the following text:

> Once there were three baby owls: Sarah and Percy and Bill. They lived in a hole in the trunk of a tree with their owl mother. The hole had twigs and leaves and owl feathers in it. It was their house.

Because students are familiar with trees, birds, twigs, leaves, and feathers, they will be able to activate background knowledge that is valuable for understanding this page. As the story proceeds, the mother goes hunting one night and the babies are lonely without her. They speculate on whether their mother will bring them a

TABLE 6.2
Sequence of Strategy Instruction and Texts for Struggling Readers
in "Birds Around the World" Unit

WEEK	STRATEGY	BOOK TITLE
1	Activating Background Knowledge	*Owl Babies* by Waddell
2	Questioning	*Living Together* by Windsor
3	Searching for Information	*Eggs and Baby Birds* by Shirley
4	Summarizing	*These Birds Can't Fly* by Fowler
5	Organizing Graphically	*How Birds Live* by Biddulph
6	Structuring Stories	*Dance My Dance* by Osakawa

mouse or be caught by a fox. She returns safely, but without food. Having read this page and successive pages aloud expressively, students gain fluency in oral reading.

With these same pages, students can activate and use their background experiences to predict and understand the story. Survival concepts in their simplest form are embedded in this narrative, including reproduction (nesting), feeding (eating the mouse), and defense (avoiding the fox). The story is about the dependence of young owls on their mother, which illustrates one phase of their life cycle, partially representing some of the processes of reproduction among owls. Students reading this book are gaining the bedrock of oral reading fluency while learning to use their background knowledge to gain new understandings from a text about basic survival processes in ecology. Likewise, books selected for the CORI struggling-reader instruction provide parallel development of conceptual knowledge and reading comprehension strategies for struggling readers in this third-grade class.

While struggling readers participate in expressive reading for purposes of fluency development, the whole class also participates in expressive reading with *On the Wing* by Douglas Florian. With encouragement, students render the text smooth, exciting, colorful, and easy to imagine. They read in different groupings, including whole class, teams, and extensively in pairs. Students may be tape-recorded or video-recorded, with the tapes serving as rewards for their diligence and feedback for their improvement. From this book, students read such texts as:

The Egret:

On morning tide the egret sat

And gave the beach a feathered hat.

The Vulture:

Two things I know about the vulture:

Its beak is strong, it's weak on culture.

The Roadrunner:

Roadrunner darts down dusty roads

In search of insects, lizards, and toads.

Past tumbleweeds it speeds for snakes

In catching them turns on the brakes.

As the whole class is involved with the expressive reading activities, struggling readers, who are spending extensive time in choral reading and reading aloud for purposes of fluency development, are given an extra opportunity for practice in reading with the whole class, rather than being pulled out and seen as stigmatized members of the classroom society.

The research literature on the use of appropriate text for teaching struggling readers is relatively limited. In a review of more than 150 studies of reading comprehension instruction for struggling readers, Gerston, Fuchs, and Williams (2001) emphasized the difficulty for learning-disabled students to comprehend expository text. The difficulty of the vocabulary and density of the information are often barriers to strategy learning. However, the authors concluded that instruction involving modeling and scaffolding, and assuring students' firm command of the strategies, facilitated their use of the strategies in comprehending other texts. In addition, emphasis on how strategies apply to different texts (teaching for transfer) and discussion of the appropriate time and place (generalization) for using the strategies provided improvements for struggling readers.

Expository text may be difficult for struggling readers to learn because there is a wide range of structures, as identified by Armbruster, Anderson, and Ostertag, (1987), such as cause–effect, problem solution, and compare–contrast. When these organizational structures for information text are taught and used, students acquire reading comprehension strategies for expository text more readily than if these organizational structures are neglected (Pappas, 1991). We concur with these findings, but our observations suggest further that selecting texts that are low-difficulty, based on criteria described elsewhere in this chapter, is a valuable step in the process of selecting suitable materials for struggling readers in a CORI classroom.

7. Incorporate Multimedia Into Each of the Previous Practices

Internet websites and CD-ROMs can be used in the classroom, much as interesting texts are, for students to obtain information on their chosen topic. Recall that a goal of CORI is to have students engaged in reading for an hour a day. One question teachers should ask when considering multimedia use is whether it will contribute toward this hour of reading. We mention this because many websites and CD-ROMs contain very little text. However, such multimedia may be appropriate for the purpose of initiating students' interest in a topic. Teachers can exploit the inherently appealing quality of multimedia to launch a new science unit. After viewing a video or working on an interesting computer activity, students are often enthusiastic about the topic and continue by reading. *Eyewitness: Bird* (Kershaw & Meehl, 1994) is a good video to launch a new unit on birds, combining striking images with interesting facts to spur students' thinking about a specific topic they would like to pursue.

However, websites may convey misinformation about science topics. Creators of websites for children include school classes, families, and other private citizens. Because these creators suffer few or no consequences if they publish inaccurate information, there is little incentive to maintain accuracy. In contrast, the reputations of scientific organizations, book publishers, and software companies can be harmed if they print inaccurate information. One way to minimize the amount of inaccuracy students are exposed to is to use websites associated with a major publisher or organization. For example, a website on birds published by National Geographic is less likely to contain inaccuracies than one published by a private source.

Selection Criteria Unique to Multimedia.   Ease of use is one criterion teachers should consider when choosing Internet websites and CD-ROMs. This refers to the use of hyperlinks, which allows users to access other parts of the software or website by mouse-clicking on text or graphics, and is unique to websites and CD-ROMs. Hyperlinks can make multimedia more appealing and easy to use, but they can also be complicated and confusing. Nielson (2000), an expert on website design, wrote that the user should always know where he is and how to get to other parts of a website. It is sensible to look for websites and CD-ROMs that children can navigate quickly and easily. Another criterion teachers should consider is the use of animation and other eye-catching effects unique to multimedia. These aspects can be appealing to students, but they can also distract students from attending to science concepts. Considerations when choosing multimedia include:

- Will the multimedia be used to engage students' initial interest?
- Can the multimedia play the role of an interesting text?
- Is the CD-ROM or Internet website easy to navigate?
- Is the website too distracting?

Because of the millions of websites that exist, it is wise to use tools that help organize the information on the Internet when searching for websites on particular topics. One popular directory is *Yahoo!* (www.yahoo.com), which contains hyperlinked topics that gradually get more specific. For example, if one is searching for websites about birds, one might first click on science, then on animals, and then on birds. The resulting page might contain further choices such as species, magazines and books about birds, and pets. When using a search engine, such as *Google*, to find websites, keywords must be specific. Typing "birds" will yield over 5 million websites. Therefore, the user must narrow the search by typing in multiple keywords, so that the number of websites listed is manageable.

One way to locate websites for children is to use an Internet directory geared toward children. *Yahooligans!* (www.yahooligans.com), the children's version of *Yahoo!*, includes only children's websites in its index. Table 6.3 is a directory of children's websites that we recommend as of 2003.

For Grade 3 students studying a unit on the pond, we recommend the website *Pond Explorer* (see Fig. 6.1), which contains an appropriate level of text and font size. This website includes colorful pictures, is easy for elementary school students to navigate, and presents ecological observations that lead to conceptual thinking.

The page in Fig. 6.1 shows links to the different pond habitats, which explain what animals live in each habitat. Another section of the site, named "Identification Key," gives detailed information about 20 different pond animals, supported by pictures and hyperlinks related to animals and concepts. This breadth of information enables teachers to use this website as a research tool for students to explore their own topics, while its attractiveness and ease of use holds students' interest, allowing it to be used as a unit introduction.

CLOSING

Because reading is complex, differing perspectives on the process are fully legitimate. If one focuses on word recognition as central to the reading process, then word recognition is a natural aim for instruction. For those who see language processing as the centerpiece of reading, then literary text that highlights language craft gains prominence in classroom instruction. When one's lens on reading embraces speaking, listening, reading, writing, and multimedia processing, then all of these communication channels are integral to instruction. Because our foreground for reading is learning concepts from text, we seek exposition and electronic text, as well as written stories and literature that en-

TABLE 6.3
CORI-Recommended Children's Websites

Directories of Children's Websites	Description
directory.google.com/Top/Kids_and_Teens	Directory maintained by *Google*
school.discovery.com/schrockguide	List of websites for educators
www.bigchalk.com	Education website that includes directory for children
www.yahooligans.com	Children's version of *Yahoo!*

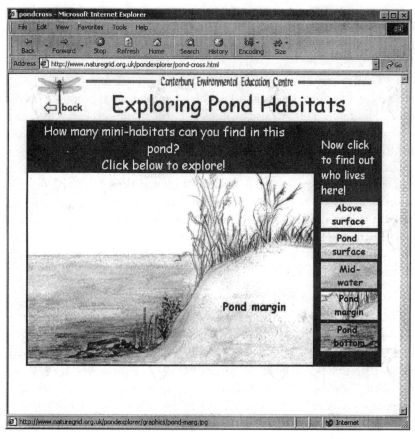

FIG. 6.1.

able students to learn and think conceptually. This conceptual learning is multigenre, connected to students' experiences, and is self-directed as it grows from prior knowledge, questioning, and inquiry. Text, then, is a way station on students' quest, and a resource for advances in self-determination in reading.

CHARACTERISTICS OF TRADE BOOKS INFLUENCING
THEIR DIFFICULTY FOR READING INSTRUCTION

Book title	Genre of book*	No.of pages	Average sentences per page	Average words per sentence	Avg. illustrat. per page	Average words per page	Avg. letters per word	Number of text feats.	Teacher ratings
Eggs and Baby Birds	I	23	2.89	8.83	1	26.5	4.17	4	1.7
Owls	I	19	11	11	0.5	60.5	4.02	6	2.6
Birds' Nests	I	7	2.14	8.1	2	11.5	4.13	1	1.5
Bird Beaks	I	11	2.0	10.25	1.5	20.5	4.15	1	1.3
Birds of the City	I	22	3.0	12.33	1	37	4.24	3	2.0
Birds of a Feather	I	14	4.5	9.22	4	41.5	4.54	5	2.5
All Kinds of Habitats	I	22	9.1	15.38	2.33	66.67	4.49	5	2.7
White Bird	L	59	16.1	8.8	0.25	145.25	3.83	1	2.3
Owl Moon	L	28	2.62	8	0.67	20.67	4.14	0	2.6
On the Wing	L	42	3.5	11.57	0.25	20.25	3.73	1	2.5
When Agnes Caws	L	30	4.5	16.5	1	24	4.53	0	3.6
Beginner's Guide to Birds	G	137	6.75	11.61	1.5	81.25	4.94	6	2.8

*I = Information; L = Literary; G = Guide

BIRDS AROUND THE WORLD
Non-Fiction

1. Bird Class Set	Author	ALL
Welcome to the World of Owls	Diane Swanson	X
All Kinds of Habitats	Sally Hewitt	X
Set Counted as One Book:	Fred and Jeanne Biddulph	X
– Eggs and Baby Birds – Feathers and Flight – How Birds Live		X
2. Bird Team Set	Author	Select 5
Birds of the City	Lynette Moon	
Birds of a Feather	Avelyn Davidson	
Owls	Susan Ring	
Birds: Desert Animals	Lynn M. Stone	
Owls	Lynn M. Stone	
Bird Beaks/Bird Nests	Diana Noonan	
Bird: Starting with Nature	Pamela Hickman	
What's the Difference: Birds	Stephen Savage	
3. Bird Field Guides	Author	Select 1
Usborne Spotter's Guide	Philip Burton	
Beginner's Guide to Birds: Eastern Region	Donald & L. Strokes	
Peterson First Guides: Birds		

4. Birds Individual		Author	Select 5
	Cactus Hotel	Megan Lloyd	
	Predators: Birds	Lynn M. Stone	
	Owls: The Silent Hunters	Sara Swan Miller	
	Animals in Disguise: Birds	Lynn Stone	
	Using a Beak	Jo Windsor	
	Birds: Eyewitness Explorers	Jill Bailey	
	Bird Watchers	Dawn McMillan	
	How Do Birds Find Their Way	Roma Gans	
GENERAL	*Bird: Eyewitness Books (H)*	David Burnie	
	Life in Your Backyard	Natalie Lunis	
	Bird Behavior: Living Together	Lynette Moon	
	Amazing Birds of Prey	Jemina Jones	
	Birds of Prey	Marilyn Woolley	

5. BIRDS Individual		Author	ALL
Polar	*Penguins: Growing up Wild (H)*	Sandra Markle	X
	Plenty of Penguins	Sonia Black	X
	Birds of America	Lynn M. Stone	X
Woodland	*Perching Birds of North America*	Sara Swan Miller	X
	Woodpeckers: Backyard Birds	Lynn Stone	X
	Welcome to the World of Hummingbirds	Diane Swanson	X
Water Birds	*Whooping Crane*	Rod Theodorou	X
	Geese: Barnyard Friends	Jason Cooper	X
	Swans	Lynn Stone	X
	Water Birds: A Picture Book	Grace Mabie	X
Grassland	*Bald Eagles*	Buck Wilde	X
	The Bald Eagle	Ryon Quiri	
	The Night Owls	Kevin Patrick	X
	All About Owls	Jim Arnosky	X
E – Easier, H – Harder			

Fiction

6. Bird Chapter Books	Author	Select 1
Falcon's Feathers	Ron Roy	
White Bird	Clyde Robert Bulla	
7. Bird Classy Story Books	Author	ALL
Owl Moon	Jane Yolen	X
8. Bird Individual Stories	Author	Select 3
* *The Birdwatcher*	Simon James	
Magic School Bus: Hops Home	Scholastic	
* *Adopted by an Owl*	Robbyn Smith	
When Agnes Caws	Candace Fleming	
Bird Watch	Jane Yoken	
Feathers and Fools	Nicholas Wilton	
*Recommended		
9. Class Expressive Books	Author	ALL
On the Wing	Douglas Florian	X

APPENDIX 6.C
SURVIVAL IN FRESHWATER HABITATS
Non-Fiction

1. POND Class Set	Author	ALL
Pond Life: Look Closer	Barbara Taylor	X
Snails	Kevin J. Holmes	X
Set Counted as One Book: – The Pond – Animal Eaters of the Pond – Plant Eaters of the Pond	Maud King	X

2. POND Team Set	Author	Select 5
What's the Difference: Amphibians	Steven Savage	
A Freshwater Pond	Adam Hibbert	
Animals in Rivers and Lakes	Moira Butterfield	
Crayfish	Phyllis Grimm	
Freshwater Habitats	Diane Snowball	
Amazing Frogs and Toads	Barry Clarke	
What is a Fish	Bobbie Kalman	
Set Counted as One Book: – How Snails Live – How Snails Protect Themselves – The Life Cycle of a Snail	Chris Brough	

3. Pond Field Guides	Author	Select 1
Pond Life: A Golden Guide	George Reid	
Aquarium Fish	Dick Mills	

4. PONDS Individual		Author	Select 5
	* And so They Build	Bert Kitchen	
	* One Small Square: Pond	Donald Silver	
	Frogs and Toads and Tadpoles, Too (E)	Allan Fowler	
	Life in a Pond (E)	Allan Fowler	
	Life in a Pond	Claire Oliver	
	From Tadpole to Frog (E)	Wendy Pfeffer	
	Around the Pond (E)	Ann Cooper	
	Tadpole Diary	David Drew	
	Frogs and Toads: I Can Read About	Ellen Schultz	
	FROG: See How They Grow (E)	Kim Taylor	
	Pond and River: Eyewitness Books (H)	Steve Parker	
	Beavers	Deboarah Hodge	
GENERAL	What's it Like to be a Fish?	Wendy Pfeffer	
	Set Counted as One Book: – The Survival of Fish, How do Fish Live, Is it a Fish	Fred and Jeanne Biddulph	
* Recommended E – Easier, H – Harder			

5. PONDS Individual		Author	ALL
Mammals	The Beaver	Sabrina Crewe	X
	Welcome to the Wold of Otters	Diane Swanson	X
	Beavers	Lynn Stone	X
	River Otter: Wild Animals of the Woods	Lynn Stone	X
	Deer	Lynn Stone	X
BIRDS	Swans	Lynn Stone	X
	Whooping Cranes	Karen Dudley	X
	Herons	Frank Straub	X
	Wading Birds: From Herons to Hammerkops	Sara Swan Miller	X
Snail	Snails and Slugs	Theresa Greenaway	X
Amphibians	Salamanders: Creepy Crawlers	Lynn Stone	X
	Tale of a Tadpole	Karen Wallace	
	Tadpoles	Theresa Greenaway	X
	Very first things to know about Frogs	Patricia Grossman	X
FISH	Angelfish	Elaine Landau	X
	Electric Fish	Elaine Landau	X
	Piranhas	Elaine Landau	X

Fiction

6. Pond Chapter Books	Author	Select 2
Junie B. Jones Smells Something Fishy	Barbara Park	
The Prince of the Pond	Donna Jo Napoli	
Jimmy: The Pickpocket of the Palace	Donna Jo Napoli	
Dolphins at Daybreak	Mary Pope Osborne	
Afternoon on the Amazon	Mary Pope Osborne	
7. Pond Class Story Books	Author	ALL
Silver Swan	Michael Morpurgo	X
8. Pond Individual Stories	Author	Select 3
Animal Lives: The Frog	Sally Tagholm	
Pond Year	Kathryn Lasky	
Beaver Pond: Moose Pond	Jim Arnosky	
In the Swim	Douglas Florian	
The Rainbow Fish	Marcus Pfister	
The Gift	Owl Goingback	
9. Class Expressive Books	Author	ALL
Pond Seasons	Ann Blades	X

REFERENCES

Alexander, P. A., Kulikowich, J. M., & Jetton, T. L. (1994). The role of subject-matter knowledge and interest in the processing of linear and nonlinear texts. *Review of Educational Research, 64*, 201–252.

Anderman, L. H. (1999). Classroom goal orientation, school belonging and social goals as predictors of students' positive and negative affect following the transition to middle school. *Journal of Research and Development in Education, 32*(2), 89–103.

Armbruster, B. B., Anderson, T. H., & Ostertag, J. (1987). Does text structure/summarization instruction facilitate learning from expository text? *Reading Research Quarterly, 22*(3), 331–346.

Baker, L., & Brown, A. L. (1984). *Metacognitive skills and reading.* In P. D. Pearson (Ed.), *Handbook of reading research* (pp. 353–394). New York: Longman.

Chambliss, M. J. (1994). Evaluating the quality of textbooks for diverse learners. *Remedial and Special Education, 15*(6), 348–363.

Cordova, D. I., & Lepper, M. R. (1996). Intrinsic motivation and the process of learning: Beneficial effects of contextualization, personalization, and choice. *Journal of Educational Psychology, 88*, 715–730.

Donovan, C. A., & Smolkin, L. B. (2001). Genre and other factors influencing teachers' book selection for science. *Reading Research Quarterly, 36*, 412–440.

Dreher, M. J., & Singer, H. (1989). Friendly texts and text-friendly teachers. *Theory into Practice, 28*(2), 98–104.

Duke, N. K. (2000). 3.6 minutes per day: The scarcity of informational texts in first grade. *Reading Research Quarterly, 35*(2), 202–224.

Gerston, R., Fuchs, L., & Williams, J. P. (2001). Teaching reading comprehension strategies to students with learning disabilities: A review of research. *Review of Educational Research, 71*, 279–320.

Guthrie, J. T., & Cox, K. E. (2001). Classroom conditions for motivation and engagement in reading. *Educational Psychology Review, 13*(3), 283–302.

Guthrie, J. T., Schafer, W. D., Von Secker, C., & Alban, T. (2000). Contributions of instructional practices to reading achievement in a statewide improvement program. *Journal of Educational Research, 93*(4), 211–225.

Holiday, W. G., Yore, L. D., & Alvermann, D. E. (1994). The reading–science learning–writing connection: Breakthroughs, barriers, and promises. *Journal of Research in Science Teaching, 31*(9), 877–893.

Kershaw, J. (Producer), & Meehl, B. (Writer), (1994). *Eyewitness: Bird* (Motion Picture). United Kingdom. BBC Wildvision.

Lapp, D., Flood, J., & Ranck-Buhr, W. (1995). Using multiple text formats to explore scientific phenomena in middle school classrooms. *Reading & Writing Quarterly, 11*, 173–186.

Miller, S. D., & Meece, J. L. (1997). Enhancing elementary students' motivation to read and write: A classroom intervention study. *Journal of Educational Research, 90*, 286–301.

Morrow, L. M., Pressley, M., Smith, J. K., & Smith, M. (1997). The effect of a literature-based program integrated into literacy and science instruction with children from diverse backgrounds. *Reading Research Quarterly, 32*, 54–76.

National Reading Panel (2000). *Teaching children to read: An evidence-based assessment of the scientific research literature on reading and its implications for reading instruction* (NIH Pub. No. 00–4769). Jessup, MD: National Institute for Literacy.

Nielson, J. (2000). *Designing Web Usability.* Indianapolis, IN: New Riders Publishing.

Pappas, C. C. (1991). Young children's strategies in learning the "book language "of information books. *Discourse Processes, 14*, 203–225.

Paris, S., Carpenter, R., Paris, A., & Hamilton, E. (2002, October). *Spurious and genuine correlates of childrens' reading comprehension.* Paper at Reading Assessment Conference, University of Michigan, Ann Arbor.

Reynolds, P. L., & Symons, S. (2001). Motivational variables and children's text search. *Journal of Educational Psychology, 93*(1), 14–22.

Rice, D. C. (2002). Using trade books in teaching elementary science: Facts and fallacies. *The Reading Teacher, 55*(6), 552–565.

Romance, N. R., & Vitale, M. R. (2001). Implementing an in-depth expanded science model in elementary schools: Multi-year findings, research issues, and policy implications. *International Journal of Science Education, 23*(4), 373–404.

Rosenshine, B., Meister, C., & Chapman, S. (1996). Teaching students to generate questions: A review of the intervention studies. *Review of Educational Research, 66,* 181–221.

Schiefele, U. (1996). Topic interest, text representation, and quality of experience. *Contemporary Educational Psychology, 21,* 3–18.

Schmidt, P. R., Gillen, S., Zollo, T. C., & Stone, R. (2002). Literacy learning and scientific inquiry: Children respond. *The Reading Teacher, 55*(6), 534–548.

Schraw, G., Bruning, R., & Svoboda, C. (1995). Source of situational interest. *Journal of Reading Behavior, 27,* 1–17.

Shymansky, J. A., Yore, L. D., & Good, R. (1991). Elementary teachers' beliefs about and perceptions of elementary school science, science reading, science textbooks, and supportive instructional factors. *Journal of Research in Science Teaching, 28*(50), 437–454.

Smolkin, L. B., & Donovan, C. A. (2001). The contexts of comprehension: The information book read aloud, comprehension acquisition, and comprehension instruction in a first grade classroom. *Elementary School Journal, 102,* 97–122.

Stahl, S. A., & Kuhn, M. R. (2002). Making it sound like language: Developing fluency. *Reading Teacher, 55*(6), 582–584.

Torgesen, J. K., Wagner, R. K., & Rashotte, C. A. (1999). *Test of word reading efficiency.* Austin, TX: PRO-ED Publishing.

CHILDREN'S BOOK REFERENCES

Biddulph, F., & Biddulph, J. (1993). *Feathers and flight.* Bothell, WA: Wright Group.

Biddulph, F., & Biddulph, J. (1993). *How birds live.* Bothell, WA: Wright Group.

Bulla, C. R. (1990). *White bird.* New York: Random House.

Davidson, A. D. (1991). *Birds of a feather.* Crystal Lake, IL: Reed Elsevier Inc.

Fleischman, P. (1992). *Joyful noise: Poems for two voices.* New York: Harper Collins.

Florian, D. (2000). *On the wing.* New York: Voyager Books.

George, J. C. (1995). *One day in the woods.* New York: Harper Collins.

Hewitt, S. (1999). *All kinds of habitats.* New York: Children's Press.

Holmes, K. J. (1998). *Snails.* Mankato, MN: Capstone Press.

Noonan, D. (1993). *Birds' nests.* Bothell, WA: Wright Group.

Noonan, D. (1995). *Bird beaks.* Bothell, WA: Wright Group.

Roy, R. (1998). *A to Z mysteries: The falcon's feathers.* New York: Random House.

Shirley, A. (1993). *Eggs and baby birds.* Bothell, WA: Wright Group.

Stone, L. M. (1989). *Owls.* New York: Rourke.

Swanson, D. (1997). *Welcome to the world of owls.* Vancouver, BC: Whitecap Books.

Waddell, M. (1992). *Owl babies.* Cambridge, MA: Candlewick Press.

Yolen, J. (1987). *Owl moon.* New York: Philomel Books.

7

Differentiating Instruction for Struggling Readers Within the CORI Classroom

John T. Guthrie
University of Maryland

Learners who struggle with reading in the third grade are often maintained within the CORI classroom. However, students at the first-grade level are frequently assigned to special education for reading outside of the regular classroom. Teachers must pay particular attention to all below-average groups to ensure that they progress to a level that is commensurate with headway of the other students in the classroom.

ORAL READING FLUENCY

Students who struggle with reading in the beginning of third grade have several needs. A prominent requirement for these students is fluency in oral reading (Kuhn & Stahl, 2002; National Reading Panel, 2000). At this level, students often have not attained automatic word recognition skills. These students read aloud with awkward pauses, stops, and starts, treating each word as a single entity, which limits the flow of the passage. At the same time, the slowness of their reading is a further barrier to meaning. Their expressiveness in reading connected text is severely limited, shown by a lack of tone, inflection, and changes of rate or speed that enable the listener to fully interpret the text (Clay & Imlach, 1971). All of these obstacles obscure the meaning of the text (LaBerge & Samuels, 1974).

As children begin to gain oral reading fluency, they read in larger chunks and phrases of continuous text (Samuels, LaBerge, & Bremer, 1978). Their substitutions are more likely to be consistent with meaning. However, although their rate may be increased, it may be forced or too constant for good expression. They may exaggerate in attempting to be expressive, or provide adjustments of tone only occasionally. At this stage of development, children have some skill in rereading and sounding out words, but frequently are bogged down in oral reading.

Advanced readers are fluent, in the sense that they can read isolated words rapidly and accurately. They can read a whole passage aloud to communicate its meaning by adjusting their inflection, rate, and speed to match the intended meaning of the author (Schreiber, 1987). Confident in showing their interpretation of the text, their reading is purposeful and may include rereading for better expression. At this level, students become artful in their communication about the uniqueness and richness of a text. Development of such oral reading fluency and expression is especially necessary for struggling readers in third grade, but it is also valuable for many learners at all levels of achievement in the later elementary grades.

RATIONALE FOR DIFFERENTIATED INSTRUCTION IN CORI

Why do we need to provide specialized forms of reading comprehension instruction for some readers in CORI? In a majority of schools in Maryland and elsewhere, a nontrivial proportion of children (we find it is at least 10% to 15%) have not established basic oral reading fluency with beginning Grade 3 text. To these students, establishing the meaning of a short page of text containing 10 to 15 words does not occur during their first reading. Their initial attempts to construct meaning are directed at decoding processes and discovering single word meanings. These learners need improvements in word recognition, as well as fluency and expressiveness in reading connected text.

To teach comprehension strategies, such as questioning or graphic organizing, students must, in one reading, be able to read a page of text with sufficient fluency to "get the main idea" relatively well. This enables them to think about what kind of question might be productive for what types of information to be entered onto a graphic organizer for a page or section of text. Forming a question, and reading a page of text with the intention of answering that question, is an abstract process. This process demands attention to conceptual information and factual statements. It demands cognitive effort, which cannot be consumed by decoding or assessing individual vocabulary meanings. Therefore, our aim is to help the reader establish the textual representation for a specific two to four page text. We attempt to accomplish this through frequent experiences with oral reading activities in a particular text. After students have gained fluency for a text, its meaning becomes apparent. They get the gist, and perceive the meaning of most of the sentences (Reutzel & Hollingsworth, 1993). However, without extensive instruction, they generally cannot use a strategy, such as questioning, on that text.

Several studies and reviews of research, including the National Reading Panel Report (2000) conclude that oral reading fluency is not sufficient for comprehension. Even though students may be taught to be fluent and expressive in their oral reading, their literal comprehension of passages and ability to summarize or use other strategies may be extremely limited. Explicit instruction in these strategies is often necessary; with perhaps only 25% of the most rapid learners in our observation able to induce strategies quite effectively, without modeling or scaffolding from teachers. However, we are not focusing on those students in this chapter.

In the CORI framework for supporting struggling readers, we intentionally merge the support for fluency development and a support for cognitive strategy learning. This practice has not been widely examined in previous investigations. The majority of studies have examined whether oral reading fluency can be developed, without attending to simultaneous instruction in cognitive strategies. Likewise, cognitive strategy teaching has frequently been investigated without explicit attention to oral reading fluency, assuming that this fluency exists. We expect that for students with low fluency, establishing the oral reading fluency for a specific text of 25 to 100 words will facilitate strategy development. We also expect that the ability to use a strategy, such as questioning, will enable students to improve oral reading fluency by focusing their attention on sentence and passage meaning.

For fluency development, the teacher provides expressive activities for a specific text of two to five pages. Students read and reread in pairs and groups to discover the sounds and meaning of the text (Samuels, 1979). Immediately following, the teacher provides simplified strategy teaching for a strategy with the texts on which fluency was established. A relatively abstract process, such as asking a question, becomes possible and productive of new learning when the student has recently read the text aloud expressively. We do not assume that gaining fluency in one text will immediately transfer to others. Generalized fluency is not necessary for initial comprehension strategy instruction. Specific, local fluency will suffice. Of course, the acquisition of generalized fluency increases with these limited expressive reading activities.

SUPPORTING INITIAL STRATEGY LEARNING

Compounding their lack of oral reading fluency, struggling readers in Grade 3 or 4 usually have not learned comprehension strategies, such as questioning, during reading or organizing text content. To help these learners, simplified strategy instruction is usually necessary. To distill the task of using a strategy, simplification begins with using easy-to-read materials and decodable text. A small amount of text, such as one paragraph, is advisable for teaching this group a strategy, such as summarizing.

Struggling readers benefit from a bridge that supports the use of a comprehension strategy. This bridge is a link between the text and the normal outcome of using a strategy. For example, if a teacher asks a student to summarize a paragraph, the struggling reader will benefit from a bridge between text and the written summary. This bridge is a scaffold that supports the process of doing this strategy. Often, without the scaffold, the learner cannot begin to use the strategy nor follow it through to its conclusion. Examples of bridges used by CORI teachers are presented in this chapter.

Opportunities to learn are especially important for struggling readers. They need multiple occasions for doing a strategy and gaining command of it. Whereas a normally achieving third-grade student may learn the basics of questioning strategy in two or three lessons, the struggling reader requires more opportunities. We observe that these students benefit from 8 to 10 occasions for learning a strategy and applying it to different text types, when other students within the same classroom acquire the strategy with fewer learning activities.

PRACTICES OF STRATEGY INSTRUCTION FOR STRUGGLING READERS

Because they need multiple opportunities with texts and materials designed for them, struggling readers need small-group, daily instruction inside or outside of the classroom. Groups of three to six students are formed and provided instruction for 30 minutes daily. While the teacher is working with this group, the remainder of the class is reading independently, writing, or pursuing an extended project. This daily instruction is maintained in the classroom until these students have proficiency in strategies that teachers are providing and are capable of initiating the strategies themselves on appropriate occasions (Strickland, Ganske, & Monroe, 2002).

Expressive Reading

Strategy instruction for struggling readers is provided in two 15-minute segments that can occasionally be varied for the sake of novelty. First, students participate in a 15-minute expressive reading activity, emphasizing oral reading fluency and expressiveness. It is an opportunity for students to develop and improve their word recognition and strategies that include rereading, sounding out, substituting, skipping over, searching for help, or asking questions to aid in word recognition (Simmons, Fuchs, Fuchs, Mathes, & Hodge, 1995). Expressive reading is an opportunity for enjoying the sound of language, expressing the meanings of exciting words, phrases, and sentences, and gaining self-confidence in reading interpretively (Worthy & Broaddus, 2002).

To foster expressiveness, teachers may involve students as participants in assisted reading. As they listen to their teacher or to a tape recording, students read along. This assures active word recognition and attention to sentence meaning. Teachers can provide feedback, encouragement, correction, and a model of reading aloud during this activity. Another assisted reading activity is "whisper reading" in which students read aloud by whispering, so only the teacher can hear them. Teachers can then provide feedback and instruction to each learner during a brief period of this activity. Finally, students may engage in group choral reading, showing as much expressiveness as possible. In each of these reading activities, individuals can participate as a full team or with partners. A pair of students can engage in "whisper reading," and develop an impressive level of harmony and effectiveness as a team. Throughout these activities, a high volume of reading is needed (Stahl & Heubach, in press).

Crossing Bridges

Small group instruction for struggling readers is extended to strategy learning in the phase called *Crossing Bridges*. This is a daily activity in which students remain in their expressive reading groups. The same text that was used for expressive reading is the basis for strategy learning. Because students have read the text aloud, they are familiar with many of its meanings, although their comprehension is not likely to be deep or thorough.

Struggling readers receive a second 15-minute segment devoted to simplified strategy instruction. Teachers use the same texts that were used in expressive reading, including stories, poems, and information books. After reading the content fluently, students are likely to have a basic comprehension of it. They are in a strong position to deepen their understanding by applying strategies to these texts. Then simplified strategy instruction can be provided with a bridge, which links the text to the expected response of a learner and a strategy task. For example, in teaching questioning, a chart may be used as a bridge to aid students in forming and recording their questions about a book.

Scaffolding for simplified strategy instruction begins with modeling. The teacher demonstrates how she would complete a reading chart for questioning with a text (see the scaffolding in Appendix A and the chart in Appendix B). At the outset, students follow the teacher. Later in the sequence of instruction, students complete the same chart on a new text with teacher guidance. After 4 or 5 days, students work as independently as possible with the same chart on new texts. Within this framework, the students will be gaining competence and confidence in using a strategy, such as questioning, for reading comprehension. This approach follows recommendations of Gersten, Fuchs, and Williams (2001), who suggested that comprehension instruction for struggling readers should consist of (a) reasons for using the strategy, (b) steps in performing it, (c) teacher modeling at the beginning, and (d) student practice with the strategy. For a single strategy they recommend four 45-minute lessons followed by practice with new and different texts. For multiple strategies, at least 2 or 3 months are needed. Our framework of instruction for 30 minutes daily over 12 weeks for 6 strategies is highly compatible with these recommendations.

For the section on *Crossing Bridges*, the teacher selects material that is compatible with the content being taught in the classroom, utilizing the lowest difficulty texts that are available so that students are able to read these texts aloud, fluently, with expression, and gain a basic comprehension of the gist, with minimal teacher support (Hiebert & Fisher, 2002). This low difficulty enables the students to think about and construct the strategies for deeper comprehension. Such texts, usually having 7 to 10 words per sentence, one to four sentences per page, and 1 or 2 illustrations on each page, enable students to activate background knowledge and confirm text meanings readily. The teacher selects two to five pages within such a text for use in a given lesson on simplified strategy instruction.

Having identified the text, the teacher selects a bridge, consisting of a guide for the learner to facilitate the use of a cognitive strategy. Appendix B presents two bridges. The questioning bridge consists of the following:

1. Look at the title and pictures. What is this about?
2. Now read the first sentence.
3. Write a question you might answer in this book or section.
4. Read to answer your question.
5. Write your answer in the space provided.

The second portion of Appendix B is the bridge for summarizing and includes the following sections:

1. Look at the following text and read it aloud.
2. What is the main idea of this page? What is the most important word on this page?

3. Circle this word with your pencil.
4. Underline two important facts about this main idea.
5. Make a sentence with the words you just circled and underlined.

Simplified Strategy Instruction

Using low difficulty text for content in a CORI unit and relying on the bridge as a support for student thinking and writing, teachers provide simplified strategy instruction, beginning with modeling. On a typical first day of a week, the teacher models all of the steps in the questioning process as the students complete the bridge for questioning. That is, as the teacher reads each step aloud with the students and says or writes the answers on a chalkboard or overhead projector, students complete their own forms. At the end of Day 1, each student should have completed her bridge showing the question she formed over this text. On Day 2, using the next several pages in the same text, the teacher provides a high scaffold, supplying students with 75% of the information in the bridge as they work to complete their bridges individually. The teacher may read most of these sentences aloud, providing a majority of the answers, while students are offering approximately 25% of the answers to the questions. The student writes the requested information for each step on a chalkboard or overhead, following the teacher's guidance. On Day 3, the teacher provides a moderate scaffold in which students are supplying 50% of the information in response to questions while the teacher is offering the other half of the material needed to complete the bridge. On Day 4, the teacher offers a low scaffold in which she may read the first sentence for the task and encourage students to complete the remainder of the bridge in pairs. On Day 5, the teacher instructs students to work individually and encourages their completion of a bridge on their own.

On each of the days, the same text has been used and students' familiarity with the content improves their ability to form interesting questions and relate their questioning to the text-based information. Through the course of this instruction, the students gain a sense of efficacy in their ability to pose questions and to write them effectively. As the teacher proceeds, she encourages students to think more globally about the content, to ask higher level questions, and to incorporate what they know about the topic into their questioning, to the degree that students are able.

SCAFFOLDING MOTIVATION FOR FLUENCY DEVELOPMENT AND SIMPLIFIED STRATEGY LEARNING

Two motivational processes are integrally connected to the development of students' oral reading fluency. At the outset, a certain level of self-efficacy in reading is necessary. Students need to believe they can read a majority of a text before they will exert sufficient effort to complete the reading of a sentence or a page. As their ability to read words rapidly and to construe meanings of sentences improves, students gain a belief in their capacity. They increase their ability to read aloud effectively, with the accuracy and expressiveness that makes a text sensible to themselves and others. The process of rereading in a whole group, in pairs, or in solo reading activities fuels the students' self-efficacy. Beginning to recognize themselves as readers, they see their oral expressions as legitimate and effective communications with others. These experiences enhance their willingness to read new texts and persevere when they encounter difficulties.

Intrinsic motivation for reading is also woven with oral reading fluency improvement. As students read information books, and begin to read full sentences, comprehension of the text emerges. Students recognize that a picture in the text is related to or represented by the sentence they read aloud. The print they decode has a link to the illustration or the mental picture they may have, making meaning an intrinsically motivating activity. When students are able to make meaning of printed language, their motivation for reading improves (Palmer, Codling, & Gambrell, 1994).

Supporting intrinsic motivation for reading among struggling learners is provided through the same principles of scaffolding used in the mainstream of CORI. For example, real-world interactions and hands-on activities support oral reading development, just as they support strategy development. If a student has observed a turtle swimming in the classroom aquarium, the sentence, "Painted turtles swim quickly," will be more interesting to read. When students read fluently enough to realize there is a bond between the printed sentence and the observation, motivation for reading is enhanced.

Motivating students by providing choice and control can occur during instruction for struggling readers, just as it occurs elsewhere in CORI. For example, students may be reading a small, illustrated book with three sentences per page. Students can be given the choice of which page of text they will read next, ensuring of course, that the choice is sensible in terms of content, vocabulary, and students' readiness. Having made a decision to read one page rather than another, students will invest more effort and show slightly more delight than if the text is always prescribed for them. With growing independence, choices can be broadened to include sections of a book, topics within a book, or books within a classroom library. The point here is that choice can be scaffolded to be cognitively appropriate and developmentally sensitive. Broader choices can be offered to students who are more advanced in their self-directed reading, whereas narrower choices can be given to students who are less capable of handling this independence. As teachers enable students to become more self-reliant in selecting text, students' fluency increases as a result of the frequency and amount of reading this independence enables.

The principle of collaborative support for reading development applies to fluency as well as to cognitive strategies. When students can discuss which words sounded "interesting" or "exciting" in a passage or sentence, they gain more interest in the text. As students hear each other read aloud, their knowledge of the content becomes clearer. Collaborating to establish the meaning of a paragraph reinforces that students can hear their classmates and can communicate effectively to be understood by them. These processes undergird interest in the text and the intrinsic motivation to read.

SELECTION OF TEXTS FOR DIFFERENTIATED INSTRUCTION IN CORI

One criterion for text selection is the content connection. When students are studying the unit "Birds Around the World," the texts relate to birds and how they may live in different biomes. It is important to maintain the conceptual theme, even when the instruction is differentiated. Texts on the conceptual theme link students to other classroom activities that may include science observation or writing personal narratives. The genre of texts for struggling readers may include both informational text and literary materials. However, the ratio is approximately 5:1, with five information books for each storybook or chapter book of literary material or fiction. As fiction books are often longer, this affords students about 50% of their time in informational and literary books.

Format and layout of text are important. For beginning third graders, we use trade books that have approximately 7 to 11 words per sentence. We attempt to identify texts with approximately one to four sentences per page. In texts of this kind, there are usually one to two illustrations per page, which consume about 50% of a four-or-five-page selection. We attempt to locate texts in which the vocabulary load and the number of unknown words to be decoded are not excessively high. Approximately 10% to 15% of the words may be nondecodable or new in meaning. At proportions higher than this, oral reading activities become excessively focused on word recognition, while fluency development at the passage level suffers. These trade books are usually about 30 pages in length, with a small table of contents, index, and possibly headings and captions. A larger font size is decidedly a factor in making the text appealing and approachable. The texts listed in Appendix C represent materials we have found to be valuable.

A final characteristic is that the texts should lend themselves to simplified strategy instruction. For example, we select materials for activating background knowledge with a few challenging words present to cause the students to stop and think. This enables the teacher to ask students to perform the activating strategy with other known words in the sentence and passage. This fosters students' construction of meaning for the unknown words, as well as their decoding of the words. We often select texts for beginning summarizing instruction in which a single page is an appropriate chunk of text for a summarizing activity. If students have to read three pages to gain a sufficient amount of information to summarize, they are easily distracted and lose focus on the strategy. If the text contains too much information, for example, 100 words on three different topics, then students often cannot focus efficiently on an appropriate unit of text. Their attention wavers and they become discouraged in this summarizing instruction. For each strategy, we select texts that lend themselves, and contain the characteristics suitable, to performing the strategy optimally, within the limits of the learner.

A VIGNETTE ON DIFFERENTIATED INSTRUCTION FROM CAROL BARRETT'S CLASSROOM

It is early October in Carol Barrett's third-grade classroom in Frederick, Maryland. Entering school in September, her students were generally on grade level in reading and were responding favorably to the CORI framework. Carol identifies, however, four students whose reading fluencies are inadequate to enable them to learn cognitive strategies easily. Unlike other students, they have not made the same headway in learning the strategy of activating background knowledge. Now, they are struggling with forming questions over text.

Carol gathers Sienna, Danielle, Ananzia, and Charlie at a table in one corner of the room, while other students are writing their own questions on the unit "Birds Around the World." Carol gives each child a copy of the colorful *Living Together* by Jo Windsor. "Let's look at the cover. What do you see there?" she asks. "A hippo," offers Charlie. "I see a big bull with horns," says Ananzia. "A bird," volunteers Ananzia. "I see a shrimp and a fish," says Danielle. "Yes, you're using your eyes today," comments Mrs. Barrett. "Now let's turn to page 2. What do we see here?"

The students continue naming the animals on pages 2 to 5, which include fish of different sizes and birds. "Now let's read the text aloud together in our whisper voices," says Mrs. Barrett. As Carol leads, they all read the following text aloud:

> Some big and little animals live together. The little animals help the big animals stay clean. This shrimp lives with this fish. The little shrimp cleans the fish. This little fish lives with this big fish. The little fish can clean the big fish's mouth.

Most of the students identify the words correctly, although several are slow in recognizing "together," "shrimp," and "mouth." The children's reading is achingly slow at the single-word level. Some ... big ... and ... little ... animals ... live ... together. None of the words in any of the sentences was grouped or associated in any meaningful way.

Carol continues, "Let's read this again, and this time, let's make it sound *interesting*. We want other people to think what we are reading is very *interesting*." They read the following text again:

> Some big and little animals live together. The little animals help the big animals stay clean.

In this reading, phrases appeared, including "little animals" and "big animals." Students associate the text with the picture, which shows a big fish with a little fish cleaning its mouth. Carol finishes reading pages 4 and 5, leading the students to make meaningful phrases such as, "little shrimp," and "big fish's mouth."

In oral reading, the students had progressed from single-word statements to phrases. These clusters gave meaning to the chunks of language. In just 10 minutes, they progressed from almost no oral reading fluency to meaningful adjective–noun and adverb–verb relations. Yet, their meanings at the sentence level were primitive.

Now that the students were fluent with these initial 3 or 4 pages of *Living Together*, Carol directed her students to the questioning chart in the Guide for Differentiated Instruction (see Appendix B: Bridge for Questioning). She asked them to look at the title, headings, and pictures in the section they had read. "What is it about?"

"Big animals," said Ananzia.

"Little animals," replied Charlie.

"Big animals and little animals living together," said Danielle.

"That's a nice way to say it," responded Carol. "Let's write that on our charts."

She turned to a chart board behind her chair and wrote, "Big animals and little animals living together." Students followed her example and wrote this statement in their bridge for questioning.

Mrs. Barrett requested, "Read the first sentence of this section." They all read together, "Some big and little animals live together."

"Write a question you might answer in this book or section," she suggested, reading the second step of the bridge for questioning with the students. "What question do you have, Ananzia?" Ananzia replied, "Why doesn't the big fish eat the little fish?" She had been cued by the picture of a large grouper having its mouth cleaned by a tiny fish.

"This is an excellent question. Let's write this question on our charts." Mrs. Barrett turned to the chalkboard and wrote the question, urging all students to write the same one on their questioning charts. It took a few minutes for them to finish. "Now, on our own, let's read pages 2 to 5, to answer this question."

After a couple of minutes, Carol inquired, "Can you answer your question?" "No," said Ananzia. Danielle responded, "Because a big fish wants his mouth clean." Mrs. Barrett asked, "Does it say this in the book?" "No," replied Danielle. Carol offered, "This is a good answer to our question, but we can't find it in the book. So, let's record on our charts that, yes, we can answer the question, but no, the answer is not in this book."

Carol concluded, "We have asked a good question about this book."

"I want to read the rest of the book," said Charlie.

"Let's keep going," added Danielle.

"We are finished for today," said Mrs. Barrett. "We will continue reading this book tomorrow. Let's go back to your teams now." This completed Day 1 of the simplified strategy instruction and Mrs. Barrett was pleased.

Two days later, on Day 3 of the questioning instruction, she took the next step with these students. She gathered the same group and directed their attention to pages 6 to 9 in the book *Living Together*. On this day, Mrs. Barrett wanted to step back from the strong direction and modeling she provided on Day 1. She decided to give the students an intermediate level of scaffolding for oral reading fluency and the development of their questioning.

Carol began, "Let's read pages 6 to 9 together," and she lead them reading aloud with "whisper voices."

> This little fish lives with this big, big fish. The little fish can clean this big, big mouth! Look at the crabs. The crabs live with the iguana. The crabs can clean the iguana's skin. This bird lives with this tortoise. The bird can clean the tortoise. This bird lives with this crocodile. The bird can clean the crocodile's back.

Carol asked pairs to read aloud. "Sienna and Ananzia, read page 6 for us and make it as *interesting* as you can," she said. They read, "This little fish lives with this big, big fish. The little fish can clean this big, big mouth!" They pounced on the "big, big" adjectives in both sentences. They smiled as they said the verb "clean" in the second sentence.

Carol asked the others, "What words did they say that made it sound interesting?"

"Big, big," offered Sienna.

"All of them," said Charlie.

"Yes, this was good reading," Mrs. Barrett observed.

"Charlie and Danielle, please read the next page," Carol requested. The students read aloud with improved expression. The other pair of students, Sienna and Ananzia, identified some of the appropriate words that gave meaning to this page. Carol continued this alternating process through the end of page 9.

"Now let's look at our bridge for questioning," Mrs. Barrett directed.

"Look at the title and pictures. What is this about?" "Helping other animals," offered Danielle.

"About being friendly," said Ananzia.

"Good, these are fine statements. Write your own statement on the chart," said Mrs. Barrett.

"Now, let's look at the first sentence of this section on page 6," said Carol. "This little fish lives with this big, big fish."

Write a question you might answer in this book or in this section. Each of you, think of your question and write it in the chart."

With determination, each student wrote the following questions:

- Danielle: What is the fish with the big mouth?
- Charlie: Why don't they get eaten?
- Ananzia: I want to know why they clean their backs.
- Sienna: Why would they eat their backs?

"Now let's read these pages and decide whether we can answer our questions," said Carol. The students decided that they could not answer their questions and they wanted to read further in the book to find more information.

"You have each asked your own very good question today. Tomorrow, we'll read to answer them. Let's return to our teams," said Mrs. Barrett, closing the session.

At a later point in October, Carol was maintaining her work with this group. Daily work was enabling them to begin to keep pace in learning strategies with the class. However, she feared that decreasing this differentiated instruction would be unwise for the students. In Week 4, she turned to summarizing.

On the first day, Carol modeled how to perform the summarizing process (see Appendix B: Summarizing). Although she had given this guideline to the rest of the class, these students were confused and unable to succeed with the directions she provided for the whole group. Sitting with the group in the corner, she opened by saying, "Let's look at our book on owls and turn to page 12." The text appeared as follows:

Owls

Owls are nocturnal hunters. This means they hunt at night. Owls eat grasshoppers, frogs, mice, rabbits, and moles. Some owls even eat skunks! During the day, owls sleep in nests, barns, or hollow trees.

Mrs. Barrett gave each student a photocopy of page 12.

"What is the main idea of this page? What is the one most important word on this page?" she asked.

"Owls," offered Danielle.

Charlie said, "Nocturnal is most important."

Sienna was following but had nothing to offer. Ananzia said, "Owls."

"Yes, Charlie," Mrs. Barrett said, "Owls are nocturnal, but the most important single idea is owls. Let's circle owls on this page with our pencils.

Now let's find important facts about owls. What are some important facts?"

"They are nocturnal," said Charlie.

Ananzia said, "They eat mice."

Danielle said, "They hunt at night and sleep in the day."

"We have lots of good ideas," said Mrs. Barrett. "Now let's underline 'nocturnal,' because that's a fact, and let's underline 'hunt at night.' We said 'eat' is an important fact. Let's underline eat. We said 'sleep' and 'day' are important facts, so let's underline those words." The students followed. "Now what is our summary of this page?

"Owls eat," said Ananzia.

"Owls are nocturnal birds," said Charlie.

"Owls are nocturnal birds. They hunt at night and sleep in the day," said Danielle.

Ananzia offered, "Owls hunt and eat other animals."

"Let's make a sentence with these ideas," said Mrs. Barrett. She turned to the chart board behind her and wrote: *Owls are nocturnal animals.* "This is what Charlie said," she noted. She continued. *Hunting at night and sleeping in the day.* "This is what Danielle said," she continued. *Eating other animals.* "This is what Ananzia and Sienna said. Now let's all write our summaries on our charts like we have it here." The students composed summaries, following Carol's model. After completing this, she asked them to step up to the board and read the sentence aloud, making it sound interesting. Most students emphasized *nocturnal* strongly. *Sleeping in the day* was read with inflection.

This activity showed that the students comprehended the passage fully. They could volunteer important words and concepts and they could read it with reasonable expression. Yet, their abilities to compose a summary were extremely limited. Mrs. Barrett's model on the board was necessary for all of these students. In the days following, they wrote summaries on their charts, on one page of text, with increasing comfort and confidence. Their sense of a summary was beginning to develop.

In Week 7, Mrs. Barrett provided instruction for combining the reading strategy of activating background knowledge with questioning for the whole class, and she continued this simplified strategy instruction for the struggling readers' group. She worked with the students using *How Birds Live* by Biddulph and Biddulph. They read a section on legs and feet, on pages 12–18. The first paragraph follows:

> You can tell a lot about birds by looking at their legs and feet. A bird's foot can tell us how it moves around, as well as where it lives or what it eats.

The next pages included the following paragraph:

> These feet all belong to perching birds. About two out of three birds sleep each night perching on a branch. Can you guess what birds these feet belong to? These feet all belong to birds of prey. These birds often use their feet to help them catch their food. Can you guess what birds these feet belong to? These feet all belong to birds that live by the water. Birds that wade in the water to catch their food have very long legs. Some water birds have webbed feet for paddling. Can you guess what birds these feet belong to?

The two previous paragraphs were accompanied by captioned illustrations. Two of these captions are as follows:

- The osprey has strong claws for grasping a fish. Its feet have rough pads so it can hold on to its slippery prey.
- Like many perching birds, the thrush has three toes in front and one toe behind.

Next, Carol said, "In one sentence, write one thing you know about this."

- Ananzia: "I know that they stick toenails in their food."
- Danielle: "All birds, big and little, have talons."
- Charlie: "Birds' feet are all different."

Mrs. Barrett continued, "You've all made a good sentence. Now, what question do you have that includes what you know? Think of what you just wrote about birds and put it in a question."

- Ananzia: "I really want to know whether they do stick their toes in their food."
- Danielle: "Do they catch fish with their talons?"

- Charlie: "How do they stay on branches?"

"Good questions," said Mrs. Barrett. "Now, on your own, read these pages we have looked at and think about your answer." The students all found that they could answer their questions with this text. Ananzia wrote her answer, "I found out that they do stick their toes in their food." Danielle recorded, "The osprey has strong claws for grasping a fish. Its feet have rough pads so it can hold on to its slippery prey." Charlie wrote, "Their claws touch into the trees so they won't fall."

Mrs. Barrett closed the session by asking the students to read their answers and to make the information sound interesting to others.

The students returned to their teams with a sense of reassurance about their reading and efficacy about their strategies. They had identified the topic of a text, recorded their background knowledge about it, and written a question. In some cases, this question made a small extension on their prior knowledge. Although some students copied the text verbatim, Mrs. Barrett accepted this as necessary to their success in using the strategy at this early stage. Students had composed an answer, based on the book, that satisfied themselves and their teacher. Their work had been substantially, although not totally, independent. The "bridge" had fostered their crossing. They had stepped onto fresh ground as strategy-users and successful text-comprehenders.

COMMENTARY ON THE VIGNETTE

With Carol's guidance, these students improved markedly in oral reading fluency. In the very first lesson, it was evident that they gained a sense of phrasing in their oral reading. They were able to say "little fish" and "big fish." Yet, their sentence structures were incomplete. On the third or fourth day of their fluency development in the questioning strategy, they gained a clear sense of sentence structures in their reading. They were able to say that the "little fish cleans the big, big fish." The subject–predicate relations became evident in their inflections and intonations. Verbs became the words that the other students noticed as carrying interest and meaning. Yet, even at this stage, students were operating at the level of individual sentences. These sentences did not necessarily merge into a total passage meaning.

By the time these students were in Week 7, they had benefited from more oral fluency and strategy instruction. While reading the passages on birds' feet in How Birds Live, they grasped passage-level meanings. Their abilities to identify main topics of paragraphs and distinguish them from supporting facts were well-formed, at least for these simple texts.

In 12 weeks, these students acquired the simplest forms of the cognitive strategies of activating background knowledge, questioning, summarizing, searching, and organizing graphically, and they began to merge these strategies. At each phase, improved oral fluency and text understanding enabled them to think at higher levels. With a strong text base, they formed the abstractions that are questions and summaries. Initially, the students were heavily dependent on a teacher model for writing a question, and not all succeeded. However, with substantial scaffolding, students improved in composing questions, summaries, and graphic organizers. This progress was sustained by the highly structured form of simplified strategy instruction. Carol gave them the limited texts, and "bridges" in the form of charts, to enable them to perform the reading strategies successfully. Some of the advancements were evident in their classwork. Danielle was transferring the strategies of summarizing to other texts in her projects. Charlie was using his questioning and searching skills gained in the simplified strategy instruction to contribute to his team projects. Ananzia and Sienna, more quietly, pursued their individual book writing within the CORI framework.

CONCLUSION

Simplified strategy instruction is provided when the teacher (a) selects a text used in expressive reading that is familiar and comfortable to students, (b) selects an amount of text that is manageable for a complete strategy instruction lesson, (c) uses a bridge to support strategy use (examples of bridges are given in Appendix B of this chapter), and (d) provides multiple opportunities for strategy learning to assure competence of the strategy for different types of texts, such as narrative and informational materials.

Resources for helping struggling readers are presented in Appendix A. Weeks 1–6 are devoted to the individual strategies of activating background knowledge, questioning, searching for information, summarizing, organizing graphically, and structuring stories. Weeks 7–12 are dedicated to combining the strategies in the following sequence: combining background knowledge and questioning, combining questioning with searching, structuring stories, combining searching and summarizing, combining reading strategies, and structuring stories.

APPENDIX 7.A: READING STRATEGIES AND RESOURCES

Week	Reading Strategy	Book Title	Monday	Tuesday	Wednesday	Thursday	Friday
1	Activating Background Knowledge	Owl at Home	Chapter 1	Chapter 2	Chapter 3	Chapter 4	Chapter 5
2	Questioning	Living Together	pp.2-5	pp.6-7	pp.8-9	pp.10-11	pp.12-14
3	Searching for Information	Eggs and Baby Birds	pp.2-5	pp.6-11	pp.12-15	pp.16-19	pp.20-24
4	Summarizing	These Birds Can't Fly	pp.3-6	pp.7-13	pp.14-17	pp.18-21	pp.22-29
5	Organizing Graphically	How Birds Live	pp.2-4	pp.5-11	pp.12-18	pp.19-22	pp.23-24
6	Structuring Story	Dance My Dance	pp.2-5	pp.6-9	pp.10-11	pp.12-13	pp.14-16
7	Combining Background Knowledge and Questioning	Life in a Pond	pp.3-8	pp.10-12	pp.13-16	pp.17-21	pp.22-28
8	Combining Questioning with Searching	How Do Fish Live?	pp.2-5	pp.6-9	pp.10-14	pp.15-19	pp.20-23
9	Structuring Story	Newt	pp.9-14	pp.16-20	pp.23-27	pp.29-36	pp.39-48
10	Combining Searching and Summarizing	Turtles	pp.5-7	pp.8-11	pp.12-15	pp.16-19	pp.20-22
11	Combining Reading Strategies	Fishes	pp.5-11	pp.12-19	pp.20-29	pp.30-33	pp.34-42
12	Structuring Story	Crocodile's Bag	pp.2-7	pp.8-12	pp.13-17	pp.19-21	pp.22-end

Instructional Practices

Instruction	Monday	Tuesday	Wednesday	Thursday	Friday
Expressive Reading Activity	Teacher reads aloud with students. Each student pair rereads.	Teacher reads aloud with students. Each student pair rereads.	Teacher reads aloud with students. Student pairs reread aloud. Alternate whole group, pairs, and individuals. Others comment on expressiveness of readers. Use diverse requests for comment, as appropriate.	Teacher reads aloud with students. Student pairs reread aloud. Alternate whole group, pairs, and individuals. Others comment on expressiveness of readers. Use diverse requests for comment, as appropriate.	Teacher reads aloud with students. Each student pair rereads. Use **Diverse Requests for Comment** on bottom half of list.
Simplified Strategy Instruction	Teacher models-students complete a chart.	Teacher highly scaffolds students working individually. Each student completes a chart.	Student pairs work to complete one chart as teacher provides moderate scaffold. Each student completes a chart.	Students work individually with low scaffolding (teacher support) to complete one chart. Each student completes a chart.	Teacher encourages individuals to work independently. Each student completes a chart.

Diverse Requests for Comment

1. What word made it interesting?
2. Name 2 words he or she said together that made it expressive.
3. Where did he or she read the *slowest*, and how did this make it good?
4. What words did he or she say the *loudest,* and how did that make you feel?
5. What did his or her reading make you feel like?
6. Could you make this sentence (or passage) *sound* different, and how would you do it?
7. Could you give this a slightly different *meaning* by reading it aloud differently, and how would you do it?
8. What is the listener supposed to think this means, and how did the reading help?
9. Can you read this so it sounds much more *boring* than he or she did, and how would you do it?
10. Could this (sentence) have a very different meaning from the one you just heard, and how would you read it to give it the new meaning?

APPENDIX 7.B: READING CHARTS FOR STRUGGLING READERS

Week 2 - Bridge for Questioning

Name _____

1. Look at the title, headings and pictures in the chapter or section.
2. It is about _____
3. Read the first sentence of this section. Write a question you might answer in this book or in this section.

_____

4. Reread the pages you read today.
5. Can you answer your question? YES NO
6. Was your answer in the book? YES NO
7. If you have an answer, discuss it in your group.

Week 4 - Summarizing

Name _____

1. Look at the first page in this book, or section. (Your teacher will supply a photocopy of one page or show pages on overhead.)

2. With your pencil, circle the main idea on this page. Circle 1–3 key words in one sentence.
3. Underline 2–3 supporting facts for this main idea. The 2–3 key words should be in different sentences.
4. Use your circled and underlined words to say a summary out loud.
5. Write your summary here.

_____

_____

_____

_____

APPENDIX 7.C: CHARACTERISTICS OF TEXTS FOR STRUGGLING READERS IN CORI

Struggling Reader Book Titles	Type*	Number of pages	Average sentences per page	Average words per sentence	Average words per page	Average illustrations per page	Average letters per word	Number of access features
These Birds Can't Fly	I	27	1.56	9.4	14.63	0.89	4.38	3
Turtles	I	19	2.84	10.4	29.7	0.53	4.77	7
Eggs and Baby Birds	I	23	2.39	10.49	25.1	2.13	4.11	5
Fishes	I	40	3.3	10.73	44.25	0.7	4.22	6
How Birds Live	I	23	2.61	9.02	23.52	1	4.22	5
How Do Fish Live?	I	23	3.74	9.17	34.3	1.35	4.1	4
Life in a Pond	I	27	1.41	10.39	14.63	0.93	4.2	3
Living Together	I	13	1.77	7.22	12.77	1.23	4.24	2
Owl at Home	L	61	3.13	12.06	37.8	0.87	2.42	3
Newt	L	41	2.45	7.74	19	1.18	3.99	3
Crocodile's Bag	L	29	8.4	3.76	31.6	0.8	3.79	4
Dance My Dance	L	15	3.8	10.19	38.7	1	4.26	1

* I = Information; L = Literary

REFERENCES

Clay, M. M., & Imlach, R. H. (1971). Juncture, pitch, and stress as reading behavior variables. *Journal of Verbal Learning and Verbal Behavior, 10*, 133–139.

Gersten, R., Fuchs, L. S., & Williams, J. P. (2001). Teaching reading comprehension strategies to students with learning disabilities: A review of research. *Review of Educational Research, 71*(2), 279–320.

Hiebert, E. H., & Fisher, C. W. (2002). *Text matters in developing fluent reading.* Manuscript submitted for publication.

Kuhn, M. R., & Stahl, S. A. (2002). *Fluency: A review of developmental and remedial practices.* Retrieved January 2, 2002, from *http://www.ciera.org/library/reports/inquiry-2/2-008/2-008.html*

LaBerge, D., & Samuels, S. J. (1974). Toward a theory of automatic information processing in reading. *Cognitive Psychology, 6*, 293–323.

National Reading Panel (2000). *Teaching children to read: An evidence-based assessment of the scientific research literature on reading and its implications for reading instruction* (NIH Pub. No. 00–4769). Jessup, MD: National Institute for Literacy.

Palmer, B. M., Codling, R. M., & Gambrell, L. B. (1994). In their own words: What elementary students have to say about motivation to read. *The Reading Teacher, 48*, 176–178.

Reutzel, D. R., & Hollingsworth, P. M. (1993). Effects of fluency training on second graders' reading comprehension. *Journal of Educational Research, 86*, 325–331.

Samuels, S. J., (1979). The method of repeated readings. *The Reading Teacher, 32*, 403–408.

Samuels, S. J., LaBerge, D., & Bremer, C. (1978). Units of word recognition: Evidence for developmental changes. *Journal of Verbal Learning and Verbal Behavior, 17*, 715–720.

Schreiber, P. A. (1987). Prosody and structure in children's syntactic processing. In R. Horowitz & S. J. Samuels (Eds.), *Comprehending oral and written language.* New York: Academic Press.

Simmons, D. C., Fuchs, L. S., Fuchs, D., Mathes, P., & Hodge, J. P. (1995). Effects of explicit teaching and peer tutoring on the reading achievement of learning-disabled and low-performing students in regular classrooms. *Elementary School Journal, 5*, 135–144.

Stahl, S. A., & Heubach, K. (in press). Fluency oriented reading instruction. *Elementary School Journal.*

Strickland, D. S., Ganske, K., & Monroe, J. K. (2002). *Supporting struggling readers and writers: Strategies for classroom intervention 3–6.* Newark, DE: International Reading Association.

Worthy, J., & Broaddus, K. (2002). Fluency beyond the primary grades: From group performance to silent, independent reading. *The Reading Teacher, 55*(4), 334–343.

CHILDREN'S BOOK REFERENCES

Biddulph, F., & Biddulph, J. (undated). *How birds live.* Bothell, WA: Wright Group.

Windsor, J. (1999). *Living together.* Barrington, IL: Rigby.

8

Inside Mrs. O'Hara's CORI Classroom

Melissa P. Sikorski
Montgomery County Public Schools, Maryland

This chapter portrays Janice O'Hara's third-grade classroom. In a case study based on extensive videotapes, observations, and personal interviews with the teacher and students, the major principles of CORI are illustrated. Two students at different instructional levels are featured to demonstrate the adaptations of CORI and the growth of students with varying ability levels.

The third-grade classroom of Janice O'Hara in Frederick, Maryland, is located in a middle to lower income neighborhood in a semirural town. Janice has been teaching more than 11 years and holds a Master's degree in reading. She began teaching CORI in her classroom after attending a 2-week summer workshop. Although she is implementing the complete 12-week CORI framework, this chapter focuses on the second unit, "Survival in Freshwater Habitats." Each 6-week unit follows the frame of *Observe and Personalize, Search and Retrieve, Comprehend and Integrate,* and *Communicate to Others,* which provides the organization for this chapter. Janice is revisiting, and beginning to teach the students to combine, the reading comprehension strategies of activating background knowledge, questioning, searching for information, summarizing, organizing graphically, and structuring stories.

Reading levels of the students in this classroom range from preprimer to fourth grade. Such diversity requires Janice to structure her teaching in ways to make the material accessible to all students. Her instruction includes a great deal of scaffolding, grouping, and the use of diverse texts ranging from Grades 1–6 in reading difficulty.

The atmosphere of the classroom is very warm and inviting. As you enter Mrs. O'Hara's room, you are immediately immersed in a literate, print-rich environment. On the right are three large bookshelves chocked full of books, both fiction and nonfiction, for the students to enjoy. Across the room is yet another bookshelf, along with a standing rack filled with even more books. All of these selections are physically accessible to the students. The books have been coded and labeled according to reading level with a sticker on the spine of each book.

OPENING THE UNIT

Janice has launched the aquatic unit and the room reflects this. Located in various places around the room are aquaria housing aquatic life. Frederick, the classroom water frog, can be found in one aquarium. In others, you will see plant life, goldfish, guppies, tadpoles, snails, and predatory bugs. The aquatic life in the room is not only attractive, but also helps bring the core concepts to life for the students. Predation is present as Frederick stalks his prey, an unsuspecting cricket. Goldfish and guppies glide through their habitat, bringing the concept of locomotion into perspective.

Janice and her students are reading books that tie in with this unit. *Pond Year* by Kathryn Lasky is a favorite. It depicts the changes and interactions in a pond over the course of one year. This book has students thinking deeply about the habitat of a pond. They are generating questions, and their curiosities have been sparked as they read and discuss the book. Janice introduces nine of the core ecological concepts including eating, locomotion, reproduction, competition, respiration, communication, predation, defense, and adaptation to habitat. These are the knowledge goals for the unit. With these terms, students discuss interactions of the animals and plants found in the pond habitat. The students' interests are building along with their background knowledge as they begin to explore aquatic life. The class is also reading fiction, such as *Junie B. Jones Smells Something Fishy* by B. Park.

Observe and Personalize: Using Hands-on Science to Initiate Reading

In preparation for the aquatic unit, it is necessary for students to activate their background knowledge about ponds and pond life. Mrs. O'Hara asks students to think about what they already know about ponds and which organisms might live near ponds. Students had the opportunity to observe and personalize the topic through a visit to Fountain Rock Park. On this trip, the class observed aquatic life in a natural habitat. Following the field trip, the students were asked what they learned about ponds. Mrs. O'Hara commented in her journal about the experience. It was a beginning and helped the students think about what they already knew. Images of this visit were constantly shared in group discussion—"Remember our pond visit."

The class further explored pond life with an activity consisting of a hands-on science investigation. After dividing into cooperative groups, each group set up a pond life aquarium complete with snails, guppies, daphnia, dragonfly nymphs, and aquatic plants. They asked questions about how the different organisms move through the water. What did they eat? How do they protect themselves? The students posted their favorite questions on sentence strips and wrote more in their CORI journals. The core concepts helped the students ask a wide variety of questions about the organisms and their interactions with each other and their habitat.

Students observed the interaction of the organisms over a two-day period, seeking answers to their questions. While finding answers for many of their questions, they continued asking additional ones. They began generating questions about predator–prey relationships. Mrs. O'Hara's questioning instruction aided learners in improving their reading comprehension strategy. Simultaneously, this teaching gave students choices about what they wanted to learn and read within the theme.

Then came the time for the investigation. What would happen if a giant diving bug were introduced into the environment? What would it eat, plants or other animals? Students made predictions. Most students predicted that the beetle would eat plants. One kind of animal at a time was placed with the giant diving beetle. The discovery was that the diving beetle had quite a voracious appetite! It was definitely a carnivorous creature, consuming the animal species but none of the plants. The students recorded the results on a histogram. They drew diagrams of their observations and worked together to communicate information about the experiment. The diving beetle experiment allowed the students to observe and personalize aquatic life. It fed their appetites to learn and read more about the topic. They are now ready to investigate through reading.

Search and Retrieve: Learning How to Locate Information

Janice O'Hara prepares her class to search for information about key concepts connected to aquatic life. Her students are gathered on the floor in the front of the classroom. On the board is a large graphic organizer divided into columns, along with icons depicting eight of the CORI core concepts: feeding, respiration, predation, locomotion, defense, communication, competition, and reproduction. Located on the floor, for easy student access, are bins of books for the students to explore on their upcoming information search on aquatic life. Janice makes sure that each student has at least one book in his hands as she prepares for instruction.

"Let's say that Mrs. O'Hara has given you the task of finding something about feeding in your book. You have to find out about how this animal eats. Where am I going to find this information?" Students respond, "In the book."

"Ok, so let's say I'm going to look for information. In this book, I want to find out what the chameleon eats and I have to read every page until I get to it, right?" Janice turns the pages slowly, modeling an ineffective method of searching for information in the text by turning page after page. "Is this how I find out?" she asks.

"No," replies Erin, "Go to the table of contents."

"Let's try Erin's idea and go to the table of contents and see if we can find anything about feeding." Mrs. O'Hara turns to the table of contents in her book about chameleons.

"Mine says what they eat. So, I can put the word *eat*, that's another word I could use for feeding, *eat*." Janice writes the word *eat* on the class chart under the heading *Feeding*.

"Is there another place in the book, besides the table of contents, to find information or look for words about feeding? Justin, how else could I find out about what they eat, what their feeding is?" Justin suggests asking someone else for the information.

Janice redirects students back to the features of the book. "Now I'm looking at my book. Is there another place in my book that has information organized, other than the table of contents? I found the table of contents, it told me the word *eat*. Where else can I find some information?"

Rebecca replies, "In the index."

"Where is the index located, Rebecca?" asks Mrs. O'Hara.

Rebecca answers, "In the back of the book."

"Ok, everyone find the back of your book," directs Mrs. O'Hara.

The index has now become a tool for locating information. Students are eagerly searching through their books, looking in the index for key words about the survival concepts. They share their findings with each other as the searching continues. As the students locate information, they are encouraged to share their findings, and Mrs. O'Hara adds the information to the class chart. Finding synonyms for concepts such as eating for feeding and fighting for defense, makes difficult concepts more meaningful and accessible to these young learners. Cody finds the word *oxygen* in his search. "What (concept) would I put that word under?" asks Mrs. O'Hara.

Cody replies, "Respiration."

Mrs. O'Hara records the word *oxygen* in the column titled *Respiration*.

The chart is well on the way to completion, with students diligently searching through text for words related to the key concepts, a key word search. As we look at this group, it is evident that students are engaged. Cody is looking through the index of his book for key words related to the core concepts. His classmates also refer to the proper sections of their books in search of pertinent information.

Janice prepares her students for more independent practice in searching for information, paired with questioning. The class has become quite competent at generating questions. "What are you going to be doing as you return to your seats today? You are going to be identifying two questions about the animals you have chosen, and then I want you to think of the key terms you are going to need in order to look up the information. You need to have key terms." Mrs. O'Hara gives an example. "Not just this word, communication, because you might not be able to find it under communication. You might need to look under a different word. You need at least two terms that you could look under to find out more about it." Janice moves on to the next part of instruction once she is confident that the students have the gist about searching and retrieving information in text. She clarifies directions for the task students will be working on at their seats, related to the morning's lesson.

As evidenced in this vignette, Janice O'Hara has prepared these engaged young learners to complete research on their own. She has modeled the importance of text and appropriate features for locating information. Janice has involved all of her students in the process of searching for information and simultaneously activated and connected the students' background knowledge to new and somewhat difficult concepts.

She has enabled students to combine the strategy of questioning with the strategy of searching for answers to their own questions. Along the way, she has motivated these learners by providing limited choices and praising students' involvement in the lesson. She has prompted students' thinking by posing questions to them, encouraging them to problem-solve on their own, as opposed to simply providing information. Prompting is prominent in this classroom as a means to get the children involved in their own learning. Students believe in themselves and in their abilities as active learners who question, read, and discuss. Teacher and classmates value their questions and ideas.

Activating Background Knowledge, Questioning, and Searching for Struggling Readers

While the majority of the class is engaged in generating questions and searching to find the answers, small reading groups are pulled together for more explicit instruction. Mrs. O'Hara meets with one of her reading groups at the reading table in the back of the room. A group of seven students is seated at the table, each with a copy of *Is It a Fish?* by Brian and Jillian Cutting. This Level 2 text, replete with photographs, illustrations, captions, table of contents, and index, is appropriate for the task at hand. The amount of print is manageable for the struggling reader, while rich with information. It contains many features of the "interesting text."

This small group instruction is based on the needs of the individual students who require more instructional scaffolding than others in the class. Janice explains that the group will be reading to find information about the core concepts, thus setting a purpose for reading. Core concept icons are posted for student reference. Janice reviews the concepts and explains that as the students read, they will be adding information about the concepts to their graphic organizers.

This group of seven students is seated in a circle at the reading table. In the center of the table is an aquarium, which houses Frederick, the class water frog. Next to the reading table is another aquarium with goldfish. As the group comes together, students are engaged in a discussion about the class frog. They are talking about how the frog hides as a means of defense, and also in preparation for feeding. They have determined that if the crickets cannot see the frog, it will be easier for him to catch his unsuspecting dinner.

Mrs. O'Hara tells the seven students that today they will be reading about fish. She asks them what they know about fish, as she nonchalantly gestures toward the aquarium of goldfish. Students share verbal responses such as: "Fish use their fins to swim through the water." "They sometimes hide behind rocks to avoid being eaten by other fish."

Next, she asks her students to take a quick picture walk through the book they will be reading, *What Is a Fish?* by Bobbie Kalman. This text is a bit more difficult than *Is It a Fish?* used by the previous group. The reading level of *What Is a Fish?* is higher, maintaining the features necessary for successful searching. As the teacher prepares her students for reading, she asks them to think about what they already know about fish and to connect that background knowledge to the core concepts in order to generate ideas and questions. The students glance at the core concept icons posted on the wall to refresh their memories and trigger their thinking. One student asks, "Why are fish in a different group than reptiles?" Another student replies to that query by stating, "Fish have gills, fish can't live on land."

Mrs. O'Hara again encourages the students to think about what they would like to know about fish. Each student writes questions on individual graphic organizers. This extensive set-up and modeling is important for struggling readers. Accessing background knowledge and getting the students focused on their upcoming reading topic is necessary for greater comprehension. The students know they will be reading more about fish and adding to their knowledge base on the subject. The stage is set for them to begin reading.

The group now begins choral reading from *What Is a Fish?* After reading one page, Mrs. O'Hara asks, "What do you notice?" as she has the students refer to the photo illustrations in the book. One of the group members recalls the recent class trip to the National Aquarium in Baltimore when noticing that the fish pictured was a species they observed there. The group continues reading, stopping frequently to discuss the new information, and to make connections to the core concepts. As Mrs. O'Hara guides the students, she poses questions such as, "What is the defense for this fish?" The students reexamine the text to locate the information that fish hide for defense. Janice encourages and extends this by prompting them to use search strategies. This choral reading improves oral reading fluency for the specific text being read. As a result, students comprehend those pages more fully and gain deeper concepts from the text.

As core concepts are unveiled through reading, the students record the information on their graphic organizers. A graphic organizer is a table to structure their new knowledge gained from texts. Mrs. O'Hara monitors the members of the group, giving guidance and assistance as needed. She does this by posing questions to guide students' thinking. After a student shares that she discovered that fish like to swim in rocky areas, Janice might pose questions such as, "Why do you think a fish might do that? What concept do you think that would fit with?" Throughout the small group discussion and reading, the students referred to their aquarium visit as a point of personal reference.

The extra scaffolding that Janice provides in her small group instruction, such as providing individual graphic organizers and guiding the students in their reading and search for information, helps these students on their road to becoming independent readers and self-directed learners. The students are beginning to initiate their own questions. Janice has helped foster this growth of questioning through her encouragement. Instead of providing answers to questions, Janice promotes independent thinking by posing additional questions to foster further inquiry.

Adjusting Instructional Scaffolding to Meet Student Needs. The next small group that Mrs. O'Hara met with was reading about snails in the text, *How Snails Live* by C. Brough, rich with photographs, as well as cartoon-type illustrations. The text has a table of contents and index, as well as subheadings throughout. *How Snails Live* is an appropriate text for the level of readers in this group and is well-suited for the focus of searching for information. It contains the necessary components for the instructional purposes. The members of this group do not need quite as much instructional scaffolding as the previous group. They are reading at a higher level and are more confident readers. The group is using the table of contents and the index to locate information. Mrs. O'Hara uses "thinking aloud" to explain the use of the table of contents and index for locating information. She models searching for concepts, using actual core concept words like respiration, as well as synonyms such as breathing, which are found in the index.

This snail book includes some cartoon illustrations, one depicting a snail pulling a dump truck. Janice says that sometimes illustrations can distract you from finding the information you are seeking. Although a snail can move things heavier than itself, it really cannot pull a truck. The group begins choral reading. One student stops to reread a sentence to the group, "Snails can burrow under things." The student comments, "I wish that word *burrow* was dark." Mrs. O'Hara asks her to explain what she means. The young reader explains that she thinks that *burrow* is important, so it should be in **bold print**. The teacher responds by saying "Isn't it fun to find those words? Why don't you circle it (on your paper) so you know it's important." The student has shown that she understands the importance of **bold print**, and the teacher has made this young learner feel that her thoughts and opinions as a reader are important.

As the group continues reading about snails, the students come across the claim that snails can carry 12 times their body weight. One of the boys in the group finds this totally unbelievable and cannot imagine how much weight that would be. Janice responds, "Let's get a scale and weigh one of our snails so we can see what types of things he might be able to move in our room."

Mrs. O'Hara embraces the student interest generated from reading the text and encourages that interest by promoting further inquiry. The interest the students have in aquatic life is a great benefit for independent inquiry on their chosen topic. They are hungry for information and motivated to find answers to their questions.

Comprehend and Integrate: Understanding and Organizing Information From Multiple Texts.   Mrs. O'Hara's students have been learning to search and retrieve information from text effectively and to ask their own questions on self-selected topics. They are ready to begin their projects on their chosen aquatic animals now that they know how and where to find information from text. In order to get acquainted with the pond biome and aquatic life, students constructed food webs (Fig. 8.1) and observed pond life in the classroom. They are now ready to deepen their understanding of the ecological concepts.

Figure 1
Name <u>Rebecca</u>   Date <u>November 27, 2001</u>

Pond Life: Food Webs I can find

Plant Eaters: herbivores	Animal Eaters: carnivores	Plant and animal eaters: Omnivores
snails	frog	raccon ducks
muskrats	snake	insects nypmphs crayfish
turtles	snakes	small fish
waterflea daphnia	ginat diving beetle	fish
water insects	newts	mallard ducks
		water strider

Draw a picture of a food web from what you know about each of the animals in our pond biome. Use as many animals as possible in your web to show what happens in nature. Use arrows to show what food goes into which animal's ➡ stomach.

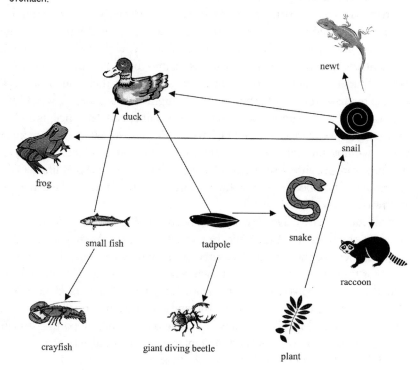

FIG. 8.1.

To begin, students were given a choice of which aquatic animal they want to learn about. They have identified the correct classification of their animal by determining specific characteristics. Is their animal a mammal or aquatic bird? Perhaps it is a reptile or amphibian. Still others may be preparing to read about fish or spineless animals. It is each student's job to determine the classification of one aquatic animal.

Mrs. O'Hara has prepared the class by teaching the characteristics of each of these animal classifications. Using direct, whole group instruction, as well as guided practice, she enables students to work in small groups to identify animal classifications. Janice has designed a graphic organizer to use in the search for information (see Fig. 8.2). The organizer gives the students a framework, making what could be a frustrating and insurmountable task manageable and accessible to students of varying ability levels.

In preparation, the students have not only been given the task of searching for and retrieving information about the core concepts associated with their animals, they have also identified their personal questions. Now they are ready for independent work. There are ample resources around the room, such as posters and books. Students begin their quest for information about their aquatic animals.

The reading strategy of summarizing is taught in this context. Mrs. O'Hara begins with one paragraph, modeling how to identify central concepts and supporting facts, or evidence. She helps the students distinguish high-important from low-important information, at the paragraph level. Students practice writing short, two- or three- sentence summaries. These become building blocks in the students' notebooks and graphic organizers, as they learn all the concepts of freshwater aquatic survival.

Students in Mrs. O'Hara's class have been working conscientiously over the course of the week, reading about their aquatic animals. As they work on their projects, they use the available resources in a confident manner. It is commonplace for them to be up and out of their seats, gathering appropriate resources from the multiple bins of books on aquatic life, such as *Pond Life* by G. K. Reid. They are confidently searching and retrieving information using the table of contents and indices. Mrs. O'Hara acts as a guide on the side, supporting students' use of strategies, as needed. As pertinent information is found, it is recorded in the proper location on individual animal classification charts (Fig. 8.3).

These charts containing valuable information are taking shape nicely. Students' notes reveal the depth of their learning about how the aquatic animals defend themselves, how each creature moves through its habitat, how it obtains food, and how it survives. All of this knowledge prepares these learners for the

Figure 2

Name _____ Date _____

Organizing My Information by Core Concepts
Name of the Animal:_____

Core Concepts	Information I learned about this animal
 **Feeding**	
 **Locomotion**	
 **Defense**	
 **Competition**	

FIG. 8.2. Animal classification chart.

(continued on next page)

Reproduction	
Predation	
Communication	
Respiration	

Fig. 8.2.   (continued)

next phase of their work, an authentic piece of writing that will showcase much of the valuable information the students are gathering.

Communicating to Others

Throughout the unit on aquatic animals, Mrs. O'Hara has been sharing stories by author Joanne Ryder. Her stories depict the life of an animal in a format where the reader actually awakens as a particular species and spends a day in the life of the creature. Although these beautiful stories are works of fiction, the factual information about each creature is accurate. Mrs. O'Hara's students will be writing similar stories about their aquatic animals.

The class is gathered on the floor in preparation for a "read-aloud" of Joanne Ryder's book, *The Sea Elf*, a story about a sea otter. Mrs. O'Hara opens by saying,

Animal Classification Chart

	Mammal	Reptile	Amphibian	Aquatic Bird	Crustaceans, mollusks, insects	Fish
Definition: What are they?	Raccoon Beaver Mouse Opossum Weasel	Turtle Crocodile Snake	Lizards Frogs	Duck Swan Goose Crane	Beetle	Goldfish
Examples of animals (pictures)						
Breathing	lungs					
Backbones (vertebrae)	yes					
Body Temperature	Warm blooded					
Reproduction	Live birth					
Primary means of locomotion	Walk, jump, run					

FIG. 8.3. Animal classification chart.

"What the person did first, in order to write this story, was to do an actual investigation, just like you did. In the front of the book, it tells me information about the investigation that was done." The teacher shares the information in the beginning of the book, stressing the importance of the accuracy of information contained within. Mrs. O'Hara acknowledges the students' hard work investigating their creatures in preparation for writing their own Joanne Ryder-style stories. She explains to her students that this will not really be a fictional story; it will be an informational story where they become the animal.

"You are changing places for one day; you are becoming the animal. What would you do if you were that animal? But you had to know the animal first, didn't you. You had to do a lot of reading. The same thing happened in *Lizard in the Sun* [another Joanne Ryder selection the class has read]."

Mrs. O'Hara explains that the information in the lizard story is also accurate.

"Each of you will have created a teaching story when you are finished, one that will teach us about your animal and the habitat in which it lives. That's an important fact to remember. First, I'm going to read the story again to you because I think it's important for you to see the flow of it. Then, we are going to start writing the first paragraph, using the information packets you have made."

She directs the students to pay close attention to how the author describes the sea otter in the story.

Teaching Story Structure and Organization

Mrs. O'Hara begins reading *The Sea Elf* aloud, pausing to think aloud as she exclaims, "Do you get a picture in your head of this animal floating in the seaweed? I can just feel it." The teacher is very animated while reading and thinking aloud, mimicking how this otter would be bobbing up and down as it travels slowly, peacefully through its water habitat. She bobs back and forth as the otter would.

As they read, children are guided in filling out a "story chart" that includes characters, setting, and problem (goals, events [plot], and ending/resolution). They discuss how these story elements fit together. As she reads, Mrs. O'Hara notices information pertinent to concepts of survival, pausing to acknowledge important factual information about feeding practices of the otter and to visualize the content of the book.

As the story comes to a close, Mrs. O'Hara comments that the reader has just experienced what it would be like to be an otter for a day. She reviews the format of the story the children will begin writing and refers to the text about lizards, pointing out information about how it moves, its locomotion. Mrs. O'Hara encourages her students to include information in their stories about each of the core concepts, just as Joanne Ryder did in her stories. She points out details in the story about mating calls, other animals present in the habitat, and competition for food. Mrs. O'Hara encourages the students to use these concepts in their stories. As the teacher further prepares her students for their writing, she asks them to close their eyes and visualize their animals. She asks, "What do you look like? Describe yourself." From this point, Mrs. O'Hara takes her students to the next step. She begins guiding these student authors.

The Writing Process for a Factual Narrative.   The children return to their seats and prepare to write, but the teacher does not abandon them. She guides them through the writing process by modeling. Again, Mrs. O'Hara has developed a framework for writing a factual narrative. Each student has a story frame from which to work. This organizer breaks down the large task of writing an entire story into manageable paragraphs (Fig. 8.4). For each paragraph, there is a reminder of the type of information and core concepts that should be included. One student's story is embedded in this framework for illustration, but cues are not included for the students.

Writing a Factual Narrative

1. Opening Paragraph (Describe yourself waking up in the morning in your warm bed.)

> *I see the sun and I wake up and stretch and rub my eyes and I look at my self and see that I am a sea otter. My pups are laying on my tummy, warm and soft in the sea with other animals around me and the sun is on me.*

2. Description Paragraph (Describe yourself as the animal you researched for your report. What do you look like?)

> *I am brown soft and smooth. I have four legs. I am wrapped up in kelp laying on the sea with the sun shining on me and my fur is warm and cozy. My fur is toasty like a quilt. I am 14 kilograms and 30 pounds.*

3. Locomotion and Respiration Paragraph (Begin to move from your cozy bed to tell the reader about your biome, or home. What does it look like in your animal's environment? Help the reader see it through your words and description what you are doing each day and how are you breathing.)

> *I am moving in the sea with the sun on me and my pups are on my tummy and I am floating in the sea with the seagulls flying above me. I breathe with my nose and mouth.*

4. Biome Paragraph (Continue to describe what it looks like when you are in your animal's world. Tell about the other animals that live in the same place and what they are doing.)

> *I live in the sea with my pups with me by my side all the time in the sea so they won't be dinner for an eagle. I see red urchins and fish to eat. The fish are swimming in the beautiful sea and red urchins laying there.*

5. Feeding Paragraph (Tell how your animal gets its food. Describe how it catches the food and what it is eating for this meal.)

> *When I stop moving I was hungry so I was hunting. I found some good crabs. It tried to get out of my paw. I still hang on. My pups want it so I get some pieces of the crab and give it to them so they can eat and they were stuffed.*

6. Predator and Defense Paragraph (Describe the predator who comes near your animal and what defenses would it use to protect itself)

> *When me and my pups were done we saw a big fish that was trying to get me and my pups but we swim across the sea and got on land with my pups. There was one missing it was right by the big fish but a male otter got him before the big fish could eat him and put him on land.*

FIG. 8.4. Writing a factual narrative.

(continued on next page)

7. Reproduction and Communication Paragraph (Describe yourself as either the adult animal or the baby animal of your species. What are you doing? Are you caring for young babies, or playing with other animals like you? Describe how you communicate to other animals.)

> *We said do you want to come over our house for dinner he said ok. Then we ate and ate. My pups said you can come tomorrow. He said no. He said I will come back another day. We want and want and want but he never came back.*

8. Competition Paragraph (How do you compete with other animals in your environment? Are you fighting for food or for space to live? Are you competing to see who can build the best home, or dig the best tunnel? Everyone likes to be good at what they are doing. Describe yourself as your animal competing with others in the environment.)

> *Then another female otter came and we both saw food. I told my mate to watch the pups.*
> *We both swam for the five red urchins. The otter missed. I got the five red urchins. The other otter swam away. I gave the urchins to my pups they needed help opening them. I helped them open them.*

9. The End of the Day Conclusion (Describe your animal in the evening as the sun goes down. Bring your animal back to your bedroom where you become yourself again.)

> *Then I was asleep in my warm soft cuddle bed and I was dreaming that I was a female otter with my pups with the sun on me and I am back to my normal self again.*

FIG. 8.4.   (*continued*)

Janice commented in her journal that the organizer was used to guide students in writing a factual narrative about their particular pond animal. Each paragraph was isolated to help reinforce separateness of idea or core concept.

Once the students are settled at their desks with their collected information at hand, Janice uses the overhead projector to model how she would begin writing an opening paragraph. The opening paragraph is focused on a description of the writer, waking as the animal. Again, Mrs. O'Hara has the students visualize themselves as they wake up in the morning. She thinks aloud as she begins her example paragraph. "I roll over in my cozy bed and begin to stretch. As I rub my eyes, I realize I am a guppy, swimming freely in the pond."

The opening sentences are written on the overhead for the students to view. Janice explains that this is the format for information that should be shared in the opening paragraph. It should be clear that the person telling the story is actually waking up as an animal in the animal's habitat, just as in Joanne Ryder's stories. The students then begin writing their own opening paragraphs as Mrs. O'Hara circulates around the room, providing assistance as needed. She guides through questioning and prompts thinking. She makes suggestions, such as deciding whether the animals are adults or babies, because this will have an effect on the information.

As the students work on their stories, many of them take their papers to the teacher for reassurance that they are on the right track. Janice not only gives the students individual feedback, she asks their permission to share what they have written thus far with the class. Jessica permits Mrs. O'Hara to share what she has written about her frog. Janice captures the attention of the class, which is very interested to hear Jessica's story opening. Janice reads the student sample aloud. "I wake up in my room in my soft bed and I stretch my arms out wide. As I stretch my arms, I realize that I am not me; I am a frog with my tadpoles in the pond. I am on a lily pad in the nice, warm sun." Janice follows the reading by pointing out the elements Jessica has included. "She has already taken us from her bed, tells us that she is an adult with baby tadpoles in the pond, and she is sitting on a lily pad." Students who are at this point in their writing are encouraged to think about and begin writing the next portion of their story, which is a self-description. Jessica returns to her seat, happy with her progress as a writer.

As writing continues, other students are anxious to have their story beginnings shared. Sereen is writing about an angelfish. She has added a twist to her writing by making her story rhyme. Mrs. O'Hara comments to Sereen, "You made your fish much better than my fish." Mrs. O'Hara says to the class, "Sereen is doing hers on angelfish and she made hers sound much nicer than mine. Can I read it to you? She says, 'I rub my eyes in my fluffy, cozy bed.' Oh, I like her bed much better than mine. Mine wasn't fluffy and cozy." She continues with Sereen's story, "and I begin to stretch my hands and when I rub my eyes, I realize that I was not me, I was an angel fish, swimming in the sea while the sun was shining on me." The class responds enthusiastically, "That rhymes!" The teacher continues by pointing out the detail in Sereen's story. "She wasn't just swimming; she has the sun shining on her. I can see glistening, sparkling water. Can you see that? She has described that for me. She is now ready to describe what she looks like in her second paragraph." Sereen returns to her seat to continue writing. She takes a moment to reread what she has written so far and then begins thinking about her next paragraph.

The classroom is abuzz with activity. The students are working on their stories, referring to their notebooks as well as to the text available to them. Their goal on this day is to finish the first two paragraphs. Mrs. O'Hara circulates among the children to assure that they are on task and have the materials they need, assisting individual students as necessary.

To write paragraph two, a physical description of their animal, students are encouraged to revisit the books they used. Many of the students scurry to retrieve their books from the bins in the front of the room, while others remain at their seats, engrossed in their writing. Students in search of books locate them very quickly because the books are organized in bins, according to animal classification. This organization not only makes materials accessible, it also reinforces the concept of animal classification.

Rayona shares her story with the teacher before moving on to paragraph two. Mrs. O'Hara reads Rayona's first paragraph and encourages her to go on to paragraph two and describe herself. The encouragement the teacher provides Rayona gives her the confidence to continue.

Octavia needs a little extra assistance with her description of a frog. "Pretend like you are looking in the mirror." As she reads Octavia's paper, Mrs. O'Hara suggests that Octavia think about her color and texture as she writes the description of the frog she has become. She helps Octavia create an image of a frog in her mind by saying, "You look in the mirror and say, oh my goodness, I'm a frog and this is what I look like." This prompting is just what Octavia needed to get her beyond a stumbling block. She returns to her desk to resume writing.

Young Authors Share.   Once their rough drafts are complete, small editing groups meet to prepare for the final draft writing. The students gather in groups of four that have been determined by the teacher. They arrange themselves in small circles on the floor. Each student has a specific editing role, which is determined by the color of the pencil that has been given to him by the teacher. Students with red pencils are responsible for checking spelling accuracy. Blue pencils are for checking capitalization and punctuation. Students with green pencils will check to see if the stories they are editing make sense, and the students with purple pencils are the paragraph finders. A chart is posted on the board as a reminder of the job associated with each pencil color. Students are accustomed to meeting in editing groups and know the expectations. Each group edits the stories from another group. The students within each group read the stories of their peers with interest and diligence, completing their individual editing jobs as they go. Once they have finished their particular editing task for one paper, they rotate the papers among their group and complete their editing job for each. By the time the rotation of a paper is complete, each story has been edited for spelling, punctuation, coherence, and paragraphing. The edited papers are returned to their authors, who prepare to write final drafts.

The editing system that Mrs. O'Hara has in place is not only efficient; it is manageable for these young authors and editors. Each student can concentrate on one particular aspect of editing, instead of all editing tasks at once. The next time editing groups meet, roles will change, providing all students with the experience of editing for different purposes. Although not all CORI teachers use this group editing, Mrs. O'Hara uses it frequently.

Writing and Communication. Once the final drafts are completed, the students in Mrs. O'Hara's class are ready to share their finished products. They now have wonderful stories about their animals, packed full of information related to the core concepts. Like many (but not all) CORI teachers, Mrs. O'Hara finds an authentic audience for her students to communicate with; in this case it is pre-kindergarteners. As an added bonus for their pre-kindergarteners, students have each illustrated their animal in its habitat and have constructed dioramas depicting the aquatic life they have been so eagerly reading about.

When the group of third graders enters the pre-kindergarten classroom, their young audience greets them with excitement. They have become very fond of their regular visits with Mrs. O'Hara's class and are anxious to hear the stories they have been told so much about. Each pre-k youngster is paired with a third-grade buddy. Each pair finds a cozy place to sit in the room and the sharing begins. The third grade *experts* begin reading to their young audience. Even the most reluctant students are reading their stories with confidence. They are reading aloud, stopping to pose a question to their buddies, or pausing to further explain a concept within the story. Rayona has a conversation with her buddy about predation. She explains that if she was a frog and her buddy was a snake, a really hungry snake, he would eat her.

In another area, Mrs. Jones, the pre-kindergarten teacher, has a conversation with Cody and Jesse, two of the third-grade authors. She inquires how they learned so much about crocodiles, their chosen animal.

Teacher: Where did you get the idea for the illustration?

Cody: We had to like, first we picked the animal, then we had to ask questions and find the answers. Then we had to write a story like we wake up and we turn into the animal like Joanne Ryder does. Then we had to draw a picture and then we made a diorama.

Teacher: Where did you find the information?

Cody: I found it in this book that was called Natural, I think it was called World Nature Crocodiles. It had all the answers to my questions in it. Cause me and him (Jesse) did crocodiles.

Teacher: You did the same animal? Did you work together to do this project or did you work by yourselves?

Cody: For some of it we had to work together.

Jesse: Then we did it by ourselves.

Teacher: You worked really hard!

Teacher: Could you pick any animal you wanted?

Jesse: Yea, but it had to be an aquatic animal.

Teacher: What did you find out about crocodiles that you didn't know before you did this project?

Cody: For defense, it would whack its tail. They like, if an elephant trying to step on him, he could bite, or if a tiger was trying to jump on
it, it could turn around and smack it with its tail.

Cody and Jesse are proud to share information with Mrs. Jones. They are
crocodile experts!

When sharing comes to a close, Mrs. O'Hara's class departs, promising another visit in the near future when they complete their next project. Sharing the
final product of the unit on aquatic life was an excellent way to celebrate the
successes of these young learners. They have accomplished so much!

INDIVIDUAL STUDENTS

To profile the progress of a variety of readers, I closely observed Rebecca and
Octavia for three 1-hour periods within the classroom in the latter part of November. I talked with them briefly in each session asking general questions such
as, "Can you tell me what you are doing?" and "How is your work going now?"

Rebecca: A Confident Reader

Background.   Rebecca is a strong, confident reader. As indicated by the Qualitative Reading Inventory (QRI) administered by her teacher in September, she is
reading at an overall level of 3^1. She reads fluently and self-monitors, making cor-
rections and rereading text when necessary. Rebecca likes reading and thinks she is
a good reader. When asked what strategies she uses, Rebecca indicates that she
chunks unknown words she encounters when reading. Rebecca says that if she
reads something and does not understand it, she sometimes asks questions or rereads the confusing portion of the text showing some level of meta-cognitive
awareness. She also says that she stops and thinks about what she has read. This is
an excellent strategy for Rebecca because comprehension was a concern at the beginning of the year. Her comprehension has improved quite a bit.

Rebecca loves to read! "Reading gets my mind working," she says. Reading is a part of Rebecca's daily life. She is an intrinsically motivated reader, reading to several members of her family, even her dog. Rebecca enjoys learning new facts when she reads, such as where animals live. She enjoys a wide variety of books, including nonfiction books about ponds, oceans, and animals, as well as humorous books. Rebecca is also aware of her dislikes. She reads Nancy Drew books with her mom, but says she does not really like them that much.

In class, Rebecca reads independently for a sustained amount of time and she transitions from one task to another smoothly, without outside direction from the teacher. She often monitors other students, encouraging them to stay on task during independent work time. When it is time for collaborative work, Rebecca jumps right in as a valuable member of the group, sharing resources and information appropriately.

Conceptual Understanding. Rebecca has a grasp of the core concepts and applies them to other situations. While pleasure reading a nonfiction book about animals, she recognizes *locomotion* as how things get from here to there. She also recognizes and identifies core concepts in fiction such as *The Silver Swan* by Michael Morpurgo, which are shown next:

Feeding:	The swan eats bread crumbs from the little boy.
Locomotion:	It gets here from there by swimming or waddling to get away from its enemies or finding food or swimming if it is a hot day.
Predation:	The fox catches the swan by darting and then dragging her by her wing away to its den to feed its cubs.
Reproduction:	The swan builds its nest with sticks big and tiny and small sticks to keep warm.
Communication:	The swan sang a song. It was quiet and true it tells about swan singing.
Defense:	The swan's defends itself by lowering her neck ready to attack.
Respiration:	The swan breathes with two holes on its beak.
Competition:	The cob came and ready to attack chased the hungry fox ran away.

When discussing core concepts in reading group, Rebecca uses the concept vocabulary comfortably, showing she brings conceptual knowledge to texts. Even though core concept icons are posted in both the front and back of the classroom, Rebecca does not need to refer to them. She easily identifies the concepts during reading without the use of the icons.

Reading Comprehension Strategy Development.   Rebecca is a strategic reader. She rereads when confused and pauses to reflect on what has been read. She consciously stays focused on the meaning of the material as she reads. She is competent in the area of questioning. Prior to reading about swans, Rebecca posed the following questions:

Feeding:	What do swans eat?
	How do swans get there [their]) food?
	How does a swan get food for itself?
Locomotion:	How do they get here from there?
	Do swans get out of the pound [pond] and walk around to get what it eats?
Defense:	How do they get there [their] food when onther [another] one whats [wants] it?
	How does it get food for its baby so the baby what [won't] be hungry?
Competition:	How does [do] swans get food for there [their] babys [babies] when other swans whats [want] it?
Reproduction:	How long do swans have to sit on their eggs?
	How many babys [babies] do swans have?
Predation:	What eats swans?
	What eats the predator that eats the swans?

Rebecca's ability to synthesize information has grown over time. In September, after reading about owls, a sample of synthesized information consisted of a list of facts she learned about the topic:

- I now [know] that owls eat mice.
- Owls sleep during the day not at night.
- Owls only take a 5 min. nap or there be eaten.
- Owls predator are hawks
- Owl sounds are whooo.
- I know that owls are feather anamials [animals].

Later summaries of information were more detailed and written in paragraph form, like this one from November:

I learn [learned] that dragonflies and the damesflie [damselflies] died long ago. Their eggs hatch into nymphs, young insects without wings that dig down under the rocks and sticks of the pond bottom. I learn [learned] in September the muskrats that live in holes on the banks get busy fixing their nest for winter. I learn [learned] that frog eggs float in clumps near the surface like clear beads of jelly. I learn [learned] that frogs and salamander [salamanders] grow slow and burrow into the quiet mud for a long winter's sleep.

Summarizing can be a difficult strategy for even the strongest reader. Rebecca shows a sense of story in her summaries and she captures a feeling of the characters, settings, and events in her Chapter 3 summary of *White Bird* by Clyde Robert Bulla, which is presented next:

John Thomes want [wants] a puppy but Luke would not let him. He try [tried] to go to the valley but Luke would not let John Thomes go. He asked Luke if we needed anything from the valley Luke said why because I just want to see the valley. Luke said are you still thing [thinking] about them dogs? I think there [there's] one that no one wants said John Thomes.

Integrating information graphically is a strategy in which Rebecca is competent. Her aquatic animal diagram of a snail shows comprehension of its parts and their functions (see Fig. 8.5 next).

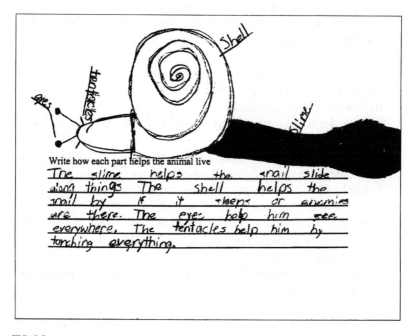

FIG. 8.5.

Writing and Communication.   Rebecca's writing is characteristically basic. She does not typically write complex sentences and her written responses tend to be brief in explanation. She avoids proofreading her writing to check for errors. Structured writing frames provided by her teacher are useful tools for the development of Rebecca's writing. A portion of her factual narrative is presented next.

Locomotion and Respiration Paragraph (begin to move from your cozy bed to tell the reader about your biome, or home. What does it look like in your animal's environment? Help the reader see it through your words and description of what you are doing each day and how you are breathing.)

I am moving in the sea with the sun on me. My pups are on my tummy and I am floating in the sea with sea gulls flying above me. I am breathing with my lungs. I breathe with my nose and mouth.

To summarize the book *Pond Life*, at the end of December, Rebecca wrote:

- In the Pond, turtles, frogs, ducks, fish, salamanders, snails, insects and toads live. Turtles have a shell to protect it. Turtles lay 50 eggs. Turtle's enemies are crabs and birds. Turtles eat frogs, plants, fish, ducks, cattails. Turtles weigh less than 10 pounds (4.5 kilograms).
- Frogs enemies are turtles, fish, birds, snakes, raccoons. Frogs defend theirselfs by going in water. Frogs weigh ten pounds or less than an inch.
- Ducks have feathers to keep them warm. Ducks have a beak to dive in the water. Ducks lay 5 eggs. Ducks eat duck weed, and insects. Ducks have webbed feet to swim.
- Fish need gills to breathe. Fish eat tadpoles. Fish lay 2 eggs. Fish swim away to protect itself.
- Salamanders eat insects. They climb in the cozy mud at winter time and come out in spring. Some salamanders have spots, and some don't.
- Snails have a shell to protect it. Snail lay a lot of eggs. Snails have a slime trail that they leave when they glide.
- Some insects have claws, a soft belly, sharp teeth, 9 legs and wings. Insects have lots of enemies like ducks, frogs, and birds. Insects eat plants and al kinds of stuff.
- Toads have some bumpy skin. They protect theirself by jumping back in the water. Toad lay hundreds of eggs.

The frame helped to keep Rebecca focused on the topic and encouraged her to include details about each concept.

In February, Rebecca's teacher administered another QRI to reassess her overall reading level. At that point, Rebecca was reading at an overall level of 4. This growth of more than a full grade level was encouraging to both Rebecca and her teacher.

Octavia: A Struggling Reader

Background. At the beginning of the school year, Octavia was a very hesitant reader. She was reading at an overall grade level of 1^1, as indicated by the Qualitative Reading Inventory (QRI) administered by her teacher. Now in November, she is willing to try reading all types of text and says she likes to read. Octavia feels that one of her strongest points, as a reader, is that she is a good speller. When asked what strategies she uses as a reader, Octavia indicates that she sounds out words she does not know. Even though she attends to punctuation, Octavia's reading is choppy and lacks expressiveness. She is beginning to self-monitor when she reads, and attempts to decode unfamiliar words, yet she spends quite a long time doing so. This large amount of decoding time negatively impacts her comprehension of text. When she does not understand what she has read, Octavia says that she asks someone, like a friend or the teacher, for help. Sometimes she will read on for more information when she is confused. She said that in order to be a good reader, you have to stay focused on the book and not play around.

In September, Octavia was given the task of writing what she knew about survival of life in oceans and forests. She wrote, "they are different because a fores [forest] has beas [bear] and foxs and the oceans has fish" She was given several texts at grade levels 2–3. After reading, she wrote about survival of life in oceans and forests by saying, "The oceans the forest are diff because the ocean has fish and the forests has bair [bear] and radit" [rabbit]. She gained no usable information from the text, despite ample time and opportunities for note taking. She could not comprehend anything in grade level text. Octavia says she likes to hear funny books, like the *Junie B. Jones* series by B. Park. She likes the way her teacher expressively reads *Junie B. Jones*. Octavia does not read much at home, but will sometimes read to her little brother or with her dad at night.

Octavia is easily distracted when reading independently, illustrating her lack of intrinsic motivation. Early in the year, she was quite hesitant to think on her own. She lacked confidence in herself as a reader and learner. Her teacher said that she would get easily frustrated and simply say she could not do it when faced with an unfamiliar task. She now tries to complete her work on her own, but often seeks reassurance and encouragement from the teacher At this point, she needs frequent urging and rewards of praise, the signs of an extrinsically motivated reader.

Conceptual Understanding. Octavia has a basic understanding of the core concepts. She is beginning to recognize the concepts, but is not yet expanding on them by including specific details. In early October, Octavia's responses on a graphic organizer, completed for the purpose of locating evidence of core concepts in *The Silver Swan* by Michael Morpurgo, illustrate her basic understanding of the concepts:

Feeding: The swan eats brad crams [bread crumbs] By moveing har nack around and the Boy fad her brad croms.

Locomotion: the swun and the foxs did move around they look at each other moveing.

Predation: the foxs grav [grab] the swun by har wing and drag har.

Reproduction: the BaBies swuns war near their Mother swun when she was moveing around.

Defense: they war fighting By moveing around and prtanking [protecting] har BaBies.

Respiration: She Bresh [breathes] rilly fast when she was fighting with the foxs.

Competition: the swun had to fight to staf [save] har BaBies from Dagner [danger].

Communication: the foxs hard [heard] the swun because she was flying that her can be herd.

Octavia is aware that locomotion indicates movement, yet she does not expand on how the swan moves. She knows that the concept of reproduction involves offspring, but she does not mention nesting or egg laying, which are discussed in the story. She is beginning to understand the concepts at the basic level and uses the reminder icons, which are posted in the room, to assist her thinking. Even though her understanding of the concepts is basic, Octavia has come a long way. At the beginning of the school year, she would not have even attempted to make connections between the story and the core concepts.

Reading Comprehension Strategy Development. Activating background knowledge is a strategy that Octavia has a fairly good handle on. When prompted, she will verbalize what she already knows about a topic, prior to reading. Her written responses about prior knowledge tend to be brief. Her oral responses are lengthier. Activating prior knowledge is becoming more self-initiated as the year progresses.

As mentioned previously, Octavia was very insecure at the beginning of the year. One strategy that she was uncomfortable with was questioning. This was a new challenge for her. She had never been expected to pose her own questions. As far as Octavia was concerned, questions were supposed to be asked by the teacher. Why should anyone value what she was thinking and wondering? It was a big step for her to pose her own questions, but she is coming along nicely, as can been seen next in the questions she asked, prior to reading about owls:

Feeding:	How do owls eat?
	How do owls feed there baby?
Locomotion:	If it was snowing and the owls had to life [leave] for the wheter [winter] how long would they fly?
Defense:	If a owl was going to get some moe food for there babys and another owl want it for baby woud they fight?
Competition:	Do owls have to fight if they don't get there food?
Reproduction:	How do owls have there baby to gather [together] and be mates?
Predation:	Does the frother [father] owl always get the food are does the mother owls?

Even though her questions may not be considered higher level, Octavia is beginning to self-initiate questioning.

Searching for information is an area in which Octavia is developing. When investigating her aquatic life animal, the frog, Octavia had difficulty staying focused while doing independent work. She was more confident working in a group with the support of other classmates. When the time came for independent searching, she was again seeking assistance and confirmation from the teacher or other adult in the room. Although she did use the table of contents and index, she had a difficult time cross-referencing topics. If, for example, she could not find information about predation in the index, she did not automatically look for a different, yet related word, such as enemies. She has not yet attained the benchmarks for beginning third-grade performance on this or other strategies.

Octavia's ability to integrate information graphically has developed since the beginning of the year. Initial graphic representations of text-based knowledge were minimal. An example of this is an early graphic representation of a woodland biome. Octavia's representation depicts two trees standing alone. This representation does not reflect comprehension of the topic. Improvement was evident later in the unit, with Octavia's graph of a food web. Although the number of organisms in the web was limited to eight, it was clear that Octavia understood the concept of a food web. She clearly indicated that energy from the sun was gathered by plants, which in turn were eaten by herbivores such as snails, which in turn were eaten by carnivores and omnivores, such as large fish and crayfish.

Writing and Communication.   Octavia uses good ideas in her writing to communicate, but she has quite a bit of difficulty with the mechanics of writing. She is working to expand her editing skills, as shown in this excerpt of her factual narrative:

> A baby frog
>
> I wake up in my bed. I open my eyes and then Im a baby frog on a lilypad. I jump and I jump highin the sky and I swim like a fish in the water. I nosedis [notice] that I have big eyes and I have four legs. And My big eyes and my legs are shong [strong]. I have big black yellow wite eyes my faces is so slimy. Im a baby frog…

While Octavia continues to work on her writing skills, she has become quite a determined learner. She sets goals for herself and follows through on her research. She becomes motivated to read when a topic interests her. Her determination is evident in her February QRI results. The overall reading level for Octavia in February was 3^1, indicating 2 full years of growth in a 5-month period. Octavia is very determined to become a better reader.

Rebecca and Octavia represent differing ability levels in Janice O'Hara's classroom. Even though there is quite a range in levels between these students, both of them showed significant growth during the classroom instruction incorporating CORI. These two students are representative of the students in Mrs. O'Hara's classroom in that they have grown to be engaged, motivated readers who are excited about learning, interested in reading, and confident in themselves.

CLOSING

Within the framework of CORI, teachers vary, each using their strengths and adapting CORI to their personalities. Like other CORI teachers, Mrs. O'Hara emphasized concepts of ecology and engaged students in reading to learn and enjoy this theme. In addition, she was exceptional in two respects. She differentiated instruction for diverse students more frequently and effectively than other teachers. Taking pride in scaffolding lower achieving readers to learn concepts and reading strategies, she enabled them to progress as well as other students. She provided expressive reading for the struggling readers remarkably well. Whereas other CORI teachers may emphasize the science processes, the support for engagement through choice, or the explicit instruction on strategies with modeling slightly more than Mrs. O'Hara, she excelled at differentiating her teaching. She was accomplished at accommodating diversity in reading strategy development within her classroom.

CHILDREN'S BOOK REFERENCES

Brough, C. (1995). *How snails live.* Bothell, WA: Wright Group.
Bulla, C. R. (1996). *White bird.* New York: Random House.
Cutting, B., & Cutting, J. (undated). *Is it a fish?* Bothell, WA: Wright Group.
Kalman, B. (1999). *What is a fish?* New York: Crabtree.
Lasky, K. (1995). *Pond year.* Cambridge, MA: Candlewick Press.
Morpurgo, M. (2000). *The silver swan.* New York: Penguin Putnam.
Park, B. (1998). *Junie B. Jones smells something fishy.* New York: Random House.
Reid, G. K. (2001). *Pond life.* New York: St. Martin's Press.
Ryder, J. (1990). *A just for a day book: Lizard in the sun.* New York: Morrow.
Ryder, J. (1993). *A just for a day book: Sea elf.* New York: Morrow.

9

Reading Comprehension for Information Text: Theoretical Meanings, Developmental Patterns, and Benchmarks for Instruction

John T. Guthrie
Nicole T. Scafiddi
University of Maryland

To begin this chapter, we define the phrase *reading comprehension*. We compare our definition to the prevailing understandings of this term in contemporary articles and reports. We attempt to clarify our definition by saying "what-it-is-not," as well as explaining what reading comprehension does entail. We distinguish between reading comprehension and learning from text, and describe their frequent overlap for students in Grades 3–5. To illustrate, we provide evidence from several hundred students over a 3-month period who are receiving Concept-Oriented Reading Instruction or Strategy Instruction, according to guidelines described in chapters 2, 3, and 5. We portray individual learners, as well as trends typical of our sample. Finally, we discuss how developmental patterns can be used to improve classroom instruction in reading comprehension.

CURRENT VIEWS OF READING COMPREHENSION

A large majority of authors on reading comprehension suggest that there are several critical elements: (a) the text, (b) the reader, (c) the interaction between the reader and the text, and (d) the mental state of the reader after the text interaction. These four elements may be emphasized to a greater or lesser degree by different researchers and in different situations. For example, van den Broek and Kremer (2000) stated;

> When reading is successful, the result is a coherent and useable mental representation of the text. This representation resembles a network, with nodes that depict individual text elements, (e.g., events, facts, setting) and connections that depict the meaningful relations between the elements. (p. 2)

This shows the mental state of a reader following the reading act. In this view, understanding a text consists of forming a semantic network of the concepts and relationships within the text. Although these investigators do not discount the processes or interactions that occur during reading, in this statement the knowledge outcomes are highlighted.

Consistent with this perspective, Williams (2002) proposed, "Full comprehension implies an understanding of … the general theme that the story exemplifies" (p. 128). This definition is intended to represent narrative with a focus on the theme, which refers to an idea that holds the story together. For example, in the tortoise and the hare fable, the theme is that "We should keep trying" or "Perseverance pays dividends." Williams suggested that successful comprehension of stories results in understanding the themes and that a variety of reader–text interactions are needed for this accomplishment. Related to this view of theme identification, Narvaez (1998) stated that comprehension of texts that contain a moral can be observed when students correctly recall moral themes or moral arguments, such as the importance of being honest with strangers. These definitions show an emphasis on the understanding that results from reading and is carried away from the text by the learner.

A slightly different emphasis on reading comprehension underscores the centrality of the processes and interactions of the reader with the text during the course of reading. The authors of the recent RAND Report (Snow, 2002) stated, "We define reading comprehension as the process of simultaneously extracting and constructing meaning through interaction and involvement with written language" (p. 11). They continued by stating that a representation of comprehension includes describing the nature of the reader's capabilities and knowledge, the text and its qualities, and the reader's activities that include the purposes or consequences associated with reading. The processes emphasized within this definition suggest that the reader is: (a) using knowledge of the world, (b) activating vocabulary, (c) employing linguistic knowledge about English, (d) using cognitive comprehension strategies, and (e) displaying motivational attributes, such as goals for reading, sense of confidence, and interest in the topic. This focus on the reader's processes as central to defining comprehension was underscored also in the National Reading Panel's Report on comprehension (NRP, 2000). That report emphasized cognitive strategies for gaining meaning that included: activating background knowledge, asking questions, summarizing, answering questions, organizing graphically, and structuring stories. As Baker (2002) observed, comprehension monitoring is a metacognitive competency, referring to students' awareness of their strategies as they attempt to understand text. She stated, "Comprehension monitoring is often considered to be a comprehension strategy in itself" (p. 79). Baker went beyond cognitive strategies to highlight awareness and self-regulation of the comprehension processes. Certainly these perspectives do not discount the value of mental states following reading, but they do not specify them in any detail. Consequently, outcome states (i.e., knowledge) are placed secondary to the processes of extracting and constructing meaning.

OUR DEFINITION OF READING COMPREHENSION

Building on these definitions, we suggest that **reading comprehension consists of the processes of constructing conceptual knowledge from a text through cognitive interaction and motivational involvement with the text.** Each of the words and phrases in this statement carries some weight. Our emphasis is placed on the conceptual knowledge that the learner builds during reading. Such knowledge consists of concepts that are related to each other structurally and associated with important examples or supporting evidence. If the text is informational or expository, this conceptual knowledge will consist of content information within a knowledge domain. If the text is narrative or literary, the knowledge consists of principles such as the theme, described by Williams (2002). In our view, a theme such as "Perseverance pays dividends" is a principle containing the concepts of "perseverance," "payment," and "dividends." Describing the increases of the learner's conceptual knowledge as a consequence of reading, and the difference between knowledge before and after reading, is explained extensively. We present a knowledge rubric that describes the levels of conceptual understanding for higher and lower comprehenders. Although the rubric is written for the topic of ecology, the levels could be generalized to other content domains. We further suggest that the development of comprehension consists of the ability to construct higher levels of knowledge as the result of interacting with text.

Our definition contains the phrase *interaction with texts*. This refers mainly to cognitive strategies that are central to reading comprehension processes. In

CORI, the cognitive strategies include: (a) activating background knowledge, (b) questioning, (c) searching for information, (d) summarizing, (e) organizing graphically, and (f) structuring stories. These cognitive strategies are the key forms of interacting with text that enable learners to build new knowledge.

Additionally, our definition includes involvement with text, which refers to motivational processes necessary to reading. If the text is interesting to the reader, cognitive processing deepens and knowledge outcomes increase (Schiefele, 1999). A learner who is intrinsically motivated to read uses cognitive strategies more effectively than a less motivated reader (Guthrie, Wigfield, & Von Secker, 2000). Many motivational processes, including self-efficacy, are vital to comprehension (see chapter 4).

Reading in many genres is covered by our definition. However, we emphasize comprehension of information text because CORI integrates reading with science, which is usually conveyed in information text. We explain information text as containing the exposition of substantive information in a subject matter. In contrast, literary text refers to fictional or symbolic content, emphasizing characters and their experiences in imagined mirror worlds. (Beach & Wendler, 1987; Rosenblatt, 1991). We do not suggest that our rubric represents aesthetic understanding or experience of the kind often gained from reading narrative literature. The extent that our view of comprehending information text generalizes to other genres and literature remains to be investigated.

Distinguishing Reading Comprehension and Learning From Text

As a reader builds knowledge from text, he brings prior knowledge to the task. The outcome of text interaction is a representation of knowledge that is partly preexisting and partly new to the learner. If a high proportion of knowledge constructed from reading is new, the reader learned from the text. If none of the knowledge is new, but it accurately reflects the text, the learner comprehended, but did not learn *new* conceptual knowledge. Therefore, we define *learning from text* as the process of constructing *new* conceptual knowledge through interaction and involvement with text.

The distinction between reading comprehension and learning from text is whether a sizeable portion of the reader's knowledge after interacting with text is *new*. For learners in Grades 3–5, a high proportion of texts encountered contain new information. In these cases, reading comprehension (building conceptual knowledge) is virtually identical to learning from text (building *new* conceptual knowledge). If the text contains a large amount of new information for a student, yet the student did not learning anything new from interacting with the text, the learner cannot be said to have comprehended the text. Comprehension and learning are nearly the same only when the text is new. However, because that condition is frequent in reading in Grades 3–5, comprehending and learning from information text are highly similar in those grades.

Roles of Cognitive Strategies in Comprehension

In this perspective, cognitive strategies and linguistic processing are necessary, but are not sufficient conditions for comprehension. For instance, a learner may question during reading, but may not gain knowledge as a consequence of reading (e.g., the question may not be answered and the benefits from activating background knowledge may be insufficient to increase new knowledge). Successful strategy use does not guarantee successful comprehension. In addition, other necessary conditions, such as retrieving word meanings, recalling individual sentences, and drawing inferences of several varieties, are not sufficient conditions for comprehension. However, if a reader forms conceptual knowledge as a consequence of text interaction, we suggest that comprehension has occurred.

SKETCHING THE FRAMEWORK
FOR CONCEPTUAL KNOWLEDGE

Our view is that reading comprehension is centrally defined by the conceptual knowledge that the reader constructs and extracts from text. This definition places an emphasis on the term *conceptual knowledge*. Although many authors have grappled with the meaning of the term, for purposes of this chapter, we suggest that conceptual knowledge refers to structured organization of concepts, supporting information, and their interrelationships. This view is not intended to be original, but to be consistent with current literature. As science educators, Mintzes, Wandersee, and Novak (2001) stated that knowledge in biology can be represented as integrated frameworks of cohesive knowledge that can be used in novel real-world settings. Relative lack of conceptual knowledge would consist of isolated bits of information that are inert and cannot serve as a basis for successive encounters with content. Elaborating on this perspective, Mintzes, Trowbridge, Arnaudin, and Wandersee (1991) suggested that knowledge is higher level when important concepts of a topic or domain in biology are present, accurately represented, and appropriately related to each other. Students with lower level knowledge lack important concepts, fail to connect concepts appropriately with each other, and introduce scientifically inappropriate information.

In cognitive science, conceptual knowledge has been represented in the form of mental models. A mental model is a visual image that "runs" like a video in the mind. For example, Chi, DeLeeuw, Chiu, and Lavancher (1994) showed that students have mental models of the circulatory system. For college students, a low-level mental model would be, "*Blood is pumped from the heart to the body, and the blood does not necessarily return to the heart.*" This statement contains three physical structures with two functions. A higher form of conceptual knowledge consists of a more complex mental model. For example, at the highest level, there are dynamic relationships among the physical features of the heart, the lungs, the body, the blood, and the blood vessels, all of which are described with physical characteristics. Chi et al. (1994) found that college students with high conceptual knowledge had models with 12 structures and 25 functions. We concur with the general view that conceptual knowledge consists of interrelationships among concepts in a network with appropriate supporting evidence, as advocated and articulated by Glynn and Duit (1995), Strike and Posner (1985), Alao and Guthrie (1999), and Alexander and Jetton (2000). We suggest that a simpler version of the same view of conceptual knowledge is viable for third graders.

An alternative way to conceptualize and represent conceptual knowledge is with semantic networks. A semantic network is like a map of words. A web of concepts, or nodes, that are linked to each other is one example of a semantic network. Links among the concepts show how closely they are related. As Novak and Musonda (1991) illustrated, students' understanding of a science topic is readily shown in a concept map or a semantic network. Differences among students can be depicted and new learning can be illustrated. Jonasson (1999) described a range of graphic organizations for showing semantic networks with diagrams and charts. We suggest that semantic networks are one viable form of representing conceptual knowledge. They can include concepts, supporting information, and the relationships among them. Consequently, semantic networks can be used to measure knowledge gained from interacting with text.

GROWTH OF READING COMPREHENSION

For both mental models and semantic networks, there are basic elements. To more fully delineate the constituents of conceptual knowledge, let us outline the meanings of concepts, relationships, supporting information, and principles. In this framework, a concept is an abstract term referring to a class of objects, events, or interactions. A concept is distinguished from the particular and the tangible. It is not a specific object, event, or interaction. For example, the concept of a chair includes dining chairs and lounge chairs. Many particular individual chairs are referred to by this class reference. Likewise, the concept of competition in ecology refers to many forms of interactions among animals and the environment or among animals with other animals. A particular competition between two zebras to win territory in a savannah represents an example. It may be used as supporting information for the concept of competition among animals in the grassland. Relationships within conceptual knowledge are formed among concepts and supporting information. For example, if we state, "Competition increases when resources are scarce," the term *scarce* depicts the relationship between the needs of a species and resource availability.

In this view, **growth of reading comprehension consists of an increase in the ability to build conceptual knowledge during text interaction**. The reader who has improved in comprehension is the reader who has advanced in the capacity for gaining knowledge from text. Several kinds of knowledge are built during reading. Individuals may construct concepts, gain supporting information for existing concepts, build relationships among existing concepts, or advance on all of these aspects of conceptual knowledge. An issue for future inquiry could focus on which of these diverse aspects of knowledge grows more rapidly at different ages or in different text interactions.

READING COMPREHENSION: A RUBRIC
FOR CONCEPTUAL KNOWLEDGE

To investigate children's levels and growth of reading comprehension, we examined children's writings about their learning from information texts. Students in four Frederick, Maryland schools participated in a 12-week reading comprehension intervention project. The tasks described were part of pre- and post-assessments. First, students wrote their background knowledge about the topic of their packet. Next, we gave Grade 3 students a packet that simulates a chapter book. Each 70-page packet, on either the topic of ponds and deserts, rivers and grasslands, or oceans and forests, contained about 20 chapter-like sections with an index, table of contents, and section headings. Students were given logs to record their notes during a 50-minute reading activity. Students spent 30 minutes writing what they knew after reading, without referring to the packet. The guiding questions for their writing (on one of three forms) included:

1. What are rivers and grasslands like?
2. What plants and animals live there?
3. How do these plants and animals survive?

Based on the written compositions, we constructed a rubric for characterizing the conceptual knowledge gained from reading these information texts. This rubric is also used to depict children's growth of reading comprehension during those 3 months.

DESCRIPTION OF THE READING COMPREHENSION RUBRIC FOR ECOLOGY TEXTS

Brief explanations of each level, with examples from third-grade children's writings, are provided next.

Facts and Associations: Simple–Level 1

A student's writing consists of very few characteristics of a biome or an organism. The statements exclude concepts or definitions and may consist only of the student's name as identifying information. Typical examples of children's writings at Level 1 consist of minimal identification and classification of organisms into biomes. These statements are often presented in the form of a list, as shown next:

"In grasslands lions, tigers, zebras."

"There are fish, grass, bear, deer, snake, otter, flowers, and trees."

In the first example, the student correctly named three organisms and the biome they inhabit. In the second example, the student only identifies organisms and does not state in which biome they reside. Common examples of students' biome descriptions at Level 1 consist of limited aspects and characteristics. No true biome definitions are presented. Students' writings usually contain a reference to one significant attribute of each biome and often mention the lack of this feature's intensity in the other biome. An example of a Level 1 biome description is: "**Forests have a lot of trees, oceans don't.**" In this example, the student has named *trees* as the defining aspect of a forest and defines *oceans* through its lack of trees.

The student may also describe an organism's presence within a biome as a characteristic of that biome, for example, "**In oceans there are no trees. In forests there are not octopuses. Octopuses live in oceans. Foxes live in forests.**" The student has described the ocean by the fact that it has octopi and that forests do not have them. Although this is accurate, an ocean is not defined by the presence of octopi, nor is a forest defined by its lack of them. Additionally, the student has classified only two organisms.

Facts and Associations: Extended—Level 2

At this level, students correctly classify several organisms. Limited definitions and universal plant and animal concept statements are often present. Information included at this level is factual and often appears in the form of a list.

A Level 2 student writes multiple classifications with more biome descriptions than at Level 1. In addition, a weakly stated concept may appear as follows:

> In forests there are more animals. For example there are deer, birds, snakes, lizards, bugs, rats, squirrels, chipmunks, and alligators. In oceans there are fewer animals. There are whales, dolphins, sea lions, fish, sharks and other animals from the sea

The student accurately classifies more than seven organisms and clearly states which biome the organisms inhabit. It is typical for the statement to lack any biome description. However, it is also possible for the qualities of a Level 2 to appear along with a limited biome definition.

Also typical at this level are extensive classifications and a limited biome definition, along with a weakly stated concept, such as the following:

> An animal that lives in a grassland is an elephant. Another animal that lives in grassland is a giraffe. An Animal that lives in grassland is a zebra. A plant that is in a grassland is grass. Another plant is trees. Also bushes are in grassland. An animal that lives in a river is the water boatmen. Also some fish and seaweed live in rivers. Grasslands are different because rivers are wet and grasslands are dry. Plants help animals live so animals can eat.

The classifications are presented in the form of a list. The limited biome description includes a minor amount of detail about the defining physical characteristics of both biomes. Limited biome statements provide slightly more detail about aspects of both biomes, not the lack of one characteristic in the other biome. The student makes a limited biome statement, referring to the grasslands as dry and the rivers as wet. A weakly stated concept is present (e.g., "Plants help animals live so animals can eat"), but is simple and over-generalized.

Concepts and Evidence: Simple—Level 3

A well-formed, fully elaborated definition of both biomes is accompanied by a substantial number of organisms accurately classified. Students may present one or more ecological concepts with minimal supporting information, but the statements are disorganized.

At Level 3, students present extensive biome definitions. Their concepts are appropriately qualified and do not contain overgeneralized physical and behavioral adaptations. Students present specific facts and patterns of information in relation to concepts, but these statements are typically disorganized and incoherent, as follows:

> I know that all deserts are not hot and dry. Some are cold, icy, and fog hides them. Ponds and desert are different because deserts are miles long and ponds are not miles long. Ponds and deserts are also different because of where they are located. I know that diving beetles and damselflies live near and in ponds. I know that it hardly any animals or plants live in the hot and dry deserts. Ponds and deserts are the same because some desserts have ice and water just like when it is winter and ponds turn into ice and the water is in the pond is underneath. Ponds and desserts are also the same because animals live in both deserts and ponds. I also know that Angelfish and piranhas live in ponds. The plants that live in ponds are seaweed, algae, moss. Ponds and desserts are the same because snakes live in the desert and snakes can also live in ponds.

Writing about ecological organisms at Level 3 centers on survival concepts. The student is not just writing a list, but is writing statements centering on the survival topic. In addition, the student includes the behavioral patterns or physical structures of specific organisms, but does not include additional supporting information and is disorganized, for example, **"What I know is golden wheel spider cartwheel. Gorillas can crawl when they are two months old. Roadrunners go 23 mph. Water – boat man uses legs like oars. Diving beetle larva eats tadpoles."**

Concepts and Evidence: Extended—Level 4

Students display conceptual understanding of organisms and their survival mechanisms in one or more biomes. Concepts are illustrated by specific organisms and the physical characteristics or the behavioral patterns that facilitate their survival. Higher level principles, such as food webs or interactions among ecological concepts, may be partially stated.

Writing at Level 4 emphasizes core concepts with references to specific organisms' behaviors, and physical structures are presented to exemplify the concepts.

> Some snakes, which live in the desert, squeeze their prey to death and then eat them. This is called a deadly hug. Bright markings on some snakes are warnings to stay away. In the desert two male jackrabbits fight for a female. Some deserts are actually cold and rocky. Both deserts' hot or cold, it barely ever rain and if it does it comes down so fast and so hard it just runs off and does not sink into the ground.

This student begins by discussing predation (a major concept) and gives minimally supported information about feeding (another concept of survival). The student writes about the concept of defense (defensive markings) and communication (how these markings communicate a warning). She demonstrates her knowledge that the jackrabbit belongs in the desert biome. She refers to the concepts of competition and reproduction among jackrabbits and briefly links them. Finally, the student provides essential biome information, referring to the fact that deserts can be icy, not just hot, and that a lack of rain is a characteristic in both the cold and hot deserts.

Patterns of Relationships: Simple—Level 5

At this level, students show command of ecological concepts by presenting relationships among and between different organisms and the biomes they inhabit. These interactions are the central element of the statement. An example of a Level 5 follows:

> A river is different from grassland because a river is body of water and grassland is land. A river is fast flowing. Grasshoppers live in grasslands. A grasshopper called a locust lays its egg in a thin case. One case could carry 100 eggs. The largest herbivores in the grassland are an elephant. In the African savanna meat-eats prey on grazing animals, such as zebra. Many animals live in grasslands. The river is a home to many animals. In just a drop of river water millions of animals can be living in it. Many fish live in the river. Many birds fly above the grasslands and rivers. A river is called freshwater because it has no salt in it.

A detailed parallel between the organisms that inhabit these biomes is the central feature of this statement of conceptual knowledge. The student begins with a brief definition of the two biomes. Next, the student selects one organism found in the grasslands, the grasshopper, and introduces it. Subsequently, she chooses a specific type of grasshopper, the locust, to discuss the concept of reproduction. She refers to the physical structure the locust uses for reproduction, the egg case. Instead of just stating that locusts lay eggs in a case, this student includes supporting details about the case

The statement contrasts one of the tiniest animals in the grassland, the locust, to the largest herbivore in the grassland, the elephant. This provides a strong parallel between the diverse organisms that reside within the same biome. Later, the student makes a specific reference to the African savannah, one of the three types of grasslands students read about. This student describes the concept of predation with minimal support: On the savanna meat-eaters prey on the grazing zebra. The grazing zebra is named as a type of specific prey in the grassland. However, details about predation are not provided. She then introduces the river biome, making a specific reference to the diverse nature of the animals in the river. She does not limit her writing to the typical animals often named when discussing the river, but instead briefly mentions the micro-scopic organisms that reside in "just a drop of river water."

Patterns of Relationships: Extended—Level 6

Students describe complex relationships among multiple organisms and their habitats. Concepts and principles presented are thoroughly supported by state-ments directly relating them to specific organisms' behaviors or physical adapta-tions. Well-supported principles of ecology are a fundamental component. An example of a Level 6 follows:

> River and grassland are alike and different. Rivers have lots of aquatic animals. Grass-lands have mammals and birds. Rivers don't have many plants but grassland have trees and lots of grass. Rivers have lots of animal like fish trout and stickle backs. They also have insects and mammals, like the giant water bug and river otters. Grasslands usu-ally have lions, zebras, giraffes, antelope, gazelles, and birds. In rivers the food chain starts with a snail. Insects and small animals eat the snail. Then fish eat the small ani-mals and insects. Then bigger animals like the heron and bears eat the fish. Snails also eat algae with grows form the sun. In the grass lands the sun grown the grass. Animals like gazelle, antelope, and zebra eat the grass. Then animals like lions eat them. This is called a food chain of what eats what. In a way the animals are helping each other live. Animals have special things for uses. Otters have closable noses and ears. Gills let fish breath under water. Some fish lay thousands of egg because lot of animals like eating fish eggs. Some animals have camouflage. Swallow tail butter fly larva look like bird droppings. That is what I know and about grasslands rivers.

This student presents two food chains, one for each biome. The first repre-sents the organisms in a river, naming a snail as a type of prey and insects as the snail's predator. He then presents fish as a predator of insects. This shows that the student recognizes that a single organism is capable of being both a predator and prey. He continues with this pattern until the end of the chain. At this point, he refers to the snails as consumers of algae that grow in the river. Next, he introduces a brief grassland chain consisting of a gazelle, antelope, and zebra as consumers of grass. The lion is identified as the predator of these animals. Continuing on the food chain, the student refers to the idea that these animals are helping each other survive. He expresses this by writing, "In a way, the ani-mals are helping each other live." Unlike many other students, he understands that the prey is not benefiting in the predator–prey relationship. He also writes detailed concept statements, introducing the idea that animals have special (physical) structures for different uses. Next, the student names specific ani-mals, the otter and fish, and describes the structures that aid these organisms in respiration, which is a core concept. Then, he addresses the concept of defense, remarks that, "Some animals have camouflage," and names the swallow-tail butterfly as one example. This knowledge structure contains multiple food chains in two biomes interconnected and characterized by core ecological concepts that are amply illustrated. We observed few Grade 3 students at this level.

This rubric could be applied to other contents in science or history. It seems plausible that students would form these six levels of knowledge in those domains. For example, *Facts and associations* are a rudimentary aspect of understanding a historical event; *Concepts and evidence* for a historical event might relate to groups in conflict or economic forces, accompanied by the particular persons and their actions; *Patterns of relationships* might refer to trends in political conflicts, the changes in economic forces over time and their mutual influences. However, we have not attempted to relate our rubric to students' reading in domains outside of ecology.

WHAT IS NEW IN THIS VIEW OF READING COMPREHENSION?

By using this rubric to describe reading comprehension, we see that higher level comprehenders differ from lower level comprehenders in several ways. It is obvious that higher level readers have expanded vocabularies and more word meanings in their statements of what they have read in text. In addition, higher level readers usually have more facts and accurately rendered propositions contained in the text than lower level comprehenders. These characteristics are seen in the differences between Levels 1 and 2, in which students report more correct facts from text. Such word and sentence (propositional level) differences are apparent in the contrast of Levels 3 and 4 and Levels 4 and 5.

In addition, higher level comprehenders (those at Level 4 and higher) gain conceptual knowledge from text. They can form superordinate concepts, supported by subordinate information, in a structured fashion. In particular, to progress from Level 2 to Level 3, students improve from representing several facts in text to representing a few major concepts from the text. This is a qualitative change. It is more than the mere addition of more words or sentences to a simpler statement. Likewise, to progress from Level 4 to Level 5, students move from understanding concepts in isolation to forming complex patterns. At Level 5, they synthesize concepts into a structured network of knowledge. Such a network can be expanded or fused with other networks.

To progress up the reading comprehension rubric, students also move from presenting facts to understanding "big ideas." This is a qualitative shift shown in the move from Level 2 to Level 3. Those big ideas, or major concepts, are refined, qualified, and supported with evidence at Levels 4 to 6 in the rubric in ways that are not shown in Level 3. It is not only the identification of main concepts that characterizes the better reading comprehender. Improved reading comprehension is shown by progress up the rubric, which contains both qualitative shifts toward more coherently formed, conceptually organized knowledge and quantitative shifts toward more factual knowledge and vocabulary meanings that undergird overarching concepts.

CHARACTERIZING GROWTH
OF READING COMPREHENSION

We distinguish between this perspective on text comprehension and comprehension defined as text recall. If a student recalls a large number of facts from an extended text, we suggest that this may be valuable, but it does not necessarily show a high level of conceptual knowledge. In our framework, learning an extended large number of facts from text places the person at Level 2. However, a reader who merely recalls a large number of facts that are isolated from conceptual content cannot score highly on our representation of conceptual knowledge. If we give a student an extended text and ask, "Recall as much as possible after reading," and we count the number of propositions recalled, we do not know whether the individual is recalling facts, concepts, or patterns of relationships. It is apparent that recalling propositions is not necessarily an indicator of learning conceptual knowledge from texts.

It is possible for a Grade 3 student to have prior knowledge of a particular text on butterflies. For instance, she may know a "fact" that "butterflies are different colors". After reading the text, the student may have learned a new "fact" that "some butterflies have spots." She entered the text with a simple fact, which is Level 1 knowledge. She departed the text with another simple fact, which is a new form of Level 1 knowledge. Although she learned one proposition from text, she did not advance up the rubric. To advance, she would have had to learn a large number of new facts (Level 2) or concepts with supporting evidence (Level 3). If the student learned that "butterflies have spots to fool predators" and they "have scales to protect their wings," she would have learned about the concepts of defense and adaptation to habitat, which would be Level 3. We define growth in reading comprehension, then, as not merely improved proficiency within a level, but as progress up the conceptual knowledge hierarchy.

Adequate texts are necessary to observe children's growth in reading comprehension. That is, we need extended texts that afford students the opportunity to learn deeply if we are to understand their knowledge construction. A text useful for this purpose must contain conceptual information that is interrelated and supported by examples or evidence. An individual is not likely to build knowledge from a list of facts, nor even from an elaborated statement describing one concept with multiple examples. Although both of these texts may lead to a learner's recall and to the acquisition of new information, they cannot provide the necessary conditions for constructing conceptual knowledge. Next, we provide examples of students who have displayed reading comprehension growth.

Growth of Reading Comprehension: Group Trends and a Case Study

This section provides an outline showing third graders' development of reading comprehension in a 3-month period, between September and December. The trends reported here are based on approximately 150 students who were randomly selected from 400 students assessed during Fall 2001 in an extended reading comprehension intervention project (see Guthrie, Wigfield, & Barbosa, 2002).

Reading Comprehension Levels. The typical reading comprehension level of students in September was Level 2 on the rubric (see Fig. 9.1). After reading, students at this level possessed a number of facts and associations about the biome or the animals. However, they possessed virtually no concepts about survival or critically important defining attributes of the biomes.

A typical example of a Level 2 knowledge statement follows:

Animals live in a desert. They like to live there because it's nice and warm. Ducks like to drink water in the pond. They are different because one of them is wet and the other

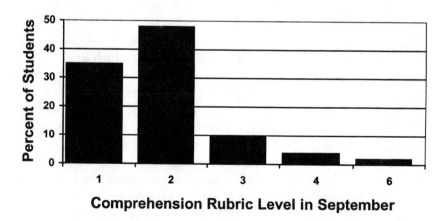

FIG. 9.1. Reading comprehension levels of Grade 3 students in September.

dry. Snake and bears, birds, live in the deserts. They help each other live by giving the animals water and some food that's what the mothers do.

This statement shows that the student has correctly classified *ducks* as living in ponds and *birds* and *snakes* as living in deserts, although she mistakenly classified *bears* as a desert creature. She defined the *desert* as warm, which is a misconception, but correctly identified the *pond* as wet, whereas the *desert* is dry. Showing such facts and associations is a Level 2.

In December, reading comprehension of students typically showed a few concepts of survival, as well as information present in previous levels, which is Level 3. A typical Level 3 on this task follows:

Deserts are different than ponds because deserts have a little bit of water and ponds have a lot of water. The animals that live in a pond are snakes, fish, bugs, ducks, and plants. The plants that live in a pond are grass and seaweed. The animals and plants that live in a desert are rattlesnakes, foxes, rabbits, owls, woodpeckers. The plants that live in a desert are cactus, little grass, small trees. Some of the animals eat plants. The plants eat the food in the soil and the little rain. The animals help the plants live by when the animals step on the ground it makes it a little soft and it is easy for the plants to grow. The plants help the animals by bringing some animals close so other animals can catch them and eat them. The animals also help the plant when some of the bugs that drink the plants nectar carry things from one plant to another.

She shows a good, simple definition of both biomes and 12 correctly assigned species. More important, she describes feeding, predation, and cross-pollination (reproduction) with minimal factual support for each concept. She builds several concepts, with examples, from the texts, which is Level 3.

In December, after reading a packet on one of the topics (ponds and deserts, rivers and grasslands, or oceans and forests), students' reading comprehension rubric level was typically at Level 3, 4, or 5. As Fig. 9.2 shows, the largest percentage of students (about 32%) was placed at rubric Level 3 in the knowledge framework. At this level, students displayed one relatively high-level concept with some supporting evidence. When reading about biomes, they defined both biomes and identified a substantial number of organisms that survive within them. These students also presented one or more ecological concepts, with examples from organisms successfully surviving within the environment, as evidence for the concepts. In December, students departed this reading and writing assessment with a conceptual understanding that was a qualitatively higher level form of knowledge than the facts they were able to gain from text in September. The majority gained concepts with supportive evidence in December, whereas they gained only factual information in September. Their grasp of the content represented in the text advanced as a result of reading, in the sense

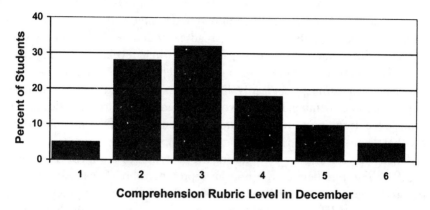

FIG. 9.2. Reading comprehension levels of Grade 3 students in December.

that their understanding progressed up the knowledge rubric that was presented previously in this chapter. Within this framework for depicting reading comprehension, we define growth. In this context, reading comprehension growth consists of the learner's increased *capacity* for constructing knowledge through interacting with text.

LEARNING FROM TEXT

Suppose we give students an extensive text and ask them to recall what they remember after reading. We place their statements onto the knowledge rubric. At one point in time, suppose a student's writing after reading is placed at Level 2 and later at Level 4. This suggests growth in conceptual knowledge constructed during reading. From this, we infer growth of *capacity* to build knowledge from text. Performing at rubric Level 4 reflects a relatively high level of reading comprehension.

However, it is possible that the individual already possessed the knowledge before reading and, therefore, learned little new from the text interaction of reading at Level 2 or Level 4. In other words, it is possible that the individual did not learn from the text in either case. To judge whether an individual learned new knowledge from a text, we must give a pretest prior to reading. Then, we can compare the entry level of information to the individual's information after reading. It is this pre–post gain in conceptual knowledge that reflects learning from text.

To measure whether students improve in *learning from text*, we give students a pretest, ask the students to read extended text, and then give a posttest. The students' pre–post gains show their levels of learning from text. We administer parallel assessments in September and December. Advancement in *learning from text* is shown when students display a gain from September to December. In other words, students' capacity for building new knowledge from text increased from September to December, if their pre–post gains increased across that time period.

Children's learning from text during the September assessment is shown in Fig. 9.3. The numbers at the bottom represent rubric levels gained from pre-assessment to post-assessment in September. The largest percentage of students (about 36%) did not change in their rubric level. Although they may have learned a few facts or new information, it was not enough for them to advance on this knowledge rubric. However, a number of students increased one to three rubric levels. It was also possible for students to show a lower rubric score after reading, as indicated by the −1 and −3. These losses may be due to lack of motivation to read or low level of investment in the writing activity. From the distribution of children's scores, it is evident that the majority of students did not construct new knowledge in this reading activity.

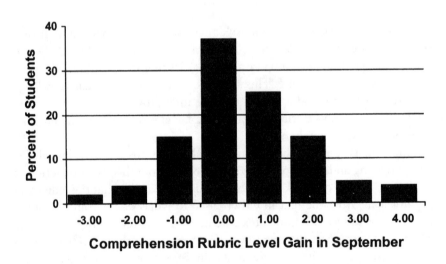

FIG. 9.3. Gains in conceptual knowledge from reading for Grade 3 students in September.

Children's learning from text in December can be compared with their learning from text in September. In December, the most frequent and typical gain for students was one rubric level from pre-assessment to post-assessment, as shown in Fig. 9.4. Also evident from the graph is that a significant proportion of students gained 2, 3, or 4 rubric levels in conceptual knowledge as a consequence of their reading. In sum, although the typical learner did not advance on the knowledge rubric as a result of text interaction during the September assessment, in December, typical learners rose one level on the knowledge rubric, as a result of their reading and writing in this packet of text materials.

Here is an example of growth in learning from text. In December, this student's prior knowledge for animal life in grasslands and rivers was as follows:

Cheetahs, lions, zebras, grass, trees, leopards, and many other things live in grasslands. Fish, alligators, and plants live in rivers.

After reading, his understanding increased to the following:

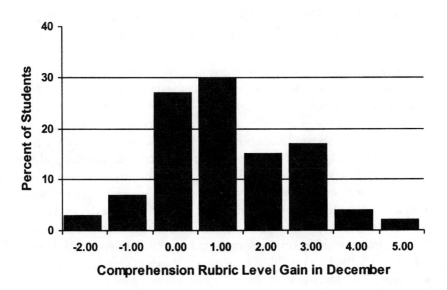

FIG. 9.4. Gains in conceptual knowledge from reading for Grade 3 students in December.

Grasslands and rivers are very different. Rivers are bodies of water. Rivers have salmon, fish, and other animals unable to live on land. Grasslands have hyenas, lions, zebras, hippos, and other animals that can't permanently live underwater. Grasslands have mostly grass, and rivers have several types of plants. Otters (river animals) hunt for shellfish, crayfish, and fish. They can chuckle, giggle, and make many other noises. They can stay underwater for two minutes. The salmon (fish) life cycle goes: egg, fry, parr, smolt, adult. That's what I learned about grasslands and rivers.

He includes good definitions of both biomes, correctly identifying species of plants and many animals that dwell there. He proceeds to describe the concept of predation among otters, with enumerations of their prey. He conveys various communications of otters, and indicates their proficiency for holding their breath, showing how their respiration restricts their hunting. He briefly depicts the life cycle of the salmon, accurately showing the basic survival processes of reproduction, even though the detail is minimal.

This student began the reading assessment in December with information about a few **facts and associations,** Level 2. He departed the reading assessment with knowledge of multiple survival **concepts and evidence,** Level 4. He conveyed a beginning understanding of the lifecycle network. His September pre- and post-assessments were both Level 2. They appeared very similar to his pre-assessment in December presented previously. Consequently, his gain in learning from text was substantial.

USING BENCHMARKS IN READING COMPREHENSION AS GOALS FOR INSTRUCTION

Our rubric for reading comprehension displays a progression from ability to construct simpler, low-level factual knowledge from text to competence in building interconnecting networks of concepts that are thoroughly integrated. Grade 3 students improved one or two rubric levels in reading comprehension during the period from September to December. As we indicated, in September, the most typical pattern was for students to construct simple facts from a complex packet of simulated trade books, which is Level 2. In December, typical students constructed concepts about the topic supported by factual information and evidence, Level 3. A substantial number of students also increased two or three rubric levels, progressing from simple facts and associations to advanced statements of relationships among multiple concepts, supported accurately by appropriate facts.

Each rubric level is a benchmark referring to the child's reading comprehension capacity at a given point in time. If a student is at Level 2, knowing an extended number of facts and associations, it is not likely he will proceed immediately to Level 4, which is knowledge of concepts with supporting information. Students are unlikely to leap across levels. Rather, they are likely to progress successively from Level 1 to Level 2, Level 2 to Level 3, and so on. Therefore, benchmarks provide forecasts for students' next level of reading comprehension ability.

As reading comprehension is a form of cognitive expertise, it is wise to scaffold children gradually toward higher levels of reading. In the large majority of cases, it is counterproductive to attempt to teach novices to become experts immediately. A more reasonable approach is a tactic of moving novices through a progression of increasing levels of competence.

We have emphasized the cognitive strategies that students use in building their understandings, such as activating background knowledge, questioning, searching, and summarizing. Teachers who are providing instruction for these strategies are giving emphasis to one crucial aspect of reading. Although it is sensible for a teacher to have a strategy goal, teaching to knowledge goals is just as important.

Teaching for knowledge building is vital to reading comprehension instruction. If students in a classroom are predominantly at Level 1, understanding a very few simple facts and associations after reading, it will be most valuable to help students focus on a single concept with supporting information. Knowledge goals for instruction can be linked to the students' benchmarks on the reading comprehension rubric. Level 1 students can be encouraged to move to Level 2, reading for knowing a few simple facts followed by reading to learn a wider number of appropriate facts and associations of the topic domain. If the classroom has many Level 5 students who can build a rich array of concepts that are linked to one another, the teacher may expand their reading comprehension by enabling them to widen the network of concepts, interrelationships, and deepen the supporting information for all of them. This would move those students toward Level 6 on this proposed rubric.

Within a given classroom, students vary in their reading comprehension competencies. We found that in December, the mean rubric level was 3 for Grade 3 students, with variations from Levels 1 to 5, demonstrating that whereas the majority of students can comprehend a few simple, basic facts and associations about a topic domain, others are able to construct higher level concepts with examples and evidence. Practically speaking, if the majority of students are at Levels 1 and 2 (able to comprehend simple facts and associations from text), it is reasonable to help them read for individual concepts and identify supporting evidence from text, which is teaching them to read at Level 3. For learners at a higher level, (e.g., Level 4—reading for general concepts and supporting information), teachers should place emphasis on higher rubric levels (e.g., reading for integrated networks of concepts and patterns of relationships). To challenge the more advanced comprehenders within the classroom, a portion of teaching could be directed to a rubric level one step higher than their current level.

According to our initial findings, many students reading at the Grade 4 level can read life science texts at rubric Level 3 or 4. This indicates that they can comprehend a number of concepts with supporting evidence for them, but show little articulation of interrelationships. Consequently, taking students to the next level in this situation requires placing an emphasis on interrelating concepts and deepening the supporting evidence for them. In Grade 4, students may be at Levels 3 and 4, and the instruction can profitably be targeted toward Levels 5 and 6. However, some fourth-grade learners may be lower in their reading comprehension of a topic; opportunities for learning should be provided to enable these students to successfully comprehend at simpler rubric levels.

Books should be selected for Grade 4 reading comprehension instruction in which the conceptual knowledge contains multiple interrelated concepts on a topic, with an emphasis on interdependences and detailed supporting information. These texts will naturally be longer, more heavily formatted, with higher vocabulary, and will be more challenging to integrate. As a consequence, the cognitive strategies needed by Grade 4 students to build new knowledge from these texts will necessarily be more complex. For example, it is more cognitively challenging to summarize a three-page text of 1,000 words on the adaptation of insects to hidden worlds in an aquatic environment than to summarize a one-page statement of 100 words on facts and simple concepts about how a zebra survives on an African savannah. There is a natural alignment between the complexity of the new knowledge to be learned from a text and the complexity of the cognitive strategies needed to build that knowledge. Our findings suggest that successful teachers of Grade 4 students attempt the coordination of strategies to enable students to build a coherent pattern of relationships among concepts learned from reading.

CLOSING

Comprehending what we read is rightfully considered the essence of literacy. Therefore, enhancing that process of comprehending should be the cornerstone of education, at least in the elementary grades. In this light, understanding what we mean by *teaching for comprehending* is a crucial journey for educators and researchers.

Our beginning point in that trek was to state one functional meaning of reading comprehension. This definition is grounded in knowledge development and is inextricably linked to text interaction and involvement. After observation, we find we can compare students to each other at one point in time in sensible ways. In chronicling students' growth across 3 months, we observed both qualitative advancements and quantitative increases. Therefore, we suggest that these relatively simple characterizations of reading comprehension and learning from text are useful. Throughout this book, we enrich the picture. We show how cognitive reading strategies, reading motivation, and classroom instruction predict and impact reading comprehension, as we have unfolded it here.

REFERENCES

Alao, S., & Guthrie, J. T. (1999). Predicting conceptual understanding with cognitive and motivational variables. *Journal of Educational Research, 92*(4), 243–254.

Alexander, P. A., & Jetton, T. L. (2000). Learning from text: A multidimensional and developmental perspective. In M. L. Kamil, P. B. Mosenthal, P. D. Pearson, & R. Barr (Eds.), *Handbook of reading research* (Vol. 3, pp. 285–310). Mahwah, NJ: Lawrence Erlbaum Associates.

Baker, L. (2002). Metacognition in comprehension instruction. In C. C. Block & M. Pressley (Eds.), *Comprehension instruction: Research-based best practices* (pp. 77–95). New York: Guilford.

Beach, R., & Wendler, L. (1987). Developmental differences in response to a story. *Research in the Teaching of English, 21*, 286–297.

Chi, M. T. H., DeLeeuw, N., Chiu, M., & Lavancher, C. (1994). Eliciting self-explanations improves understanding. *Cognitive Science, 18*, 439–477.

Glynn, S. M., & Duit, R. (1995). Learning science meaningfully: Constructing conceptual models. In S. Glynn & R. Duit (Eds.), *Learning science in the schools: Research reforming practice.* Mahwah, NJ: Lawrence Erlbaum Associates.

Guthrie, J. T., Wigfield, A., & Barbosa, P. (2002). *Increasing reading comprehension, motivation and science knowledge through Concept-Oriented Reading Instruction in a district-wide experiment.* Annual report to Interagency Education Research Initiative. University of Maryland, College Park, MD.

Guthrie, J. T., Wigfield, A., & Von Secker, C. (2000). Effects of integrated instruction on motivation and strategy use in reading. *Journal of Educational Psychology, 92*(2), 331–341.

Jonasson, D. (1999). Designing constructivist learning environments. In C. M. Reigeluth (Ed.), *Instructional-design theories and models: A new paradigm of instructional theory, Vol. II* (pp. 215–239). Mahwah, NJ: Lawrence Erlbaum Associates.

Mintzes, J. J., Trowbridge, J. E., Arnaudin, M. W., & Wandersee, J. H.. (1991). Children's biology: Studies on conceptual development in the life sciences. In S. M. Glynn, R. H. Yearny, & B. K. Britton (Eds.), *Psychology of learning science* (pp. 179–205), Hillsdale, NJ: Lawrence Erlbaum Associates.

Mintzes, J. J., Wandersee, J. H., & Novak, J. D. (2001). Assessing understanding in biology. *Journal of Biological Education, 35*(3), 118–125.

Narvaez, D. (1998). The effects of moral schemas on the reconstruction of moral narratives in 8th grade and college students. *Journal of Educational Psychology, 90*(1), 13–24.

National Reading Panel. (2000). *Report of the National Reading Panel: Teaching children to read—An evidence-based assessment of the scientific research literature on reading and its implications for reading instruction.* (NIH Publication No. 00–4769). Jessup, MD: National Institute for Literacy.

Novak, J. D., & Musonda, D. (1991). A twelve-year longitudinal study of science concept learning. *American Education Research Journal, 28*(1), 117–153.

Rosenblatt, L. M. (1991). The reading transaction: What for? In B. M. Power & R. Hubbbard (Eds.), *Literacy in process* (pp. 114–127). Portsmouth, NH: Heinemann.

Schiefele, U. (1999). Interest and learning from text. *Scientific Studies of Reading, 3*(3), 257–279.

Snow, C. E. (2002). *Reading for understanding: Toward a research and development program in reading comprehension.* Arlington, VA: RAND.

Strike, K. A., & Posner, G. J. (1985). A conceptual change-in-view of learning and understanding. In L. H. West & A. L. Pines (Eds.), *Cognitive structure and conceptual change* (pp. 211–230). New York: Academic Press.

van den Broek, P., & Kremer, K. E. (2000). The mind in action: What it means to comprehend during reading. In B. M. Taylor, M. F. Graves, & P. van den Broek (Eds.), *Reading for meaning: Fostering comprehension in the middle grades* (pp. 1–31). Newark, DE: International Reading Association.

Williams, J. P. (2002). Using the theme scheme to improve story comprehension. In C. C. Block & M. Pressley (Eds.), *Comprehension instruction: Research-based best practices* (pp. 126–139). New York: Guilford.

10

The Development
of Motivation for Reading
and How It Is Influenced
by CORI

Allan Wigfield
Stephen Tonks
University of Maryland

Walk into any elementary school classroom during a reading lesson and the differences in student reading engagement are obvious. Some students are actively engaged in reading. They eagerly turn to their books when it is time to begin the lesson, and concentrate fully on them. They enjoy talking about what they are reading to their classmates and teachers. They use the different reading strategies they are learning to discover the meaning in the text. When the lesson is over, they reluctantly put their books away, eager to return to them at the first opportunity. When they have free time at other times during the school day they reach for a book and spend time reading.

Other students take a much different approach. They dawdle in getting out their books, and spend as little time with them as possible. If asked to read aloud they do so hesitantly and rarely, if ever, volunteer to read aloud. While reading on their own, they are easily distracted by things around them and can quickly lose their focus. They do not have a clear understanding of important reading strategies, and have difficulty applying them in appropriate situations. They are happy to put away their reading books at lesson's end, and do not return to them in their free time. Still other students are somewhere in between these two groups. They become engaged in reading at some times and for some books, but often are less engaged. They work to apply some of the strategies they are learning at times, but at other times only read superficially. They may return to their books at other times during the day, but often do not. What produces these differences in student reading engagement?

FOCUS OF THIS CHAPTER

In this chapter we discuss the development of children's reading motivation and how motivation contributes to reading engagement. *Reading engagement* is defined as the "simultaneous functioning of motivation, conceptual knowledge, strategies, and social interactions during literacy activities" (Baker, Dreher, & Guthrie, 2000, p. ix). As many authors in this book have discussed, reading engagement is a major goal of CORI, and to understand why children are engaged or not, we need to understand children's motivation for reading. We focus on the aspects of motivation described in chapter 3 in this book, and explore their definitions in more detail in this chapter. We also consider some other aspects of motivation that may influence children's reading engagement. We review research on how these aspects of motivation develop during the elementary school years, and connect this research to our work on fostering reading engagement in CORI.

The question of why some children become engaged readers and others do not is fundamental to motivation because motivation theorists seek to understand the reasons for people's behavior, and for the choices individuals make among the different options available to them. Each day, children are faced with many choices, such as whether to read a book, watch TV, do homework, or call a friend. Once the individual chooses an activity to do, such as to read a book, motivation theorists also try to understand how individuals direct their energy to do the activity. Are individuals actively involved in the activity, persisting when challenges arise, or do they put in minimal effort?

Researchers studying children's reading have become increasingly interested in children's motivation to read (see Guthrie & Wigfield, 2000; Turner, 1995; Wigfield & Guthrie, 1997). For many years reading researchers focused primarily on the cognitive aspects of reading. This research contributed much to our understanding of both the nature of reading and how children can be taught to read. Because reading is an effortful activity that often involves choice, motivation is crucial to reading engagement. Even the reader with the strongest cognitive skills may not spend much time reading if he is not motivated to read. For struggling readers, motivation can be an especially important factor because these readers often try to avoid reading (see chapter 7). Thus, our engagement perspective on reading includes cognitive skills, strategy use, and motivation as crucial parts of reading (see Guthrie & Wigfield, 2000).

We organize the chapter in four sections. First, we define aspects of reading motivation that others and we have assessed. Second, we discuss how motivation links to reading comprehension by influencing the amount of reading that children do. Third, we discuss how children's motivation changes over the school years, and some of the reasons for these changes, including how different kinds of instructional practices influence children's reading motivation. We also present some information in this section about how CORI influences children's reading motivation. Fourth, we discuss our idea that children's intrinsic motivation to read can be enhanced by first creating interest in a topic through hands-on science activities and then connecting this interest to reading. We call this the *situational-to-general* hypothesis.

ASPECTS OF MOTIVATION INFLUENCING READING ENGAGEMENT

Currently, many researchers think of motivation as being determined by the beliefs, values, and goals the individual has (Eccles & Wigfield, 2002). In line with this general approach, Guthrie and Wigfield (2000) defined reading motivation this way: "Reading motivation is the individual's personal goals, values, and beliefs with regard to the topics, processes, and outcomes of reading" (p. 405). From this definition, we can see that the individual is in control of his motivation because it is determined by his beliefs, values, and goals. The definition also implies that motivation is multifaceted and complex, which means that there are different aspects of motivation (see Wigfield & Guthrie, 1997).

We focus in this chapter on the following beliefs, values, and goals associated with motivation: self-efficacy, intrinsic and extrinsic motivation, and mastery goals. We chose these because they have a solid base of support in the research literature as being key to student motivation and achievement (see Wigfield & Eccles, 2002). In addition, several of these are aspects of motivation that we attempt to enhance in the CORI program described in this book. We measure a number of these aspects of motivation in our research, and Table 10.1 presents these aspects and sample items from our Motivation for Reading Questionnaire (MRQ). Our purpose in this chapter is to discuss these particular beliefs, values, and goals, rather than provide a complete review of the broad array of constructs in the motivation literature. More comprehensive reviews of motivation constructs can be found in Eccles, Wigfield, and Schiefele (1998), Pintrich and Schunk (2002), and Stipek (2002). We begin our discussion with self-efficacy.

TABLE 10.1
Motivational Dimensions Assessed in CORI

Dimension	Explanation	Example items
Reading Efficacy	Belief that one can be successful at reading	I know that I will do well in reading next year.
Intrinsic Motivation		
Curiosity	Desire to learn about a topic through reading	If the teacher discusses something interesting, I might read more about it.
Involvement	Enjoyment of different kinds of reading	I make pictures in my mind when I read.
Challenge	Satisfaction gained from reading difficult books	I like hard, challenging books.
Extrinsic Motivation		
Recognition for success	Publicly visible symbols of one's reading accomplishments	I like having the teacher say I read well.
Competition	Reading in order to do better than one's classmates	In reading, I try to get more answers right than my friends.

Reading Self-Efficacy

Self-efficacy is defined as individuals' assessments of their ability at different activities, and their sense that they can accomplish the activity (Bandura, 1997; Schunk & Pajares, 2002). There are two important parts of this definition: the belief that one is capable, and the explicit connection of that belief to the accomplishment of an activity. For Bandura, the link between belief and action is central to his definition of self-efficacy, and so self-efficacy clearly links to children's behavior. A child believing he is efficacious at reading not only has that belief, but also effectively engages in reading activities.

Bandura (1977, 1997) stated that there are several main sources of information that individuals use in forming their efficacy beliefs; we discuss three of them in this chapter. The first is previous performance. When individuals do well on an activity, such as reading, they begin to develop a positive sense of efficacy for that activity. When they do less well, their sense of efficacy is less positive. An important implication of this point is that children's early experiences with reading in school have a strong influence on their developing sense of self-efficacy for reading.

The second source of information is watching peers do the activity. When a child's peers can do an activity, such as read a page in a book, this helps the child think she can do the activity, too. This is particularly likely to happen when the child thinks the peer is relatively similar to herself (see Schunk, 1990). Thus an adult successfully reading has less impact on a child's self-efficacy than a peer whom the child judges as similar.

The third source of information is encouragement from others. When teachers, parents, and peers tell children they can accomplish an activity, children's sense of efficacy increases. Thus it is important for teachers to provide positive feedback about children's performance whenever they can, a point we return to later. However, because children's performance is the strongest influence on their efficacy, this encouragement from others cannot be a substitute for children's own successful performance.

Researchers have shown that children with high self-efficacy do better on different achievement activities, choose more difficult activities to try, and persist at them even if they are having trouble completing them (e.g., Bandura, 1997; Schunk & Pajares, 2002). Furthermore, research has shown that children's self-efficacy in subject areas such as reading can be enhanced by providing children with skills necessary to do the activity better, as well as by direct feedback that they are capable of doing the activity (see Schunk, 1990; Schunk & Zimmerman, 1997).

How does children's self-efficacy influence their approach to reading? Here are two examples, based on children we observed in classrooms in which we work. Jamal is a third-grade reader with a strong sense of his reading efficacy. Because he thinks he is a good reader, he likes to choose long books with difficult words in them. Some of the words in these books sometimes slow him down and disrupt his reading, but he continually strives to improve his reading. When he understands the new words and phrases, his sense of his reading efficacy grows stronger. His reading efficacy helps him continue to pursue his reading interests.

By contrast, Dawn does not believe strongly in her capabilities as a reader. Reading is difficult for her, and when she encounters a new book, she is apprehensive about her ability to understand the material in it. Because she lacks confidence in her reading, she does not volunteer to read aloud in class and tries to avoid reading when she can. She stops reading when she encounters words she does not understand, and often will not ask for help with her reading, even though the assistance would be beneficial to her. Instead, she stops reading and sits quietly at her desk, waiting for the class reading period to be over.

Because of self-efficacy's influence on motivation and performance, it is essential that students develop a strong sense of their efficacy for reading for them to be engaged in reading. Thus, in our instructional programs we emphasize the development of self-efficacy for reading. We do this primarily through strategy instruction, to provide students with the tools they need to become good readers. Teachers provide strategy instruction, opportunities for success, and feedback that emphasizes how their competencies as readers are developing. Chapter 3 discusses how teachers foster children's self-efficacy through reading strategy instruction. In a nutshell, giving readers strategies to utilize develops their *expertise* as readers, which helps them develop a sense of efficacy for reading.

Intrinsic Motivation

When individuals are intrinsically motivated, they do activities for their own sake and out of interest in the activity. Their motivation comes from inside themselves rather than from external sources. When they are intrinsically motivated to learn, students become deeply involved in the activity they are doing and devote much time and energy to it (see Deci & Ryan, 1985; Gottfried, 1990; Ryan & Deci, 2000). They also seek to improve their skills and build on what they know. A substantial body of research indicates that intrinsic motivation relates to long-term engagement in activities, as well as deeper learning (see Deci & Ryan, 1985; Hidi & Harackiewicz, 2000; Lepper & Henderlong, 2000).

In our work on reading motivation, we have defined different subcomponents of intrinsic motivation for reading and measure some of them in the MRQ (see Table 10.1). We defined these subcomponents based on the general definitions of intrinsic motivation in the literature and our experiences working with children in reading. The first is *curiosity*, which we define as a desire to gain understanding about a topic or author of particular interest to a student. Curiosity is an integral part of intrinsic motivation for reading because it refers to the quest for learning about a person, topic, or event for its own sake (Harter, 1981). A child does not attempt to satisfy a curiosity in order to receive an external reward.

Preference for challenge refers to the desire to read relatively difficult or challenging texts. Csikszentmihalyi (1988) discussed how intrinsic motivation is optimized when individuals believe they can master the challenges they face. Thus, a preference for challenge is indicative of intrinsic motivation. Children who prefer to take on challenges in reading are likely confident in their reading skills. They enjoy the challenge of mastering new words and complex ideas presented in text. By taking on more challenging reading materials, their reading comprehension skills grow along with their motivation to read.

A third part of intrinsic motivation for reading is *involvement*, which means deep engagement with a text. Involved readers may be so absorbed that they lose track of time during a text interaction. The content, whether literary or informational, is so intriguing that they concentrate closely, without much effort, and attend to details that bring to light the full meanings the author intended. Deep involvement in text means a high level of cognitive engagement with the text. While reading, the learner is thinking and pondering material, sometimes slowly and sometimes rapidly. This cognitive engagement leads to full experience of the text and deep understanding of content after reading. An involved reader is frequently satisfying a curiosity and will choose books that provide this experience of immersion in favorite topics and pursuits (Wigfield & Guthrie, 1997).

Researchers studying intrinsic motivation emphasize *perceived autonomy's* importance to intrinsic motivation. Perceived autonomy refers to children's beliefs that they have some control over their own learning. When children perceive that they have control over their actions, as compared to being controlled by others or the environment, they are more likely to be positively motivated (Skinner, Zimmer-Gembeck, & Connell, 1998). Children who are autonomous learners are aware that they can find books that interest them and are empowered to give themselves satisfying experiences through reading. The development of perceived autonomy is an important milestone in children's development. As they get older, children desire and need more opportunities to control their own actions and make their own decisions (see Eccles & Midgley, 1989). These decisions include things like what kinds of activities to do in school. When they are given these opportunities, their intrinsic motivation can grow (see chapter 3).

These subcomponents of intrinsic motivation interrelate. For instance, curious readers are likely to be highly involved in their reading and choose more challenging texts to read. They probably have a relatively high level of perceived autonomy because they seek out books and information tailored to their interests. They make choices and control their reading activities for the purposes of gratifying and expanding their curiosity. When children are intrinsically motivated, they enjoy the experiences of collaborating with others (see chapter 3). Research on relations among these components shows they are related (Stipek, 1996; Wigfield & Guthrie, 1997).

What does an intrinsically motivated student in elementary school look like? Jenny is a third-grade student who is intrinsically motivated to read. From the time she was a baby, she always has enjoyed interacting with books, first with her parents and later on her own. In her third-grade class, she reads avidly and grabs a book when there are breaks in classroom activities. One of her favorite activities in school is going to the library to choose a new book to read, and she often chooses books that challenge her. She enjoys sharing what she is reading with classmates and her teacher. She often reads at home after she goes to bed because she says she becomes very involved in the characters and plots. This excitement sparked by books keeps Jenny reading even when other activities are available to her. Her involvement in reading contributes strongly to the development of her reading skills.

Extrinsic Motivation

When extrinsically motivated, individuals do activities in order to receive some benefit, such as a reward. Their motivation comes from what they will receive for doing the activity, rather than from inside themselves. They do not do the activity in their free time, and once they receive the reward, they may stop doing it altogether.

We have defined different subcomponents of extrinsic motivation as well (see Table 10.1). One of these is *recognition for success*. Incentives provide students with publicly visible symbols, such as gold stars, points, or announcements of their success. Many children strive to attain these kinds of rewards in classrooms. Another aspect of extrinsic motivation is *competition*. Students who enjoy being the best in the class, or who seek to outperform their peers, are competitive. Their reward for reading is fulfilled by outperforming other classmates. Success in reading means doing better than others, whereas doing worse may be viewed as failure. These students depend on the external condition that they read better, by some criterion, than their classmates. For these students, internal gratification from knowing the content or enjoying the language of text is not viewed as a valuable reason for reading.

Last, rewards may come in the form of privileges in the classroom, money from parents, or grades. Students who read in order to gain a good grade in the classroom are dependent on the teacher for their reward. If the teacher awards them high grades for a reading activity, their motivation is satisfied, but if the teacher awards them low grades, they are likely to be frustrated and believe that their attempts at reading were unsuccessful. Their criterion for a beneficial reading event is the attainment of a high grade.

James' motivation for reading is primarily extrinsic. When participating in programs that offer rewards for reading a certain number of books, James reads the number required, but no more. He reads the books quickly, instead of enjoying and lingering over each one. Unless there is a reward or some kind of recognition, James does not choose to read. In class, his teacher has to work hard to keep James involved in reading and often needs to provide him with extrinsic rewards to keep him reading.

Extrinsic Versus Intrinsic Motivation

The value of extrinsic motivation compared to intrinsic motivation continues to be debated, sometimes fiercely so (e.g., Cameron & Pierce, 1994; Deci,

Koestner, & Ryan, 1999). This debate centers on whether the use of extrinsic rewards undermines intrinsic motivation. From this debate, we are learning about the conditions under which this can occur. A major factor is how *controlling* the reward is. When children believe teachers use rewards to control them, their intrinsic motivation is more likely to decrease when given rewards of this nature. However, when the reward provides information about how they are doing, children's intrinsic motivation can be enhanced, such that extrinsic and intrinsic motivations work together.

Indeed, a number of authors now argue that intrinsic and extrinsic motivations can coexist (Lepper & Henderlong, 2000; Wigfield & Guthrie, 1997). Correlational studies looking at relations of intrinsic and extrinsic motivation find moderate relations between the constructs, with the relations sometimes positive and other times negative (Lepper & Henderlong, 2000; Wigfield & Guthrie, 1997). For instance, students who enjoy reading, and pursue it on their own time, also seek high grades and recognition for their success. Likewise, students who do not read frequently, nor find gratification in text interaction for its own sake, are unlikely to read frequently for the purposes of high grades and recognition. However, some students with no intrinsic motivation do read to get good grades, in which case the two forms of motivation relate negatively.

In CORI classrooms, children also can read for both intrinsic and extrinsic reasons. For instance, when reading a book about snakes as part of a CORI unit on survival, a student may be intrinsically motivated by a personal curiosity about snakes, and may frequently read books at home on the topic. In addition, this student may be motivated to read about snakes to do well on tests and achieve a high grade. Thus, the student is motivated to read about this topic by curiosity, an intrinsic motivator, and grades, an extrinsic motivator.

Is this view that intrinsic and extrinsic motivation can coexist compatible with Ryan and Deci's (2000) idea that intrinsic and extrinsic motivation form a continuum that is based on the perceived self-determination of a behavior (i.e., the extent to which one feels in control of a behavior such as reading)? These authors state that extrinsic motivation is at one extreme of the continuum and is characterized by very low self-determination. An example is reading to follow the classroom rules or because a reward is given. Intrinsic motivation is at the other extreme and is defined by very high self-determination: The child chooses to read for personal reasons. Between the extremes there are three types of extrinsic motivation that are increasingly self-determined. Ryan and Deci (2000) labeled these as *introjected, identified,* and *integrated,* with integrated representing the most self-determined of these extrinsically motivated behaviors. As self-determination increases, reasons for behavior become more personal. More self-determined reasons that are not purely intrinsic include wanting to learn about something because it has value to a future career (identified motivation), or wanting to study because one believes it is important (integrated motivation). Finally, we arrive at the highly autonomous reasons for behavior, or intrinsic motivation, which include pure interest in a topic or the inherent enjoyment of an activity. Ryan and Connell (1989) found evidence for such a continuum by analyzing reasons children gave for performing school-related behaviors, such as doing assigned homework and answering questions in class. The children's reasons fell at different points on this continuum, and individual children tended to give more extrinsic or more intrinsic reasons for their behavior.

We think this continuum view of intrinsic motivation is at least somewhat compatible with the idea that intrinsic and extrinsic motivation can coexist, and evidence has been found for both models. As noted earlier and as Ryan and Connell (1989) found, students likely have both extrinsic and intrinsic reasons for many of the activities they do. Although both forms of motivation can coexist, we are in strong agreement with Ryan and Deci (2000) that fostering intrinsic motivation in classrooms should be emphasized. As previously discussed, intrinsic motivation relates to many positive outcomes, and we believe it is a major contributor to reading engagement, as we discuss in more detail in a later section of this chapter. Although not all activities in school are intrinsically motivating (see Brophy, 1998), teachers can structure classroom environments to foster children's intrinsic motivation. In particular, they can stimulate students' interests in different topics, support their autonomy for learning, and provide opportunities for social interaction and collaboration. We discuss later in this chapter how children's interest can be stimulated through hands-on activities connected to books. Chapter 3 presents numerous ways teachers can foster students' intrinsic motivation for reading, through autonomy support, providing opportunities for social interaction, providing interesting texts, and teaching reading strategies and conceptual knowledge.

Mastery Goals

When students have a mastery goal orientation, they focus on improving their skills and developing their competencies. They are intrinsically motivated to learn and put a lot of effort into their learning. These students take on challenging tasks in order to improve their skills (Anderman, Austin, & Johnson, 2002). In the motivation literature, such goals often are contrasted with performance goals, which reflect a students' concern to outperform others, demonstrate that they are able, and focus on getting high grades. Although many students have both kinds of goal orientations and there now is evidence that some kinds of performance goals can facilitate children's achievement (see Pintrich, 2000), research clearly shows that a focus on mastery facilitates children's learning and motivation (Anderman et al., 2002).

CORI teachers work to establish a mastery goal orientation in their class-rooms, particularly through their focus on conceptual themes in science. We can see many examples of this in Jean Samuel's classroom. As soon as students walk through the door, they see a range of activity stations, which encourage students to initiate their own research and learn about different science themes. Examples include a live bird and a working aquarium. Each station includes books on the theme, so that students can observe animals first-hand, ask questions, and then answer them with the resources, all in one place. Children can often be seen at these stations working on their own, and the products of their work can be seen on the walls of the classroom. These stations provide opportunities for children to challenge themselves, thus promoting one aspect of mastery goals. Another key aspect of this classroom is the lack of focus on competition between students. There is no need to try and outperform each other, as the atmosphere is supportive of students' individual and cooperative learning efforts. In this environment, students can focus on the concepts they are learning in both science and reading.

Optimal Motivational Beliefs, Values, and Goals

We just defined separately each aspect of motivation that we think is essential to reading engagement. We also noted some of the ways the different aspects of motivation relate to each other, particularly the different components of intrinsic motivation to read, as well as intrinsic and extrinsic motivation. There are other relations among these different aspects of motivation (see Wigfield & Guthrie, 1997). For instance, students with high self-efficacy to read are more likely to be intrinsically motivated to read. When students believe they are capable of doing an activity, they enjoy it more and often pursue it for intrinsic reasons. Mastery goals also relate closely to intrinsic motivation. Generally, students who focus on learning and improvement are intrinsically motivated to learn as well. Thus the different aspects of motivation operate together and influence one another.

Students see these connections as well. During our CORI and SI interventions, we asked students how good they thought they were at using each strategy, and how much they enjoyed reading. Many students connected these two concepts in their answers. Julie, a student in Sally Trent's CORI class, had this to say about how good she was at searching for new information: "I was good at searching for information in books this week because I enjoy reading information and because I like learning about rainforests." Julie's sense of efficacy for searching clearly relates to her enjoyment of reading.

Furthermore, we think that there is an optimal pattern of these motivational characteristics. Students who are intrinsically motivated to read, efficacious about their reading, focused on mastery goals, and socially interactive will be more engaged in reading. Amy illustrates these relations in Sally Trent's class: "I liked the question a lot because it was a lot of fun. Also, it was easy [high self-efficacy!]. Last, I worked with my friends." Students like Amy are more likely to master the various reading strategies taught in their classrooms and ultimately become better readers (Guthrie & Wigfield, 2000). So the goal of CORI is to foster these different aspects of motivation so that children become engaged, strategic readers (see chapter 3).

Reading Motivation, Reading Frequency, and Reading Achievement

We have defined different aspects of motivation and discussed how they relate to one another. We noted (in a general way) that motivation is important to students' engagement in reading. In this section we discuss motivation's importance to engagement in more detail. Why is it necessary to consider motivation's contribution to children's engagement in reading? We think there are a number of reasons. First, motivation influences children's choices of which activities to do. If children are motivated to do an activity, like reading, they will more often choose to do it. Jenny, the student we introduced earlier, can be used to illustrate this point. She has strong intrinsic motivation to read, so she chooses to read whenever she can. She reads in her spare time at school, at home, and in other situations. Reading is one of Jenny's favorite activities, and her love of reading directly influences her choice to read as much as she can.

Second, motivation activates children's behavior. When children are motivated to do an activity, they bring much more energy to it. This is true of individual children and those working together in groups. In our CORI classrooms, we often find children energetically engaged in their science activities and in reading, as vignettes presented in this volume have shown.

Third, children's motivation influences how committed they are to the activity. Whenever children (or adults!) do an activity, they eventually run into challenges or difficulties to overcome to complete the activity successfully. Teachers often hear students say, "This is too hard" or "I can't do this." Some children say such things soon after they start an activity. Such statements mean that the children are not confident they can do the activity, but also that they are not strongly committed to completing the activity. Motivation is one of the key factors that helps students persist when these challenges arise. Students' sense of efficacy is especially important here. Recall Jamal, who has a strong sense of his reading efficacy and so chooses challenging books with difficult words in them. The challenges spurred him to stronger efforts, rather than to giving up.

Along with their efficacy, students' interest in the activity (in this case, reading) also is key. With stronger interest, persistence is greater. In CORI classrooms, children have a wide range of interesting texts to choose from to maintain and build their interest in reading (see chapter 6).

To summarize, children's motivation influences their choice of which activity to do, the energy and enthusiasm with which they approach the activity, and their persistence at it, even when the activity becomes important. This implies that children who are motivated to read will read more frequently. Our research has shown just that. Wigfield and Guthrie (1997), using our Motivations for Reading Questionnaire (MRQ) and a self-report measure of amount of reading called the Reading Activity Inventory (RAI), found that children who were motivated to read reported reading more than three times as much as children less motivated. This was particularly true of children who were intrinsically motivated to read. Furthermore, children's reading motivation measured in the fall predicted *growth* in the amount of reading children did at the end of 3 months. The more highly motivated children increased the amount of reading they did to a greater extent than did less motivated students. From these and other results, we conclude that children who are motivated to read will read more frequently.

But why is reading frequency important? Many studies have shown that the amount of reading children do is important because it relates strongly to their reading comprehension and achievement, and knowledge of the world (see Cipielewski & Stanovich, 1992; Guthrie & Wigfield, 2000). Reading amount also relates to the *growth* over a school year in children's reading comprehension. All schools have as a goal increasing children's reading comprehension. The research we just discussed shows that increasing the amount of reading children do should help schools attain this goal.

How do reading motivation, reading amount, and reading comprehension connect? We suggest that children's reading motivation increases the amount that they read, which then increases their reading comprehension (see Cox & Guthrie, 2001; Guthrie & Wigfield, 2000). Our research has shown this to be the case (Cox & Guthrie, 2001; Guthrie, Wigfield, Cox, & Metsala, 1999). So motivation does not *directly* influence children's reading comprehension. Instead, children's motivation leads them to read more, which in turn increases their comprehension. Thus, motivation provides the energy, but the amount of reading children do is what develops the cognitive skills necessary for stronger reading comprehension. By reading more, children develop stronger vocabularies and also develop the crucial reading strategies necessary for good comprehension. The cognitive aspects of reading comprehension are discussed more fully in chapters 4, 9, and 11.

Importantly, when we look at the relations of reading motivation to reading amount, it is the *intrinsic* aspects of motivation that relate most strongly to amount of reading. The implication of this finding is that enhancing students' intrinsic motivation for reading is crucial to their reading engagement; we return to this point later in the chapter, and it also is discussed in chapter 3.

In summary, children's motivation influences their choices of which activities to do, the enthusiasm and energy with which they approach these activities, and their persistence at them even when the activities get challenging. Reading motivation influences the amount of reading children do, which in turn influences their reading comprehension. Thus, maintaining and enhancing children's motivation for reading is critical for children's reading engagement and comprehension. However, a number of studies have shown that children's motivation *decreases* across the school years, which does not bode well for continued engagement in reading. We discuss this research in the next section.

The Development of Reading Motivation

Most children come to school expecting to do well, curious about learning, and ready to make friends with their classmates. They are excited about starting school, and think of it is a big adventure. Many children form close bonds with their teachers, bonds that can sometimes rival those that they have with their parents. When the first author's daughter, Noelle, was in first grade, she had a teacher that she liked and admired very much. If her parents ever contradicted something the teacher said about a topic, Noelle was quick to take the teacher's side, because Miss Brooks' word was gospel on whatever the topic was.

With respect to the motivation variables we just defined, many young children tend to have an elevated sense of their competence for different activities they do in school. One research study provided a clear example of this. Nicholls (1979) asked first-grade children who was the best in their class in reading, and nearly all of the children identified themselves as either the best or second-best. He asked the same questions of fourth graders and the spread in answers was much greater. Children also find most of the activities they do interesting and exciting, so they are enthusiastic about a wide variety of things they do each day at school. They also greatly enjoy working in groups with other children. Because of their age, they are not yet autonomous learners, nor are they able to self-regulate their learning; these are capabilities that must be learned in the first few years of school. Their confidence in their abilities and enthusiasm for school should help pave their way toward later autonomous learning.

Unfortunately, this optimistic beginning does not last for all children. Children's competence beliefs and intrinsic motivation for learning tend to decline across the elementary school years, especially in academic subject areas like reading and math (Eccles et al., 1998). For instance, researchers studying the early development of children's competence beliefs and intrinsic motivation for different subjects (including reading) found that both decrease during the early elementary school years (Wigfield et al., 1997). Children's extrinsic motivation often increases throughout elementary school and into middle school, sometimes at the expense of their intrinsic motivation (Gottfried, Fleming, & Gottfried, 2001; Harter, 1981; Maehr & Midgley, 1996). Studies looking at reading motivation in particular present a somewhat mixed picture, with some showing these declines and others not (see Wigfield, 2000). In studies where such declines are observed, the largest decreases in reading motivation seem to occur across Grades 1–4, the time when many children work to develop competent reading skills.

Brian's experiences in school can be used to illustrate these points. He enjoyed kindergarten and mastered the different tasks and activities he had to do. He came to first grade eager and excited to learn more about reading and numbers. The first few weeks of school went well for him. He fit in with his classmates and enthusiastically completed his work. As the year went on, however, he began to experience some difficulty. Although he could decode some words, he had a hard time with others. He became hesitant to read aloud in class or at home with his parents. He was placed in the low reading group, where he continued to struggle with his reading. His excitement about attending school was gradually replaced by apprehension, and he sometimes resisted the work given to him. He would respond to rewards for his efforts, but would not often pick up a book in his free time. He was relieved when the school year was finally over.

Brian began second grade with renewed excitement about school. However, he started the year in the low reading group and quickly could tell that other children in the class were reading much better than he. As he continued to struggle with reading, his confidence fell and his apprehension about school increased. He volunteered infrequently to answer questions or to read aloud. His difficulties decoding the harder words he encountered made it hard for him to understand the meaning of the books and stories he tried to read. He avoided reading when he could, so his intrinsic motivation also decreased. These declines in Brian's sense of competence in reading and intrinsic motivation to read continued through the spring of his second-grade year. As the year drew to a close, Brian sometimes wondered what would happen in third grade, when the books became even harder. During third grade, Brian's sense of efficacy for reading continued to decline and he became less interested in reading.

Such changes in children's sense of competence and intrinsic motivation have been explained in two main ways. One explanation focuses on changes that occur within the child. Through the school years, children's capacity to understand their own performance increases. They receive more and more feedback about their performance in school, and become much more sophisticated at understanding its meaning. Two examples, one from the first author's experience and one from research, illustrate this point. When the first author's son, Dennis, was in first grade, the family went out to dinner to celebrate the good grades he received at the end of the first marking period. One of Dennis' friends was at the restaurant and the boy asked Dennis about his report card. After hearing about Dennis' grades, the boy proudly told Dennis that he had received "all S's and NAs" (S- satisfactory; NA- not applicable). At subsequent marking periods, the boy probably learned that NAs are not relevant to his evaluation of his performance in school. A number of research studies show that when young children receive feedback that they did poorly on a task, they continue to think they will do very well if given the task again. As children get older, however, they adjust their expectations in light of such feedback (Eccles et al., 1998). Report card grades, feedback about performance on different school projects and tests, and other evaluative information can lead some children to the realization that they are not as capable as other children. The realization that one is not as capable as others can decrease intrinsic motivation to learn (see Wigfield, 1994).

Children also learn how to compare themselves to others. These comparisons have implications for their own sense of competence. Children engage in social comparison more frequently once they enter school, because they spend all day with same-aged peers. At first, they do not seem to understand how these comparisons reflect on their judgments about themselves, but soon understanding begins to occur (Ruble, 1983). For instance, even in first grade, children are quite aware of which groups they are assigned to and what that means regarding their capabilities (Weinstein, 1989).

The initial excitement children experience in school can start to wear off. The tasks and activities that once were so fresh and new become familiar and sometimes boring. Each school day follows a similar pattern, making school very routine for many children. As a result, their intrinsic motivation for learning and interest in the activities they are doing can decrease.

In sum, as they go through school, children develop a clearer sense of their own competence, based on the kinds of feedback they get from teachers. They also begin to learn how competent they are compared to other children. Their initial excitement in school can fade as the school routine takes over. Despite these changes, many children maintain a strong sense of competence and intrinsic motivation for learning. Others, however, do not. It is important to remember that children's sense of competence and intrinsic motivation are related to each other. If one starts to decline, the other often does as well.

A second explanation focuses on how changing teaching practices may contribute to a decline in some children's motivation. A variety of such practices have been discussed; we present a brief summary here (see Stipek, 1996; Wigfield, 2000). We just noted that children get better at interpreting the evaluative information they receive. They also receive increasing amounts of this information as they go through school. Furthermore, this information gets more specific and focused. For instance, points replace stars and letter grades replace O's for outstanding and S's for satisfactory. Practices that emphasize social comparison and excessive competition between children, may lead children to focus too much on how their skills compare to others. Examples of such practices include public evaluations of students, public displays of students' graded work, teachers making direct comparisons of how different students are doing, and competitive activities, such as spelling bees. Such practices can deflate the competence beliefs of children doing less well.

Grouping practices also can have a strong impact. In elementary schools, children are often grouped by ability within classrooms for instruction in subjects such as reading and math. Later, students often are tracked, so that they are grouped together with children of similar ability levels throughout the school day. These practices are controversial and have attracted much attention (see Oakes, 1985). A major concern is that children in the lower ability groups will perceive they are not very able. As noted before, children often are very aware of their group membership and what it means, despite best efforts not to label the groups in obvious ways (Weinstein, 1989). Research on ability grouping shows it may have benefits for higher-ability students' motivation, but weakens the motivation of children in the lower groups (Fuligni, Eccles, & Barber, 1995; Oakes, 1985). Because of the potential negative effects of ability grouping, especially on children in the low groups, such grouping should be used with care. Teachers should reevaluate group membership on a regular basis. Children should know that they have the opportunity to move into different reading groups.

Instructional practices can influence children's intrinsic motivation for learning as well. Instruction that makes few attempts to spark children's interests in different topics can decrease children's intrinsic motivation (see Brophy, 1998; Stipek, 1996). Children's motivation to read can be enhanced when interesting texts and materials are used in class including trade books, Internet websites, and CD-ROMS (chapter 6; Chambliss & McKillop, 2000). These materials can be used to supplement, or possibly replace, basal reading series, and can be a powerful influence on children's intrinsic motivation, particularly when children also have some choice about which texts to read. When teachers are overly controlling and do not allow children much choice, intrinsic motivation and autonomy can be stifled (see chapter 3).

The evidence for the decline in motivation is convincing in many ways. However, there are some important issues with respect to this research that should be mentioned. Most importantly, many of the measures used to document this decline assess children's motivation at relatively general levels, using questions such as, "How much do you like reading?" and "Are you a good reader?" These questions provide important information, but they may be too general to provide a nuanced sense of the development of children's reading motivation. Younger children may respond to these questions positively, in part because their ideas about reading are general and still taking shape. As they get older, children may develop particular interests about what they love to read; love of mystery books is one example of this. Children also may decide there are other books and topics they do not enjoy as much. In this way, children's views of their own reading become more differentiated. In response to questions such as, "How much do you like reading?" children who hold such differentiated views of their reading may say that overall they do not like reading that much. If asked about their particular topic, however, they likely would report a strong liking or high intrinsic motivation to read. General questions about liking reading may not capture the subtleties of the development of children's motivation to read. Children who have found a niche, or several niches, about which they like to read actually may be highly intrinsically motivated to read. We need to develop measures that assess reading motivation in more specific ways to explore the development of different aspects of children's motivation to read.

Second, we noted earlier, and other authors have discussed, how many children become increasingly autonomous and self-directed as learners as they go through school. They can do more tasks and activities on their own, organize themselves to get their work done, make good choices of books to read when they go to the media center, and so on. In the self-determination theory of motivation (Deci & Ryan, 1985; Ryan & Deci, 2000), such self-determined behaviors are indicative of intrinsic motivation. So why does the research suggest that children's intrinsic motivation and sense of competence declines, when they appear to become more capable and self-determined as they get older? Ryan (personal communication) suggested that it may be because of the changes in school environments previously discussed. Although children's capabilities, perceived autonomy, and self-determination are developing, school and classroom environments often are not supportive of these developments and so may frustrate children, leading to the decline in intrinsic motivation and sense of competence so often reported in the literature (see Eccles & Midgley, 1989; Wigfield, Eccles, & Rodriguez, 1998). As Eccles and Midgley argued, there may be a mismatch between students' desire for autonomy and self-determination and the kinds of controlling behaviors they often experience in school, leading to a decline in their intrinsic motivation.

Classroom environments can be changed, and there are discussions in the literature of how classrooms can be structured to enhance motivation (see chapter 3; Stipek, 1996; Wigfield et al., 1998). So, how does CORI influence students' motivation? We recently addressed this issue using data from the first year of our study of CORI and SI's effects on students (Tonks, Wigfield, Guthrie, & Perencevich, 2003; Wigfield, Guthrie, Tonks, & Perencevich, in press). Third-grade children in both groups completed the MRQ and the RAI before and after the 12-week intervention phase of the project. We looked at change in children's self-efficacy and intrinsic motivation to read in children experiencing CORI and SI. Our statistical analyses showed that children in the CORI group increased significantly in their reading self-efficacy and in their intrinsic motivation to read. Children in the SI group did not increase in either of these aspects of motivation. Thus it appears that CORI fosters children's self-efficacy for reading and their intrinsic motivation to read, the aspects of motivation on which we focus in the CORI program.

These findings show how changes in classroom instructional practices can enhance children's reading motivation. The declines in motivation found in many research studies thus are not inevitable, but can be ameliorated by changing instructional practices. How does CORI foster children's intrinsic motivation to read (also see chapter 3)? In the final section of this chapter, we discuss one important way teachers in CORI classrooms foster students' intrinsic motivation, by connecting students' situational interests to their intrinsic motivation.

Connecting Situational Interest to Intrinsic Motivation in CORI Classrooms

One fundamental way that teachers foster children's intrinsic motivation to read is by connecting hands-on science activities to reading. As discussed in other chapters in this volume, we chose to connect science and reading because science provides many opportunities for active involvement on the part of students. These science activities stimulate children's immediate (or situational) interest in what they are studying. We then build on children's situational interest by providing interesting trade books about the science activity they just did, as detailed in the example that follows. We believe the reading connection is necessary to translate children's situational interest in the topic or activity to longer term motivation to learn; we call this the *situational-to-general hypothesis.*

Motivation theorists define situational interest as a temporary, affective reaction to an activity or a set of conditions, a reaction that may not last (Hidi & Harackiewicz; 2000; Schiefele, 2001). Children's situational interest also can be sparked by an interesting book, website, or video. Thus, situational interest is something that is sparked by an activity or activities that children experience, but it may not extend much beyond the duration of the activity. Hidi and Harackiewicz (2000) called situational interest the "catch" that gets students engaged. Because it may not last, situational interest's effects on learning can be limited. In order for deeper learning to occur, students' situational interests must be connected either to their personal interests or to their intrinsic motivation, because both of these are more permanent (Hidi & Harackiewicz, 2000). This is termed the "hold." What translates situational interest into deeper personal interest and/or intrinsic motivation? Hidi and Harackiewicz discussed how the situational interest can lead a student to want to learn more about a topic. As the student's knowledge deepens, the reasons for engaging in an activity may become intrinsic. Thus, there is a connection between the deeper learning and subsequent motivation.

Hidi and Harackiewicz's (2000) discussion of how the "catch" of situational interest translates into the "hold" of intrinsic motivation is fascinating; however, their analysis is relatively general. We need to develop a better understanding of these linkages to help teachers make the translation from catch to hold. We have begun to do this in our CORI classrooms. In general, we think this process involves generating situational interest by creating specific classroom environmental conditions that foster this interest. These specific conditions include the following (see Table 10.1): hands-on science activities, interesting trade books and multimedia to build on these activities, opportunities for student autonomy concerning which books to read and which questions to answer, opportunities to increase their knowledge and thereby foster both their self-efficacy and mastery goals, and opportunities for collaboration with other students, both in group work and by presenting what they have learned to the class (see chapter 3 for further discussion). Note that these environmental conditions are designed to foster the different aspects of motivation we defined earlier in this chapter.

In each CORI unit, teachers design hands-on-science activities to capitalize on students' interest in active participation in such activities. It is well known that elementary school children love hands-on and other active learning activities, in which they get to participate directly. One example of such an activity in CORI is the habitat walk described in chapter 1, where students take a walk outside their classroom to observe the surrounding habitat and the birds and animals in it. There are many other examples as well; we present a detailed example later in this section. The common thread across these activities is that they are designed to spark students' interests in important science topics and concepts.

Following the activity, students generate their own questions about the activity that they would like to investigate further. Students' creation of their own questions gives them a sense of autonomy over their own learning; this is much different from responding to teacher-generated questions. As a group, they then choose which of the questions to investigate more thoroughly. Because choice can be difficult for some children, teachers monitor the question-generating process closely to ensure that children's questions are ones that can be answered and that follow from the activity. This scaffolding is especially important the first time that children generate questions.

Following the activity and generation of questions, CORI teachers immediately connect students' interest to books. We provide CORI teachers with a large number of books directly relevant to the science topics that are the central focus of the CORI unit "Survival of Life on Land and Water" (see chapter 6). After students participate in the particular activity, they immediately turn to these books to connect their experiences to information they can gain from text. The books available to students include both expository and narrative texts. We chose the books in collaboration with the teachers; the book selection procedure is discussed in chapter 6. Students choose which books to read either individually or in groups, with appropriate scaffolding from the teacher as needed. They compare the information they gain from both sources in order to reach a deeper understanding of the topic. They learn that information from doing the activities, and reading about them are complementary, and that both kinds of information are key to deepening their understanding of the topic, as well as their motivation to pursue it.

Students then often work together in groups to answer their questions and develop a presentation for their class on what they have learned. These activities foster collaboration in two ways. First, children learn to work together in small groups. Second, the whole class becomes a learning community, sharing what they have learned and asking further questions about it.

As mentioned earlier, the science–reading connections and activities that follow influence all of the aspects of motivation we have discussed: intrinsic motivation, self-efficacy, mastery goals, and autonomy. The crucial, initial link for these science–reading connections, however, is translating the situational interest generated by the science activity to students' intrinsic motivation. We see this as the key to building students' motivation to read.

CONCLUSION

We discussed, in this chapter, important aspects of children's reading motivation, how reading motivation develops, and how reading motivation relates to the amount of reading children do. We ended the chapter with a discussion of how different instructional practices influence children's reading motivation, focusing in particular on how CORI teachers work to enhance children's intrinsic motivation to read by creating conditions that spark their situational interest and working to translate these interests into long term intrinsic motivation to read. We continue to believe that motivation is key to reading engagement, and that reading engagement is key to many positive outcomes for children. We will continue to work with teachers to foster children's intrinsic reading motivation.

REFERENCES

Anderman, E. M., Austin, C. C., & Johnson, D. M. (2002). The development of goal orientation. In A. Wigfield & J. S. Eccles (Eds.), *Development of achievement motivation* (pp. 197–220). San Diego: Academic Press.

Baker, L., Dreher, M. J., & Guthrie, J. T. (2000). Preface. In L. Baker, J. T. Guthrie, & M. J. Dreher (Eds.), *Engaging young readers: Promoting achievement and motivation* (p. ix). New York: Guilford.

Bandura, A. (1977). Self-efficacy: Toward a unifying theory of behavioral change. *Psychological Review, 84,* 191–215.

Bandura, A. (1997). *Self-efficacy: The exercise of control.* New York: W. H. Freeman.

Brophy, J. E. (1998). *Motivating students to learn.* New York: McGraw-Hill.

Cameron, J., & Pierce, W. D. (1994). Reinforcement, reward, and intrinsic motivation: A meta-analysis. *Review of Educational Research, 64,* 363–423.

Chambliss, M. J., & McKillop, A. M. (2000). Creating a print- and technology-rich classroom library to entice children to read. In L. Baker, M. J. Dreher, & J. T. Guthrie (Eds.), *Engaging young readers: Promoting achievement and motivation* (pp. 94–118). New York: Guilford.

Cipielewski, J., & Stanovich, K. E. (1992). Predicting growth in reading ability from children's exposure to print. *Journal of Experimental Child Psychology, 54,* 74–89.

Cox, K. E., & Guthrie, J. T. (2001). Motivational and cognitive contributors to students' amount of reading. *Contemporary Educational Psychology, 26,* 116–131.

Csikszentmihalyi, M. (1988). The flow experience and its significance for human psychology. In M. Csikszentmihalyi & I. S. Csikszentmihalyi (Eds.), *Optimal experience* (pp. 15–35). Cambridge, MA: Cambridge University Press.

Deci, E. L., Koestner, R., & Ryan, R. M. (1999). A meta-analytic review of experiments examining the effects of extrinsic motivation on intrinsic motivation. *Psychological Bulletin, 125,* 627–668.

Deci, E. L., & Ryan, R. M. (1985). *Intrinsic motivation and self-determination in human behavior.* New York: Plenum Press.

Eccles, J. S., & Midgley, C. (1989). Stage/environment fit: Developmentally appropriate classrooms for early adolescents. In R. Ames & C. Ames (Eds.), *Research on motivation in education* (Vol. 3, pp. 139–181). New York: Academic Press.

Eccles, J. S., & Wigfield, A. (2002). Motivational beliefs, values, and goals. *Annual Review of Psychology, 53,* 109–132.

Eccles, J. S., Wigfield, A., & Schiefele, U. (1998). Motivation to succeed. In W. Damon (Series Ed.) & N. Eisenberg (Volume Ed.), *Handbook of child psychology* (5th ed., Vol. III). New York: Wiley.

Fuligni, A. J., Eccles, J. S., & Barber, B. L. (1995). The long-term effects of seventh-grade ability grouping in mathematics. *Journal of Early Adolescence, 15,* 58–89.

Gottfried, A. E., (1990). Academic intrinsic motivation in young elementary school children. *Journal of Educational Psychology, 82*(3), 525–538.

Gottfried, A. E., Fleming, J. S., & Gottfried, A. W. (2001). Continuity of academic intrinsic motivation from childhood through late adolescence: A longitudinal study. Journal of Educational Psychology, 93, 3–13.

Guthrie, J. T., & Wigfield, A. (2000). Engagement and motivation in reading. In M. L. Kamil, P. B. Mosenthal, P. D. Pearson, & R. Barr (Eds.) *Handbook of reading research* (Vol. 3, pp. 403–422). Mahwah, NJ: Lawrence Erlbaum Associates.

Guthrie, J. T., Wigfield, A., Cox, K., & Metsala, J. (1999). Predicting text comprehension and reading activity with motivational and cognitive variables. *Scientific Studies of Reading, 3,* 231–256.

Harter, S. (1981). A new self-report scale of intrinsic versus extrinsic orientation in the classroom: Motivational and informational components. *Developmental Psychology, 17,* 300–312.

Hidi, S., & Harackiewicz, J. M. (2000). Motivating the academically unmotivated: A critical issue for the 21st century. *Review of Educational Research, 70,* 151–179.

Lepper, M. R., & Henderlong, J. (2000). Turning "play" into "work" and "work" into "play": 25 years of research on intrinsic versus extrinsic motivation. In C. Sansone & J. M. Harackiewicz, (Eds.), *Intrinsic and extrinsic motivation: The search for optimal motivation and performance* (pp. 257–307). San Diego: Academic Press.

Maehr, M. L., & Midgley, C. (1996). *Transforming school cultures.* Boulder, CO: Westview Press.

Nicholls, J. G. (1979). Development of perception of own attainment and causal attributions for success and failure in reading. *Journal of Educational Psychology, 71,* 94–99.

Oakes, J. (1985). *Keeping track: How schools structure inequality.* New Haven, CT: Yale University Press.

Pintrich, P. R. (2000). Multiple goals, multiple pathways: The role of goal orientation in learning and achievement. *Journal of Educational Psychology, 92,* 544–555.

Pintrich, P. R., & Schunk, D. H. (2002). *Motivation in education: Theory, research, and applications* (2nd Ed.). Columbus, OH: Merrill-Prentice Hall.

Ruble, D. (1983). The development of social comparison processes and their role in achievement-related self-socialization. In E. T. Higgins, D. N. Ruble, & W. W. Hartup (Eds.), *Social cognition and social development: A sociocultural perspective* (pp. 134–157). New York: Cambridge University Press.

Ryan, R. M., & Connell, J. P. (1989). Perceived locus of causality and internalization: Examining reasons for acting in two domains. *Journal of Personality and Social Psychology, 57,* 749–761.

Ryan, R. M., & Deci, E. L. (2000). Intrinsic and extrinsic motivation: Classic definitions and new directions. *Contemporary Educational Psychology, 25,* 54–67.

Schiefele, U. (2001). The role of interest in motivation and learning. In J. M. Collis & S. Messick (Eds.), *Intelligence and personality: Bridging the gap in theory and measurement* (pp. 163–194). Mahwah NJ: Lawrence Erlbaum Associates.

Schunk, D. H. (1990). Goal setting and self-efficacy during self-regulated learning. *Educational Psychologist, 25,* 71–86.

Schunk, D. H., & Pajares, F. (2002). The development of academic self-efficacy. In A. Wigfield & J. S. Eccles (Eds.), *Development of achievement motivation* (pp. 16–31). San Diego: Academic Press.

Schunk, D. H., & Zimmerman, B. J. (1997). Developing efficacious readers and writers: The role of social and self-regulatory processes. In J. T. Guthrie & A. Wigfield (Eds.), *Reading engagement: Motivating readers through integrated instruction* (pp. 34–50). Newark, DE: International Reading Association.

Skinner, E. A., Zimmer-Gembeck, M. J., & Connell, J. P. (1998). Individual differences and the development of perceived control. *Monographs of the Society for Research in Child Development (Serial No. 254, 63, No. 2–3).* Chicago: University of Chicago Press.

Stipek, D. J. (1996). Motivation and instruction. In D. Berliner & R. Calfee (Eds.), *Handbook of educational psychology* (pp. 85–113). New York: Macmillan.

Stipek, D. J. (2002). *Motivation to learn: Integrating theory and practice* (4ᵗʰ ed). Boston: Allyn and Bacon.

Tonks, S., Wigfield, A., Guthrie, J. T., & Perencevich, K. C. (2003, April). *Instructional influences on children's reading motivation.* Paper presented at the Annual Conference of the American Educational Research Association, Chicago, IL.

Turner, J. C. (1995). The influence of classroom contexts on young children's motivation for literacy. *Reading Research Quarterly, 30,* 410–441.

Weinstein, R. S. (1989). Perception of classroom processes and student motivation: Children's views of self-fulfilling prophecies. In R. E. Ames & C. Ames (Eds.), *Research on motivation in education* (Vol. 3, pp. 187–221). New York: Academic Press.

Wigfield, A. (1994). Expectancy—value theory of achievement motivation: A developmental perspective. *Educational Psychology Review, 6,* 49–78.

Wigfield, A. (2000). Facilitating young children's motivation to read. In L. Baker, M. J. Dreher, & J. T. Guthrie (Eds.), *Engaging young readers: Promoting achievement and motivation* (pp. 140–158). New York: Guilford.

Wigfield, A., & Eccles, J. S. (Eds.). (2002). *Development of achievement motivation.* San Diego: Academic Press.

Wigfield, A., Eccles, J. S., & Rodriguez, D. (1998). The development of children's motivation in school contexts. In. A. Iran-Nejad & P. D. Pearson (Eds.), *Review of research in education* (Vol. 23, pp. 78–118). Washington, DC: American Educational Research Association.

Wigfield, A., Eccles, J. S., Yoon, K. S., Harold, R. D., Arbreton, A., Freedman-Doan, C., & Blumenfeld, P. C. (1997). Changes in children's competence beliefs and subjective task values across the elementary school years: A three-year study. *Journal of Educational Psychology, 89,* 451–469.

Wigfield, A., & Guthrie, J. T. (1997). Relations of children's motivation for reading to the amount and breadth of their reading. *Journal of Educational Psychology, 89,* 420–432.

Wigfield, A., Guthrie, J. T., Tonks, S., & Perencevich, K. C. (in press). Children's defining motivation for reading and how it is reading influenced by two reading instructional programs. *Journal of Educational Research.*

11

Growth of Cognitive Strategies for Reading Comprehension

Ana Taboada
John T. Guthrie
University of Maryland

As children's reading engagement develops, many aspects of their reading improve. In their advancement, children become more motivated to read, more conversant in using their current knowledge to gain new understanding, more adept in socially exchanging their ideas with classmates, and more strategic in their reading. In this chapter, we discuss what it means to become increasingly strategic as a reader. Acknowledging the difficulty of learning to use and transfer strategies to new contexts (Smolkin & Donovan, 2001), we present children's performances across time in this chapter. These performances are examples of children's proficiency in using various strategies.

Performances of strategic reading by children at different ages can be viewed as benchmarks of development. We present developmental benchmarks for children at three points in their education: beginning of third grade, end of third grade, and end of fourth grade. We suggest that these benchmarks are useful in setting goals for instruction. When teachers know more specifically what performances to expect from children, or their developmental benchmarks, they can set realistic aims for teaching that will be successfully met.

STRATEGIC READING: THREE ASPECTS

Previous authors have portrayed students' strategic reading in several ways (Collins-Block & Pressley, 2002). Strategic readers are deliberate in their use of strategies (e.g., questioning) as a tool to improve their understanding of text. To be accomplished in the use of strategies, such as questioning, students need to be capable of performing strategies, be aware of how strategies will help them in different circumstances, and be motivated to use the strategies. We refer to the three qualities of the strategic reader as *competence* (knows how to do the strategy), *awareness* (knows when and how to apply the strategy during reading), and *self-initiation* (chooses to use the strategy frequently on appropriate occasions). Next, we discuss each of these qualities.

Competence

Competence in using a reading strategy refers to performing the strategy well. The student who is competent in self-questioning during reading is capable of asking a sensible number of questions at appropriate times. The reader does not simply ask one general question that is not useful and then stop. On the other hand, the competent reader does not ask an endless number of questions that are low in quality or irrelevant to the reading activity. Those are examples of nonadaptive, less relevant forms of self-questioning. The competent questioner knows an appropriate question, distinguishes an interesting and probing question from a boring and useless one, and asks high-caliber questions.

The student who is competent in a reading strategy implements it effectively and appropriately. If the strategy is summarizing, the student provides a full and complete summary, without omitting important portions and without obsessing inappropriately on the task of summarizing. In other words, students who are competent in using a strategy are successful in implementing it completely with appropriate texts. They use the strategy effectively to deepen their knowledge. Although students may be competent in using one or multiple strategies, they nevertheless may not be highly developed in their awareness or self-initiation.

Awareness

Good readers tend to employ reading strategies frequently in an appropriate and effective way (Pressley, Goodchild, Fleet, Zajchowski, & Evans, 1989). To do this, they depend on their awareness. Aware readers believe their strategies are effective tools. Because they possess awareness, these readers can be deliberate. They can use the strategy when they need it to understand a text. For example, awareness of concept mapping as a reading strategy entails knowing that this strategy will assist with integrating information from multiple texts. Aware readers know how one strategy will help them in one situation (graphic organizing to integrate multiple texts), whereas another strategy may help them in a different situation (searching for information to locate important concepts for a project). This awareness is grounded in one's sense of competence. Aware, competent readers know what strategies they possess, and the times and places for using them appropriately.

Self-Initiation

To this point, we have discussed students' capabilities as strategic readers. One capability is competence in doing strategies well and another capability is awareness of strategies as tools for understanding text. These capabilities are indispensable to the strategic reader, but they are not sufficient to enable a student to be an effective comprehender. To take the next step toward being a proficient reading comprehender, students must be self-initiating. They must make deliberate choices to perform a strategy when it is appropriate.

Self-initiation is the motivational aspect of being a strategic reader. Performing a strategy well requires effort and perseverance. Strategies demand thinking and active learning that call for energy and commitment. Without the commitment to use strategies for understanding, a student's competencies are underutilized. If students possess the skill of using a strategy, such as summarizing, but never elect to make a mini-summary during reading, the strategy is inert. In its dormancy, the strategy is not productive and the students' text comprehension suffers. Many students possess the competence to perform several strategies. Also, they are aware that those strategies improve understanding. Nevertheless, they are nonstrategic readers because they are not self-initiating. These students rarely think to use a strategy or decide to complete one.

Being self-initiating is tied to motivational goals and dispositions. Students who are curious to learn about a topic initiate strategies to satisfy their curiosity. Intrinsically motivated students, who put concepts together from texts that they are reading, are more likely to self-initiate than students who find the content to be boring. Intrinsic motivation and interest in topics are the strongest motivational sources of self-initiated strategy use. Because using a strategy carries the risk of possible failure, self-efficacy is valuable. Students who believe they can complete a strategy are more likely to use one than students who doubt their abilities. Lack of confidence and self-doubt can undermine a student's strategic reading because they prevent self-initiation. Why begin something that you do not believe you can finish? In brief, the self-initiating, strategic reader has attained independence in reading comprehension.

DEVELOPMENT OF READING COMPREHENSION STRATEGIES

Previous researchers have described children's growth in reading comprehension strategies using several abstract principles. One of these principles is that students improve in performing strategies successfully (Pressley & El-Dinary, 1997). During Grades 3–5, children improve their ability to complete a requested strategy with relatively little teacher assistance on how to implement the strategy effectively with a given text. This principle refers to the aspect of competence discussed previously that well-developed readers are more competent in successfully performing a given strategy.

Growth of awareness has also been highlighted as a principle of children's strategy development. Paris, Wasik, and Turner (1991) suggested that effective strategy users have the awareness of whether to apply a given strategy before, during, or after reading. For example, it is often valuable to activate background knowledge before reading, whereas it is somewhat less useful to use this strategy afterwards. Metacognitive awareness, the sense of when and where to use a strategy, improves across the elementary grades.

Improvement in self-initiating strategies has been emphasized as a principle in development. It has been shown that students who are proficient in self-monitoring during reading are better comprehenders than students who rarely or incompetently self-monitor (Baker & Brown, 1984). Students who self-monitor regularly stop reading when they are confused, use fix-up strategies to repair their misunderstandings, and resume the reading process appropriately. Embedded in this complex array of processes is self-initiation. Students start and stop their strategy use appropriately.

Development of comprehension strategies is also expressed in the principle of increasing complexity. For example, graphically organizing information from multiple texts is a more complex strategy than asking a single, simple question on the same multiple texts. The more complex strategy of organizing graphically requires students to perform more steps with larger segments of texts and to self-regulate their reading more frequently during the process.

Growth of strategies proceeds as children use increasingly complex texts. A brief text of 50 words on a single topic, such as butterflies, that is suitable for a second-grade student, may be relatively easy for a fourth grader to summarize. In comparison, a more complex text of 500 words on an abstract concept, such as how different species occupy complementary environmental niches, that may contain many concepts and supporting details, demands more strategic expertise. Children improve in the complexity of their strategies and the text to which the strategy is applied.

DEVELOPMENTAL BENCHMARKS
FOR READING COMPREHENSION

The principles of strategy development referring to growth of competence, awareness, self-initiation, and complexity are valuable, but are extremely abstract. What do they mean in terms of children's actions or reading behaviors in the classroom? It is not self-evident what tasks a third grader can or cannot perform with particular texts if she possesses awareness. The principles can be supplemented with students' reading practices at different ages. We refer to these as *developmental benchmarks*.

Developmental benchmarks for strategy use in reading refer to performances of students at different levels of proficiency. A benchmark is a typical performance from students at a given point in their development or schooling. For example, a benchmark for the strategy of questioning during reading is the student's performance of the strategy with an appropriate text at a given point in time, such as the end of third grade. In the next section, we present developmental benchmarks for reading strategies as we have observed them. These benchmarks are based on the performances of approximately 150 students of extremely diverse reading competencies. We observed these students as they progressed from the beginning of Grade 3 to the beginning of Grade 4.

Each strategy included in CORI for Grades 3–5 is presented from a developmental perspective. We include developmental benchmarks for the following five strategies: activating background knowledge; searching; summarizing; organizing graphically, and questioning. Questioning is treated in more detail because we have investigated it more thoroughly. We describe and illustrate the strategy at three stages: (a) beginning of Grade 3, (b) end of Grade 3, and (c) end of Grade 4. End-of-third-grade benchmarks represent instructional goals for typical Grade 3 students. End-of-fourth-grade benchmarks represent instructional goals for students at the end of Grade 4.

Activating Background Knowledge

Definition. Activating background knowledge refers to the recall of experience and knowledge of a text topic before and during reading for the purpose of linking new text content to prior understanding (Anderson & Pearson, 1984). Students who are proficient in this strategy reveal what they know about a topic and relate it to the text at hand. Their knowledge is interconnected and specifically related to the reading topic; it is neither disconnected nor too vague. When students are not familiar with activating background knowledge, their statements might not necessarily be relevant to the main topic. Statements may be too general or based on trivial text cues, rather than the main topic. Initially, the teacher must prompt students on a frequent basis (Prince & Mancus, 1987; Spires, Gallini, Riggsbee, 1992). Later, students learn to self-initiate their knowledge activation.

Example.   When presented with a text on "Grasslands and Rivers," students were prompted to state their background knowledge. Prompts consisted of such questions as: *How are grasslands and rivers similar? How are they different? How do plants and animals live?* The following are samples of the background knowledge statements presented by two third graders at the beginning of the school year:

S1:   *I know that there's lots of animals in the grasslands and rivers and animals drink from the river.*

S2:   *Rivers have plants and animals. The animals that live in the river are fish.*

For several reasons, this type of background knowledge denotes early performance in activating background knowledge. First, students had to receive very specific prompts (questions in this case) in order to activate what they knew about grasslands and rivers. They did not self-initiate the use of the strategy. Second, the knowledge lacks detail and specific reference to the topic; knowledge about the presence of animals is not specific to these biomes but to *all* biomes. Additionally, their knowledge does not reveal any type of causal understanding, but only states factual information.

On the other hand, later in Grade 3, performance of activating background knowledge shows that knowledge is topic relevant. It is related to the *specific* topic at hand. Knowledge may be elicited by the important text cues, such as titles or headings. Moreover, knowledge shows interconnections among its different facets and contains causal understandings. An example of a prior knowledge statement that is more developmentally advanced at the middle of Grade 3 follows:

Grasslands and rivers are different because grasslands do not have water in them but rivers do. Fish, bugs, snails and algae live in the river. Bugs, cat tails, leaves and caterpillars live in the grassland. They live by water, food, plants and nectar. They help each other by providing food and water for each other. I also know that you can find cray fish in a river. You can also find snails on plants in grasslands. Grasslands are also very wet in the water. They are also usually cold in the grasslands to keep the plants growing and so that they will not die. Because if they do die they will stop the food chain.

This statement of background knowledge shows specific aspects of the two biomes in the text, as opposed to generalities that can be applied to any biome. Although this knowledge statement does not refer to defining features of the biomes (i.e., they are rather broad statements such as *"Grasslands do not have water in them but rivers do"*), it mentions specific aspects that pertain to rivers and grasslands, rather than to any other biome, thus making prior knowledge topic-relevant. The list of animals for each biome is another instance of the relevancy of background knowledge in relation to the text topic. Integration of knowledge is also evident in sentences such as: *They live by water, food, plants and nectar. They help each other by providing food and water for each other.*

Students who are proficient with prior knowledge activation tend to use it frequently. They activate background knowledge before and during all major reading events. More advanced prior knowledge activation also implies reader awareness of its purpose. Such a reader is fully aware that prior knowledge is useful for better and deeper understanding of text. The reader uses it in relation to other reading strategies, such as questioning and searching.

Benchmarks for Activating Background Knowledge at the End of Grade 3
Background knowledge statements by the end of Grade 3 are characterized by:
- A few simple concepts that might serve as organizing ideas.
- Limited descriptive information supporting or illustrating the concepts.
- Basic definitions of central concepts.
- Relevance to the topic to be read.
- Distinctions of the topic from similar topics.

Students at this stage:
- Usually require teacher prompting.
- Activate background knowledge thoroughly with little teacher guidance.
- Show beginning awareness of how the strategy supports comprehension.

Benchmarks for Activating Background Knowledge at the End of Grade 4
Background knowledge statements by the end of Grade 4 are characterized by:
- Several facts and/or concepts that are related to the topic.
- Significant illustrative information supporting concepts (supporting details for more than one concept).
- One or more causal explanations included.

Students at this stage:
- Think about background knowledge to build new understanding during reading.
- Invoke the strategy appropriately (i.e., when they do not understand text).
- Self-initiate the strategy frequently.
- Make some decisions to consult their background knowledge before reading.

Developmental Pattern.   The growth pattern for activating background knowledge emphasizes the increase in breadth of knowledge used to understand new text. During the third grade, students become much more elaborate in their recall of text-relevant information that helps their reading comprehension. Students' growth of awareness is also evident. In the beginning of Grade 3, students have a sense that their background knowledge is useful and that it increases as they read a new text. However, their awareness is not sufficient for them to know when it is valuable to activate their previous experience or how extensively to engage in this strategy. Finally, self-initiation of background knowledge activation is rare until the end of Grade 4.

Searching for Information as a Reading Strategy

Definition.   Searching for information refers to students seeking and finding a subset of information in the total text by forming specific goals, selecting particular sections of text, extracting information accurately, combining new and old information, and continuing until goals are fulfilled (Guthrie, Weber, & Kimmerly, 1993). Searching for information is a strategy that students use when they are reading to learn specific topics in a content domain or studying a subject area. The process of searching refers to finding specific information within a large amount of text. For example, we search encyclopedias, reference books, and information books. Only occasionally do we read to comprehend the total text of these books. As the strategy of searching is driven by the goal of the reader, the goal is an information need or a question the reader brings to the task. Searching is unlike text comprehension because only a limited portion of the total text is examined, understood, and used to advance the learner's knowledge.

Students first encounter the need to search when they begin learning in content areas. They are expected to answer important questions and may need to look in multiple parts of a large book or resource. Searching requires students to form a goal, navigate text features, and integrate information. Early performance in search consists of a lack of awareness about when it is relevant to search, or how to establish good goals. A student who initiates search for the first time might use one text feature, such as the table of contents or pictures, but might not use the multiple features in a text that can help with search. For instance, a student might not know how to use macrotext features, such as headings or subheadings, or microtext features, such as captions, to assist and guide him in his search.

Success in search depends on alignment between the search goals and the text features. Some goals may be too broad, driving an imprecise search where words in the index may not relate to the goal. Also, goals may be too specific for the type of text at hand. If the book lacks abundant text features and the search goal is highly specific, then the search will be frustrating.

Students who are proficient with search as a reading strategy show awareness of the need for a specific piece of information (Dreher & Sammons, 1994). Instruction in searching can help students form necessary goals (Dreher & Brown, 1993) that are multiple and task-relevant; they include several questions, synonyms, or paraphrases. Good searchers select useful sections within texts and reject those that are irrelevant. An advanced searcher frequently makes use of multiple text access systems (e.g. table of contents, index, glossary) and continues until questions are answered as fully as possible. Search at this stage is mostly self-initiated. All the processes of goal setting, selection, and extraction of information, as well as integration, are fulfilled with little prompting (Symons, McLatchy-Gaudet, & Stone, 2001).

Examples. Melissa, a beginning third grader, initiated a teacher-requested search in a book about birds' feeding. It had only an index, page numbers, and big pictures. Melissa's goal for this search was "to learn all about birds." She learned a bit about beaks, but skimmed in vain for other topics, like nesting and the color of feathers. The text was a misfit, too narrow for her broad goal. Frustrated due to the vagueness of her goal and the inadequacy of the book for this purpose, Melissa disengaged from the activity.

Matt enjoyed a more successful search. Having read the word *blubber* in a book about penguins, he decided to find out what *blubber* was. The first book Matt located had very limited text features that were not helpful in his search. The second book, *Birds of Antarctica* (Stone, 1995) had good text access systems and Matt was aware that by using the index, he could look for information in a fast and organized (alphabetical) manner. He knew that he needed to look up the word *blubber* alphabetically. Using the index, Matt located the page number, turned to the indicated page, and discovered that *blubber* keeps penguins warm. However, he still did not know *what blubber was*. He was aware of the glossary's location in the book and that this section could help him with word definitions. Matt found the word in the book's glossary and discovered that *blubber* is "*a layer of fat that helps animals who live in very cold places keep warm.*" Now, he not only knows that penguins have *blubber*, but he knows its function and that other animals have it as well. Matt was satisfied with his search and accomplished his goal.

Benchmarks for Searching for Information at the End of Grade 3
Student characteristics by the end of Grade 3 include:
- Initiating searches at teacher request without teacher assistance.
- Students focus on several goals or questions to guide a search.
- Beginning knowledge of organization of resources (books).
- Competence in using several text features to locate goal-relevant information
- Use of one or two texts or resources in a search.
- Careful reading of selected sections of books or information sources.
- Integration of information gleaned from one or two locations in a book.

Benchmarks for Searching for Information at End of Grade 4
Student characteristics by the end of Grade 4 include:
- Selection of texts appropriate to students' reading (word recognition) level with minimal teacher assistance.
- Ability to adjust to the goals by adding relevant synonyms or new terms.
- Knowledge of how diverse expository books are organized (table of contents, index, sections, headings).
- Use of most features of books (topic sentences, captions, side bars, illustrations as examples, etc.).
- Use of two to five texts or resources in a search.
- Accurate, critical reading of selected sections of books or information sources.
- Integration of information gleaned from multiple locations in books or sources.
- Monitoring processes of searching.
- Knowing when to search versus when to fully comprehend a text.
- Initiating searches when it is appropriate to the task or purposes of a project.

Developmental Pattern. The developmental pattern for searching for information in Grades 3–5 begins with rapid gains in competence. Because students have rarely searched in previous grades, they are not familiar with the organization of information books. With brief instruction, however, students can form a goal (e.g., a question), identify a relevant book section from the table of contents or index, and locate their answer if it is present in the text (Symons, McLatchy-Gaudet, & Stone, 2001). This primitive search competence is achieved readily. More complex forms of search develop more slowly during Grades 3–5. As students gain command of this strategy, they learn to form multiple goals (neither too few nor too many) at an appropriate level of detail and select an appropriate number of texts and resources. Furthermore, students develop self-regulation of the searching process. They learn to use relevant material and discard the irrelevant. They pursue multiple text interactions until their goals are achieved and their information needs are met.

Acquisition of self-initiation for searching is vital. The importance of self-initiating all of the processes within searching cannot be overstated. When students are in command of this strategy, they integrate information, seek more resources, and pursue their search goals resourcefully. In contrast, less self-initiating searchers require teacher prompting to integrate across texts. Intrinsic motivation for learning from text increases students' effectiveness in the search process. Motivated students persevere in reading for longer periods of time, find more relevant information, and culminate their search conclusively (Reynolds & Symons, 2001).

Summarizing

Definition. Summarizing refers to students forming an accurate abstract representation (summary) of text after reading all, or a substantial portion, of text material (Brown & Day, 1983). Beginning third graders may not have a clear mental framework for writing a summary. They may copy verbatim from a text or may use text-explicit information only. Often, they follow the sequence of information in a text, rather than form their own coherent conceptual organization.

Examples. After reading the following text, here is an example of a beginning third grader's summary. This child wrote, "*Otters can hold their breath staying under water up to four minutes.*" Her summary mentions one isolated concept that was transcribed verbatim from the text. Even though it is an important conceptual idea, it has no relation to other concepts. It seems to have been chosen due to its location as the last line in the shortest section of the text. The text is a section of an unpublished assessment packet (Guthrie, 2001a, 2001b).

Otters. River otters live near rivers and lakes. They spend much of their time swimming. Otters feed on fish and small animals such as crayfish. They can crush shells and slice fish with their strong sharp teeth. They also eat snakes, clams, snails, frogs, and even earthworms.

Legs, Feet, and Ears. Otters have short legs with five toes on each foot. Elastic skin called webbing between the toes helps them swim. Except for pads on their toes and soles, their feet are covered with fur.

Otters use their front paws like hands to handle food and other objects. (Picture caption).

They use their paws to feel for crayfish under rocks in muddy riverbeds. They hold food in their front paws while they eat it. Special muscles allow otters to close their small ears and nostrils to keep water out.

Breathing. Otters are good swimmers. Otters can hold their breath and stay under water up to four minutes.

Communication. River otters have good eyesight and a very keen sense of smell. They make many different sounds. They chatter, chuckle, grunt, snort, and growl. They also warn other otters of danger with a shrill whistle.

In another case, a student at the end of third grade wrote, "*River otters eat crayfish, clams, snakes, fish. Otters can hold their breath to four minutes. Otters use their front paws to feel for crayfish under muddy rocks. Otters call each other when there is danger.*"

This summary integrates and merges information from all four sections. Even though the summary comprises only explicit text information, it does not follow the exact sequence of the text, showing the student's ability to express information succinctly in his own words. An example of such ability is shown in the last sentence, "*Otters call each other when there is danger.*" This sentence precisely captures the essential information in this text section.

Students who possess advanced summarizing skills present ideas in an organized fashion based on importance. They denote levels of abstraction and generalization and display information that is relevant and comprehensive. The organization may be conceptual, conforming to the student's knowledge organization rather than to the text sequence. Ideas and concepts make use of inferences and integrate knowledge across sections, rather than merely using text-explicit information.

Students who have advanced summarizing skills can also encapsulate multiple genres and text representations (i.e., diagrams, tables, etc.). They can distinguish information within different texts in terms of intratext facts, conclusions, or opinions. Advanced students can also use either the persuasive or informative text style to denote different prioritizing of ideas. In summarizing this text, a student at the end of fourth grade wrote:

> Otters live near rivers and lakes. They swim a lot. They eat fish and crayfish. With their strong teeth they can crush shells. Otters have webbed feet with five toes that help them swim. They use their paws to catch fish. They can stay under water for four minutes. When they want to keep water out they use special muscles in the nostrils and ears. They make many different noises and tell each other when they are in danger using noises.

This summary captures the essence of the text. It taps all text sections and all the major ecological concepts. Information often follows the text sequence, but it has its own coherence. There are instances of integration of information across text sections, which are revealed in the linkage between some sentences (e.g.: *They can stay under water for four minutes. When they want to keep water out they use special muscles in the nostrils and ears.*). This integration of information across sections denotes a level of conceptual order that is imposed by the reader over the text structure. The language used is not verbatim transcription from the text; rather it is the reader's own language. The reader's words are appropriate and true to the ideas in the text; they convey a level of abstraction essential to good summaries. The last sentence of the summary is a good example of an inference from the information in the last section in the original text on communication.

The following is another summary from an end-of-fourth-grade student:

> Otters are river animals that do different things to survive. They eat river and land animals, such as crayfish, clams, snails and even snakes. They use their front paws to catch food and other things. Otters have special webbed feet that help them swim this might also help them to escape from enemies that want to kill them. They are excellent swimmers and can hold their breath under water up to four minutes. Otters can close their nostrils and ears using special muscles to keep water out. They have a good sight and sense of smell. And they can also make many noises to tell each other when they are in danger.

This summary is presented in a conceptually ordered manner. The text concepts drive the organization or structure. The first sentence that states that otters *"do different things to survive,"* exemplifies the level of abstraction the reader extracted from the text. Nowhere in the text is this information explicitly stated. The reader probably inferred it from reading the four text sections. Statements on what otters eat, and that their webbed feet help them swim and escape from enemies, support the overarching concept of survival.

Information is presented in a conceptually organized way. The sentences *"They are excellent swimmers and can hold their breath under water up to four minutes"* and *"Otters can close their nostrils and ears using special muscles to keep water out"* are conceptually organized as they integrate ideas from across different sections in the text and tend to be centered around similar concepts (i.e., locomotion [swimming]). *Breathing* in the first sentence is linked to the ability *to keep water out* in the second sentence. This shows that information is based on conceptual thinking, rather than on explicit text information or sequence. Although these summaries are relatively long and substantive, by the end of Grade 4, students also form brief mini-summaries of text segments. Such 2 to 3 sentence summaries are part of synthesizing multiple texts.

Benchmarks for Summarizing at the End of Grade 3
Student characteristics by the end of Grade 3 include:
- Summaries are written for a page or a chapter of an information book.
- Central idea is accurately identified.
- Supporting facts and details are identified for the central idea.
- Most unimportant information is omitted.
- Summary is organized around key topics, not original text sequence.
- Frequent teacher prompting, but not teacher guidance or scaffolding.

Benchmarks for Summarizing at the End of Grade 4
Student characteristics by the end of Grade 4 include:
- Summaries are written for a chapter or for full information book.
- Central idea is accurately identified.
- Several supporting facts and details are identified for the central idea.
- Unimportant information is omitted from written summary.
- Summary is organized around key concepts, not original text sequence.
- Students compose summaries with minimal teacher prompting.
- Students can evaluate the quality of a summary (self or peers).
- Students use mini-summaries of a portion of text to write summary of full book.
- Students appropriately initiate a mini-summary activity to aid in their synthesis of multiple texts.

Developmental Pattern.   From the beginning of third grade to the end of fourth grade, students' development of summaries reflects all aspects of the summarizing process. During this time, students improve in their identification of all important text concepts to be summarized. They locate supporting information and examples that are critically important and highlight essential features of the concepts. One of the last aspects to be learned is organization. During the latter portion of this time period, students gain competence in framing their summary in a coherent organization of ideas that may differ from the presentation in the text. Although summarizing requires a high amount of cognitive effort, students develop the disposition to write mini-summaries during their work on an extended project. They gain the conditional knowledge of when to write smaller summaries to provide them with a resource for pulling together and integrating a large amount of information for a report or presentation.

Organizing Graphically

Definition. Organizing graphically refers to students' construction of a spatial representation of text-based knowledge, which may include drawings, concept maps, and diagrams (Armbruster, Anderson, & Meyer, 1991). This process consists of: (a) reading an extended text thoroughly, (b) identifying key concepts in the form of words, (c) locating supporting information in the form of words or phrases, (d) defining the relationships among key ideas and supporting information, and (e) organizing this information onto a concept map, chart, diagram, or visual display. Such organizing is valuable in all content domains (Darch, Carnine, & Kameenui, 1986).

At the beginning of Grade 3, students display a few concepts with little or no overall organization. The selection of concepts does not reflect importance of the text. Few relationships are depicted. Their graphic structures may show some misconceptions and scientific inaccuracies.

Third graders who received the text *The Amazing Snake* (Guthrie, 2001a) demonstrated an illustration of organizing graphically. This text is organized into four subtopics: (a) snakes' feeding; (b) hunting and killing; (c) snakes' locomotion, and (d) snakes' defense. The four sections represent four central ecological concepts subsumed under the overarching concept of survival. In each section, a concept is supported by details. Figure 11.1 shows a beginning third-grade student's concept map.

The concept map displays some concepts (*eating, hiding, hunting, and killing*), but the map lacks overall organization. A limited number of concepts are displayed, whereas some important concepts, such as *locomotion* and *defense,* that are present in the text, have been omitted. The map lacks interconnection between concepts and the central topic. Additionally, some of the concepts do not display the same level of inclusiveness or generality that others do, yet they are still located in equal positions in relation to the main topic (e.g., *hide* is a means of *defense* and it is displayed at the same level as *hunting and killing* which are both more encompassing than *hide*). Other limitations might be attributed to the fact that some concepts are supported by salient facts, whereas others are not. Lastly, the link between the words *squeeze* and *fangs* may represent a misconception or, perhaps, just a mistake.

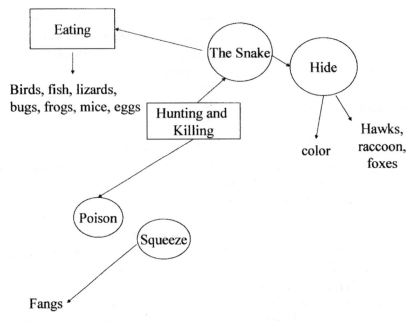

FIG. 11.1. Beginning Grade 3 student's concept map.

More advanced third-grade graphic organizers display several main concepts with supporting details that are linked to them. These graphic displays show information organized in different ways. Hierarchical organizations are typical of graphic organizers, with concepts denoting inclusive relations among them. To use graphic organizers as strategies for comprehending text, students need to understand about the conceptual knowledge structure of the content and the organization of the information text itself (Taylor & Beach, 1984).

A hierarchical form implies that each level on the concept map is expressing a similar level of generality and inclusiveness. From top to bottom, the map gets progressively more specific and less inclusive in the types of relationships represented. Thus, the more levels a concept map has, the higher the degree of differentiation of meaning and conceptual refinement (Novak & Musonda, 1991).

A student at the end of Grade 4, with a more advanced graphic organizer, might represent the text with a concept map as seen in Fig. 11.2. The hierarchical organization of this map is shown in the display of a main central concept (in the triangle) and related, less inclusive, concepts displayed in boxes. Features of these concepts are located in the ovals (e.g., *swallowing whole, hide, squeeze,* etc.). These

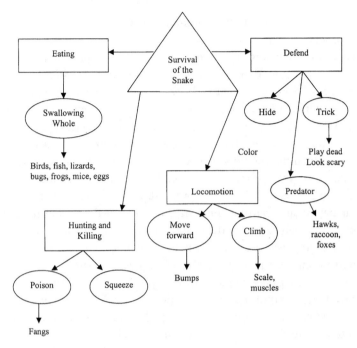

FIG. 11.2. Grade 4 students' advanced graphic organizer.

features represent the actual behaviors that enable the interaction of the organism with its habitat (i.e., the ecological concept). Finally, at the lowest level of inclusiveness, supporting details are depicted as linked to these features.

Many concept maps have links explicitly labeled with connecting words such as *for, because, have,* for example, to help students organize their thinking when making their maps. However, some students might choose not to use these labels, as is the case of the map in Fig. 11.2. A map that is hierarchically well organized should convey these relationships, even if the links are not explicitly labeled. From the center outward, the map gets progressively more specific, to the least inclusive level of supporting details that help with a high degree of conceptual differentiation.

Organizing Graphically in Amy Broomall's Classroom

We now visit a third-grade classroom in a middle-income neighborhood school. Stepping into Amy Broomall's classroom, you enter a stimulating, literacy-rich environment. Extensive wall displays of written materials describe the different purposes for reading and writing. Students' works are exhibited, another sign that this is a classroom environment where literacy has a central place.

Today, Amy is teaching her students how to build graphic organizers; in particular, she is teaching concept maps, a reading strategy essential to gaining knowledge from text. Amy begins her lesson by using a concrete example to illustrate the steps of graphic organizing. Students have congregated into a large group and Amy selects one of her students' folders. She seizes the papers in the folder and mixes them up. Then, she opens the discussion by asking her students what difficulties they might encounter when asked to look for a paper in a messy folder. Amy stresses that they would be wasting their time if they could not find their papers right away. She proceeds to tell the class that by categorizing their papers and putting them in order, they will be able to find them promptly. Amy then addresses the lesson's main point: *"What are we doing when we categorize our papers and put them in the right order?"*

Almost in unison, the students reply, *"We are organizing."*

"Why is organizing important?" Amy asks.

Her students respond that if you do not organize, you are unable to know where things are. Once students have grasped the idea at a concrete level, Amy goes on to explain the strategy at a cognitive level.

"Today we are going to be organizing some information from the story that you read to make your learning easier. We need to learn to organize our knowledge because, if I just gave you a whole bunch of information and asked you to organize it, that would be difficult."

Amy leads whole group instruction for the first section of an information text entitled, *What's the Difference?: Birds* by S. Savage (2000). She explains, *"We call this strategy 'Organizing Graphically' and what we'll use to organize it is called a concept map."* She asks the children to give examples of webs they have constructed in the past. Students open their books to the story, *"What Makes a Bird a Bird?"* Amy continues, *"Now, we are going to work on the text section that talks about birds. After that you will work with your partner on the section about feathers."*

Amy puts the word *birds* in the middle of the concept map and circles it. She also has about 15 words displayed on the side of the board that relate to *birds* and emphasizes that she picked those words because they are important to learning about birds. She then asks her students to choose a word from the list that could be "connected" to *birds*. A student picks the word *egg-layers; she asks for a reason that this word might be related to birds,* stressing the type of relationship between the words: *"Yes, birds are egg-layers,"* says Amy. Before continuing with the concept map, Amy asks her students to locate where it says that birds are egg-layers. In this way, she points out to them how the links in the graphic organizer are related to content in the text. This is an important relationship students need to remember in order to build effective concept maps.

Students continue to choose words from the list. The next word they choose is *habitat*. Like the word *egg-layers*, *habitat* is placed in a box linked to the central word, *birds*. Amy also draws attention to the differences between this concept map and other webbing activities they have done previously.

One student chooses the word *penguin* and chooses where to place it. Another picks the words *can't fly* and Amy places those at the same level as *penguins*, both branching out from the central topic, *birds*. Some students shake their heads; they seem to disagree with the placement of these words. Students have begun to realize that the map is disorganized. Some linkages between words are appropriate and some are not. So Amy asks, "*Why shouldn't words like* penguins *and* can't fly *be in boxes branching out from the central topic,* birds, *at the same level?*" Her students conclude that *penguins* are a **type** of bird, whereas *can't fly* is a **characteristic** shared by some birds, including *penguins*. Thus, *can't fly* is of a higher level of abstraction than *penguins*. While slightly guiding students toward this conclusion, Amy asks the children to decide on the location of these words on the map. Students locate *can't fly* in direct linkage to *birds*, and *penguins* as a linkage to *can't fly*.

By shifting the location of the boxed words and involving her students in discussing the reasons for the shift, Amy is scaffolding and modeling how to organize concept maps in a conceptual way. Words are linked to each other because of conceptual relationships among them, rather than because of their order of appearance in the text. In addition, by asking students to find information that corroborates the linkages depicted graphically in the text, Amy stresses the correspondences between the concept map and the text, and teaches them the use of symbols and links in an economic and systematic way.

When the concept map is complete, Amy points out its similarity to a *web* (a term more familiar to students). She also emphasizes that the boxes could be changed to other shapes, such as triangles, as long as the words that belong to the same level or category (in reference to the central topic) are all within the same shape or are comparably color-coded, to show these relationships. She then highlights that the next task is to figure out how these words are linked. Amy prompts the students to write connecting words on the links to help them make sentences. Using *that* and *are*, students formed the sentence *Birds that can't fly are penguins*. With connecting words *makes* and *like*, they come up with the sentence *Birds make habitats like trees*. Her students start to see the connections between words in a more explicit way. Amy notes that the words added to the map can be changed. To finalize the whole group activity, the students read the sentences from the concept map. This activity reiterates that the concept map is linked to text and is a method of organizing text information graphically. Fig. 11.3 shows the final concept map co-constructed by the whole group.

As a second phase of this lesson, Amy's students work on concept maps in pairs. Their concept maps are on the text section of *feathers*. She asks what the map's central topic is and provides some word-cards that relate to the topic of *feathers*. Some of the word-cards provided are: *light, beautiful, water, oil, mating,* and *preening.* Amy also points out that the students must continue to look for words in the text, and that they will decide on the words that go in the boxes and how to organize them. To provide flexible arrangement and reorganization of words, students work with word-cards. As students put their concept maps together, Amy walks around scaffolding their work and asking for rationales for the locations of different words. She also monitors students' selection of words. While building their concept maps, children are working with the text. They use the text as a source for words and to help lay out their maps. Amy continues monitoring; she inquires about word groupings and the rationale for certain links. Once again, she is developing awareness of the types of links among words and of their conceptual relationships.

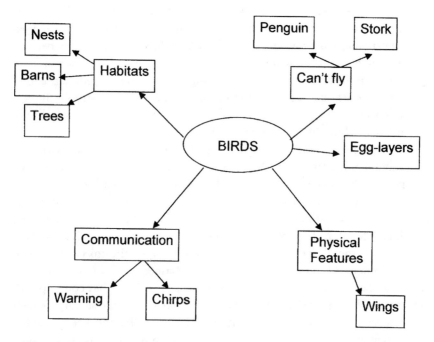

FIG. 11.3. Final concept map contructed by Amy's class.

Benchmarks for Organizing Graphically at the End of Grade 3
Student characteristics by the end of Grade 3 include:
- Students compose graphic organizer at teacher's request.
- Students supply the words and links for the organizer provided by the teacher.
- Students make graphic organizers for a page or section of book, but not the total book.
- Spatial display of text information is internally consistent.
- The hierarchy, time sequence, and cause–effect relations are clear.
- Superordinate concepts and subordinate information are present.
- Links among concepts show key relationships (labeled or unlabeled).
- Students are aware of text sources for the concepts and links depicted in their organizers.

Benchmarks for Organizing Graphically at the End of Grade 4
Student characteristics by the end of Grade 4 include:
- Students supply all aspects of organizer, including main concepts, support, and organization.
- Students make graphic organizers for sections or books.
- Organization is internally consistent.
- Organizers are structured in a hierarchy, such as by time, sequence, cause–effect, or others.
- Organizers contain multiple superordinate concepts and several subordinate ones with additional supporting information.
- Labeling or word links among concepts show key relationships.
- Students compose graphic organizers by supplying the words, links, and organizing structure.
- Students critically discuss the qualities, inclusiveness, and relationships of a graphic organizer.
- Students diagnose misconceptions of organizers as representation of text.
- Students occasionally compose organizers for a text on their own initiative.

Developmental Pattern.   Two major aspects of organizing graphically are especially sensitive to development. First, the ability to state explicit relationships among the elements in a graphic display is learned later than other aspects. For example, the links in a concept map are statements of relations. At the beginning of the Grade 3–4 span, students are limited in stating these relations, but later in the span they can form such connections, provided adequate instruction and opportunity are available. Second, students improve in their ability to manage all the processes without scaffolding. Being able to generate all processes including the central content, supporting details, spatial organization, and statements of interrelationships is extremely rare at the beginning of Grade 3, but is quite common for end-of-Grade-4 students.

Questioning as a Strategy for Reading Comprehension

Definition.   Questioning refers to students asking or writing *self-initiated* questions about the content of a text before and during reading, to help them understand the text and topic (Dreher & Gambrell, 1985). By asking their own questions, students invest themselves in reading. Self-generated questions come from children's own knowledge and desire to know more about a topic. In this way, questions function as a bridge between children's interests and curiosities and new knowledge contained in text.

Student questions have several advantages over teacher questions. In some cases, teacher-posed questions tend to constrain students' reading. These teacher-posed questions attempt to satisfy the teacher's purposes, rather than the students' (Singer & Donlan, 1982). Teacher questions often emphasize evaluation of students' responses. When the emphasis is solely on answering questions for evaluation and recall, the opportunity for students' meaning construction process is diminished. When students ask their own questions in relation to a text, they grapple with text ideas as they construct meaning (Beck, McKeown, & Sandora, 1996). Posing and answering their own questions enables students to engage in more active and deeper processing of text. They must inspect text by identifying ideas and tying parts together.

Students who have learned to ask questions in reading can better comprehend text than students who have not learned to generate their own questions (National Reading Panel, 2000). It is likely that questioning enhances comprehension, due to the deeper processing of text that questioning generates. By asking questions related to a text, students set a purpose of inquiry that enables them to focus on text content.

Building a Questioning Rubric

We developed a questioning rubric to describe students' growth and to guide instruction (see appendix). We expect that teaching students to generate and ask high-level questions may improve their comprehension. However, it is important that a guide for such instruction be grounded in students' performances. In this discussion, we emphasize questions in relation to text. Students should find text-based answers to their questions. This does not mean that answers have to be limited to one text. On the contrary, high-level questions may result from the integration of information across different sources.

To form an information base, we sampled questions from a pool of 170 Grade 3 students in September and December of a school year. Students asked questions in relation to two different texts that were part of two different tasks within a performance assessment. Texts varied in length and content, although both were based on ecological science content and included information on ecological concepts. The longer text version was a 75-page booklet that included information on two particular biomes. Three sets of texts were provided (rivers & grasslands; ponds & deserts; forests & oceans). These texts were constructed with equal difficulty levels. Nine ecological concepts are included in the longer texts. Shorter texts were used for a computer-based passage comprehension task, containing three alternate versions (sharks, bats, or bears).

Questioning and reading took place on two different days. Students were prompted to browse through the text for a few minutes and to write questions in relation to the topics of the texts. Students were given approximately 15 minutes to write a maximum of 10 questions on the longer text and 5 to 7 minutes to write a maximum of four questions on the shorter text.

Students' questions were first grouped broadly into a large number of different categories. Narrowing of categories based on similarities and differences among questions followed, until four categories emerged from the data. These four categories (rubric levels) were also based on our theoretical understanding of conceptual improvement and differentiation. We examined interrater reliability for our rubric. After training, a graduate and an undergraduate student independently rated 353 questions. Their agreement with the researcher was 95% (adjacent) and 84% (exact) for questions on the short passages, and 96% (adjacent) and 84% (exact) for questions on the long texts.

Our studies have shown that third graders ask different types of questions, evincing individual differences in their questioning. Questioning instruction improves their ability to ask higher level questions that are conducive to deeper text processing and better comprehension. Some of these results are included in a later section. Next, we present examples of the different types of questions asked by third graders.

Developmental Shifts.   At the beginning of third grade, students' questions tend to focus on simple facts and basic information that do not always refer to the central topic of a text. These are questions peripheral to the main topic that inquire about commonplace features in the form of a factual proposition. For instance, children's questions at this stage might include: *How big are polar bears? How much do whales weigh? What colors are crabs?* These are factual information questions, Level 1 on the questioning rubric, and can be answered by factual information that is concrete and simple.

Alternatively, low-level questions can request a simple classification or a "yes/no" answer: *Are there male and female polar bears? How many ponds are there in the world?* These naïve questions require a simple *yes* answer in the first case and a numerical answer in the second case. They are Level 1 questions because they do not lead to any further learning. Rather, their answers are constrained to simple facts that do not involve explanations.

Toward the middle and end of third grade, as students gain knowledge about different topics and become more familiar with texts, their questions change significantly. First, they become less fact-based and more focused on concepts and processes within the topic. Examples of these Level 2 questions are: *How do whales have babies? How do fish breathe under water? How do birds fly?* Second, the improved quality of Level 2 questions lies in their request for a description of an ecological concept, rather than for a piece of factual information. *Concepts* refer to a class of objects, events, or interactions. Thus, a question about how fish breathe taps into a series of interactions and events (e.g. use of gills in place of lungs; lack of oxygen under water; difference of air composition, etc.). To provide an answer to this question, it is necessary to explain the interactions and events that constitute a concept. Questions at this level also inquire about classifications or characterizations of organisms by emphasizing the interaction of the organisms and their habitats. For example: *What kind of places can polar bears live in? What kinds of bugs live in the desert? What kind of algae are in the ocean?* A clear request for taxonomies or classes is evident in these questions. Therefore, Level 2 questions call for information about descriptions of concepts or classifications, rather than mere factual information.

At the end of third grade, students often pose Level 3 questions about concepts or processes at a more specific level than those questions at Level 2. They do so by providing information within a question that probes into the concept itself. Rather than asking about an ecological concept at a global level, the question identifies some specific aspect or feature of an ecological concept. Students asking these questions need elaborated explanations on a concept by expressing knowledge about the concept in the question itself. For example, rather than asking, *"How do sharks swim?"* (Level 2), students probe into the concept of *swimming* by asking: *"Why do sharks sink when they stop swimming?"* Or, in relation to *feeding* they ask: *"Why do sharks eat things that bleed?"* The questions denote knowledge about specific aspects of the organism in relation to that concept and they inquire about those aspects.

By the end of fourth grade, students ask questions at a higher level of complexity. Questions are identified as Level 4, the highest level on our questioning rubric. Level 4 questions are mostly characterized by requests about interrelationships between concepts in reference to an organism or species. At this level, questions not only refer to individual concepts, but request principles that link concepts into relationships. Such principled understandings are evident in the request for explanations that imply complex interactions among concepts or between the organism and its environment. A teacher's example of these questioning levels is shown in Fig. 11.4.

A qualitative shift in questioning occurs from Levels 2 and 3 to Level 4 by moving from inquiry about an individual concept to inquiry about how different concepts interact in reference to one organism (i.e., a plant or an animal). Examples of Level 4 questions are: *"Why do salmon go to the sea to mate and go to the river to lay eggs?"* or, *"How do polar bears feed their babies and protect them from the cold if the food is in the snow?"* These questions are complex because they focus on the interrelationship between the concepts of *reproduction* and *feeding*. Questions at Level 4 tap into networks of relationships among concepts, and by doing so, show the depth and breadth of the knowledge they inquire.

Question levels increase in difficulty from 1 to 4 because of changes in the type of knowledge complexity they seek. Low-level questions request information about simple facts, whereas at the highest level, questions require information about networks of relationships among concepts.

Benchmarks for Questioning at the End of Grade 3.
- Students ask or write questions with teacher request, but not teacher assistance.
- Questions probe concepts and explanations.
- Information within questions enables them to probe deeply.
- Several questions are asked that are linked and integrated.
- Questions are related to text available to students.
- Questions presume and request classifications and contrasts.

What makes a good question?
-It has a capital letter and a question mark.
-It can be answered.
-It asks about something we don't already know.

<u>Levels of Questions:</u>
Level 1: Question asks about a specific feature or characteristic.
Ex.: How many toes does a bird have?
Level 2: Question asks about the function of a feature.
Ex.: How do swans use their long necks?
Level 3: Question asks about a core concept & seeks
evidence/example.
Ex.: How do penguins swim?
Level 4: Question asks about relationships among core concepts.
Ex.: How does a bird's singing help it defend itself from its
enemies?

FIG. 11.4. A teacher's example of the questioning rubric levels.

Benchmarks for Questioning at the End of Grade 4.
- Students can write questions in good form (full sentence with punctuation).
- Information within the questions allows students to probe deeply about concepts.
- Questions are related to a variety of texts available to students.
- Questions integrate information from different sources and can contrast information from different sources.
- Questions presume contrasts and classifications across species, organisms, biomes, etc.
- Students are aware of the difference between conceptual/explanation questions and factual questions and see the relationships among these (i.e., factual questions subsumed under conceptual questions).
- Students evaluate the quality of questions (their own and classmates) for improving learning from text.
- Students can relate the content of questions to content of their new learning from text. (They know how well they answered their questions.)
- Students can generate questions with minimal teacher prompting before, during, and after reading.

Developmental Pattern. Children's development of questioning over text expands on several dimensions simultaneously. Questions improve through a sequence of requests for **facts, descriptions, explanations** of concepts, and **patterns of relationships** among concepts and evidence. Fundamentally, higher level questions call for higher levels of conceptual learning from text. Increasing complexity of questions is based on students' expansion of knowledge about a topic that permits probing inquiries. Advanced questions also depend on at least partial understanding of the major themes or concepts of a topic, permitting the pursuit of knowledge about important, rather than trivial, matters.

Relationship of Questioning to Reading Comprehension

To investigate the relationship between questioning and text comprehension, we examined the questions posed by third graders before reading a text on a specific animal. The text was approximately four pages, with two paragraphs, illustrations, and captions on each page. Text content was organized around three aspects of survival (i.e., ecological concepts) that pertained to the animal. Students were prompted to browse the text for a few minutes and then to ask any questions they might have on the animal in the text. After writing their questions, students read the text and proceeded to take the computer-based assessment.

Students' questions were categorized according to our questioning rubric. According to these categorizations, students evinced individual differences in their questions. Students' questions toward the middle of third grade ranged from Level 1 to Level 3. Very few students were able to ask Level 4 questions, showing the complexity and difficulty that formulating these questions entails.

Our results show a very interesting pattern in the relationship between students' questions and their reading comprehension levels. As shown in Fig. 11.5, students who asked lower level or factual questions (Level 1) showed lower levels of comprehension on the passage comprehension task (about .35 on a scale of 0–1.0). Students who asked simple description questions (Level 2) had higher levels of comprehension, as shown on the graph (about .40). Students who asked complex explanation questions (Level 3) had the highest levels of comprehension, as shown by their scores (about .50). These findings suggest that students' question levels are associated with their reading comprehension levels.

CLOSING

It is valuable for teachers to understand students' benchmarks of strategy development. One reason is that benchmarks, such as those offered here, can be-

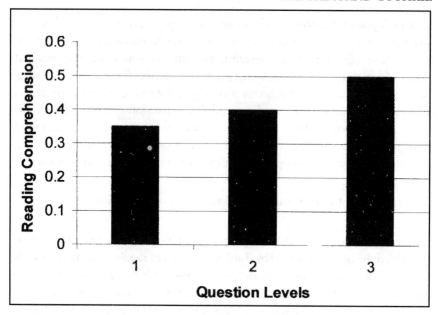

FIG. 11.5. Relationship between students' questions and their reading comprehension levels.

come goals for teaching reading comprehension strategies. These benchmarks are fairly specific student performances because teachers need more than abstract principles. For instance, one abstract principle of strategy development is that students should become more independent in using all strategies, such as summarizing, in their reading. Although true, this is an insufficient guide to the texts, scaffolding, expected student responses, and detail of teacher's role in fostering students' reading engagement. Simultaneously, a script for teaching strategies is unlikely to be helpful in engaging learners in reading. A script with one set of texts, teacher actions, and expected student responses is usually too rigid to be responsive. A script cannot cope adequately with diversity among students' reading, writing, language, self-directedness, and preexisting engagement. Therefore, we use these benchmarks as goals for instructional activities. They are a middle ground between principles of instruction, which may be too abstract to use easily, and curricular scripts, which are not sufficiently adaptable to students' needs. The research base for these benchmarks is descriptive and initial. We need additional investigations that provide refinements to these benchmarks, based on wider and deeper inquiries.

APPENDIX 11.A

QUESTIONING RUBRIC

Level 1: Factual Information

Questions are simple in form and request a simple answer, such as a single fact. Questions are a request for a factual proposition. They are based on naïve concepts about the world rather than disciplined understanding of the subject matter. Questions refer to relatively trivial, nondefining characteristics of organisms (plants and animals), ecological concepts, or biomes.

Text about animals

These questions may inquire about or take the form of:

- Commonplace or general features of animals that require simple and factual answers: *How big are bats? Do sharks eat trash? How much do bears weigh?*
- Simple classification that only requires a yes/no type of answer or a one-word answer: *Are sharks mammals? What is the biggest shark? Are there male and female polar bears? How many coats of fur do polar bears have?*

Text about biomes and organisms

These questions may inquire about or take the form of:

- Commonplace or general features of a living organism (plants or animals) in the biome. These questions request yes/no answers or simple factual (e.g. numeric) answers: *Are there crabs in a river? How old do orangutans get?*
- Commonplace or general features of the biome itself that are *not* defining attributes of the biome: *How big do rivers get? How big are grasslands?*
- Simple classification or quantification that only requires a yes/no type of answer or a one-word answer: *How many grasslands are there? How many rivers are there in the world? How many plants live in ponds?*

Level 2: Simple Description

Questions are a request for a global statement about an ecological concept or an important aspect of survival. Questions may also request general information that denotes a link between the biome and organisms that live in it. The question may be simple, yet the answer may contain multiple facts and generalizations. The answer may be a moderately complex description or an explanation of an animal's behavior or physical characteristics. An answer may also be a set of distinctions necessary to account for all the forms of species.

Text about animals

These questions may inquire about or take the form of:

- Ecological concepts in their global characteristics. Usually the question inquires about *how* and *why*, so an explanation can be elicited: *How do sharks mate? How do sharks have babies? How do birds fly? How do bats protect themselves?*
- A global distinction to classify the animal (general taxonomy): *How many types of bats are there? What kinds of sharks are in the ocean?*
- A global distinction or classification about the animal's habitat: *What types of places can polar bears live? What kinds of water do sharks live in?*
- Simple description of an aspect of an ecological concept: How many eggs does a shark lay? How fast can a bat fly? How far do polar bears swim in the ocean?

Text about biomes and organisms

These questions may inquire about or take the form of:

- Classification or taxonomy of organisms (plants or animals) that live in the biome. The specification of the organism living in that biome is explicit in the question: *What bugs live in the desert? What kind of algae are in the ocean?* rather than: *What types of algae are there?* (i.e., biome is not specified in the question).
- Global/general explanation or description of an ecological/biological concept in reference to organisms that live in the biome. Usually the question inquires about *how* and *why*, so an explanation can be elicited: *How do desert animals live?*
  How do grasslands get flowers and trees?
- Description or explanation that involves or makes reference to a defining or critical attribute of a biome: *How come it almost never rains in*

the desert? (i.e., reference to dryness); *How long do sandstorms last?* (i.e., reference to a sandy region); *Why do rivers start at a hilltop? What makes rivers fast and flowing?*

Level 3: Complex Explanation

Questions are a request for an elaborated explanation about a specific aspect of an ecological concept with accompanying evidence. The question probes the ecological concept by using knowledge about survival or animal biological characteristics. Questions may also request information that denote a link between the biome and organisms that live in it. Questions use defining features of biomes to probe for the influence those attributes have on life in the biome. The question is complex and the expected answer requires elaborated propositions, general principles, and supporting evidence about ecological concepts.

Text about animals

These questions may inquire about:

- An ecological concept of the animal interacting with the environment. The question probes into a specific concept by showing prior knowledge on a significant aspect of the interaction: *Why do sharks sink when they stop swimming? Why do sharks eat things that bleed? How do polar bears keep warm in their den?* Alternatively, the question can address physical characteristics that enable the interaction or biological process to occur: *Why do sharks have three rows of teeth? Why is the polar bear's summer coat a different color? Why do all bats have sharp teeth?*
- Requests a distinction among types of organisms within a species to understand the concept at hand. Either information about the ecological concept or the animals' interaction with the environment is used as the basis of an analytical process: *What kinds of sharks lay eggs? What kinds of bats hide in caves?* Or the question may be directed to a structural or a behavioral characteristic necessary for the concept to be understood: *Do fruit-eating bats have really good eyes? Do owls that live in the desert hunt at night?*

Text about biomes and organisms

These questions may inquire about:

- Description or explanation of an ecological concept of an organism that lives in a biome, with probed information about the organism *or* the biome. The question denotes prior-knowledge by including a level of specificity not included in questions in Level 2. The question may, for example, focus on a behavioral pattern that is typical of the ecological concept: *What kinds of animals* that eat meat live in the forest? Why do Elf Owls make their homes in cactuses?

- Explanation of the influence a defining feature of the biome has on life (animals and plants) in the biome. The question is not just on the defining feature itself as in Level 2 (e.g., *What makes the river fast and flowing?*) but on the *effects* the defining feature has on the biome: *How do animals in the desert survive long periods without water? If the desert is hot, how can animals get so active?*

Level 4: Pattern of Relationships

Questions display science knowledge coherently expressed to probe the interrelationship of concepts, the interaction with the biome, or interdependencies of organisms. Questions are a request for principled understanding with evidence for complex interactions among multiple concepts and possibly across biomes. Knowledge is used to form a focused inquiry into a specific aspect of a biological concept and an organism's interaction with its biome. Answers may consist of a complex network of two or more concepts.

Text about animals

Descriptions of animals' survival process in which two or more ecological concepts are interacting with each other: *Do snakes use their fangs to kill their enemies as well as poison their prey? Do polar bears hunt seals to eat or feed their babies?*

Text about biomes and organisms

- Description or explanation of an organism's biology in which two or more ecological concepts are interacting: *Why do salmons go to the sea to mate and lay eggs in the river? How do animals and plants in the desert help each other?*
- Description or explanation of the interaction of two biomes in relation to an organisms' survival: *How does the grassland help the animals in the river? How are grassland animals and river animals the same and different?*
- Alternatively the complexity of the question might lie in the inquiry for relationships of multiple organisms in relation to a single concept:

Is the polar bear at the top of the food chain? The scope of the answer to this question is vast as the relationships among multiple organisms are described in reference to one concept (i.e., feeding).

REFERENCES

Ambruster, B. B., Anderson, T. H., & Meyer, J. L. (1991). Improving content-area reading using instructional graphics. *Reading Research Quarterly, 26*(4), 393–416.

Anderson, R. C., & Pearson, P. D. (1984). A schema-theoretic view of basic processes in reading. In R. Barr, M. L. Kamil, & P. Mosenthal (Eds.), *Handbook of reading research* (pp. 255–291). New York: Longman.

Baker, L., & Brown, A. L. (1984). Metacognitive skills of reading. In P. D. Pearson (Ed.), *Handbook of reading research* (Vol. 2, pp. 353–394). New York: Longman.

Beck, I. L., McKeown, M. G., & Sandora, C. (1996). Questioning the author: A yearlong classroom implementation to engage students with text. *Elementary School Journal, 96,* 385–414.

Brown, A. L., & Day, J. D. (1983). Macrorules for summarizing texts: The development of expertise. *Journal of Verbal Learning & Verbal Behavior, 22*(1), 1–14.

Collins-Block, C., & Pressley, M. (2002). *Comprehension instruction: Research-based best practices.* New York: Guilford.

Darch, C. B., Carnine, D. W., & Kameenui, E. J. (1986). The role of graphic organizers and social structure in content area instruction. *Journal of Reading Behavior, 18*(4), 275–295.

Dreher, M. J., & Brown, R. F. (1993). Planning prompts and indexed terms in textbook search tasks. *Journal of Educational Psychology, 85*(4), 662–669.

Dreher, M. J., & Gambrell, L. B. (1985). Teaching children to use a self-questioning strategy for studying expository prose. *Reading Improvement, 22,* 2–7.

Dreher, M. J., & Sammons, R. B. (1994). Fifth graders' search for information in a textbook. *Journal of Reading Behavior, 26*(3), 301–314.

Guthrie, J. T. (2001a). *Concept-Oriented Reading Instruction reading assessment: The amazing snake.* Unpublished assessment.

Guthrie, J. T. (2001b). *Concept-Oriented Reading Instruction reading assessment: Rivers and grasslands.* Unpublished Assessment.

Guthrie, J. T., Weber, S., & Kimmerly, N. (1993). Searching documents: Cognitive processes and deficits in understanding graphs, tables, and illustrations. *Contemporary Educational Psychology, 18*(2), 186–221.

National Reading Panel. (2000). *Teaching children to read.* (NIH Publication No. 00–4769). Bethesda, MD: National Institute of Child Health and Human Development.

Novak, J. D., & Musonda, D. (1991). A twelve-year longitudinal study of science concept learning. *American Educational Reserach Journal, 28*(1), 117–153.

Paris, S. G., Wasik, B., & Turner, J. C. (1991). The development of strategic readers. In M. L. Kamil, P. Mosenthal, & P. D. Pearson (Eds.), *Handbook of reading research,* Vol. 2 (pp. 609–640) Mahwah, NJ: Lawrence Erlbaum Associates.

Pressley, M., & El-Dinary, P. B. (1997). What we know about translating comprehension-strategies instruction research into practice. *Journal of Learning Disabilities, 30*(5), 486–488.

Pressley, M., Goodchild, F., Fleet, J., Zajchowski, R., & Evans, E. D. (1989). The challenges of classroom strategy instruction. *The Elementary School Journal, 89*(3), 301–341.

Prince, A. T., & Mancus, D. S. (1987). Enriching comprehension: A scheme altered basal reading lesson. Reading Research & Instruction, 27(1), 45–54.

Reynolds, P. L., Symons, S. (2001). Motivational variables and children's text search. *Journal of Educational Psychology, 93*(1), 14–22.

Singer, H., & Donlan, D. (1982). Active comprehension: Problem-solving schema with question generation for comprehension of complex short stories. *Reading Research Quarterly, 2*(7), 166–185.

Smolkin, L. B., & Donovan, C. A. (2001). The contexts of comprehension: The information book read aloud, comprehension acquisition, and comprehension instruction in a first-grade classroom. *Elementary School Journal, 102*(2), 97–122.

Spires, H. A., Gallini, J., & Riggsbee, J. (1992). Effects of schema-based and text structure-based cues on expository prose comprehension in fourth graders. *Journal of Experimental Education, 60*(4), 307–320.

Symons, S., McLatchy-Gaudet, H., & Stone, T. D. (2001). Strategy instruction for elementary students searching informational text. *Scientific Studies of Reading, 15*(1), 1–33.

Taylor, B. M., & Beach, R. W. (1984). The effects of text structure instruction on middle-grade students' comprehension and production of expository text. *Reading Research Quarterly, 19*(2), 134–146.

CHILDREN'S BOOK REFERENCES

Savage, S. (2000). *What's the difference?: Birds*. Austin, TX: Steck-Vaughn.

Stone, L. M. (1995). *Birds of Antarctica*. Vero Beach, FL: Rourke.

Appendix

Description of Research Project Assessing CORI's Effects on Reading Comprehension and Reading Motivation

In various chapters we have described our implementation of CORI in elementary school classrooms, and also referred to our ongoing research project assessing the effects of each reading program on elementary school-aged children's reading comprehension and reading motivation. This appendix provides a summary of the design of this project and the measures being used.

PROJECT DESIGN

We are conducting this project in third, fourth, and fifth grade classrooms in five schools, in a middle-sized town in Maryland. In two of the schools teachers are implementing CORI, and in two of the schools teachers are implementing strategy instruction (SI). The fifth school is a control school in which teachers are implementing their traditional reading and science instructional practices. The general design of the project is as follows. During the summer, teachers implementing CORI and SI receive training in workshops run by the University of Maryland staff. The CORI workshops last 2 weeks and the SI workshops 1 week. The CORI workshop is longer because teachers have to learn science instructional practices along with reading instructional practices. Teachers in each school implement CORI or SI for 12 weeks of instructional time in the fall of the school year. Before and after implementation, students complete assessments of their reading comprehension and reading motivation.

In the first year of the project (2001–2002 school year), the two instructional programs were implemented on a pilot basis in third-grade classrooms in the participating schools. As part of the pilot, students completed the pre and posttest assessments. In the second year (2002–2003), teachers provided full implementation of the instructional programs in third grade. Fourth-grade teachers administered the programs on a pilot basis. During the 2003–2004 school year, fourth-grade teachers will provide full implementation of the instructional programs. During the 2004–2005 school year, the programs will be implemented in fifth grade.

The research questions for this investigation are as follows:

1. To what extent does CORI produce higher gains than SI and traditional instruction (TI) on reading comprehension, reading motivation, and science knowledge, controlling for initial Reading Program Quality (RPQ)?
2. To what extent does the implementation quality of CORI and SI predict gains in reading comprehension, reading motivation, and science knowledge?

We now present fuller details of the project and each instructional program.

CORI AND SI INSTRUCTIONAL PROGRAMS

The CORI Instructional Program

The CORI instructional program was portrayed throughout the book; we provide here a summary of how the implementation occurs. CORI integrates reading and science instruction, and teachers use science activities to engage children in reading. During reading instruction, students are explicitly taught comprehension strategies consisting of the following: activating background knowledge, questioning, searching for information, summarizing, organizing graphically, and learning story structure. Explicit instruction of these strategies, and extended practice using them, is inherent within CORI. In science, students are taught science inquiry skills (observation, experimentation, data analysis) and also science concepts dealing with survival. The particular concepts taught (e.g., feeding, locomotion, defense, predation, reproduction, competition, communication, respiration, and niche) are described in detail in chapter 5 of this book.

The 12 weeks of instruction are organized into two units at each grade level. In third grade, teachers teach two 6-week units, "Birds Around the World" and "Survival in Freshwater Habitats." The different science concepts described in chapter 5 are taught to children across these two units. During

"Birds Around the World," teachers focus on one reading strategy per week, in the following order: activating background knowledge, questioning, searching for information, summarizing, organizing graphically, and communicating to others. During each week of "Survival in Freshwater Habitats," teachers instruct students on how to combine these reading strategies, focusing on combining two or three per week.

In fourth grade, the first 6 weeks of CORI focus on "Hidden Worlds of the Woodlands," and the second 6 weeks focus on "Hidden Worlds of the Wetlands." In each unit, the same ecological concepts continue to be emphasized (feeding, locomotion, defense, predation, reproduction, competition, communication, respiration, niche, adaptation to habitat, and habitat conservation), and there is a new emphasis on students' understanding of plant and animal adjustments to their habitats and ecological niche. Teachers also help students see how these concepts relate (e.g., how does locomotion influence feeding?), which is a new emphasis in fourth grade. The Grade 4 instructional program continues to emphasize the reading strategies of activating background knowledge, questioning, summarizing, searching, organizing graphically, and there is a new emphasis on interpreting stories. In Grade 3, we emphasize basic competencies at using these strategies. In Grade 4, we introduce the ideas of *awareness* of when to use the strategies, and *self-initiation* of strategy use, to foster students' independent self-regulatory reading.

At both Grades 3 and 4 there is a strand of CORI devoted to struggling readers. In this strand, oral reading fluency is emphasized through assisted choral reading, expressive reading, and readers' theater. In addition, this strand uses simpler books to teach the various reading strategies as well as reading fluency, which is a necessary prerequisite to being able to use the strategies. Teachers identify struggling readers in their classrooms, and these children then get additional instruction from the classroom teacher or another reading specialist in each CORI school in both fluency and the strategies. By becoming more fluent readers, these students can master the reading strategies.

In CORI, students' reading motivation is supported through five major classroom instructional practices discussed in greater detail in chapters 3 and 10 in this book. First, students are taught reading comprehension in the context of knowledge goals related to ecology, which provides a purpose for activities such as questioning. Second, teachers optimize student choice in reading comprehension activities in the classroom in order to develop student self-determination. Third, teachers provide a variety of hands-on experiences related to texts and reading activities. Fourth, there is an abundance of interesting texts for comprehension instruction. We refer to interesting texts as trade books possessing the macrostructure of a book, including table of contents, index, illustrations, bold headings, and a coherent array of subsections. Fifth, teachers support student collaboration in a diversity of reading and science activities. The five aspects of motivational support are combined with the systematic explicit instruction in reading comprehension strategies, and science instruction and activities, to comprise the CORI context for reading development.

Strategy Instruction and Traditional Instruction

Our study compares the effects of CORI on students' reading comprehension and motivation to the effects of strategy instruction and traditional instruction. Strategy instruction consists of teaching the same comprehension strategies as taught in CORI (activating background knowledge, questioning, searching, summarizing, organizing graphically, and identifying the structures of stories) over a 12-week instructional period. These strategies were taught singly in the first 6 weeks of SI, in the sequence just given. During the second 6 weeks, teachers taught the strategies in conjunction and coordination with each other, emphasizing the combination of two or three strategies at a time. Teachers are provided workshops to learn and refine this strategy instruction. These reading comprehension strategies are taught in the reading and language arts block with the materials and other language arts activities that are used in the school.

Traditional instruction provided in reading/language arts in the participating school consisted of guided reading with flexible groups and writer's workshop activities. Some comprehension strategies, such as predicting, may be taught but are not explicitly supported by the project.

PARTICIPATING SCHOOLS AND CHILDREN

Participating Schools

Year 1. During the first (pilot) year of the project, CORI was implemented in two schools, to all third-grade students in eight classrooms. The program was administered from the second week in September to the third week in December, for a total of 12 weeks of instruction. Class size in the two schools averaged 24 students. The model was taught for 90 to 120 minutes daily, at one school in the morning and one school in the afternoon.

Strategy Instruction was implemented in 11 classrooms for all third graders in two different schools, from the second week in September to the third week in December. Class size in the two schools averaged 23 students. Both schools implemented the model for 90 minutes daily in the morning.

For both models, students who were reading at the-end-of first-grade level or below in September of Grade 3 were pulled from classrooms and taught by special education teachers for 30 minutes, approximately three times per week. Struggling readers, who were not eligible for special education or were not more than 2 years below in reading, were taught within classrooms.

Year 2.   CORI was implemented in the same two schools, to children in eight third-grade classrooms and nine fourth-grade classrooms. The program again was administered for total of 12 weeks of instruction, from early September to early December. Class size in the two schools averaged 24 students. The model was taught for 90 to 120 minutes daily.

SI also was implemented in the same two schools, to children in ten Grade 3 and nine Grade 4 classrooms. As in Year 1, there were 12 weeks of instruction in SI, for 90 minutes per day.

One school served as a traditional instruction comparison. Children in four third-grade classrooms were included in the study, with an average class size of 20 per class. They received the reading instructional program for third grade that was given in the school, for 90 minutes per day.

Description of Participants   Students from five schools in Frederick County, Maryland participated with permission from their parents. In the sample, 48% were boys and 52% were girls, which closely resembles the district as a whole in which 50% were boys and 50% were girls. In the sample of CORI schools, 76% were Caucasian, 21% were African-American, and 2% were Asian. In the sample of SI schools, 73% were Caucasian, 22% were African-American, and 5% were Asian. These proportions are typical of the district as a whole, which had 87% Caucasian, 8% African-American, 2% Asian, and 2% Hispanic. On the indicator of poverty, CORI schools had 18% qualifying for free and reduced means; SI schools had 22% qualifying, and the district had 13%, showing comparability for the sample and the district population.

In Year 1, approximately 450 third-grade children participated in the two instructional programs. In Year 2, there were approximately 540 third-grade children and 580 fourth-grade children participating.

ASSESSMENTS OF READING COMPREHENSION AND MOTIVATION

Assessments consisted of a pretest in the first week of September and a posttest in the second week of December, following the 12 weeks of reading comprehension instruction. The assessments included the following tasks: (a) eliciting prior knowledge, (b) student questioning, (c) searching for information, (d) writing knowledge gained from text, (e) reading a shorter passage for computer-based assessment, (f) performing the computer-based assessment of reading comprehension, (g) completing a reading activity inventory (RAI) to obtain information about what children read, (h) completing a motivation for reading questionnaire (MRQ), and (at Year 2), (i) completing the Gates MacGinitie Reading Comprehension Test.

The cognitive portions of the test (activities 1 through 6) were administered in two ways. The Long Form was given over 4 days and required more extensive reading and writing by students. The Short Form relied more on multiple choice and computer-based assessments of reading comprehension. During the Year 1 pilot, the Long Form was given to students in all classrooms in the September pretest and to six classes in the December posttest. The Short Form was given to the remaining students in the December posttest. During Year 2, the Long Form was given to students in four CORI classrooms, four SI classrooms, and two TI classrooms across third and fourth grades. The remaining students completed the Short Form.

Reading Comprehension Long Form

In the Long Form, students received one of three parallel reading packets that contained information about one of the following three ecological topics: ponds and deserts, rivers and grasslands, and oceans and forests. Students received one packet at the pretest and a different packet at the posttest. Each packet contained about 75 pages of reading material. The assessment was organized in the following manner.

Prior Knowledge. Students first wrote what they knew about life in the biomes to which they had been assigned (e.g., ponds and deserts, rivers and grasslands, oceans and forests). They were given 15 minutes in an open-ended writing activity.

Searching for information. In each classroom, all students were given a packet that represented a simulation of multiple trade books, covering one of the three ecological topics. Each packet contained 75 pages in 22 sections, 16 of which were relevant to the topic and 6 of which were distracters. Each packet contained an equal number of easy (Grade 2) and difficult (Grade 4) texts, which presented 9 of the 11 ecological concepts and defining information on the biomes. Students searched the packets and took notes on what they learned in one 10-minute activity on the first day, and a subsequent 40-minute activity the following day.

Questioning.   After briefly reviewing an assessment packet of information on life in the biomes, students wrote their questions. Students were encouraged to write as many good questions as possible in 15 minutes about what the biomes were like and how animals survived in them.

Reading Comprehension.   Following the continuation of the search activity just described, students were asked to write what they knew about their biome after reading. They were given 30 minutes to express their knowledge, with two statements of encouragement after 7 and 13 minutes.

Passage Comprehension.   Students were given a passage on an animal (sharks, polar bears, bats). The four-page text was 400 words with illustrations. Sentence length was 7 to 24 words and word difficulty was Grade 3, according to teacher ratings. Students were given 7 minutes to read it. For Grade 4, some classrooms received a reading packet with one additional page, to make the task longer for the older students.

After students read the passage in their classrooms, they went to the school's computer lab to complete the assessment. Students performed a task in which they rated the relatedness of pairs of words drawn from the reading passages. In this task, experimenters identified nine key words that represent the conceptual structure of the reading passage. These nine key words were presented to students in pairs on the computer; students rated 36 word pairs. The fourth graders who received the longer reading passage rated 77 word pairs formed from 13 key words drawn from the passage. Students made one of three responses: highly related (9), a little bit related (5), and not related (1). In research using this assessment tool with adults, a nine-point rating scale is used. For children, we reduced this to the three responses just described. Students' responses to the pairs generate a concept map (created by a computer program called Pathfinder) that shows their understanding of the passage.

Reading Comprehension Short Form

The Short Form relied more heavily on the computer-based assessment of reading comprehension. Students were given a reading passage about one of three animals (sharks, bats, or bears), and the assessment was based on that passage.

Prior Knowledge.   Students were given a 22-item multiple-choice task that assessed their prior knowledge of the animal assigned to the student. Each item contained a word or phrase describing some aspect of the animal. Students then chose one word out of four that was most like the word about the animal.

Questioning. Students were given 3 minutes to scan the reading passage. The passage was removed, and then they were allotted 10 minutes to write questions they had about the animal.

Passage Comprehension. Students completed the same reading comprehension task previously described. First, they read a passage about one of three animals (bat, shark, or bear) in their classrooms, and then went to the school's computer lab to do the ratings of how related they thought the key words taken from the passage were.

Reading Comprehension Scales. From these tasks, the following measures were derived from the different forms: (a) prior knowledge, long form, coded 1–6 to a knowledge rubric (described in Chapter 9 of this book); (b) prior knowledge, short form, total number of items correct from the multiple choice assessment; (c) questioning, both forms, coded 1–4 to a questioning rubric (see chapter 11); (d) searching, long form, number of correctly identified relevant sections in notes from the searching task; (e) reading comprehension, long form, coded 1–6 to a knowledge rubric (that was the same as the rubric used for prior knowledge), (f) passage comprehension (a score ranging from 0-1.0 derived from Pathfinder algorithm, and (g) computer passage knowledge organization (the coherence score derived from the Pathfinder algorithm ranging from 0–1.0). These scales are being used to evaluate growth in children's reading comprehension.

Reading Motivation

Motivations for Reading Questionnaire. All children completed portions of the Motivations for Reading Questionnaire (MRQ), which is designed to assess different aspects of children's motivation to read. The particular aspects of motivation assessed were reading self-efficacy, intrinsic and extrinsic motivation to read, and efficacy at using reading strategies. Three components of intrinsic motivation to read were assessed: curiosity, involvement, and preference for challenging reading. Two aspects of extrinsic reading motivation to read were assessed: desire for recognition, and reading for grades. Items assessing these aspects of motivation to read were read to children, and they indicated the extent to which the item was like them or not.

Reading Activity Inventory. All children completed a Reading Activity Inventory (RAI) that asked children how frequently that they read different kinds of books for their own enjoyment. They were asked about the following book types: story books (like a mystery or adventure), sports books, science books, comic books or magazines, or any other kinds of books. First, children were asked if they read such a book last week, and also how often they read each kind of book.

Standardized Measure of Reading Comprehension

During Year 2 posttest, all children completed the grade-level-appropriate comprehension portion of the Gates MacGinitie Reading Test.

TEACHER PROFESSIONAL DEVELOPMENT

To optimize implementation fidelity for the CORI and SI models, workshops are given during the summer preceding the implementation for each grade level. Workshops provide the teachers with the following: (a) a theoretical overview of the instructional program, (b) a mini-instructional model learning experience, (c) videotapes of model implementation, (d) portraits of excellent practices, (e) a description of instructional materials, and (f) unit planning guides and activities. For CORI teachers, the workshop lasted 10 days. For SI teachers, the workshop lasted 5 days. The workshops are of different lengths because of the science training needed for the CORI model.

Each workshop experience has five major elements for both groups. First, teachers experience each of the six reading strategies as students in the classroom are expected to perform it, using either adult text or student texts. Second, extended lectures or discussions on the dynamics of engaged reading, with an emphasis on strategies, motivations, conceptual knowledge, and social interactions, are accompanied by a discussion of the principles implemented within each model. Third, teachers observe exemplars of instruction on videotapes of CORI and SI classrooms and are provided presentations of units and lessons from teachers who have implemented these models previously. Fourth, teachers participate in the instructional practices as students might within their classrooms. For example, teachers performed some of the hands-on experiences in CORI as they would do it themselves. Fifth, teachers are engaged for 60 to 90 minutes daily, preparing plans for the full 12-week unit and for two specific weeks in detail. In planning, teachers work collaboratively in their teams to merge instructional models with the requirements of their school, the texts available for instruction, and the needs of the students in their individual classrooms.

As a follow-up to the workshops, project staff meets with teachers four times during and immediately after the 12-week intervention to provide professional development and monitor the progress of the intervention. These full- and half-day meetings enable teachers to exchange their techniques and approaches, ask questions about the programs they are implementing, and develop solutions to any problems that emerge. In each meeting, teachers write their reactions to reflection questions and exchange perspectives on teaching. The meetings also help ensure the fidelity of the CORI and SI interventions.

Assessing Implementation of Instructional Models

To determine the nature and degree of implementation, we videotape lessons provided by each teacher and conduct an interview with the teacher as she views the videotape. During Year 1, all but one CORI and SI teacher were videotaped, and many were videotaped twice. During Year 2, all but one CORI, SI, and TI third grade teacher were videotaped once. One fourth-grade CORI and one fourth-grade SI teacher were videotaped.

Teachers were asked to demonstrate their teaching techniques with an emphasis on reading. Cameras were focused on the teacher and one group of students, with a microphone on the teacher and a zoom microphone to capture student dialogue. Vignettes in this book were frequently drawn from these videotapes. In addition, we conduct interviews with each teacher as she watches the videotape and responds to questions that inquire about teaching practices outside of this videotaping session. Each teacher in CORI and SI completes an 80-item self-report questionnaire that asks about his or her teaching practices.

Instruction in the CORI model was defined by six instructional practices consisting of the following: strategy instruction, knowledge goals for instruction, use of interesting texts, autonomy support, collaboration support, and science process skills integrated with reading. Instruction in SI was defined by strategy instruction and support for self-efficacy. For each teacher, the videotape of instruction, and the interview based on that videotape, were simultaneously coded to describe the extent to which those six instructional practices appeared. Each practice was rated as follows: **four** (thoroughly implemented), **three** (partially implemented), **two** (limited implementation), and **one** (not visibly implemented).

Analyses testing the hypotheses presented here will be presented in articles submitted to research journals.

Author Index

Subject Index